FOR CRYING OUT LOUD

FOR CRYING OUT LOUD

Women's Poverty in the United States

edited by Diane Dujon and Ann Withorn

SOUTH END PRESS

Boston, Ma

Cover design by Mark Vallen

Text design and production in Kabel DemiBold and Garamond typefaces by the South End Press collective

Printed in the U.S.A.

Library of Congress Cataloging-in-Publication Data

For crying out loud: women's poverty in the United States/edited by Diane Dujon and Ann Withorn.
p. cm.
Includes index.
ISBN 0-89608-529-5 (alk. paper). —ISBN 0-89608-530-9 (alk. cloth)
1. Women-United States—Economic conditions. 2. Poor women—United States—Attitudes. 3. Sex discrimination against women—United States. 4. Public welfare—United States. I. Dujon, Diane II. Withorn, Ann, 1947-.
HQ1426.F758 1996
362.83'08'6942—dc20
96-30126CIP

South End Press, 116 Saint Botolph Street, Boston, MA 02115
02 01 00 99 98 97 96   1 2 3 4 5 6 7
GCIU 745-C

ABOUT THE EDITORS

DIANE DUJON, a former welfare recipient, has been on the front lines of the welfare rights struggle for almost 20 years. Currently she works as an administrator at the University of Massachusetts, Boston, College of Public and Community Service. In 1980, as a student at University of Massachusetts, Boston, Dujon became a founding member of the college's welfare rights group, Advocacy for Resources for Modern Survival (ARMS). She is a former board member of Jobs with Peace and the Women's Institute for New Growth and Support.

Dujon is a founding member and has served on the editorial board of *Survival News* since 1986. She is also a member of the National Welfare Rights Union.

ANN WITHORN is a professor of social policy at the College of Public and Community Service, University of Massachusetts, Boston. She is a long time speaker, activist and popular educator for feminist, labor and welfare issues. She has been an editor and associate editor of *Radical America* magazine and a member of the executive committee of the Bertha Capen Reynolds Society, a national organization of progressives in social welfare. She is the author of *Serving the People: Social Services and Social Change* and *The Circle Game: Human Services in Massachusetts* as well as of numerous articles in academic and progressive journals including: *The Women's Review of Books, The Journal of Progressive Human Services, The Nation, The Journal of Orthopsychiatry,* and *Otherwise.*

CONTENTS

PREFACE
Still Crying Out Loud
Ann Withorn

BACK IN 1986, ROCHELLE LEFKOWITZ AND I EDITED THE
original version of *For Crying Out Loud: Women and Poverty in the
United States,* with Pilgrim Press. At that time we hoped to offer a
corrective to the new attention to women's historic poverty that was
occurring under the catch phrase, the "feminization of poverty."
Therefore, the major purpose of that book was:

> to unsnarl the tangled skeins of women's poverty and to provide a more
> complex picture than has emerged in the media or in the recent literature.
> Unifying all the essays and individual accounts is the recognition that
> we live in a society where women's work is never done—and never paid
> in full, with either economic or social and psychological recognition.

Although pleased that welfare and single mothers' poverty were
receiving some sympathetic mainstream notice, we thought that both
media and policymakers were trying to make women's poverty into
a "manageable" problem. Our fear was that all the hoopla would
ignore the variety and depth of women's poverty and miss a chance
to consider a full-scale set of responses. We worried about "creaming,"
whereby only women who fit a *Newsweek* version of feminized
poverty—white, formerly middle-class women who found themselves newly divorced and unable to find employment with adequate
wages, benefits, and childcare—would get any help. We were
concerned that women who had come from poor families, especially
women of color, whose men were also poor, would be disregarded
because their problems were more structural, and because they had
"always been poor." We tried to show the inadequacy of stressing all
women's increasing vulnerability to poverty because—while true on
one level—such logic often denied the racial and class dynamics that
made climbing out of poverty much more difficult for some women

than for others. We also spoke directly to organized feminists, and urged them not to forget women's need for income security in the continued fight for workplace equality.

Especially because of the mix of voices it presented, the original *For Crying Out Loud* was well received, positively reviewed, and used in many women's studies and sociology classes. Several of the pieces were reprinted in other anthologies.

At the same time as the original version was struggling to be heard, and in spite of the ongoing efforts of welfare rights groups and organized feminists, the world facing poor women became even more bleak and forbidding. Job security for all lessened, as the rich got richer and the poor got poorer and more demonized. As the level of real benefits declined, welfare bashing increased along with a general cultural assault on single mothers. Ascendant Republican right rhetoric normalized the linking of criminality, drug abuse, poverty, and "welfare dependence." Fantasies about the viability of employment for low-income single mothers became institutionalized as feasible goals for successive rounds of punitive policies. Longtime friends of welfare rights became confused and, in the throes of a relentless realism aimed at meeting their own needs to feel effective, began to recommend "compromises" that low-income women could not accept and still remain responsible to their children.

During this time, I joined the rising activism that emerged around the nation to combat the ever more virulent attacks. Lessons learned from juggling my own parenting demands gave special energy to talks to feminist groups, church groups, labor unions and university students: talks about the need to respect the choices of women on welfare—indeed, to see them as "mother heroes." I have been on radio and television talk shows and participated in state and national efforts to fight the assault on poor women, wrongly called "welfare reform." Everywhere, I have felt the hardening of hearts from the general public, the frustration of advocates, and the increasing pain and anger of women on welfare.

So, 10 years later, with a new coeditor who has herself been on welfare and is a nationally recognized welfare rights activist, I make a renewed effort to cry out loud. The original book, which was remaindered in 1995, suffered from lack of marketing because Pilgrim Press, in 1986, decided to return to its roots as a primarily religious publisher. The result was that my mother could find the book in a religious bookstore in Florida, but it was available only by special order at most urban bookstores. It was also not marketed for classroom use. Now, with South End Press, this new volume will be marketed to a wider audience. It really is a new book with a new purpose—far more than an update and revision of the earlier collection.

The book changed because now is not the time to broaden our perspective, but to sharpen our focus: to try to explain why, as all the problems have worsened exponentially, sympathetic mainstream and "liberal" attention to women's vulnerability to poverty has nearly disappeared. How did it happen that, in 1995, an anthology by a mainstream writer, entitled *Extremism in America* can present the statements of the National Welfare Rights Organization and the Welfare Bill of Rights as coming from the "extreme Left"?

Few women on welfare today were on the rolls 10 years ago. Many of those who are remember that times were tough because of Reaganism's assaults and the weakness of liberal responses. But not even Reagan dared to propose seriously that AFDC be ended as a federal obligation, or to recommend "drop dead" time limits on how long a child could receive assistance. Today, no matter what their circumstances, single mothers who dare to seek welfare find themselves blamed for their poverty, with little talk about the structural issues that were thought, even by many conservatives, to have "feminized" poverty only a decade before. If, as teenagers, they have babies without husbands, they find themselves branded as mothers of "illegitimate" (a term feminists thought had been banished) children. Instead of being seen as deserving of help, they are blamed for every social ill from urban crime to drug abuse to the general decline of "personal responsibility." The public assistance that helped women escape abusive marriages, irresponsible partners, and low-wage employment is labeled a "social blasphemy" by politicians like Governor William Weld of Massachusetts. Most painful of all, as more and more women in two-parent families are employed to help their families stay slightly out of poverty, the societal willingness to respect, much less help, single mothers who must put the work of caring for their children before any other work has declined drastically.

So this volume is both a sequel to the first and a new version, with a sharper vision: less a second verse than a new jazz variation, emerging after a long night of hard performing. Its purpose is not so much, as in 1986, to present varied voices of women—older women, rural women, women defined first by their ethnicity, as well as welfare mothers—in the hope that if their voices were heard a responsive public would listen. Instead, this book is more sober and strategic. It attempts, by looking at varied experiences, to unravel how women who are the most poor—women who use AFDC to support their families—are so jeopardized by current assaults. It presents fewer critiques of welfare as it has been implemented and more ideas for understanding how we can defend income support for women who are responsible for their children. The links between welfare, work, and education are still explored. My coeditor Diane Dujon and I dare to spend a quarter of the volume ourselves exploring why so many have turned on the poorest women, and considering possible strategies for change, from policy proposals, to organizing strategies, to better ways of conceptualizing the issues.

Last year my 12 year old daughter, Gwyne, to whom the first *For Crying Out Loud* was dedicated, wrote a paragraph in an essay on "Hope" It said:

> Hope is a mother who cares for you. The world would not be if mothers were not who they were and are. The givers of life, the makers of hope. No one would be if a mother had not cared just enough to give even a little love. I would not be. And I, with so much love and caring inside me, can and will be somebody, thanks to a mother who loves me.

It is risky for me, as an academic with the option to hide behind distanced analysis, to write so much and so personally about welfare. But there seems no other choice, given how much I now understand about how necessary it is for any woman who finds herself a mother to be able to care for her child, regardless of the cost, and to give her child hope.

INTRODUCTION
Talking Across the Tables

In spite of public censure, welfare mothers graduate from school, get decent jobs, watch their children achieve, make good lives for themselves, and marry men they love. I feel that I am now in a position to make that process a little bit less of an uphill struggle. But what I now give is small compared to what I receive in return. Welfare mothers continue to be my inspiration, not because they survive, but because they dare to dream. Because when you are a welfare recipient, laughter is an act of rebellion...

—Janet Diamond,
former welfare recipient and welfare policy analyst

THIS IS A BOOK ABOUT WOMEN AND POVERTY IN THE United States, but it is not a book that considers the lives of all women who are poor. Older women's voices are not here, even though many women face poverty as they age. The voices of women without children are not present, even though, just as in days when they were feared as "witches," single women may be outcast in their communities if they are too openly "deviant." It is a book about women who are mothers vulnerable to poverty, but it does not include the voices of women who are living with husbands who earn low wages, even though more poor women are married and not on welfare than are single mothers on welfare.

How, then, can this be a book about "women's poverty in the United States?" Our answer is that to "cry out loud" about all women's poverty means to understand that no woman is any more secure than a single mother is secure. We, and all the authors in this volume, assume that almost all women can be mothers, that all mothers can be single mothers, and that most single mothers are vulnerable to poverty because of the demands of childrearing. Therefore, the security available to single mothers becomes a central measure of how well our society supports all women. If single mothers are expected to care for their children with little or no assistance from public programs, if they are expected always to find either jobs or men to provide full economic support, then they are not safe. Their lives are full of worry and pain that is created, not by all the troubles that come from their personal situations, but by the actions and inaction of politicians and bureaucrats.

Furthermore, we believe that to be really secure, all of us should appreciate the unique lessons that a woman on welfare can teach us.

By claiming her rights to ask the public to assist her in raising her child, she affirms that a dependable society distributes its resources so that women and children can claim food, shelter, and dignity when they ask for it.

By claiming her rights to satisfy her own sense of obligation to her children before she must fulfill obligations to an employer, she reminds us that there are more important duties to society than earning a profit.

By claiming her rights to create a legitimate family for her children without a man when men have failed her or are not available or do not satisfy her more intimate needs, she insists that society value women's contributions and choices as equal to men's.

By claiming her rights to support for her children while she charts a path to a better future that is hers alone to envision, she helps remind everyone to value what is most important in the world.

Interconnecting Themes

We are not babes in the woods. We are veteran writers, speakers, and activists in the cause of welfare rights, women's rights, workers rights, and civil rights. We have been "in the struggle" for more than two decades. Yet we are still able to be surprised that women who are doing the hardest and most important work of this society—raising their children alone—are treated so badly. Especially as we did the public speaking associated with preparing this book, and as we read the statements of politicians and pundits who felt so able to prescribe glibly cruel solutions for "welfare dependency," we found ourselves continually dismayed that it was so hard to get people to make the simple identification with poor women that makes all the difference. Whatever the differences in political strategy, we kept being taken aback by how hard it has become for people to see, in the words of the old song, that "there but for fortune go you and I."

So the first, and most overarching theme of this collection is that "you're next": that the problems that women on welfare face are connected to the dilemmas that low-income workers encounter, and that the troubles that low-income workers experience are not that different from those confronting more "middle-class" workers. Similarly, while no one expects to choose a violent or psychologically abusive man as a lover, it can happen to any woman. The results of being with such a man can be scars and patterns of self-protection that get in the way of finding solutions to one's pain, or of charting a different course. It takes time and support to think of a better future.

We know that it's scary for people to admit that their own lives are almost as vulnerable and out of control as those of welfare recipients. As Diane often says, "Denial is more than a river in Egypt; it is a deep stream in the American culture." There are real reasons that folks don't want to face their own dependence on bosses—or husbands who, for critical reasons, are less and less able to be dependable in the last decade of the 20th century. But we know too that if most people could admit to how insecure their jobs and marriages are, then they would be asking for better and more inclusive welfare programs, not fewer and more punitive ones. This is the trick that has been played on all of us: As the U.S. economy and family structures, have become less secure, somehow we have been bamboozled into reducing, not increasing, the only trust fund that most of us have—public programs. So, over and over again, *For Crying Out Loud* makes connections and shows the links between women on welfare and all women, between families seeking assistance and all families, between mothers working at home and all workers. We try not to threaten, but it seems to us only a short time before those who now think they will be secure when "welfare cheats are forced to work," will find themselves needing the very assistance that has been taken away.

A second theme that ties the essays and narratives in this book together is that the identification with low-income women is not a simple one, and that solutions to women's poverty must be varied due to the differences in cultural backgrounds of women themselves, even as the struggle for economic and political power for all must be joined. We try always to show how women of color and women who are immigrants, experience poverty and welfare differently from white women, and how solutions may look different from different vantage points. We know this is sensitive ground. Far too many people are still willing, for example, to agree with Lawrence Mead and others of his ilk that "the world view of blacks makes them uniquely prone to the attitudes contrary to work, and thus vulnerable to poverty and dependency." So we want to proclaim the universality, and normality, of poverty. But we know too that, since both women of color and the fathers of their children have been so often denied equal access to education and employment, they may view job and life "opportunities" differently. For example, if the descendants of slaves had all waited to have children until they could reasonably expect economic security, then there would be few black people in the United States today. For many poor women, then, having children becomes a statement of hope undefeated by circumstances—not the unwise choice it may appear to be from the perspective of middle-class "rationality."

A third theme is that the failures of the welfare system, which no one knows better than poor women, should lead to calls for a better, more fully accountable welfare state not to demands for less government. All the authors in this book try to temper their criticisms of how bad welfare has been with the caveat that the problems are not inevitable, but rather often stem from policy compromises made with opponents of *any* accountable government. At the same time, our authors do show how destabilizing, demeaning, and disrespectful the system can be, and do not accept that somehow, if we are to have a public bureaucracy, people will inevitably be treated this way.

Fourth, this book maintains throughout that women can speak for themselves, regardless of their situation. The obvious expertise of the welfare recipients in this volume is as powerful as the professional knowledge of the economists, social workers, or sociologists. All too often we have seen professional advocates be unable to give up their self-appointed role as judge of what is politically feasible or theoretically appropriate. They then lose the trust of welfare recipients, despite their good will, and desperately needed coalitions collapse as a consequence.

In our conclusion we argue that only when "the veterans of poverty" take leadership will successful strategies for change be adopted. At every point in the book we try to present the knowledge and meaning that comes from experience as of equal weight with the conceptualizations that come from professional methods.

Finally, the point of this volume is that the problems facing poor women, facing all women, facing everyone, are *political* in their solutions, no matter how deeply economic, structural, gendered, moral, or cultural their cause. We all argue that "crying out loud," banding together, organizing, strategizing, and educating ourselves together *can* make a difference. Better policies are possible, and broader movements can demand them. We are not sure how exactly to do this, although different authors here propose different strategies. We *are* sure that current welfare reforms passed at the federal level and anticipated by state reforms across the nation are wrong—dead wrong and we try to explain why. Moreover, we attempt to suggest ways to make arguments that will allow people—across a wide political spectrum—to look again in the mirror and see their fate as tied to that of women on welfare. We restate the problems so that people from vastly different situations can perceive them as their own, and not be afraid of facing the moral implications of sounding "utopian" or demanding.

Structure and Assumptions of the Book

This collection is divided into four sections, each with an overview written by us to show the links among the selections. This first brief section allows us to "put ourselves in the picture" by showing some of our history with welfare. The second section explains why women are differentially poor and how complexity and double binds keep them from solving their "personal" problems by themselves, either by just getting a job or by finding a better mate. The third section focuses especially on the welfare system, how it works to divide and destabilize people, and, through its overdetermined failures, to provide a wedge for the Right to gain power and legitimacy as it attempts to dismantle the welfare state. The concluding section makes suggestions about how the differing groups who must be in any real coalition for change can listen to, talk with, and teach one another more effectively.

Throughout the book, our image is one of talking across tables:

kitchen tables where women so often share their hopes and fears with each other, seminar tables where people come to learn and analyze with each other, meeting tables around which coalitions are built or fall apart, even negotiating tables where people come together to try to hammer out alternative policies. Here we briefly place "on the table" our basic agenda in presenting all the sections and suggestions:

♦ There is an absolute *need to personalize poverty* and welfare when we talk about it. Whoever is talking will think more clearly and connect more effectively if we bring the issues home for ourselves and for the audience.

♦ *Welfare rights activists have not been paranoid* all these years. Once liberals decided that it was all right to force women to work for a welfare check rather than to provide income as a right, we started down that "slippery slope" (made easier by Clintonian promises to "end welfare as we know it") that has led to today's authoritarian and punitive policies.

♦ We *can't avoid talking about media-generated but real examples of undesirable personal behavior,* or people will think we don't care about the costs to those people and communities closest to the problems. We can't deny that some folks are in real personal trouble and may act in ways that no one can defend. Our task is to find ways to get people to see how structural poverty sometimes creates the sense of hopelessness that can cause destructive behavior, and certainly makes it harder to help people change undesirable patterns. At any economic level, addictions or other personal failures are deeply unsettling, but when we give in to cruel, punishing responses then matters only get worse. The point of public policy is to create a floor that society doesn't let you fall below—whether luck, or personal mistakes, or structural problems bring you down.

♦ For almost all audiences we *must find ways to engage with the hard discussion about jobs.* Employment must provide money, as well as allowing time and energy for necessary caregiving work within the home, or it is not a viable option for single mothers. We have to keep seeking arguments that push people to realize that no mother "can do nothing all day" and, for the good of women and their children, society must support single mothers in having the baseline option of attending to the needs of their children first, if they so choose.

♦ We cannot just talk about policy options and facts about welfare as if empirical information alone will settle the issues. We *have to discuss and challenge deeply held moral convictions.* Today there is profound disagreement about how to set the moral floor of basic support and respect that members of this society owe to each other, regardless of whether anyone's behavior breaks cultural taboos regarding sexual, economic, or marital behavior. Unless we are willing to address questions in a moral frame, and openly debate "values" which are punitive (or not shared by all), then we won't engage the real issues, nor mobilize many who are on the sidelines.

◆ On the other hand, *facts about poverty and the welfare system will be useful* to help advocates, women on welfare and potential friends make arguments that convince themselves and motivate allies. So it is vital to speak from the heart, but it is critical to have the facts to back ourselves up.

◆ The *logical conclusions of right-wing assaults must not be avoided.* The success of the conservative agenda may have finally allowed others to see how central welfare is and to marshal attention to women's poverty. But we cannot assume that some natural "pendulum swing" will permit going back to the old existing system of only slightly less punitive programs and denial of consequences. While the welfare state did not create poverty, its contradictions and inadequacies did create the "logic" for dismantling what is, in fact, a basic floor that more people will need as capitalism lurches down its self-destructive path. We need to propose ways to build a real floor, not a sea of water for single moms to miraculously walk upon.

Acknowledgments

Most of all, we want to acknowledge each other. Sometimes we stare at each other surprised that two women born the same year, but in such different places, have come together in such sisterhood. Diane's family is African American, with deep roots in the northern black community and in the tradition of the black church and Civil Rights movement. Ann was born in the white, lower-middle-class South, into a family proud of Confederate ancestors and fundamentalism. Yet both of us found lasting visions in the struggles for racial and social justice that defined our coming of age in the 1960s. We share a common energy for change—which Diane finds rooted in her mother, her community, and her church, and Ann traces to rebellion against religious and social beliefs of her childhood and to her sister's collaboration in the struggle. Since we met in 1978, before either of us was a mother, we found great richness in exploring the meaning of our differences and similarities. As a leftist feminist professor who found protection in history and theory, Ann introduced Diane to perspectives that moved her to teach and make new connections between ideas and actions. As an activist, believer, and organizer, Diane helped Ann to find ways to move out into the world, to engage and listen to ideas that challenged her political preconceptions. As we have raised children, and faced the increasing stresses of middle age, we have encouraged each other. Our joint work on this book has pushed both of us, and given each of us profound pleasure at the official excuse it gave for long hours of conversation, even after we should have stopped talking and just finished.

Joanne Pearlman played a special role as editor, friend, and organizer during the last phase of pulling the book together. She did more than edit and fix our disks; she gave comments and optimism that held us together. Without her immense skill, patience, and talent, we simply would never have finished. And she, in turn, found technical support and rescue from Charlotte Corbett, to whom we all owe a great debt.

We also must acknowledge our many colleagues and students at the College of Public and Community Service at the University of Massachusetts at Boston. They were always there to give us ideas, inspiration, and support as we tried to fit the work of this book around our obligations to them. Especially important here were Marian Darlington-Hope, James Williams, Jim Green, David Rubin, Angela Lopez-Fleming, Clark Taylor, Margaret Rhodes, Anna Madison, Evonne Hill Sheppard, Ismael Ramírez-Soto and Shoshanna Erlich.

Of course, we want to thank all our contributors not only for writing for us, but, more important, for putting up with our less than tightly organized style of creating this book. We *were* overwhelmed, and sometimes made it almost impossible for anyone to write for us. Jean Thomas Griffin, Kathy Kautzer, Sister Pat Lambert, Molly Mead, Debbi Levine, Jackie Pope, and Renae Scott deserve special recognition for being victims of our failure to act on their earnest responses to our solicitations. Our new friends at South End Press, especially Dionne Brooks, never gave up either.

And we cannot give enough back to our children; Lisa, Gwyne, and Bronwen, and our sisters; Sylvia White and Barbara Marlowe, or to Diane's mother, Agnes White, and Ann's husband, George Abbott White, in return for their never-ending patience, support, and love.

OUT OF THE FRYING PAN
Reflections of a Former Welfare Recipient
Diane Dujon

I HAVE BEEN TRYING TO OUT-SWIM POVERTY ALL OF MY LIFE. Sometimes I'm lucky and a forceful wave propels me forward, but that wave produces a powerful undertow, which drags me back into the depths of poverty once again. It becomes a case of *"the aheader I go, the behinder I get!"* I've been swimming a long time, but the shore seems no closer. I'm getting tired and I am scared because I know exhaustion could cause me to drown.

Many people consider me a welfare success story. But if I am, it is in *spite* of welfare, not because of it. The success I have had is due in large part to the fact that my mother lives with me. She does most of the cooking and housework and is there when my daughter arrives home from school or is sick—in effect, I have a *"wife."* The other major reason I have achieved some success is that I was able to obtain a college degree. I had to constantly fight the Welfare Department to earn my degree while continuing to receive benefits. I was determined to be in a position where I could have a chance to become self-sufficient when I rejoined the workforce.

In 1984, I was offered a professional staff position at the university I had attended. In addition to my degree, I had more than 15 years of previous office experience in positions ranging from file clerk to secretary to administrative assistant, but my degree enabled me to earn a breadwinner's wage. The reality is that while I was fortunate enough to find employment immediately upon graduation, I still had to rely heavily upon the organizing and networking skills I had developed while surviving on welfare.

Another reality is that I had much less time for myself and my daughter Lisa. Too much of our "quality" time has been spent coaxing her to get ready for school, church, Girl Scouts, or bed. It's easier now because she's 17, but it's important in a different way for me to be there for her. In fact, in many ways, she needs me even more. I often work long hours, sometimes even bringing work home. Right now, I am taking graduate courses two evenings a week. I spend at least two nights a week attending parent meetings for Lisa's school or meetings in the community. My union activities also consume a considerable amount of my time. Then, my spirit needs to be replenished. I nourish it through my church activities and my community activism.

Even on weekends and holidays, I am usually busy trying to catch up on housework, homework, the laundry, or clothes and food shopping. Too much time is spent being the breadwinner, and the nurturing falls by the wayside. I am always tired because I never get enough rest.

While I was on welfare, I looked forward to completing my degree and re-establishing myself in the workforce. However, I soon found out that working was not the panacea that everyone would have you to believe. In fact, I am struck by the similarities between trying to survive on welfare and striving to thrive on a paycheck.

Conditions had changed radically for workers since 1979, when I had last been in the workforce. (As Stephen King would say, "The world had moved on.") No longer could workers expect to obtain full-time work, or paid health insurance, or job security. The term "steady job" had become obsolete. Does anybody remember company picnics or holiday parties? Although my job included health benefits, reasonable flexibility, liberal vacation and sick time, and increased earnings, I was still living in poverty.

At first, daycare and rent swallowed up my pay. By the time I paid for clothing, health and dental care, utilities, school loans, and transportation, I was broke again. Once my daughter was enrolled in public school and daycare expenses were saved, I had a desperate need to buy a car so that I could attend meetings, conferences, and potluck dinners at my daughter's school, and to allow me to get to her in cases of emergency, and to take her to doctors' appointments.

Once I got a car, my rent began an annual 5 percent climb and, then, my annual raises stopped coming. The university faced deep budget cuts, and layoffs were imminent. Hiring freezes resulted in fewer people working harder and longer hours. My health insurance premiums jumped from 40 cents a month to $40 a month, and then, to $80. My copayments leaped from $3 per visit to $10. After five very uncertain and turbulent years, I finally got a promotion and a raise. That same month, rent control was voted out and my rent was raised by $300 more per month—nearly double what I was paying previously!

It's been more than 12 years since I re-entered the workforce, and I still continue to be limited in my day-to-day decisions and choices. Although I am no longer dependent on a welfare check and the whims of politicians, I am now dependent on a paycheck and the whims of bosses. I have committed 40-plus hours a week of my precious time to a job to make my landlord rich. I still cannot afford to buy a new car, or go away on vacation to visit family and friends more than every three or four years. Yet, I'm one of the lucky ones in my community, so far.

I feel fortunate to have been on welfare because I learned how to survive using my wits. This type of creative thinking is invaluable to all poor people, especially single, female heads of households. I became an expert shopper, cook, and stitcher. I learned how to prioritize and set my own agenda. I also got to know my daughter in a way that would have been impossible if I had worked full-time while she was younger. I concentrated on obtaining my degree and succeeded against a myriad of odds. I believe that these skills helped me to maintain my self-esteem and buoyed my sense of dignity through all the frustrations. I also grew spiritually while on welfare. I learned to rely on God when humankind was neither human nor kind. I call on these resources as much today as I did then.

When I was on welfare, I always felt that the Welfare Department was continuously probing to find out if I had received a crust of bread to which I was not entitled; now, however, I feel that no one even cares if I get a crust of bread! The idea that because I work I need no supports is ludicrous, especially as a single mother.

I essentially have two jobs—one that pays and one that doesn't. My primary job is "mother" and I am determined to do all that is within my power to be the best mother I can be. The second job is the one I get paid for, but it is subordinate to and, in fact, is meant to be a support to my first job. If my paid position detracts from (or interferes with) my role as a mother, or doesn't pay the rent, it is of no use to me. I work to live; I don't live to work.

Life has taught me that none of us is omnipotent—we are all vulnerable at one time or another and we have needs that must be met if we are to survive. Some, but not all, of these needs, can be provided through the job market.

I have lived four lives since becoming an adult: as a single working woman, as a woman married to a poor man, as a welfare mother, and as a working single mother. I can truly say that in all of these lives I have needed supports at one time or another.

It is up to us to do the wise and right thing to ensure our future. Children are only loaned to the families that raise them—they belong to all of us. Our children are our greatest resource, and we must do whatever it takes to make sure that they get the adult guidance and discipline they need to develop into responsible individuals so that they can face the problems of adulthood and develop worthwhile solutions. To properly achieve this goal, we should value the entire family and help each member to live a life of value.

WHY MOTHER SLAPPED ME
Ann Withorn

IN OUR HOT SOUTHERN KITCHEN, AS ALWAYS, MOTHER WASHED dishes. I dried while Sister Barbara put away.

I was a senior in high school, taking "Problems in American Democracy," finding out about a new issue every week that needed to be fixed, in time for Mr. Morrow's standard Friday paper: "Facts about the problem; disputes about the problem; what is being done now; proposed solutions to the problem; what you would do to solve it." Weekly, the droll retired navy captain drilled us in a class that was my first introduction to public policy—outside of church and Sunday school, where return to Jesus, prayer, and avoidance of sin were the perpetual answers. I joked about how we should send our papers to President Johnson, so that he could get on with it.

That week we were studying poverty. Usually, I avoided discussing politics with Mother. She was so sure of her beliefs, and we would fight so easily about so much. But this time I assumed, given the childhood poverty, which had shaped her life, that we could have a discussion.

Wrong.

She was adamant that people who took welfare were lazy, and just didn't want to work hard like she and my father did. "Good people can find jobs if they aren't so picky. Women who have made their bed must lie in it," she insisted.

No radical yet, but I was always willing to react to that tone of dismissal in her voice, heard in so many criticisms of me: "Good girls who try to look pretty, and go to church, and don't read so much will be fine. They won't turn out weird like you."

So I took the bait. "But Mother, I thought you would be more sympathetic. After all, you grew up on welfare."

Mother was not a hitter. Words were her weapons. So when the slap in my face came it was almost an involuntary spasm, accompanied by words hissed between closed teeth. "Don't you *ever* say that again. My family did *not* grow up on welfare. Your grandfather was ill, in the hospital, and received veterans benefits. We earned what we received from the government because he fought in the war. We were *never* on welfare." Then she left, yet another night when my "disrespect" left me with the washing *and* the drying of the dishes.

In our household of denial, the incident would never be discussed again. I was left alone to ponder how my grandmother's poverty—caused by Pop's mental illness after tough service in World War I, followed by his life-long hospitalization beginning when Mother was five—was so different from welfare. The Veteran's Administration never sent enough money, and the checks sometimes just did not come. Grandmother had to live, with three kids, in rummy apartments, share space with questionable relatives, and never have enough. People would look down on her; even her cousins would taunt that her children's father was a "crazy man." Why wasn't that like welfare?

I still wonder and still cannot discuss welfare with Mother.

But I can talk and teach and continually try to figure out why it is that welfare is such a hot zone for people.

Talking about anything can set off some people. But welfare is a sure-fire fight almost anywhere it is discussed. Even people who agree about it get agitated.

Once, on a bus, I sat behind two men who were talking about "welfare queens." Both agreed that it was pathetic that the government was giving them money to do nothing, raise criminals, and get fat. But as they talked, their voices got louder, echoing my mother's deep fury. "Who do they think they are?" one man almost shouted to his friend as he left the bus, "having babies with no fathers, expecting *me* to pay for them?"

It has even affected me. An old friend was in my kitchen, trying to express his doubts to me about whether welfare is good for the Black community where he works. Somehow the idea that I have to defend women on welfare even in my own home, with my own friends, makes me furious. I yelled that he didn't know what he was talking about, how I wouldn't listen to such ignorance in my own kitchen.

I don't usually do this. But I, too, find it hard not to take welfare as a personal issue. When I hear people say cruel things about women on welfare, I want to jump up and scream about how they do not know Debby or Mary or Juanita (or my grandmother?). They work so hard, with so little, and manage so well, or sometimes not so well, in spite of stresses and pressures undiscussed by any "Problems in American Democracy" class.

Over the years of studying poverty, I have come to see that talking about welfare is not about public policy, about how much money should be or can be spent to provide basic economic security to families with children in an uncertain economy. It is about deeply based assumptions about how we view women, and work, and the meaning of the compromises we are supposed to make in this life.

Sometimes I feel weird about doing it, but increasingly, even as an academic who could easily retreat behind facts and figures, I talk personally about women's poverty. I talk about how the latest round of "reforms" reminds me of my family, where plans were promoted and discussed based on denial of what everyone knew to be reality. I cannot help but tell audiences—even as I fear they will think I am as crazy as my grandfather—how in my family we ignored and reframed problems like an uncle's drinking himself to death, or my father's loss of a job. We found ways to deny how serious the problem was, or to go to family picnics and recast the adversity as "the best thing for us." I try to get people to see how the Right is trying to lull everyone with ill-conceived proposals, because pretending they will work makes it appear as if there *are* jobs available for everyone if they seek them; there *are* families that can take in a pregnant teen; there *are* ways to get men to provide for their children—if we just insist on it. Not to deny, not to pretend that these false reforms will work, is to call into question even bigger, even more frightening falsehoods: that jobs alone provide adequate security, or that all women want to raise their kids with a man.

It was scary to admit that my uncle was hopelessly heading down a path of no return. It was terrifying to think that, at 40, my father had held four jobs in six years and might be in real jeopardy of being able to convince anyone else to hire him. But I say to people that just as it was not healthy for my family to pretend that some new scheme to take Uncle Robert on vacation would "turn him around," or to pretend that Daddy was simply taking advantage of another opportunity when we moved yet again, so it is extremely dangerous to deny the reality to which welfare is such a meager response. Many families *do* fail women who can't survive with bodies and souls intact if they remain either with birth families or with the fathers of their children. Most jobs fail single mothers because they cannot provide the income, benefits, and flexibility they need to raise their children. So welfare, which also fails women, still becomes the best solution. At the cost of continued poverty, disrespect, and bureaucratic indignity, it provides at least time and some flexibility to face, and not deny, the life that one has.

Welfare is so personal because, if we think about it, we cannot escape thinking about how insecure jobs are within this capitalist economy and how so many families are not the source of love and support we wish them to be. It also suggests that there could be another way. At heart, bad as we have indeed made the system, AFDC means that there is an option besides doing one's duty within abusive families or in life-destroying jobs. It is terrifying to admit that our acceptance of suffering with bad bosses and our tolerance of intolerable intimate injustices within the home could have been otherwise.

Right now, almost the whole society is trying to slap down women on welfare, telling them, with a societal hiss stronger than any mother could conjure up: "Don't you *ever* say we could have chosen assistance rather than stay in bad marriages; don't you claim that we could have done anything besides take two jobs, never seeing our children and making ourselves sick; don't you *ever* say it because then nothing we've endured makes any sense."

Somehow I knew then, and I know even more clearly now, that even if I have to do the dishes and dry, and get slapped sometimes, it is better to try to say what has to be said, to make such claims, to cry out loud.

TO A SINGLE MOTHER
Susan Eisenberg

When the just-changed diaper
    must be changed
                again,
when a plate of spaghetti is dropped
    deliberately
             onto the kitchen floor
             noodle
                by
                  noodle,
when the phone ringing at bedtime
snaps the spell of stories and songs,
tension topping a hundred three —

I think of you two sharing a one-room flat.
        Mother and Child:
        the Madonna Myth.
No partner to cut the burdens by half.
No family to step in at overload.
No door to quietly close   crying infant
safely in her crib   for a moment's
solitude, a cup of tea.
Who honors your marathon of
                    daily life?

THERE BUT FOR FORTUNE
The Failures of Our Dreams and Back-up Systems

LONG BEFORE THE WELFARE STATE, THE "SCOURGE" OF TEEN pregnancy, or the decline in family values, there was persistent poverty and myths surrounding it. In fairy tales Hansel and Gretel were abandoned in the woods by a poor couple unable to feed them. Neither goodness nor beauty saved Cinderella from having to clean chimneys after her mother died and her father remarried in order to find someone, anyone, to care for her while he traveled. Sister upon sister, in fiction and fact, was married off unhappily to save families from poverty. Orphans could find no safe home. Even in the biblical story of Ruth, poor, unmarried women had to glean the wheat fields, picking up the droppings after male harvesters were done. Indeed, poverty among women is an abiding theme in legend and history.

In myth and story, things could end happily ever after: poverty ended with a good marriage. Today, women are offered another option, with roots as much in fantasy as in reality: Poverty can end with a good job.

But woe still betides the woman with children who can't make the good marriage. And, SuperMoms still find kryptonite everywhere: in "job packages" that lack the time flexibility, adequate health benefits, and/or adequate wages to sustain families; in training programs that lead nowhere; in unsafe neighborhoods that demand Mom be home more, not less, than her suburban counterpart. Indeed, the cultural metaphor that springs most to mind to define the world facing today's mothers is a perpetual game of "Jumanji"—one where every roll of the dice yields yet another unplanned disaster. This month it is two children with consecutive cases of chicken pox and no back-up childcare. Next month it is a returning mate who falls off the wagon and wreaks havoc with family peace, so that kids miss school and Mom can't think. By summer it is a sister's car that breaks down so that she can't take the kids to day camp as planned. And then there is the landlord whose rent must be raised, plus the new welfare rule that demands monthly recertification of one's poverty. And, in this game, no sensitive Robin Williams ever materializes to wrestle the crocodiles or finally turn back the clock on the nightmare.

This section collectively paints the scenario for just such destabilization. The media, as Laura Flanders explains, helps create lies that blame women for their poverty. Instead, women are poor, Elaine Donovan and Mary Stevenson argue, because they were born into lower-income families whose ability to offer back-up support when men or jobs disappear is quickly used up. Fong Yee Lee shows how women get poorer because, as immigrants, they are expected to be poor but "proud" of the opportunity to suffer in America. Women become poorer still because, if they are not white, the education they and the men they know received may have stifled access to options, or they may not have been welcomed or trusted by employers for so long that grasping for yet one more brass ring has lost its appeal, as Lisa Catanzarite and Vilma Ortiz demonstrate. Randy Albelda and Chris Tilly explain that women stay poor because jobs do not pay enough, nor offer enough benefits and flexibility to be affordable, especially if even one child is suffering the aftershocks of damaging relationships. The welfare system to which women rightfully turn for help betrays them. When benefits are 40 percent below the poverty line, with changing and demeaning rules and constant suspicion of fraud, a woman is blocked in her efforts to make progress, even before "reformers" begin their meat cleaver approach to her complex needs. Margaret Cerullo and Marla Erlien go further to help us understand why single mothers are so feared—because, by their very existence they open up cultural options and questions about the meaning of a healthy society.

Laura Walker; Beth Harris and Susan James; Marion Graham; and the Roofless Women in narratives edited by Marie Kennedy all examine the complex ways in which cultural "facts of life" have created hard choices and self-defeating circles for so many women. Robin A. Robinson suggests how we can find hope by listening to the dreams of teen mothers, even when we are fueled by anger at understanding how they have become political pawns. And, again, Lisa Catanzarite and Vilma Ortiz add further to our understanding that women of color whose first language is not English, face double jeopardy as they try to maneuver through a system where every rule works against them, and almost every expectation cannot be met.

Most important, however, the women who tell their stories in this section make us wonder, again why can't others see the strengths buried underneath all the pain? Why isn't the media's Big Story the strength that single mothers bring to their astoundingly difficult task? For us, one key to changing the contemporary social dynamic is to begin to recognize that single mothers are the "mother heroes" of our age, women to be acknowledged for their trials and supported through their tribulations, not demonized and blamed for circumstances far beyond their control.

IF WE COULD, WE WOULD BE SOMEPLACE ELSE
Laura Walker

I AM A SINGLE MOTHER WITH A 13-YEAR-OLD AND A 14-YEAR-old. I was married for about four years. We had an income of thiry to forty thousand dollars a year. I worked part-time at nights; he worked full-time during the day. We had our two children 15 months apart. When the youngest was six months old and the oldest was 20 months old and after a very abusive marriage, including attempted murder when my former husband tried to poison me, I finally had restraining orders taken out against him. I found out that restraining orders are only good if the cops find him in my presence—if he isn't, too bad!

My husband left and not only cleaned out the bank account, but forged my signature on our last income tax return as well. There was obviously nothing I could do about either, since everything was in both our names. He also took the car and left me with the two children. I didn't even have a stroller that worked properly, and I was living in a three-room apartment. We had planned to buy a house in order to move, but I was left there alone with my children and had to experience the welfare system and found it to be very dehumanizing.

I was called a "good welfare recipient." To this day, I still can't figure out what that means, but I guess it was because I was totally intimidated and always expressed my gratitude for the too little the welfare worker did for us. Shortly after going on welfare, the phone was shut off and sometimes the lights were shut off as well.

I called DSS asking them for counseling help; and since my phone was shut off, they just showed up at the door. The DSS worker said she didn't have to come in because I wasn't under any suspicion. I told her she could come in if she didn't mind the breakfast mess. She came in and found the kids in the bathtub, where they kind of got their quick physical. The DSS worker said that I was articulate, the house was clean, and that the boys seemed very healthy. However, there were no services that they could give me.

I told her I really felt that there was something wrong with me, even though I wasn't hurting my children. (I guess poverty was getting to me.) I really needed to go to counseling, but I had no one to watch these two babies, even to let me out of the house for two hours. Things were very tough, so I tried it again eight months later with the same results; there were no services, and the welfare office said there was nothing they could do.

Finally, I started out in a Head Start Program. I thought my oldest child was active and I was very tired, but after a core evaluation at Head Start's insistence, it turned out that my son was gifted but had a really bad attention deficit disorder and was very hyperactive. We then started with the system, and my kids were in two different programs at two different times of the day. There was no childcare available, and there was no way that I could hold down a job and get someone to pick up the kids at separate times; so I stayed on welfare. I received job training once the boys started school on a fairly regular schedule.

After four years of doing that, my son seemed to be somewhat stable. There was constant counseling, occupational therapy, and there were home evaluations—you name it. When your child has what they call an "emotional problem" and you are a low-income woman, they kind of look at you like you must be doing something wrong. There has got to be something hidden, no matter how open you are.

In time I got a job and finally moved into subsidized housing. I worked as an organizer for 50, sometimes 60 hours a week to get flex time to meet my childrens' needs, and to hold on to this job. I was throwing nickels in the bus by Thursday so you couldn't see that I wasn't putting 50 cents in the slot. It was a constant struggle. I had to work on Saturday and Sunday nights, but at least I was able to meet the childrens' needs and I was able to keep that job. It was hard, but it was possible. It turned out that my younger son had a blood lead level of 40. The landlord had denied that there was any lead in the apartment. So, being the dummy that I was, until the day I moved and the inspectors came in, I didn't even know that there really was lead in the apartment! By then, my youngest son started to act up, and to add to that, my older son was having what I call "normal" issues. The childcare center kept punishing my child by throwing him out three or four days at a time. I thought, "How can I hold down this job?"

Then my son began hiding under his desk at school, and it turned out that, with all the counseling and examinations by everyone, he had become profoundly depressed and suicidal. It became necessary for me to pull him out of childcare or it would seem as though I was neglecting his needs—so we went back on welfare. My son was hospitalized for his depression.

It has been three years now since I stopped working outside of my home, and it looks as though I am going to have to stay home until my son doesn't need me. Even at 14 years old, he is afraid to be at home alone. I live in a neighborhood with over 100 children. My 13-year-old is now acting up and turning on to what's going on in the streets. So I find my priority is my children.

I am kind of happy today because my kids earned some money shoveling during the last snowstorm, and they bought themselves new pairs of pants and new shirts. While I am really glad that they have a strong work ethic, they constantly rub my nose in it all day long. "I bought this pair of pants myself; you didn't!" This is what I hear, yet I tell them to be proud of that. I am often aware that their opinions of me are being shaped by their friends in the neighborhood. I am also glad because I have been feeling pretty bad because I haven't been able to meet their needs. They have also been beaten up for wearing "bobos" (sneakers without a brand name), and that doesn't help an emotionally troubled child as it is, it really doesn't.

So for me, I guess a typical day starts at 5:00 a.m. My oldest son is on 100 mgs. of Elevil for his depression, which kind of gives him a hangover in the morning. I have to throw a glass of cold water on his face and then put up with him telling me off, put up with him telling me how the world stinks and how his life wouldn't be so bad if I had been an effective parent. He got straight A's for the third term in a row and wants to know why he can't get $5 for an A as his friends do. I can only give him praise; I can't give him anything else.

I try to find something besides macaroni and cheese to feed them for the third night in a week. A good day (and this sounds awful) is when they had a candy bar and they don't feel like having supper. Then, it is a little less on me.

I go shopping four times a week. That sounds great, but it is only because I have to carry the bags home so that my kids will not be seen with food stamps anymore. The last time we needed change, the cashier hollered across the store that they needed food stamp singles. So my boys refused to go through that again. They just said, "No, (we are) not!"

I also do my laundry in the bathtub quite often because I can't afford the laundromat, nor do I have the stamina to drag it three blocks. Clothes don't always squeeze out too well, so they may not look so clean; but you don't want to give people these excuses. So when the teacher complained, I just took it like a dummy. It's another very depressing thing.

I don't know if people realize that we *feel*. There is nothing wrong with us. It is so depressing, you know, to look at my life. I've got a 10-year-old sofa and a recliner that sinks on the left side. Well, it is *still* a recliner and I have no idea where I would possibly ever get another piece of furniture. There is just *no* way; even simple things are hard to get.

We found a bureau on the side of the road. I used rope for drawer handles and my older son now has a bureau to keep his clothes in. Before, he didn't even have that! Because of my son's special needs, I got a place where the boys could have separate bedrooms, so they couldn't even share the same bureau anymore.

In all this time, my husband earned good money; but no matter how hard I pursued him, I have never received one cent of child support. I am considered a liberal, but I think I am really a conservative when I think of men who don't give at least emotional support to their children. If a father leaves the state, or just simply goes underground and works without giving a social security number, he still has his, and his children still go without. Something has to be done; the system has a lot of problems. They are happy to blame us as women, but it goes much deeper than that. We are just a symptom of the way things are being run in this state.

I also need to get out of my financial crisis. As soon as I do work, with the way the system runs now, my wages are garnished immediately because of a loan my husband and I took out when we got married. It was in both our names. I am considered the responsible party no matter how many facts I put to a judge's face, because my ex-husband just left the state. Easy as that! Too hard to get him; easier to get me. Why? I am not a deadbeat! I never ran up another bill after he left, but I got stuck with a cleaned-out bank account, no income tax return, and a loan. Every time I go to work, within a month I get a letter pulling me into court, and when I don't show up for court, I end up having my wages garnished directly. There is no winning this!

I would like to be able to go to school to earn enough to provide for myself and my children. Things have just been crazy. I don't sit around eating bon-bons, but I don't know how I would be able to *think* long enough to get a homework paper done. Unless someone helps, I don't know how I can manage this. I don't own any clothes; I've got three or four shirts, another pair of jeans and sneakers, and that is it. There is not enough money to get myself more clothes. There is not even enough to go to the Salvation Army and get things! So how am I supposed to go to work and look like someone even wants to hire me?

People think we are too stupid or we really enjoy this life that we find ourselves in. Maybe they should put themselves in our position and realize that if we could, we would be somewhere else, believe me!

MEDIA LIES
Media, Public Opinion, and Welfare
Laura Flanders with Janine Jackson and Dan Shadoan

THE 1994-95 DEBATE OVER WELFARE POLICY GAVE THE MAIN-stream news media an opportunity to revive some of the longest-running and most beloved myths in the misogynist repertoire: the myth of out-of-control teen pregnancy; the notion that the (relatively small) AFDC program is the engine driving the United States into debt; the image of the "irresponsible" poor female as disproportionately black; and "morality"—not money—as the media's chosen explanation for the problems of the poor.

Much of the media's reporting on welfare and its "reform" featured familiar scapegoating, but in the wake of the '94 elections some reporters managed to score new highs in the game of blame-the-victim. *Newsweek*'s Jonathan Alter, for example, set some sort of record for targeting teenage moms when he wrote, "Every threat to the fabric of this country—from poverty to crime to homelessness—is connected to out-of-wedlock teen pregnancy" (12/12/94). Blaming poor, pregnant teens is a neat way to explain toxic waste, corporate corruption, AIDS, unemployment, cancer, and crime. But it's also shoddy journalism.

For the record, teenagers aren't the big drain on the welfare program: Less than 6 percent of AFDC recipients are under 20; only 1 percent goes to people under 18 years of age. *USA Today* printed the data (1/20/95), but didn't use the facts to refute the rhetoric. Instead, reporter Leslie Philips parroted the politicians: "Rising teen pregnancies and out of wedlock births are an alarming trend." The number of teenagers having babies has actually dropped significantly in the last few decades: from 9.1 percent of 15- though 19-year-olds in 1958 to 6.2 percent in 1991. As for the so-called "out-of-wedlock" births, to make the figures sound more alarming, news accounts focus not on actual numbers but on the percentage of births to unmarried mothers. That figure has less to do with unmarried "children wanting children," as syndicated columnist Charles Krauthammer put in the *Washington Post* (11/19/93), than with the tumbling rate of childbirth by married women.

Contrary to "conventional wisdom," the general public tends to be generous. "The suspicion that poorer people are getting something for nothing is much harder to bear than the visible good fortune of the richer," wrote columnist Mary McGrory (*Washington Post*, 1/15/95). But a December 1994 poll by the Center for the Study of Policy Attitudes (CSPA) showed that 80 percent of respondents agreed that the government has "a responsibility to try to do away with poverty." When asked about their support for AFDC, described as "the federal welfare program which provides financial support for unemployed poor single mothers with children," only 21 percent said funding should be cut; 29 percent said the government should pay out more.

These facts, and many more like them, were repeatedly ignored by reporters covering welfare in the wake of the November 1994 elections. In a bizarre column about the "sexually irresponsible culture of poverty," *Newsweek*'s Joe Klein provided accidental insight into what might have been going on. "Television is the only sustained communication our society has with the underclass," wrote Klein. "It is the most powerful message we send" (2/16/95). Given that relationship to poor people, it's no wonder that many in the mainstream media made their first priority not informing the public of economic reality, but indicting women, people of color, youngsters, and the poor.

What they mostly lacked in data, news reports made up for in "messages." Reporting on welfare was rife with communiqués shot from "us" to "them"—and reporters left little doubt as to who was who. In one vivid example, multi-million-dollar earner Diane Sawyer of ABC, devoted a segment to grilling a group of teenage mothers receiving Aid To Families with Dependent Children ("PrimeTime Live," 2/16/95). Explaining that "to many people these girls are public enemy No.1," Sawyer harangued them on behalf of "taxpayers" who were "mad as hell." "Answer their question," she demanded: "Why should they pay for your mistake?"

Sixteen-year-old Lisa Wright, one of "PrimeTime"'s interviewees, tried to point out that when it comes to taxpayer dollars, AFDC is "such a small percentage now, you know, of the amount of money taxpayers send in. Most of the money is going for defense." But Sawyer was having none of it: She dragged the discussion right back to female "irresponsibility." If only ABC's star anchor was as tough with CEO's and heads of state.

Sawyer was not the only one burying the economic lead on the welfare story in favor of a discourse on "shame." A three-month study by Fairness and Accuracy in Reporting (FAIR) suggests that the mainstream media have made a practice of slanting the story against poor women—and habitually have echoed the conservative Republicans' anti-AFDC agenda at the expense of analyzing the economic facts.

FAIR surveyed the sources used in welfare coverage in half a dozen of the most influential news outlets (the *New York Times*, the *Washington Post*, ABC News, PBS's "McNeil/Lehrer NewsHour," *Time*, and *Newsweek*) from December 1, 1994 to February 24, 1995. Revealed was a truncated spectrum of political opinion, a skimpy selection of experts, and a lot of moralizing that favored conventional wisdom over dissent. It comes as no surprise that the debate on welfare was male-dominated. Of sources whose gender could be identified, 71 percent (608 sources) were men—discussing policy proposals that will disproportionately affect women. Not counting welfare recipients, 77 percent of the sources were male.

Some of this gender imbalance resulted from reporters' reliance on government sources. Having accepted the arbitrary timeline of the "First 100 Days" of the new Republican Congress, reporting on welfare policy became primarily a story about politicians and parties, not women and kids. The specious nature of some of the lawmakers' positions got lost in the thrill of the congressional chase. In the period studied, reporters used current and former government officials as sources more than any other group, making up 59 percent of sources. Twenty-four percent of all sources were members of the U.S. Congress (72 percent Republican, 28 percent Democratic), 24 percent were state and local officials, while 9 percent represented the Clinton administration.

With specific proposals being debated in Congress, it's natural that Capitol Hill would provide the lead for many stories. But the Washington, D.C.-driven nature of coverage also limited the debate.

For example, since the Republican and Democratic leadership agreed that spending on the poor ought to be restricted, differing only on details, it was easy for reporters to emphasize consensus. The *New York Times'* David Rosenbaum (2/10/95) consigned any dissenters from the bipartisan view to invisibility, declaring that "politicians and scholars from all points of the political compass agree...that, as Rep. E. Clay Shaw, Jr. said today, "[the welfare system has] destroyed responsibility, diminished personal dignity and created economic disincentives that bar people from success."

Of course, plenty of scholars and some politicians do not agree with Clay Shaw, chair of the House subcommittee that drafted the "Personal Responsibility Act," which was passed by Congress in 1996. But Shaw's critics were way outnumbered. With 37 appearances, Rep. Shaw (R-FL.) was the single most quoted media source on welfare in the period. Shaw, who described the current welfare system as "pampering the poor" (*New York Times,* 2/16/95), was followed by Newt Gingrich, who racked up 34 appearances. President Clinton showed up 26 times.

Cited as frequently as members of Congress were state and local officials—largely the Republican governors who run "conservative state-of-the-art welfare reform programs," as they were called by the *Washington Post* (2/10/95). While a careful look at the track record of some of those state programs could be instructive, the largely uncritical attention given Governor John Engler of Michigan (21 appearances) and Wisconsin's Tommy Thompson (17 appearances) only promoted the idea that "success" in dealing with welfare should be defined as cutting government assistance; "expertise" was equated with "getting tough."

An ABC "World News Tonight" show "American Agenda" feature on Governor Thompson (1/13/95), for example, didn't include a single nay-saying source—no one to contradict correspondent Rebecca Chase's claim that "Wisconsin has virtually turned its welfare offices into employment offices." Other reporters (*Sacramento Bee,* 2/17/95) have found plenty of people critical of California's new "Work Not Welfare" programs—but those criticisms weren't permitted to interrupt the flow of the World News.

With the united front of Capitol Hill "consensus" standing at one end of the media's spectrum, recipients of welfare and other social services stood at the other. Recipients made up 10 percent of the media's sources in the period that FAIR studied. And their roles were strictly confined. Reminiscent of much reporting on the AIDS crisis, stories on welfare drew a stark distinction between poverty's "innocent" and "guilty" victims. The acceptably "innocent" were children, the "guilty" were their moms. Although most of the AFDC-receivers quoted were young women, mainstream reporters were emphatic in their rhetorical distinction between these "bad" aid recipients and the "good" poor child.

A *New York Times* headline (12/18/94) made no bones about it: "Despising Welfare, Pitying Its Young," Jason DeParle's article, pinpointed the central problem of welfare reform: "The more one seeks to punish the parent, the greater the risks to the child." While poor children certainly need defenders, most welfare rights advocates agree that poor children come from poor families. In the media, however, "innocent children" were often ominously separated from their guilty moms (just as "AIDS babies" were often described as more or less self-conceived.) Cutting off aid to young mothers, reported the *Washington Post* (2/14/95), "has drawn sharp criticism from advocates for the poor, who say innocent children would suffer." So much for the mothers. They weren't even in *Newsweek*'s equation: "Almost everyone agrees that millions of kids are in jeopardy" (12/12/94). Not a poor woman in sight.

For centuries, U.S. culture has demonized "outsider" groups by associating them (African Americans, queers, feminists, commies, immigrants) with sex. In the media's welfare debate public enemy number one was sexualized too—and no group was presented as more "guilty" than the lascivious teenage girl. Unmarried teenagers were linked to "every threat to the fabric of this country" by Jonathan Alter (*Newsweek,* 12/12/94.) In February 1995, Alter and *Newsweek* frankly gloried in the theme of "shame" for poor young women, comparing them to "drunk drivers," and claiming that "the public is game for a little humiliation."

The relegitimization of such outmoded terms as "illegitimacy" reflected an eagerness to resurrect top-down blaming and shaming. But women were disproportionately targeted for punishment. According to sociologist Mike Males, 70 percent of so-called "teen" pregnancies are the result of sex with men over 20. Males' widely published research suggests that 50,000 teen pregnancies a year are caused by rape and two-thirds of teen mothers have histories of sexual abuse by a perpetrator averaging 27 years of age. And if, as syndicated columnist George Will has written, the welfare crisis is "a crisis of character development," the statistics suggest that at least half of the problem lies with the impregnators—most of whom are not female or young.

When men were mentioned in the welfare debate, it was usually only as a source of quick-fix dollars. On CBS, Clay Shaw told "Face the Nation" that "the irresponsibility of male partners is killing the American family" (1/29/94). Certainly, $34 million should *not* be owed in unpaid child support to women with children, but evidence suggests that what's killing the family is poverty, not just bad dads. According to the Census Bureau, a two-parent family living in poverty is *twice* as likely as its middle-class equivalent to break up during a period of two years. As for extracting the money owed to poor mothers, discussion of welfare in isolation from tax codes, the minimum wage, labor law enforcement, and the bigger economic picture puts blame on poor parents, male and female—and keeps the focus off a system that benefits from keeping workers desperate for even low-paid jobs.

Direct interviews with welfare recipients could have contributed complexity to the coverage and might have helped to put a "human face" on welfare. But the poor women (and a few men) who appeared as sources for reporters during the period FAIR studied were given certain, limited roles. At worst, as with Diane Sawyer, receivers were cast as the "embodiment" of a "problem" or a "pathology," and forced to defend themselves.

At best, the selection of certain women to represent "welfare mothers" reinforced misleading stereotypes, especially with regard to teenagers and AFDC. When the age of welfare recipients was given in media reports, they were generally 17, 18, or 19 years old—even though only 6 percent of mothers who receive AFDC are younger than 20.

Although the number of white women roughly equals the number of African Americans on AFDC, photo-editors consistently skewed the picture in a racist way. When *US News & World Report* (1/16/95) illustrated a cover piece on welfare—six of the seven pictures were women of color, mostly African Americans. The only white woman pictured was described as clinically depressed, as if poverty only affects white people who are in some way handicapped.

Some recipients were used to confirm "expert" opinion, as when, explaining that some legislators hope to reduce pregnancies by cutting off benefits, *Newsweek*'s reporters declared (12/12/94): "Sure enough," Julia Lestido, a 17-year-old welfare mother from Elizabeth, New Jersey says that if the government abolished aid, "I would prevent myself from having more children."

Families receiving government assistance were set against the "respectable" middle class, who, it was suggested, did not get public help. "A family that works does not get a raise for having a child," wrote columnist Ellen Goodman (*Boston Globe,* 4/16/95). "Why then should a family that doesn't work?" In fact, families recognized by U.S. law *do* receive a premium for additional children, in the form of a $2,450 tax deduction. (In 1996, that deduction is likely to increase.) There are also tax credits to subsidize childcare expenses, up to a maximum of $2,400 per child. No pundit suggested that middle-class families base *their* child-bearing decisions on these publicly funded "perks." No columnist wrote about childless taxpayers, angry at being denied the breaks that go to taxpayers who have kids.

One other role for the woman on welfare was the "walk-on part," playing a "temporarily misguided" but ultimately "recovered" mom—like the women cited in the *New York Times* (2/17/95) who "hated [welfare] more than [they hated] the ex-husbands…who left them or beat them."

Even when these stories are sympathetic, as they sometimes are, they confirm the conventional wisdom that poverty is a personal problem: Like "dependency," "poverty" is a curable disease. A listener to FAIR's radio program, "CounterSpin," decried this depiction:

> My experience of welfare single moms is of heroines…women who are courageous, hard-working and creative, I would like to hear stories of these women in the media. Not just the ones who graduate from college and become a 'success,' but the ones who keep on doing their best for their kids under conditions that would daunt some of their better-off sisters.

Cogent analysis could have provided a welcome intervention between the rhetoric of politicians and the anecdotal stories of welfare receivers. Indeed, research and advocacy groups made up only 9 percent of media sources during the December to February period, and even though reporters talked to people from a variety of think tanks, a very limited range of policy proposals were permitted to direct the media debate. In an ideal world of reporting, journalists covering the Republican plans would have sought out alternative proposals to contrast with the congressional leadership's. Instead, the press restricted critics to responding to this or that aspect of conservative ideas, and no poverty-solving proposals other than cutting welfare were seriously explored. A job-creation program, or even a raise in the minimum wage, might do more for welfare recipients' economic futures than simply throwing them off the rolls—but progressive alternatives were virtually never given a space to be heard.

What critics there were of the Republican plan usually spanned a spectrum from A to B: Referring to a cut-off of benefits to unwed mothers under 18 and their children, the *New York Times* reported (2/10/95), "Liberals object to this idea because they think it punishes innocent children, and many conservatives are opposed because they fear it would encourage abortions." Harshly critical voices—which neither defend the current welfare system nor embrace conservative plans—were not excluded from the discussion; the facts they presented just weren't used to challenge the rhetorical rules that had been set up. Articles might occasionally mention the fact that studies show no relationship between benefit levels and birth rates—for example—but reporters wouldn't be so rude as to confront a policy-maker with that fact. Even intermittent references to crucial issues like the health care needs of people on welfare—by people like Robert Greenstein from the Center on Budget and Policy Priorities (4 appearances)—weren't enough to derail the Republican-led discussion about teenaged moms' morality.

Sometimes critics of welfare cuts contribute the punch line, long after a discussion that their comments contradict. The final paragraph of David Rosenbaum's 1,100-word story on "The Welfare Enigma" (*New York Times*, 2/10/95), for example, quoted the Urban Institute's Isabel V. Sawhill, who warned that welfare cuts wouldn't save money and would "leave people homeless." With Sawhill's perspective having been left for the wrap-up, no other source had to respond to her point—and no follow-up story appeared in which the Urban Institute's experts got the lead.

Similarly, no one was invited to respond to the charge made by religious leaders in the *Washington Post* (2/22/95) that, despite politicians' claims, donations to churches and charities "would do precious little to offset the cuts to social programs." Undaunted, mainstream outlets heralded volunteers like Carol Doe Porter, of Kidcare, Inc. (named ABC's "Person of the Week" after the study period had ended—3/24/95). Porter, according to the *New York Times* (2/6/95), was the "embodiment of the increasingly popular maxim that not all the country's problems need to be solved by throwing government money at them." Porter was singled out for media attention not because she feeds the hungry—thousands of people across the country do that—but because she personified a right-wing political argument. The implication of stories like the *New York Times'* profile—headlined "Mother Teresa of Houston' Fights Hunger and Government Aid"—is that we can have *either* "communities that care" *or* government spending on programs for the poor.

After participating in two hours of a "Firing Line" debate leavened with smug male jokes at the expense of poor women, economist Frances Fox Piven commented to the *St. Petersburg Times* (5/8/94), "I am struck by how little evidence matters in talk about welfare." The fact that so many myths prevailed in the media's coverage proved, again, that it's easier to state the "conventional wisdom" than to counter it. ABC "World News Tonight's" Rebecca Chase (2/9/95) illustrated the phenomenon when she "examine[d] the premise" that welfare benefits are an incentive for poor women to have babies. Having opened with the analysis of Robert Rector of the Heritage Foundation (without having identified it as a right-wing think tank), she noted a statement from 79 social scientists whose combined research found little or no impact on birth rates from welfare benefits. "But numbers can be deceiving," she warned—and returned to Rector, who claimed that "the best study on this" showed that a 50 percent increase in benefits led to a 42 percent increase in out-of-wedlock births.

Faced with conflicting claims from comparable researchers, Chase declined to examine their methodologies to see what studies were more persuasive. Instead, she threw up her hands —"the correlation between benefits and babies is complex," she concluded—and returned to analysis by anecdote. (Chase to mother: "Do you think some women have babies just to get on welfare or get more money?" Mother: "Yeah, I know a couple that do").

It's not that journalists don't know they're trading in stereotypes and personal impressions; sometimes they acknowledge as much.

Here's ABC "World News Tonight's" Peter Jennings, introducing a lead segment on the crackdown on "fugitive felons" who've been "receiving welfare checks while hiding from the law": "This problem of welfare fraud does not eat up a particularly large portion of the money spent on welfare, but public anger at what fraud does occur has helped drive the movement for reform." A good lead's a lead, in other words, regardless of whether or not it's relevant.

Had the cast of commentators been broadened to include some wholly excluded groups, the debate, and the degree of veracity, might have been improved. Had an individual who cared about civil rights for all minorities been asked to take part in the discussion, she or he might have mentioned that the Republican welfare plan was not just dismally short-sighted, but clearly discriminatory. Of 890 people quoted, if even one had been an out lesbian, for example, she could have made the point that punishing people for not getting married discriminates against a class of people whose partnerships are not recognized under U.S. law, and against children who are denied "legitimacy" even if they come from the most stable (lesbian) family.

In the months of FAIR's survey, outspoken advocates from the conservative ranks were heard from regularly. Conversely, "radical" advocates of women's rights were nowhere to be found. *Bell Curve* author Charles Murray was cited five times during the period. He told *Newsweek* his opinion of teen mothers (12/12/94): "A great many of them have no business being mothers and their feelings don't count as much as the welfare of the child." But no feminist expert was heard from to offer the opinion that a poor woman has a right to live and feed her children even when she is not married to the father of her child.

A handful of different groups dedicated to defending the rights of children were cited, but apart from one "women's rights advocate" who appeared briefly on "20/20" (12/23/94), women's rights organizations were virtually absent from the source list. Groups such as Planned Parenthood, for example, with its decades-long history of helping women to plan their pregnancies, appeared to be missing from reporters' rolodexes.

Union representatives were cited in only five stories (all but one in the *New York Times*). If reporters had sought out labor's voice more regularly, they might have resisted the invidious portrayal of welfare as a battle between workers and the unemployed. Many welfare recipients do work, but if they all did, there might be trouble. The U.S. Federal Reserve has a policy of raising interest rates whenever unemployment falls below a certain point; if all the unemployed women on welfare were to find a job today, currently employed folks would quickly find themselves on the street to prevent the economy from what the Feds call "overheating." It's not a point that comes up often in conjunction with talk about welfare receivers, who, it is assumed, can get off welfare whenever they want to: *Just get a job.*

On January 29, 1995, at the end of a week consumed by discussion of welfare, all three commercial broadcast networks focused on Congress's plans to "reform" (that is, cut) the nation's insurance program for mothers who are poor. Surfing from CBS's "Face the Nation," to NBC's "Meet the Press," to "This Week with David Brinkley" on ABC, the guest lists (and the reporters featured) included no people of color, no poor people, no consumer or workers' organizations, and no recipients of AFDC. On ABC, David Brinkley introduced California Governor Pete Wilson this way: "I think you know everyone here…" "I do indeed," said Wilson, and no wonder. For his interview with the governor, Brinkley was joined by conservative columnist George Will and ABC's centrist Sam Donaldson— what FAIR calls classic cronyism and an array of opinion that barely gets past A.

Governor Tommy Thompson got the last word on "Face the Nation": He called welfare a "matter of values." Had they been on the program, someone from the labor movement, a feminist, or an advocate of civil rights might have asked "which ones?" That person might have pointed out that so-called "welfare" is a tiny 1 percent of the federal budget (3 percent, max, if food stamps are counted). The money drained away by the bailed-out executives of failed Savings and Loans could have covered all AFDC payments in all the states for almost seven years, according to the *Boston Globe* (5/17/94.) Or they might have mentioned that tackling poverty, not poor people, can be a question of rights. But no one such as that was present, and for the sake of "consensus" or "conventional wisdom," that was just as well. If mainstream media let people talk like that more often, the public might start beating up on "Corporate Welfare Kings." Now, wouldn't that be a shame.

A HOLE IN MY SOUL
Experiences of Homeless Women
Roofless Women's Action Research Mobilization
Researchers: Deborah Clarke, Delores Dell, Brenda Farrell,
Deborah Gray, Betsy Santiago, and Tesley Utley
edited and narrated by Marie Kennedy

In my soul, I'll always be formerly homeless. It changed me so much.
Homelessness was probably one of the very roughest experiences of my
life other than losing a child and it forced me to change because I couldn't
be that person anymore and it forced me to grow and become strong to
get out. That was the only positive thing that came out of it, that I'm the
strong person that I am now, but that part of me will always be there,
like a scar; there's a hole in my soul...

—Brenda Farrell

THE FASTEST GROWING SEGMENT OF THE HOMELESS
population in the United States is women and their children. The
Massachusetts Department of Public Welfare (DPW)[1] estimated that
3,000 families would enter the state-funded shelter system in 1995.
This year, about the same number of women and children will seek
refuge at battered women's shelters across the state. In response, a
vast network of emergency shelters and services has developed to
address the needs of homeless people. In fact, there are 40 individual,
49 family, 15 specialized, and 12 scattered site programs funded by
DPW. There are 17 battered women's programs supported by the
Massachusetts Department of Social Services (DSS). Yet the problems
are not being solved. Since 1991 there has been a 36 percent increase
of homeless women and children in the DPW system and a 57 percent
increase of women and children in battered women's shelters. The
very services that are supposed to help homeless people are often,
perhaps unwittingly, part of the problem. As Kip Tiernan, founder of

the first homeless shelter for women in Boston, put it: "Providing shelter is becoming an alternative to providing a decent standard of living for people, and the shelter industry has become a self-perpetuating industry."[2]

Despite the enormity of the problem and the resources being used to address immediate needs (however ineffectively), there has never been a comprehensive effort to consult directly with those who have experienced homelessness to seek their expertise on how to restructure the current system to effectively combat homelessness. Roofless Women's Action Research Mobilization (RWARM)[3] aims to do just that. RWARM is a participatory action research project investigating causes and solutions to women's homelessness in Massachusetts and mobilizing for solutions as identified by homeless women themselves.

The driving force of the project is the RWARM researchers, six formerly homeless women: Deborah Clarke, Delores Dell, Brenda Farrell, Deborah Gray, Betsy Santiago, and Tesley Utley.[4] Through RWARM, these women have become B.A. students at the College of Public and Community Service (CPCS), University of Massachusetts at Boston. In developing the skills and knowledge necessary to do the research, analysis, and organizing agenda of RWARM, the researchers are becoming powerful advocates and are earning academic credit toward their degrees. Working with Lynn Peterson from the Women's Institute for Housing and Economic Development; Nancy Bristel, formerly of the Boston Emergency Shelter Commission, and Marie Kennedy, a professor at CPCS, they have designed a survey that they are currently administering to 150 homeless women in various circumstances throughout Massachusetts. The interview process is an opportunity to educate and organize homeless women. The results of the study will inform the advocacy efforts of RWARM and supporting agencies and will be the core around which to mobilize currently homeless women.

RWARM researchers' experiences of homelessness and of working with homeless women were the starting point for the design of the survey, and these shared experiences encourage openness on the part of the homeless women being interviewed. What we want to do in these pages is to share the stories of a few formerly homeless women in order to promote understanding of reasons women become homeless and of issues faced by women once they are homeless. While the stories are real, names printed in italics have been changed.

The Slippery Slope to Homelessness

Women become homeless by a variety of routes, but usually the underlying cause is the lack of safe, affordable housing, compounded by inadequate income and lack of services such as daycare, health care, and good legal advice. For some, mental illness, substance abuse, or domestic violence is a catalyst. But, as RWARM researcher Delores Dell says:

> There's always going to be a certain segment of the population that has mental illness, that has drug addiction and violence and stuff. They could still be housed! O.K., I have problems, but can I still have an apartment, a place to live where I can work? I think the real problem is the lack of affordable housing. We don't have a system that says housing is a human right; we have a system that says housing is a commodity that gets bought and sold. And if you can't afford it you go without or you live in substandard housing.

When *Betsy*, her two-year-old daughter, and her mother were forced to leave their apartment, having lost their rent subsidy because their landlord refused to remove the lead paint, she decided to find a place with her boyfriend. Following a discouraging and ultimately unsuccessful search for an apartment, she had no choice but to go into a homeless shelter. The DPW was of no help.

> We looked at basements, things like that. We really looked. He was working but he made very little money. We couldn't really afford it. We could afford the rent, but we couldn't afford the heat, the light, the food—you know, we couldn't really afford anything else *but* the rent. I went to Welfare and they told me to fill out applications at all the housing authorities and the low-income places. I didn't know where any housing authorities were at; I didn't know where any of the offices were. And it's not like they said, "Here's the list." They didn't tell me anything; they just said, "Go fill out applications." Well, where, where do I call? Where do I go? They didn't tell me anything.

Joan's story illustrates how easy it is for people of modest means, even if they're employed, to become homeless. All it takes is a few pieces of bad luck to get you started on that slippery slope:

> We had taken over the mortgage on my mother-in-law's house, the house from hell. We couldn't get tenants who'd pay the rent. Part of it was that it was near Franklin Field. It's a war zone. We just got really deeply into debt, and then we lost our house. We moved to an apartment and were so in debt that we just couldn't pay all of our bills and our rent. So that's how we became homeless. I was working two part-time jobs. My husband was driving a bus.

I think if we had had some help in learning how to organize our money better and if we had had better legal advice when we lost our house...we declared bankruptcy and it turned out that this was our lawyer's first bankruptcy case and she gave us all the wrong advice. Then also, my husband ended up having a drug problem for a little while, too. His brother had died of AIDS and then his mother died and I think he sort of had a nervous breakdown. At the time, I was working 11 a.m. to 7 p.m. waitressing at Howard Johnson's and I was just so tired that it just didn't dawn on me, but a lot of the money was just missing. So, it wasn't any one thing; it was just a bunch of things that happened. And then we got into illegal loans, 27 percent, you know....I think it's a sort of similar story for a lot of people who own houses in minority neighborhoods. Then you get the loan sharks and everything like that.

Sandra has been homeless twice. First, she lost her home to fire, and then to the bank.

My mate, my two kids and I had a nine-room house. We were really comfortable; we had a dog and a cat, nice neighborhood. One night we had a fire. Before I knew it, I was in a hotel downtown paid for by the Red Cross for a couple of nights. After that we were sent to one of the notorious welfare hotels where we stayed for about six months. I finally got an apartment in a city-owned building, but it was in a totally different kind of neighborhood from what I was used to. I can't say I grew up really privileged, but we were comfortable. I was used to hearing birds in the morning, having trees, having a backyard....The apartment that we moved into, there were drug dealers and shootings and loud music....After a couple of months I was a nervous wreck, because I could just hear bullets. It was my worst nightmare.

After sending her daughter to Boston, *Sandra* and her son moved in with her mother in upstate New York. Shortly afterwards, her mother's house was foreclosed and she was again homeless.

I got a job paying $4.25 an hour; my mother was living on Social Security. She had bought another house up there, a nice house, a nice neighborhood. But, she had some problem with the mortgage. There was a leak in the basement and somehow that built onto her mortgage. I don't know how it happened, but then the mortgage shot up from $600 to $1100 a month and there was no way we could do it. So, we left, we left the house. We just packed up. Because we knew we were going into foreclosure. My mother came up [to Boston] to live with my sister and I went into the shelter.

After her mother died, *Tess* went to live with a brother. When he kicked her out, she began a journey that would take her to many areas of the country. Sometimes she stayed in shelters, sometimes she had her own place, but with few resources and no family to depend on, she easily slipped back into homelessness whenever she hit a spell of bad luck:

When I was 18, I was living in Tennessee with my mother. She became terminally ill and I took care of her. When I was 19, she passed away and I went to live with my oldest brother. I had not had freedom before. As the youngest of nine, my mother sort of spoiled me, but she kept me close to home. When I moved in with my brother, my nephew, who was a year older than me, and I used to go out to parties a lot, come in 2 or 3 o'clock in the morning. My brother decided we weren't going to do that anymore, so he kicked us both out. Well, my nephew, being my brother's son, he could talk his way back in, but I didn't have much choice.

Not knowing what to do, I hitchhiked to Nashville, which was 32 miles away. I found a shelter there. It was the first time ever I'd stayed in a shelter. It was run by a church; you had to go to church at night to get a meal and a bed. The shelter was unbelievable; it was something I had never in my life seen before. There were alcoholic men and women; it was almost like an alcoholic mental ward. I met a woman there and she was from Boston and she was telling me that there were lots of jobs in Boston. I was always looking for some kind of job in Nashville. So, we hitchhiked to California and we hitchhiked to Oregon and in '86 we hitchhiked to Boston.

I've been here ever since; I've sort of made Boston my home. I've stayed in the shelters around Boston; some allow you to work, some have what they call contract beds—you can work, save your money, and get a place. Well, I did for awhile. I worked day labor, found a rooming house. I was a window washer, I stuffed envelopes, I mopped floors, I washed dishes, I worked for Creative Gourmet. I had a really good printing job but I was only there nine months. I got tired of the way the woman kept treating me—she knew I had been homeless and she was really ugly about it, demeaning—so I just told her to screw off and I left the job.

There were times when I thought that my mental and emotional health were more important to me than a job and a place to live. I've been in and out of shelters a lot. I think I've stayed at every shelter that's in Boston and probably every one in Cambridge. It's hard to decide what to do. There were times when I just wanted to keep going, to keep running and not stop.

About three years ago, I decided I'm not going to run anymore, I'm going to settle down and I'm going to do something. I was sharing a place with another woman...she decided without telling me that she was moving out. She took the month's rent money with her and half my things. I didn't know I had any choice; I didn't know what it would be like to go through an eviction, so I left the apartment and moved in with some friends. I slept on their couches, on their floors. Then the hints began, little hints that your time is up, you've been here too long. So, I called the shelter and they had a spot and I went there on Christmas night.

Given the lack of safe, affordable housing and inadequate income under their control, many women have to choose between being beaten or being homeless. For *Janice*, who ended up living in her car with her eight- and nine-year-old daughters, this was a hard choice:

At the very end of my marriage, things got very bad violence-wise. My birthday is in November and this year it happened to be on Thanksgiving Day. I woke up to "Happy birthday, honey," and he shoved a shotgun down my throat. It's still really vivid and really painful. I don't even remember all of the incident other than [that] I ended up being thrown out on the front yard in just a t-shirt. The police came—this was many, many times the police had come to my house—and just said, "Why don't you leave?" I didn't think I *could* leave. I didn't think I could afford it. We were struggling at that point, because he was drinking and doing drugs really a lot. And I thought, I can't even make it with his income; how am I going to make it alone? He just got worse and worse. I had been going to counseling for battered women and I met this other woman who gave me a little bit of strength and I decided I was going to move out.

I moved into a new place on December 29 and immediately he stopped giving me any money. In three months, I was behind in my rent. I went to the housing authority and tried to get a Section 8 [rent subsidy]; when I had filled out the application, they said, "O.K., in about five years you can expect something." In the meantime, my husband was stalking me. He actually got an apartment that backed up to mine so that our back yards met. He set up a telescope and followed me. He broke into my apartment and raped me and physically beat me really bad and then passed out because he was so stoned out on crack. So, the police came and I got some friends and we rented a truck and pulled a midnight move. I moved in with this woman I had met through this rape survival thing. But, it didn't really work out. My husband tracked me down through my kids' school records, which was one base we didn't cover. And, this woman said that I had to leave. She felt that her children's lives were in danger, and, of course, they were.

So, I went back to Welfare and they told me that there was no place available and that I wasn't really homeless, that I was leaving this place by choice. So, I did the bouncing thing. I couldn't go to my family, because there was this lunatic running after me and I can't put my family in danger. And, I'm going to friends who I don't think he knows about, but I can't stay anywhere too long because I'm afraid he's going to track me down. I basically lived in my car; we just drove around, and I'm looking in the rearview mirror every time headlights came in my view. I tried to get into a battered women's shelter, but they said, "Well, it's been three weeks since the last incident of violence so you're technically not an emergency case anymore." Eventually, I got into a homeless shelter.

Barbara's situation was aggravated by a legal and law enforcement system that acted as a barrier rather than as a help in getting her and her four children to safety. She tells her story:

I was married 12 years and my husband got deep into drugs...It took a long time for me to break through the denial—this is crazy, it's not going to work. But, once the divorce was final he started doing everything he could think of to bring me down. He lied to get me kicked off of Section 8. I almost lost my job because of him and he only paid child support when he was picked up by the marshals. I was dealing with everything that came. I was going through the legal system. I had detectives from homicide working with me. I was stalked and harassed and threatened, the whole works. My house kept being broke into...but, the police would come to the house and say, "Well, there's nothing we can do unless he hits you, puts his hands on you." One time he broke into the house and I guess he cut his arm or something, there was blood dripped all over the house. That was the final straw; we had to go into a battered women's shelter. For me and my kids to have to see that and go through that continuous terrorism was just too much.

What I felt the most was that as hard as I tried to go the right way, go through the courts, work with the police, everything they told me to do I did and, still, by the end, it turned out that they turned everything against me and they said, "He's the kids' father; you are denying him his rights to see the kids." I said, "Well, we're living in a battered women's shelter; why would I meet him and bring him the kids?" It turned out that I still had to make arrangements to drop the kids off so that he could have his visitation rights, regardless of his not paying child support and threatening to see me dead. My rights didn't matter. It got to the point where he was questioning my kids about where was I living, what was I doing, which told me that I was still in danger. When they said they were going to lock me up if I didn't bring the kids to him, I decided I'm out of here and began planning our escape from the nightmare we were living in.

Bureaucracy and Rules as Punishment

Once homeless, most women face a system that strips them of their self-esteem, limits their ability to parent their children, and, in general, delivers services in a punitive way that encourages self-blame. For homeless women with children, the abuse frequently starts with the welfare office. Most homeless shelters are funded directly by the DPW, and, to get in, you have to be approved for Emergency Assistance. Having fled for her life back to her home town of Boston, Barbara was told by the DPW housing search worker, "There's nothing here for you. The best we can do is pay your way back to the South where you came from." For *Barbara* this was like "a slap in the face."

Women often have to prove to Welfare that they are, indeed, homeless before they can get Emergency Assistance. Knowing there was nothing she could do to prevent her eviction, *Joan* went to Welfare to be placed with her two children in a shelter:

> ...they want to give you a hard way to go and tell you, "Well, you know, we're not going to do anything for you." And I got really mad and I said, "I've never been on AFDC, I've worked all my life and it's my right to have housing." So, they made me wait until the day I got evicted at 4 o'clock before they told me where I was going to go.

Many have their families pressured by Welfare to take them in, even if, as in *Janice's* case, there has been little contact for years.

> When you apply to get into the shelter, they call your family to see if they'll take you back—your mother, your father, your brothers, and your sisters. My mother had to sign a release saying that I could not live with her. I hadn't had any communication with some members of my family, and then to have the Department of Public Welfare call and say, "Could she come to live with you?" Like, "I haven't talked to her in seven years." Click. That's disgusting. It all gets back to that they think you're trying to deceive them. There's this perception that if you have to apply for welfare, then you are a crook.

Of course, many shelters are not much better. When *Sandra* went to her first Boston shelter, the only identification she had was her passport. After flipping through it, the intake worker sarcastically commented, "You've been to all these places and you're still homeless?" Upon learning that *Sandra* had also been to college, the worker continued in her sarcastic vein, "Four years of college and you still couldn't manage to not become homeless!" Then she encouraged Sandra to return to New York, rather than be a burden on Massachusetts.

Once in a shelter, women face rules and staff behavior that are frequently demeaning and that undermine their efforts to get back on their feet. Shelters for women without children are infamous for treating clients like nonpeople and preventing them from having any sense of security or community. Most shelters for single adults kick everyone out by eight in the morning, even on the coldest days. Some shelters require that clients be back too early to be able to work a normal job. Delores Dell describes one example:

> There's this shelter in Somerville that drops the women off in Central Square [a commercial area in the next city] at 7 or 7:30 in the morning and they have to be back at a certain location at 4 p.m. in the evening to be shipped out to Somerville. If you miss that bus, you don't have a shelter to stay at that night. Also, there are 21 beds there and if there are 22 women, they have to have a lottery and whoever gets the "X"—the dreaded "X"—they give them tokens to find another shelter to stay in for that night. It doesn't matter if you've been staying there for six months every night; if you draw the "X," you're shelterless for the night.

And, where do women go on a cold day when they've been kicked out of the shelter? *Sandra* describes what she faced before a women's drop-in center opened:

> ...you go someplace to keep warm, and that was the drop-in at [large shelter]. The minute you walk in, a hundred people run up to you and they make all kinds of weird propositions. It's a scary place even for someone who has street smarts as I do; it's not a safe place for women. People are attacked from time to time. Drug use is rampant in the bathrooms and things that I'm not even going to mention occur in little nooks and crannies.

Although many shelters talk about the empowerment of their guests, too often it does not mean trusting guests to know what's best for them, Delores Dell points out, but rather things like "letting the guests do their own laundry." Meanwhile, shelter rules constrain behavior, and the threat of losing shelter is used to keep people in line. For *Tess,* this meant that she couldn't even enjoy a sociable weekend away with friends:

> You'd be there every night, but if someone invited you to stay over on the weekend, the shelter said that if they have a room for you on a weekend, then they must have room for you all the time, so, if you go, don't bother coming back.

The culture in rule-bound shelters encourages even well-intentioned staff to treat clients like bad children. *Sandra* related an all-too-typical incident:

> One of the workers—a nice person—got into a disagreement with one of the other women staying in the shelter and said something like, "I'm

not homeless. I have a place to go to. And, if you give me a hard time, I'll put you out right now." The woman was just trying to explain her side of the story and the staff person said, "That's it, I'm not having any more. Get your things and get out. You've got two minutes or I'll call the cops."

Many shelters seem to encourage a culture of dependency. Even if they don't evict a woman because she shows some independence, they can make her life more difficult. *Janice* never felt welcome in her shelter and felt that the threat of eviction was always there:

When they were doing intake, they told me they didn't even want me there and that they were taking me only because they were short on funding and they needed the money from AFDC—the $2,000 or $2,200 a month they got to keep me there. It was like a constant threat. If I didn't do what they told me, I wouldn't be able to put my kids in the bed that night. And, they told me what my needs were: "This is what you need to do." And, I said, "That's not what I need to do." Their focus was to teach me how to live on welfare. They had budgeting classes…I already knew how to budget. I didn't want to live on welfare. My goal in life was not to get a $200-a-month apartment and live on welfare. My goal was to get back on my feet, go back to work, and start my life over. But, because I didn't go to the classes, because I wasn't following what they wanted me to do, I was an outcast. I was out trying to find housing and that wasn't their plan. The whole system is set up not to treat you as an individual, but as one of a mass. How can you feel any self-esteem when you're cattle? You're basically herded through this system and they have this gate you're supposed to go through and end up here; that's what they're projecting for you, but that may not be where you want to go.

The routine invasion of privacy is another way that homeless people are treated as objects or nonentities. Whether in a single or family shelter, your life is an open book. The interest of staff members in knowing personal details can be a way of exercising power, a type of voyeurism that is not connected to job requirements. Staff in *Janice's* shelter felt free to ask detailed questions about the spousal abuse she had suffered. She feared she would be kicked out of the shelter if she didn't answer. As she put it:

They're discussing me and my violence and all that stuff and I'm thinking, they have no right. Except, they felt they did. And that whole power thing—it was like a constant threat: "If you don't do what we say, tell us what we ask, we're going to take your shelter away."

Homeless Women With and Without Children

The major concern of homeless women with children is usually their children's well-being, rather than their own. Unfortunately, shelters often exacerbate the problems that a homeless mother faces trying to be a decent parent. *Janice* talked about the emotional toll of homelessness on her children:

As a parent, you're supposed to be providing a solid base so that your children can become upstanding citizens, and, all of a sudden, you don't even have the ability to take care of them anymore, not even have a roof to put over their head or a bed to put them in at night, let alone what it does to them emotionally to be homeless. At eight and nine, my kids were older than the other kids in the shelter. One of my daughters started wetting the bed again and my other daughter started sucking her thumb and sleeping in the fetal position and having nightmares. So, they regressed in that way, but in other ways, because they were subjected to people shooting up heroin in the closet—and terms they were using—all of sudden they became these adults.

In *Janice's* case, rather than helping her with what her kids were going through, shelter staff made the situation worse:

When my nine-year-old daughter was wetting her bed, one of the staff came into the living area, where all the people were, and threw a plastic sheet at me and said, "Put this on her bed; she's ruining the mattress." Imagine what that was like! They had absolutely no regard for how my child felt. And these were kids who had been through so much trauma. The lack of sensitivity and caring is just incredible, because you're just not a person, you're a way for them to get money to fund their shelter. I was so angry. And you can't yell at them; you can't say anything to them, because they won't let you in that night. I just had to take the plastic sheet and take her upstairs and cry...

Betsy resented it when she was forced to clean up a mess that her child was mistakenly blamed for, and she found it hard to control her two-year-old to the standards of the shelter staff, including keeping her child with her every single moment, "even when I went to the bathroom." But *Betsy*, who had also been homeless with her mother as a child and who was a mother herself at age 17, felt that she did gain some parenting skills in the shelter. For example, the rule of having children in bed by 8 p.m. meant that she read to her child, which she didn't think she otherwise would have, because, as she put it, "I wasn't raised that way. Nobody in my family read books to their kids...I still read a book at night...I like that as a parent and I'm proud of myself that I do that." For *Betsy*, this rule helped her structure her family life, but this type of rigor doesn't work equally well for all parents. Janice felt shelter rules limited her ability to parent her children—for example, her shelter enforced a bedtime of 7:30 for all children, although her bedtime for her children was 8:30. The earlier bedtime was a hardship for her children who, unlike the other younger children in the shelter, had homework to complete.

With their every move monitored by shelter staff, women risk having their children taken away from them for relatively minor infractions. *Janice* told the story of a woman in the shelter where she stayed:

> This woman, like everybody else, was living in an incredibly stressful situation and she hit her child. They [shelter staff] called the DSS and DSS took her children away. Took them away! They were twins, little girls about five. The kid was being annoying...just think about where your head is at that point. Who isn't going to snap at their child? But this woman wasn't in any way, shape or form beating her kids. I mean, she slapped her child and she lost her children.

As hard as it is for women to go through homelessness with their children, it may be worse for single women. A woman with children is a more sympathetic victim in society's eyes. As RWARM researcher Brenda Farrell put it:

> If you look at a mom with children that are homeless, it's real easy to say, "Well, they're homeless because of the circumstances, because of the divorce or abuse, or whatever." But if you see this single woman homeless, well, she's homeless because she's incapable.

Shelter rules are more rigid for single women, and no program like AFDC is available to the single woman. But, perhaps the most unrecognized factor is the degree to which having children dependent on her keeps her emotionally together. As Delores Dell discussed:

> Even though it's painful to see children going through homelessness, at least a mother has something—her children—to help keep her stable and focused. Single women, sometimes they drift. They may have children, but the children might be in DSS custody or in the care of a parent or relative. I can't say they forget about their children, but they start leading a life as if they no longer had children.

From her personal experience, *Barbara* commented on this theme:

> I often blamed myself for our situation and then I would get depressed, but the kids always snapped me back because I had to keep my head straight for them. That was powerful for me.

Trauma and Recovery

The circumstances that lead to an individual's homelessness are nearly always traumatic, and the experience of being homeless adds greatly to that trauma. Yet there are few mental health resources for homeless people and even less for the formerly homeless. The emphasis in our homeless service system is on the physical—whether one has a physical place to live or not. While this is important, it isn't nearly enough. *Sandra*, who has had her own place to live for the last several years, still says, "I don't feel I've had a normal day since the fire [eight years ago]; in some ways I've been in shock ever since."

Janice, who was suffering from post-traumatic stress syndrome, not only was not provided help by her shelter, but her own efforts to find help were hampered by the shelter's rules.

> You had to be in the shelter at 7:30 unless you were at an AA meeting. I couldn't go to a battered women's support group because it wasn't AA and they felt that wasn't an issue but alcohol was. So, I started going to AA meetings because I needed some kind of support.

For children, recovering from homelessness and the events leading up to becoming homeless can be a difficult journey. *Joan*, who became homeless a second time when her transitional housing burned, said that her son is still afraid of the dark and that her kids insisted on sleeping with her for a year afterwards. Additionally, her daughter lost her scholarship to a private school once the school found out she was living in a homeless shelter. The stigma of being homeless is bad enough for adults, but it can be devastating for children. *Janice* talked about the experience of one of her daughters:

> The worst thing about living in a small town afterwards is that everybody knew I was homeless, which was O.K. with me, but everyone knew my kids had been homeless. My daughter came home one day crying; her eyes were red, her nose was running. She said the kids at school were making fun of her, saying that she got her clothes at the Salvation Army and she never wanted to go back to school. It left scars, probably even more so than the shelter did, having to face the town and the kids, dealing with being ridiculed and being poor.

Generally, after a homeless woman has a place of her own to live, that's the end of whatever services were provided to her. For many, it's also an abrupt end to whatever sense of community they had begun to have in the shelter, and it can be a very disorienting transition. It's a rare shelter that continues to care about and maintain ties with former guests. Betsy was one of the lucky ones, and she expressed how much it meant to her and also how rare it was:

> My two-month-old [who had been born while Betsy was living in the shelter] was in the hospital with croup...and then Sister *Katherine* [the shelter director] walked in and I felt like an angel had just walked in...We had had this connection when I was living in the shelter, but I've never known anyone to have a connection after you've left the shelter. It's like, all right, I'm your friend because you're living here; you leave, I don't know you no more. So, to see her walk in and to hug me and to be there for me...I started to cry. It was really emotional for me because I felt like they didn't disown me.

Conclusion

The roots of homelessness lie in a complex web of economic and social structures in U.S. society. Safe and affordable housing is in increasingly short supply. Housing is treated as a commodity, not a right—if you can't pay for it, you can't have it. Education in life skills and job training that might prevent homelessness are unavailable to those who most need them. Services to materially poor people in general and to homeless people in particular are delivered in a punitive and miserly way. Frequently, officially as well as in the public's eye, the victim is blamed for her own situation; often this attitude leads to self-blame. Solutions to homelessness are seen in purely physical and quantitative terms, not in terms of human and community development.

Homeless and formerly homeless women, by discussing and analyzing their experiences, can provide new insights into this complex of causes. This process also adds a document of human experience that may itself influence the attitudes that have been so destructive to homeless women.

RWARM is working to expose and correct the problems noted in these pages. Moving away from a dependency model of providing services to materially poor people toward an interdependency model based on human dignity and a sense of connectedness and community would go a long way toward improving the situation for homeless people. But in the long run, as Delores Dell says:

> The objective is to do the kind of work that will remove homelessness from the vocabulary because there won't be any. The goal is not to work with homelessness, but to work to get rid of it.

Acknowledgments

RWARM wishes to thank the following groups for financial support: Boston Foundation, Boston Safe Deposit, Boston Women's Fund, Carlisle Foundation, Charitable Insurance Company, Fund for Self-Reliance, Jane Doe Fund, Polaroid, Roxbury Technical Assistance Project (U-Mass/Boston), Anne and David Stoneman Charitable Foundation, and WCVB-TV (Channel 5 in Boston area).

Notes

1. In this chapter, we are continuing to refer to the Department of Public Welfare (DPW) although the name has recently been changed to Department of Transitional Assistance. The new name reflects recent changes in Massachusetts' approach to providing public assistance. With the current emphasis on "two years and you're out," the new name emphasizes the temporary nature of the state's commitment to the welfare of children in materially poor families.

2. Quoted in "Justice Not Charity," *Dollars and Sense*, September 1992.

3. The creation of our name is a story in itself. Initially the project was called the Homeless Women's Study Action Project. At one meeting an RWARM researcher said, "I don't want to be known as formerly homeless. I always had a home; I made a home for my children even if it was only in my car. What I didn't have was a roof over my head." The brainstorming that followed produced the name Roofless Women's Action Research Mobilization, or RWARM for short.

4. RWARM is guided by a steering committee, of which formerly homeless women comprise the majority. RWARM researchers are joined by representatives of the Massachusetts Coalition for the Homeless, the Coalition of Battered Women's Service Groups, the Community Outreach Project, The Women's Institute for Housing and Economic Development, the College of Public and Community Service at the University of Massachusetts at Boston, the Boston Emergency Shelter Commission, and the Boston Women's Commission. United in a mutually agreed upon agenda, this broad coalition has the capacity to act on the results of the research project.

GIMME SHELTER
Battering and Poverty
Susan James and Beth Harris

NOW THAT OPEN SEASON ON WELFARE MOTHERS HAS BEEN declared, this country's politicians have been busily proposing welfare restrictions. There's Bridefare, rewarding women who get married—and punishing those who don't—and the notorious Workfare, requiring recipients to work off their grants at menial jobs. Underlying these proposals is a presumption that women on welfare are lacking in moral fiber and initiative, and need a "kick in the pants" to get motivated to join the workforce.

Among these policymakers, there's been no mention of truly helpful modifications to the current welfare system. There's been no mention of a Safetyfare, or Freedomfare, to address the enormous risks and obstacles faced by financially strapped women who are experiencing domestic violence. In contrast to the immoral image projected by politicians, many of these women make quite courageous and moral decisions to protect themselves and their children under the economic umbrella of welfare. There's been little recognition of how vital public assistance can be for women trying to leave abusive relationships. Nor do policymakers seem to comprehend that living with a jealous, controlling partner often creates barriers for women trying to develop economic independence through employment.

For many women living in domestic terror in this country, current proposed changes in welfare allotments threaten to slam shut an already narrow door to freedom. Domestic violence is such an epidemic that the U.S. surgeon general in the 1980s declared domestic violence a major health threat for women.[1] Battering by a partner or ex-partner remains the single greatest cause of injury for women,[2] and accounts for nearly one-third of female homicide victims.[3]

Many of us have witnessed, or experienced, the precarious

process of trying to extricate oneself emotionally and logistically from a relationship that hurts. For many women, especially those with young children or marginal job skills, public assistance may be the only economic road out. Survivors of domestic violence often require time and support to recover from emotional, and sometimes physical, injuries. Lack of access to public assistance due to increased restrictions is yet another obstacle being placed between a battered woman and her freedom.

To explore the relationship between welfare and the ability to leave an abusive relationship, the authors spoke to dozens of women in discussion groups drawn from programs for battered and low-income women in Seattle, Washington. These women offer perspectives largely absent from the political debate regarding the future of welfare.

Three significant issues emerge. First, for many survivors of domestic violence, welfare is an economic lifeline. Those women who have financial resources often have to leave everything behind, including jobs, in order to break free safely. Others may have no means of support other than what their partners had provided.

Second, many survivors of domestic violence report that they tried to join the workforce, but were thwarted by jealous partners who repeatedly called, or stalked the women at work after they had fled.

Third, a woman who has escaped an abusive partner may be contending with tremendous fallout that may prevent her marching fresh and ready into the workplace. The aftermath of abuse may include physical injuries, post-traumatic stress disorder, depression, and severely diminished self-esteem. To a bystander, a woman's reluctance to leave an abusive partner can seem puzzling, even maddening. Why would someone stay in a situation where she is being hurt? Usually, questions of economic survival take precedent. "I've had women literally in hysterics when they think about how they're going to support themselves and their children," noted an advocate for battered women at New Beginnings, a Seattle shelter for battered women. "They're terrified."

Take Mara (not her real name), who left her physically abusive partner when her daughter was an infant. Mara wanted to work, but couldn't find a part-time job that would pay for childcare and support her family of two. Her only choice for survival, which she turned to reluctantly, was public assistance. "I don't think any of us want to be on it [public assistance]," she said tearfully to members of her group. "You have to do what you have to do."

Another woman noted that she had relied on her boyfriend to provide childcare. After she left the relationship, her child became ill. Her employer was unsympathetic, and she was forced to choose between losing her job to care for her child or returning to her abusive boyfriend to allow her to keep her job.

The women noted that a domestic violence survivor is even less likely to get child support, especially if revealing her whereabouts places her and her children in danger. They talked about abusers insisting on placing utilities in the women's name, and then running up huge phone bills after the women had fled. They talked about joint credit laws that left women responsible for their abusers' financial excesses.

Some women said that their attempts to establish economic independence through employment were thwarted by controlling partners intent on undermining the women's independence. Their struggles to continue working despite these pressures corroborate a recent study of battered women that found that three-fourths of the sample who worked were harassed on the job by abusive partners.[4] "I had a job, and my boyfriend sabotaged my job so I'd get fired," said one woman in our discussion group. "I just decided to leave the relationship anyway. But it's been hell since then trying to support myself."

These women are understandably apprehensive about making it on their own financially. Their ambivalence is not surprising considering recent studies that indicate as many as one out of three homeless women was pushed into the abyss of homelessness by an abusive partner.[5]

And women leaving partners today face a far bleaker economic situation than their counterparts 10 years ago. A recent Census Bureau study found that the percentage of Americans working full-time but earning less than the poverty level for a family of four has risen by 50 percent in the past 13 years.[6] Three-quarters of the nation's 12 million women who lack health insurance are employed but don't receive health benefits at work.[7] As relative wages and availability of health care have declined, the cost of housing and childcare has risen dramatically. Federal and state social spending cuts in subsidized housing, childcare, and job training programs have further narrowed women's options.

These changes in the economic landscape are even more disturbing considering recent social science studies that suggest that the perception of the ability to support oneself economically is a powerful variable in determining whether a woman leaves, and stays away from an abusive relationship.

Social science researchers Michael Strube and Linda Barbour conducted several studies exploring women's decision-making process as they considered leaving abusive relationships.[8] In the first study, 62 percent of the 98 women stayed away from their abusive partners; in the second study, 70 percent did. Women's employment status was the strongest predictor of who made the break for good. Women who perceived they would face greater economic hardship from separation also were less likely to leave. Although these researchers did not specifically include public assistance as a form of income for women, we can speculate that the subjective measurement of "economic hardship" could have included the women's evaluation of the role public assistance might play in their survival.

In a study of 426 women who sought refuge at a Florida battered women's shelter, researcher Ida Johnson also found economic variables factoring into a woman's decision to leave. The most prominent variables included the victim's annual income, employment status, severity of abuse, and the victim's level of self-esteem.[9] Fifty-five percent of these women didn't return home after staying at the shelter. An abused women who was unemployed was more likely to return to her partner when his contribution to the family income was relatively high, in this case between $10,000 and $20,000. Even women who had suffered severe physical abuse were more likely to return home when the women were unemployed and their partners made a liveable income. Women whose partners did not make a liveable wage were more likely to leave and not return.

Another study of 6,000 battered women in Texas who stayed at battered women's shelters reinforces the importance of women's economic independence in their ability to escape.[10] Most of the abusers in this study had very little income. In fact, 58 percent of the abusers had no income whatsoever. The severity of physical abuse among the Texas women was striking: 42 percent had sought hospital care for their injuries and two-thirds had partners who had threatened to kill them. Nonetheless, the degree of physical abuse was not a critical factor in these women's decisionmaking process. Instead, the best predictor of whether a woman would stay away from her abuser was her degree of economic independence.

Perhaps the most directly relevant data on this topic comes from a recent study of 141 women who had stayed at a Michigan battered women's shelter.[11] Sullivan found that more than six months after leaving the shelter, only 12 percent of the women had returned to their abusers. It was the women who had been the most economically dependent on their partners before entering the shelter who were the most likely to stay involved with the men. Only 22 percent of the women who were dependent on their abusers for at least half their incomes were able to permanently leave. In this study, 79 percent of the women who brought in more than half of their family's income were on public assistance. And most (81 percent) of them were still living below the poverty level. Only 65 percent of women primarily dependent on their partners' income were living below the poverty level.

Finally, this study suggests that women are more likely to leave a batterer when they have an independent source of income, even public assistance. This was especially true if their abusers were unemployed or providing very little income.

Now imagine what a battered woman's choices might be with the welfare changes. Take the five year limits in the federal legislation that passed in the summer of 1996. Say a woman has been on public assistance in the past for two years, and then finds herself in an abusive relationship. Unless she has an independent income, or exceptional family support, she may find herself examining her options, as the women in the above-mentioned studies did, and finding the only economically viable choice is to return. Domestic violence advocates will tell you that battering violence usually spirals upward, and as time goes on, the lethal risks increase.

Some of the Workfare proposals also pose problems for survivors of domestic violence. If a woman and her very young children have been emotionally and physically abused by a partner, and she leaves, it would be inhumane to expect the mother to immediately enroll the children in full-time daycare to enable her to "work off" her welfare grant somewhere.

"It's hard to raise children and work," one woman in our discussion groups noted. "Some people just want to focus on one thing, like raising kids and recovering from a bad relationship and not compromising parenting. We don't want to repeat the [domestic violence] cycle."

If there is a silver lining to these draconian welfare reform measures, it is the growing recognition that advocates for battered women and advocates for economic justice no longer survive in separate spheres. In the past, many advocates for battered women, while working admirably to help women extricate themselves from abusers, were remiss in addressing the economic pressures facing survivors of domestic violence. Women came to shelters, often signed up for public assistance to survive, and attended support groups focusing on the cycle of violence and ways to emotionally resist a batterer's enticements to return. There were many copies of *Women Who Love Too Much* around, but no *Women Who Starve Too Much* or *Women Who Worry About Being Homeless Too Much* books to be found. Educational workshops on domestic violence emphasized that battering is an equal opportunity problem, affecting women from all walks of life, regardless of class background. Certainly, cultural attitudes that give men of all classes permission to batter play a significant role in abuse. Yet research studies have found that un- or under-employed men are at least twice as likely to beat their partners as those employed full-time.[12] In Massachusetts, which has been beset with economic woes in recent years, the frequency of domestic violence-related murders rose from once every 22 days in 1989 to once every eight days in 1992.[13]

One can suppose that with increasingly punitive welfare reforms that deny women access to public assistance, the incidence of such murders is certain to grow. For advocates for battered women, these developments amount to a feeling of bailing even faster on an ever leakier boat. We must come to grips with the fact that battering of women, and children for that matter, is likely to cut more deeply and more often into the lives of poor families. Women not only need support to escape battering but also economic resources to keep them going after they leave.

Addressing the complexities of this situation will require more coalition work between domestic violence workers and advocates for social and economic justice. These advocates are also discovering the limitations of single-issue solutions. An example of this is found in a recent study of 500 participants in a Chicago-based literacy and job-training program for welfare recipients, which found much higher drop-out rates for participants struggling with abusive partners. The study found that "once AFDC participants extricate themselves from the violence and have some time to sufficiently recover from past [domestic violence] trauma, great gains occur in literacy levels and employability. Training programs, however well-intentioned, that do not address this issue are doomed to failure."

We are beginning to better understand and communicate that these current welfare "reforms" are not about improving women's lives, but controlling them. Welfare restrictions offer an easy out for politicians because these so-called "reforms" create the illusion of control over social and economic problems that can't be solved simply or cheaply. As politicians have been shining the searchlight on welfare recipients, women on welfare have been erroneously typified as single mothers who deliberately have lots of children and refuse to work. Welfare recipients are often depicted as women of color (in reality, the majority of women on welfare are white), which provides short-sighted Americans with a convenient scapegoat while playing into racist stereotypes.

Enter "Bridefare," which supposes that if only women would get off their high horse and get married, the yellow brick road would rise up to greet them. There's an assumption that women on welfare resist relationships, hence the need to encourage marriage. Ostensibly, marriage will both tame a woman and provide her with economic support.

The reality beyond the cardboard caricatures is that most women on welfare are in relationships. Given the high incidence of abusive, or just plain unreliable partners, many are trying to beat the odds and find relationships that are both stable and non-hurtful. And contrary to the fairy tale of Bridefare, marriage, even to a nice guy, does not guarantee economic security. Likewise, many women are trying hard to join and stay in the workforce, but are up against a host of obstacles that have little to do with lack of will or drive.

Real solutions would require stepping out of this paradigm of moralistic finger-pointing, which further victimizes women, while it casts extremely complex problems into seemingly neat little formulas. Genuine solutions would require new spending, for which few policymakers are willing to advocate these days. Federally subsidized childcare and health care, along the lines of European models, would be a good beginning. Creating liveable wages and reforming tax structures that presently favor the wealthy would help even more. As long as parents lack the economic resources to enable them to raise their children, whether because of unemployment or extremely low-paying jobs that won't cover childcare, health care, and basic needs, public assistance should be available as a resource.

If women and children find through their experiences that society has abandoned them, especially when they are trying to protect themselves from abuse, they may come to regard themselves as inhabiting a separate terrain. What does it mean to grow up as a child in a world that fails to protect and provide, but instead treats you with the studied indifference accorded, say, toxic waste?

The seeds of frustration and anger already were evident in the discussion groups we convened. Noting that welfare outlays make up a tiny fraction of the federal budget (less than 2 percent), some women wondered about politicians' motives. The reforms don't seem connected to budgetary concerns, offered one woman. Another woman noted that, like the batterers these women left behind, the government seemed intent on "cutting choices." As women in the room nodded vigorously in agreement, one woman suggested that some male politicians are threatened by the example of women, even those who are dirt poor, possessing the ability to leave abusive relationships. Might the hidden, barely conscious worry fueling welfare restrictions be that some politicians' wives, in turn, might follow these women's courageous example?

Notes

1. N. Van Hightower and S. MacManus, (1989) "Limits of State Constitutional Guarantees: Lessons from Efforts to Implement Domestic Violence Policies," 49, *Public Administration Review* 269, May/June.

2. *Ibid.*

3. K. Rose and J. Goss, (1989) "Domestic Violence Statistics," *National Criminal Justice Reference Service*, Bureau of Justice Statistics 12.

4. Joan Zorza, (1991) "Woman Battering: A Major Cause of Homelessness." *Clearinghouse Review*, Special Issue.

5. *Ibid.*

6. Jason DeParle, "Sharp Increase Along the Borders of Poverty," *The New York Times*, 31 March 1994, p. A18.

7. Barbara Presley Noble, "Unhealthy Prospects for Women," *The New York Times*, 22 May 1994, p. B23;

8. Michael Strube and Linda Barbour, (1983) "The Decision to Leave an

Abusive Relationship: Economic Dependence and Psychological Commitment." *Journal of Marriage and the Family*, 46, p. 785-93; Michael Strube and Linda Barbour, (1984), "Factors Related to the Decision to Leave an Abusive Relationship." *Journal of Marriage and the Family*, p. 837-44.

9. Ida M. Johnson, (1992) "Economic, Situational, and Psychological Correlates of the Decision-making Process of Battered Women," *Families in Society: The Journal of Contemporary Human Services*, p. 168-76.

10. Edward Gondolf with Ellen Fisher. *Battered Women as Survivors: An Alternative to Treating Learned Helplessness, (Massachusetts: Lexington Books, 1988)*.

11. Cris M. Sullivan, Rebecca Campbell, Holly Angelique, Kimberly K. Eby, and William S. Davidson, (1994) "An Advocacy Intervention Program for Women with Abusive Partners: Six-month Follow-up." *American Journal of Community Psychology*, vol. 22, no. 1, 1994.

12. Murray Strauss and Richard Gelles, (1986) "Societal Change and Change in Family Violence from 1975 to 1985 as Revealed by Two National Surveys." *Journal of Marriage and the Family*, 48, p. 465-79.

13. Patricia Horn, (1992) "Beating Back the Revolution: Domestic Violence's Economic Toll on Women," *Dollars and Sense*, 8 December 1992, p. 12.

HOW THE U.S. ECONOMY CREATES POVERTY AND INEQUALITY

Mary Huff Stevenson and Elaine Donovan

ANY CAPITALIST ECONOMY CREATES WINNERS AND LOSERS, and the United States is no exception. What is noteworthy about the U.S. economy in the 1990s is that the gap between the winners and the losers is larger than it has been in the past 50 years, and that the United States is now generating more inequality than any other advanced capitalist nation.[1] These features of the contemporary U.S. economy have undermined the standard of living for many U.S. households, and are particularly threatening to households that depend heavily on women's earnings.

At the end of World War II, the U.S. economy was about to start on an expansion that brought higher living standards and greater economic security to a wide range of families. From 1945 until the early 1970s, most households could expect that their purchasing power would grow from one year to the next. In heavy industries such as automobiles or steel, a male wage earner without a high school degree could support a family with an income not only above the poverty line, but high enough to purchase a single-family home and still have enough left over to save for retirement or for the kids' college education.

Even in those expansionary times, however, there were households that did not share in the general prosperity. Observers spoke of the "paradox of poverty amid plenty." In 1960, Michael Harrington described "the other America," the people the expansion left behind.[2] They included the elderly, families in economically deserted areas such as Appalachia, minority households that faced economic discrimination, and families without access to a working man's wages.

Much of the optimism with which the "War on Poverty" was launched in the mid-1960s was based on the notion that poverty and economic insecurity were aberrant, and could be fixed with the proper combination of income security for the elderly, economic development for depressed areas, job training for those lacking skills, and anti-discrimination legislation to overcome a legacy of prejudice.

From the vantage point of the mid-1990s, that optimism seems sadly unfounded. Economic insecurity is rapidly becoming the norm, not the exception, for many U.S. households. Real wages (that is, the actual purchasing power of a worker's paycheck—the amount of goods and services it will buy) have been declining since the early 1970s. Like the gerbil inside the running wheel, who has to run faster just to stay in place, many households have responded to the decline in real wages by increasing the amount of time their members spend working, just to be able to afford the same standard of living. This also means that compared to a generation ago, many households need to have more members who are working for wages, and/or members who are working more hours, to avoid falling below the poverty line.

What has happened over the last 20-odd years to change the course of the post-World War II expansion that improved living standards for many (but not all) U.S. households? What accounts for the phenomenon that Harry Bluestone and Bennett Harrison have called "the Great U-turn?" Experts cite a number of factors, but chief among them is a change in the structure of the U.S. economy.[3] This change is the product of several forces, including technological innovations that have reduced transportation and communication costs, and have given many companies much wider latitude (literally and longitude as well) in deciding where to locate their production facilities. While the story of mobility of capital is an old one in regions such as New England, which saw its shoe and textile industries move south in the 1920s in search of cheaper and more pliable workers, the freeing of economic constraints that formerly tied companies to a specific location has occurred at a dizzying pace in recent years. As companies find it easier to make their location decisions on a worldwide basis, workers (organized, if at all, on a local or national level) find it harder to protect their economic position from erosion. Some observers worry that jobs providing decent wages and steady work for workers with no more than a high school diploma will soon be as scarce as the proverbial hen's teeth. As these jobs flow from central city to suburb, from Rustbelt to Sunbelt, from the United States to other nations, or as they simply evaporate—made obsolete by new technology—they leave behind a group of workers with grim prospects. Moreover, as companies restructure internally, even those employers who stay put are less likely to offer a lifetime employment commitment, as they come to rely more heavily on "contingent" (that is, part-time, part-year, temporary, or independent contractor) workers.[4]

While the expansion of the global economy and its attendant mobility of capital and internal workplace restructuring has accounted for much of the change that has contributed to the growing economic insecurity facing many U.S. households, public policy decisions of the last 20 years have exacerbated the problem. Sins of commission, such as the "supply side" economics of the Reagan years (deliberately reducing the tax burdens of corporations and wealthy individuals, and increasing payroll taxes that fall most heavily on the working poor) and sins of omission, such as failure to pass labor law reform or meaningful increases in the minimum wage, are public sector problems that have aggravated the inequalities produced by the private sector.

These economic realities of the late 20th century cut a wide gap through many U.S. households, including those with male wage earners, female wage earners, and no wage earners. They affect older workers whose post-layoff prospects are grim and younger workers who face far more limited opportunities than their counterparts of the previous generation. Though higher education is not an iron-clad guarantee, they fall harder on those without college degrees and affect people of color disproportionately. It is against this backdrop of growing economic insecurity that we must examine the way the U.S. economy produces poverty and economic insecurity for many women.

Paradoxically, the story of women's role in the paid labor force in the last half of the 20th century can be told as one of dramatic, revolutionary change; it can also be told as one of relative stagnation. It all depends on which indicator you're using.

If the indicator is labor force participation—the role of paid work in the lives of most women—it is undeniably true that compared with mid-century, a far larger proportion of all adult women work, and they work for a far larger proportion of their adult lives.[5] In earlier generations, young, white, native-born single women may have worked in large numbers, but many left the labor force when they married, or when they had children (even then, African-American women and immigrant women tended to work more continuously, as a matter of necessity). After World War II, and through the 1960s, the labor force re-entry of married women with older children garnered some attention, but the majority of mothers with pre-school-aged children still did not work for pay outside the home (it would be inaccurate to say that they simply did not work—raising children is hard work, even if it does not command a wage). The most dramatic change of the last 20 years is the entry of mothers with pre-school-aged children into the workforce. Currently, even among mothers with infants (defined as children less than a year old), the majority are in the paid labor force. Truly a revolutionary change.

If, however, we ask what happens to women when they enter the workforce—what are the labor market outcomes for women, in terms of risks and consequences, unemployment, access to a wide range of occupations, and remuneration for their skill and effort—the story is not one of revolutionary change, but of slow and uneven progress.[6] Images of molasses, icebergs, and snails are called to mind.

On the first Friday of every month, the Department of Labor announces the official unemployment rate for the previous month. This "First Friday" statistic is widely reported, and by this measure, unemployment rates for men and for women have been similar in recent years. In fact, women have often had a lower unemployment rate than men. On the surface, women's unemployment wouldn't seem to be a topic of special concern. The problem, though, is that the official measure of unemployment tends to understate labor market problems for all workers, and especially for women workers.

The official unemployment rate is calculated from the results of a monthly telephone survey of a carefully chosen nationally representative sample of households, in which several questions are asked about the activities of each household member aged 16 or older. On the basis of answers to these questions, people are categorized as either "employed," "unemployed," or "out of the labor force." To be considered employed, an individual must have worked at least one hour for pay in the week previous to the survey (there are other ways of qualifying—such as being on temporary leave from your normal job, or being an unpaid employee of a family business). Therefore, people who are working part-time but would like to be working full-time (the involuntary part-time workers), people who are working at jobs that do not reflect their training or experience (the laid-off aerospace engineer who is driving a cab), and people who are working full-time for wages that would not keep a family out of poverty (like many minimum-wage workers) are all categorized as "employed," despite their labor market difficulties.

To be considered "unemployed," one must not meet the criteria for being "employed," and in addition, one must also have taken active steps to search for a job within the last four weeks. Therefore, if someone has gotten discouraged by the lack of job openings and has given up active search, even if he or she is able and willing to work and would accept a job if offered, that person is not considered "unemployed," but is considered to be "out of the labor force." Unsurprisingly, these "discouraged workers" tend disproportionately to be women. As the official unemployment rate rises, the number of discouraged workers also rises, and the gap between women's actual and official unemployment rates widens. This phenomenon is not announced on "First Friday."

If the nation were truly committed to a policy of full employment, the discouraged-worker issue would be moot. But one of the consequences of the structural change in the economy over the last 20 years is that many economists and public policymakers no longer even give lip service to the notion of full employment, and speak instead of a NAIRU—a Non-Accelerating Inflation Rate of Unemployment. In the expansionary 1960s, many economists and policymakers accepted the goal of bringing the rate of unemployment down to 3 percent (defined as full employment—the assumption being that at that rate, most unemployment would be voluntary and short term, as workers left jobs to pursue better opportunities elsewhere). Now, many economists and policymakers get jittery about the dangers of inflation when the unemployment rate falls below 6 percent, which they have defined as the NAIRU rate, and call for measures to slow down the economy and prevent further declines in unemployment. Since each percentage point in the official unemployment rate stands for more than a million workers who meet the official definition of unemployment, under current circumstances, the discouraged worker issue is far from moot.

A final note on gender differences in unemployment: It is

especially troublesome to older workers who lose their jobs, and face special difficulties in finding new jobs that are comparable to those they lost. Both men and women face age discrimination in the labor market. The difference, however, is that women face it earlier. Labor market experts say that age discrimination is a factor for men beginning at age 50, but for women beginning at age 40.

What about the workers who get beyond the hurdle of unemployment? What can we say about the man and woman who stand next to each other, doing the same job for the same employer? We can say that this man and woman are mostly hypothetical, and that for the most part, men and women workers do not do the same job for the same employer. The labor force is segregated by gender, and that segregation has many dimensions. There are some occupations that are overwhelmingly male (coal miner), others that are overwhelmingly female (file clerk). Within occupations, there is segregation by industry (factory operatives in the automobile industry tend to be male, those in the apparel industry tend to be female). Even within specific job titles, some segregation occurs at the level of the firm, with some firms employing mostly men in a given job title, while others employ mostly women. There are also hierarchies within occupations: Among schoolteachers, for example, elementary schoolteachers are overwhelmingly female, while secondary schoolteachers are more evenly split along gender lines. What has remained true over time is that for the most part, men and women do not occupy the same jobs.

Social scientists use a technical measure called the Index of Dissimilarity to measure the degree of difference in the distribution of women across occupations compared with the distribution of men. By this measure, there was virtually no change in the degree of difference from 1900 to 1960, and a relatively slow and modest reduction over the last 30 years. Moreover, most of the positive change that has occurred has improved opportunities for more privileged and highly educated women, leaving opportunities for most ordinary women workers untouched.

Despite the opening up of some opportunities for more privileged women, they continue to face barriers on the way to the top—what has been called the "glass ceiling." However, as Randy Albelda and Chris Tilly point out, while some of the more privileged among women workers face a glass ceiling, the economic prospect for a far larger group of women is more aptly described as a "bottomless pit."[7]

The problem of gender segregation in the labor force is not simply that most men and most women do not work side by side doing the same job for the same employer. It is that gender segregation is almost always accompanied by pay differences. The Equal Pay Act of 1963 requires that an employer must pay the same wages to his other male and female employees, if they do the same work, and if a pay difference cannot be justified on grounds of seniority or merit. This law has not made much of a dent in the wage differential between men and women, for the simple reason that most male and female workers are not in the situation that the law presumes.

If wage rates are attached to jobs, and if men and women are in different jobs, they will have different wage rates. If women are systematically assigned to work that is less skilled and therefore less valuable, or if the skills and responsibilities of women's jobs are systematically undervalued, the consequences of gender segregation will be persistent wage differences between men and women. Indeed, the fundamental cause of pay differences between men and women is not failure to pay equal pay for equal work, but failure to provide equal work, or to pay equal wages for work of comparable value.

In 1993, women who worked full-time the year round had median annual earnings that were 71.5 percent of men's. In other words, in comparing the woman who was in the middle of the female earnings distribution (above half of women earners and below the other half) with her male counterpart, such a woman earned 71.5 cents for every dollar earned by such a man. This relative-earnings figure showed little change from the mid-1950s through the 1970s (when it was about 60 percent), and began rising in the 1980s.[8]

With regard to household income, however, this rise in relative earnings has something in common with those corny good news/bad news jokes. Mathematically, the measure of relative earnings is a ratio—a fraction—and like any fraction, its value can increase either because the numerator has gone up, or because the denominator has gone down (or some combination of the two). If the relative-earnings ratio had gone up purely because women's wages had gone up (that is, an increase in the numerator), that would have been purely good news for improvements in household income. If it had risen specifically because men's wages had gone down (that is, a decrease in the denominator), that would have been purely bad news—households would be receiving a smaller contribution from male wage earners, while the contribution from female wage earners would have remained unchanged. In reality, the change in relative wages is a mixture of good and bad news. According to calculations made by the Institute for Women's Policy Research (IWPR), about 61 percent of the reduction in the earnings gap between 1979 and 1993 is attributable to the decline in men's real wages; that leaves only 39 percent attributable to the rise in women's real wages.[9]

Median wages are higher for workers with more years of education, but the benefit of additional years of education is not the same for women as for men. Data from the Bureau of Labor Statistics on median weekly earnings for workers age 25 or older show that women with some college or an Associates degree earned $423 per week in 1994, while men with only a high school diploma earned $496. Similarly, women with Bachelors degrees earned the same as men with some college or Associates degrees ($587), while women with advanced degrees earned the same as men with Bachelors degrees ($756).[10]

If we take the weekly earnings data provided by the Bureau of Labor Statistics and extrapolate from it yearly earnings (by assuming that workers receive these wages continually for 52 weeks without any spells of unemployment), a grim picture emerges for full-time wage and salary workers with no more than a high school diploma. As Table 1 shows, among full-time workers without a high school diploma, women, both black and white, earned below the poverty line for a family of four ($14,800 in 1994).

Moreover, if we look at the bottom 25 percent of the earnings distribution for high school dropouts, we find that while none of these workers, male or female, could support a four-person family above the poverty line, the women workers would not even be able to support a three-person family above poverty. Even among high school graduates, neither black men, white women, nor black women could bring a four-person family above the poverty line.

A final reality check: Table 1 shows the upper limits of the bottom 25 percent of the distribution. These numbers, though appallingly low, are still substantially above the $8,500 yearly income that a worker earning the minimum wage of $4.25 per hour would earn. As the IWPR points out, a full-time year-round minimum wage worker

Table 1

1994 Annual Earnings for Full-time Wage and Salary Workers Age 25 and Over, By Selected Characteristics

	White Men	White Women	Black Men	Black Women
Median Earnings				
Less than High School	$18,252	$13,520	$16,640	$12,896
High School, No College	$26,572	$18,772	$19,916	$15,808
Bottom 25 % of Earners				
Less than High School	$13,416	$10,348	$12,168	$9,984
High School, No College	$19,344	$14,092	$14,612	$11,908

Footnote: Calculated from Table 8 of "Usual Weekly Earnings of Wage and Salary Workers: Fourth Quarter 1994," U.S. Department of Labor, Bureau of Labor Statistics, February 9, 1994. The calculation extrapolated from weekly earnings to yearly earnings by assuming all workers had these earnings over a period of 52 weeks.

Source: The U.S. Department of Commerce, Census Bureau's 1994 poverty thresholds were: $7,551 for a single person, $9,655 for a family of two, $11,817 for a family of three, and $14,800 for a family of four.

would not earn enough to bring even a two-person family above the poverty line. Nearly two-thirds of the minimum wage workforce is female, the vast majority of whom are adults, not teenagers.[11]

It is these realities of the U.S. labor market that must be kept in mind during debates about welfare reform. At the low end of the earnings distribution, the prospects are already quite bleak. Forcing mothers off Aid to Families with Dependent Children and swelling the ranks of job seekers will only make things even bleaker.

Within the economics profession, there are many economists who would not agree with the foregoing assessment. By and large, it is not the data itself that would be disputed, but the interpretation of that data. Conservative, liberal, and radical economists start from very different assumptions about the nature of the U.S. economy, and therefore reach very different conclusions.

Conservative economists emphasize the importance of individual choice, and the desirability of a competitive market economy, with its own self-correcting mechanisms. In this neoclassical framework, government intervention is not only unnecessary, but undesirable.[12] Liberal economists admire the workings of a competitive economy under ideal circumstances, but argue that the operation of markets is far from ideal. These economists point to constraints, barriers, and noncompetitive elements in the real world that prevent the market from functioning the way an economics textbook might describe it. The implication is that government intervention is necessary to correct the abuses of a private market mechanism that is malfunctioning.[13] The radical approach shares with the liberal approach a rejection of the neoclassical framework, but is more explicitly concerned with understanding the dynamics of a capitalist system as it changes over time. Radicals also examine the confluence of economic and political power in a society divided along lines of class, race, and gender.[14] Although they share the liberals' disaffection with private markets, radicals are less optimistic about government intervention in a system where the elite have undue control of the reigns of government. True progress for ordinary people would depend on their ability to exert economic and/or political power.

To a conservative economist, the market outcome is the correct one, and if the market produces gender inequality, there must be a good reason for it. Women must be making choices about how they spend their time, or about which occupations to enter, that reduce their value to employers. If women want higher earnings, they should make different choices. Conservative economists have a difficult time reconciling the dramatic changes in women's labor force participation with the modest changes in occupational segregation and relative wages.

Liberal economists acknowledge systematic labor market discrimination against women and prescribe government intervention in the form of anti-discrimination legislation, affirmative action requirements, and the need to pursue full employment policies. Such interventions exist, but enforcement has ranged from unreliable, in the case of affirmative action, to nonexistent, in the case of promoting full employment. The modest gains attributable to government intervention give credence to the radical view that real progress depends on ordinary people organizing in their workplaces and communities to gain more control over the economic and political forces that affect their lives.

Notes

1. Keith Bradsher, "Gap in Wealth in U.S. Called Widest in West," *New York Times,* 17 April 1995.
2. Michael Harrington, *The Other America: Poverty in the United States* (New York: MacMillan, 1962).
3. See, for example, Barry Bluestone and Bennett Harrison, *The Great U-Turn: Corporate Restructuring and the Polarization of America* (New York: Basic Books, 1988) or Robert B. Reich, *The Work of Nations* (New York: Alfred A. Knopf Inc., 1991).
4. Virginia duRivage, "Flexibility Trap: The Proliferation of Marginal Jobs," *The American Prospect,* Spring 1992.
5. Francine D. Blau and Marianne A. Ferber, *The Economics of Women, Men, and Work,* 2nd ed. (Englewood Cliffs, NJ: Prentice-Hall, 1992).
6. *Ibid.*
7. Randy Albelda and Chris Tilly, *Glass Ceilings and Bottomless Pits: Women, Income, and Poverty in Massachusetts* (Boston: Women's Statewide Legislative Network, 1994).
8. "The Wage Gap: Women's and Men's Earnings," briefing paper, Institute for Women's Policy Research, Washington D.C., 1995.
9. *Ibid.*
10. "Usual Weekly Earnings of Wage and Salary Workers: Fourth Quarter 1994," U.S. Department of Labor, Bureau of Labor Statistics, 9 February 1995.
11. "Women and the Minimum Wage," briefing paper, Institute for Women's Policy Research, Washington, D.C., 1995.

12. Milton Friedman and Gary Becker are examples of economists who write from a conservative perspective.
13. John Kenneth Galbraith and Lester Thurow are examples of economists who write from a liberal perspective.
14. David M. Gordon and Samuel Bowles are examples of economists who write from a radical perspective.

IT'S A FAMILY AFFAIR
Women, Poverty, and Welfare
Randy Albelda and Chris Tilly

HATING POOR WOMEN FOR BEING POOR IS ALL THE rage—literally. Radio talk show hosts, conservative think tanks, and many elected officials bash poor single mothers for being too "lazy," too "dependent," and too fertile. Poor mothers are blamed for almost every imaginable economic and social ill under the sun. Largely based on anecdotal information, mythical characterizations, and a recognition that the welfare system just isn't alleviating poverty, legislatures across the land and the federal government are proposing and passing draconian welfare "reform" measures.

It is true that current welfare policies do not work well—but not for the reasons usually presented. Welfare "reform" refuses to address the real issues facing single-mother families, and is heavily permeated by myths.

Aid to Families with Dependent Children (AFDC), the government income transfer program for poor non-elder families in the United States, serves only about 5 percent of the population at any given time, with over 90 percent of those receiving AFDC benefits being single mothers and their children. In 1993, 14 million people (two-thirds of them children) in the United States received AFDC. That same year, just under 40 million people were poor. Despite garnering a lion's share of political discussion, AFDC receives a minuscule amount of funding: It accounts for less than 1 percent of the federal budget and less than 3 percent of the state budgets.

Single mothers work. Not only do they do the unpaid work of raising children, they also average the same number of hours in the paid labor force as other mothers do—about 1,000 hours a year (a full-time, year-round job is about 2,000 hours a year).[1] And while close to 80 percent of all AFDC recipients are off in two years, over half of those return at some later point—usually because their wages in the jobs that got them off welfare just didn't match the cost of health care and childcare needed so they could keep the jobs. In fact, most AFDC recipients "cycle" between relying on families, work, and AFDC benefits to get or keep their families afloat.[2] That means that, for many single mothers, AFDC serves the same function as unemployment insurance does for higher-paid, full-time workers.

And, contrary to a highly volatile stereotype, welfare mothers, on average, have fewer kids than other mothers. And once on AFDC, they are less likely to have another child.

Poverty and the "Triple Whammy"

Poverty is a persistent problem in the United States. People without access to income are poor. In the United States, most people get access to income by living in a family with one or more wage-earners (either themselves or others). Income from ownership (rent, dividends, interest, and profits) provides only a few families with a large source of income. Government assistance is limited—with elders getting the bulk of it. So wages account for about 80 percent of all income generated in the United States. Not surprisingly, people whose labor market activity is limited, or who face discrimination, are the people most at risk for poverty. Children, people of color, and single mothers are most likely to be poor (see Boxes).

In 1993, 46 percent of single-mother families in the United States were living in poverty, but only 9 percent of two adult families with children were poor.[3]

Why are so many single-mother families poor? Are they lazy, do they lack initiative, or are they just unlucky? The answer to all of these is a resounding "No." Single-mother families have a very hard time generating enough income to keep themselves above the poverty line for a remarkably straightforward reason: One female adult supports the family—and one female adult usually does not earn enough to provide both childcare expenses and adequate earnings.

To spell it out, single mothers face a "triple whammy." First, like all women, when they do paid work they often face low wages—far lower than men with comparable education and experience. In 1992, the median income (the midpoint) for all women who worked full-time was $13,677. That means that about 40 percent of all working women (regardless of their marital status) would not have made enough to support a family of three above the poverty line. Even when women work year-round full-time, they make 70 percent of what men do.

Second, like all mothers, single mothers must juggle paid and unpaid work. Taking care of healthy and sometimes, sick children, and knowing where they are when at work, requires time and flexibility that few full-time jobs afford. All mothers are more likely to earn less and work less than other women workers because of it.

Finally, *unlike* married mothers, many single mothers must juggle earning income and taking care of children without the help of another adult. Single-mother families have only one adult to send into the labor market. And that same adult must also make sure children get through their day.

The deck is stacked—but not just for single mothers. All women with children face a job market which has little sympathy for their caregiving responsibilities and at the same time places no economic value on their time spent at home. The economic activity of raising children is one that no society can do without. In our society, we do not recognize it as work worth paying mothers for. For a married mother, this contradiction is the "double day." For a single mother, the contradiction frequently results in poverty for her and her children.

Denying the Real Problems

The lack of affordable childcare, the large number of jobs that fail to pay living wages, and the lack of job flexibility are the real problems that face all mothers (and increasingly everyone). For single mothers, these problems compound into crisis.

But instead of tackling these problems head on, politicians and pundits attack AFDC. Why? One reason is that non-AFDC families themselves are becoming more desperate, and resent the limited assistance that welfare provides to the worst-off. With men's wages falling over the last 30 years, fewer and fewer families can get by with only one wage earner. The government is not providing help for many low-income families who are struggling but are still above the AFDC eligibility threshold. This family "speed-up" has helped contribute to the idea that if both parents in a two-parent household can work (in order to be poor), then all AFDC recipients should have to work too.

Instead of facing the real problems, debates about welfare reform are dominated by three dead ends. First, politicians argue that single mothers must be made to work in the paid labor market. But, most single mothers already work as much as they can. Studies confirm that AFDC recipients already do cycle in and out of the labor force. Further, as surveys indicate, mothers receiving AFDC would like to work. The issue is not whether or not to work, but whether paid work is available, how much it pays, and how to balance work and childcare.

Second, there is a notion of replacing the social responsibilities of government assistance with individual "family" responsibilities: Make men pay child support, demand behavioral changes of AFDC recipients, or even pressure single women to get married. While child support can help, for most single mothers it offers a poor substitute for reliable government assistance. Penalizing women and their children for ascribed behaviors (such as having more children to collect welfare) that are supported by anecdotes but not facts is at best mean-spirited.

Third, there is an expectation that people only need support for a limited amount of time—many states and some versions of federal welfare reform limit families to 24 months of aid over some period of time (from a lifetime to five years). Yet, limiting the amount of time women receive AFDC will not reduce or limit the need for support. Children do not grow up in 24 months, nor will many women with few skills and little education necessarily become job ready. But more important, many women who do leave AFDC for the workplace will not make enough to pay for childcare or the health insurance they need to go to work.

In short, welfare "reform" that means less spending and no labor market supports will do little beyond making poor women's lives more miserable.

Beyond Welfare Reform

What could be done instead? Welfare reform in a vacuum can solve only a small part of the problem. To deal with poverty among single-mother families, to break the connection between gender and poverty, requires changing the world of work, socializing the costs of raising children, and providing low-wage supports.

If we as a nation are serious about reducing the poverty of women and children, we need to invest in seven kinds of institutional changes:

◆ *Create an income-maintenance system that recognizes the need for full-time childcare.* Policies that affect families must acknowledge the reality of children's needs. To truly value families means to financially support those (women or men) who must provide full-time childcare at home or to provide dependable, affordable, and caring alternative sources of childcare for those who work outside the home.

◆ *Provide support for low-wage workers.* If leaving welfare and taking a job means giving up health benefits and childcare subsidies, the loss to poor families can be devastating. Although high-salary workers receive (or can afford) these benefits, low-wage workers often don't. Government should provide these supports; universal health care and higher earned income tax credits (EITC) are a first step in the right direction.

◆ *Close the gender pay gap.* One way to achieve pay equity is to require employers to re-evaluate the ways that they compensate comparable skills. Poor women need pay equity most, but all women need it. Another way to close the pay gap is to increase the minimum wage. Most minimum-wage workers are women. An increase from the current $4.25 an hour to $5.50 would bring the minimum wage to 50 percent of the average wage.

◆ *Create jobs.* Create the opportunity to work, for poor women and poor men as well. Full employment is an old idea that still makes sense.

◆ *Create jobs that don't assume you have a "wife" at home to perform limitless unpaid work.* It's not just the welfare system that has to come to terms with family needs; it's employers as well. With women making up 46 percent of the workforce—and men taking on more childcare responsibilities as well—a change in work styles is overdue.

◆ *Make education and training affordable and available for all.* In an economy where the premium on skills and education is increasing, education and training are necessities for young people and adults, women and men.

◆ *Fix the tax structure.* Many of these proposals require government spending consistent with the ways our industrial counterparts spend money. Taxes must be raised to pay for these programs: the alternative—not funding child allowances, health care, and training—will prove more costly to society in the long run. But it is critically important to make the programs universal, and to fund them with a *fairer* tax system. Federal, state, and local governments have taxed middle- and low-income families for too long without assuring them basic benefits. Taxes paid by the wealthiest families as a percentage of their income have fallen dramatically over the last 15 years, while the burden on the bottom 80 percent has risen; it's time to reverse these trends.

Box 1

Who's Poor in the United States?

In 1993, one person in six was living below the official poverty line. The poverty line is an income threshold determined annually by the Department of Commerce's Census Bureau. The dollar amount is based on the price-adjusted determination of the 1960s cash value of a minimum adequate diet for families of different sizes multiplied by three (at the time, budget studies indicated that low-income families spent one-third of their incomes on food.) In 1993, the poverty threshold for a family of four is about $11,631.

While 10 percent of all men are poor, 16 percent of women and 25 percent—a full quarter—of all children in the United States are poor. Further, 36 percent of all black persons and 34 percent of Latinos are poor, versus 17 percent of Asians, and 13 percent of white persons. Does education help stave off poverty? Yes—but not very evenly. Consider the table on the next page. Those with low levels of education are much more likely to be poor—but gender matters. For men, getting a high school diploma cuts the chances of being poor by half—20 percent versus 10 percent. For women, poverty rates are more than halved by getting that degree, but the rates are still high—15 percent. For women to lower their likelihood of poverty to that of men with high school diplomas means getting some college education.

Percent Poor Persons in the United States
(All Ages) by Selected Characteristics, 1993

All	All	Men	Women	Children
	16.4%	**10.2%**	**16.1%**	**25.2%**
By race				
White	13.2%	8.6%	13.2%	19.8%
Black	35.9%	20.6%	34.5%	50.8%
Asian	17.0%	14.3%	17.4%	20.0%
By ethnicity				
Non-Latino	14.5%	8.9%	14.5%	22.0%
Latino	33.7%	22.2%	32.5%	45.2%
By residence				
City	24.1%	14.4%	22.6%	38.8%
Suburb	11.4%	7.1%	11.2%	17.4%
Rural	18.1%	11.8%	18.4%	25.9%

Source: U.S. Census Bureau, Current Population Survey, 1994

Box 2

Poverty Rates for Adults in the United States
By Educational Attainment, 1993

Poverty Rates

Years of Education	All Adults	Men	Women
8 or less	31.6%	26.4%	36.7%
9-11	27.5%	19.9%	34.3%
12	13.1%	10.0%	15.6%
13-15	9.0%	6.8%	10.9%
16	4.3%	3.8%	4.8%
17+	2.9%	2.8%	3.1%

Source: U.S. Census Bureau, Current Population Survey, 1994

The changes proposed are sweeping, but no less so than those proposed by the Republican Contract with America. With one out of every four children in this nation living in poverty, all our futures are at stake.

Notes

1. These data, and others throughout the paper, were calculated by the authors using current population survey tapes.
2. Five recent studies have looked at welfare dynamics and all come to these conclusions. LaDonna Pavetti, "The Dynamics of Welfare and Work: Exploring the Process by Which Young Women Work Their Way Off Welfare," paper presented at the APPAM Annual Research Conference, 1992; Kathleen Harris, "Work and Welfare Among Single Mothers in Poverty," *American Journal of Sociology*, vol. 99 (2), September 1993, pp. 317-52; Roberta Spalter-Roth, Beverly Burr, Heidi Hartmann, and Lois Shaw, "Welfare That Works: The Working Lives of AFDC Recipients," Institute for Women's Policy Research, 1995; Rebecca Blank and Patricia Rugggles, "Short-Term Recidivism Among Public Assistance Recipients," *American Economic Review*, vol. 84 (2), May 1994; pp. 49-53; and Peter David Brandon, "Vulnerability to Future Dependence Among Former AFDC Mothers," Institute for Research on Poverty discussion paper DP1005-95, University of Wisconsin, Madison, Wis., 1995.
3. U.S. Department of Commerce, Census Bureau, "Income, Poverty and Valuation of Noncash Benefits," *Current Populations Reports*, 1995, pp. 60-188. p. D-22.

BEYOND THE "NORMAL FAMILY"
A Cultural Critique of Women's Poverty
Margaret Cerullo and Marla Erlien*

> We live in and with a bourgeois society, its history, its traditions and
> prejudices, its confrontations and wicked laughter. Anyone who tries to
> behave well and play by what seem for the moment to be the rules of
> the game passes judgment on others who are outside the mainstream
> because they break the rules or don't bother to acknowledge them.
>
> —Hans Mayer, *Outsiders* [1]

TO THINK CRITICALLY ABOUT THE CAUSES OF POVERTY AND
to respond politically to it, a perspective is needed that includes, but
goes beyond, an economic understanding of the welfare state.
Poverty, welfare, and "dependency" are never simple social facts or
economic realities. Consciousness, culture, and politics play a crucial
role in defining their meanings—for poor people and their friends as
well as their antagonists.

Poor people's movements in the 1960s achieved two related goals.
First, they increased benefit levels. But, second, and as a crucial part of
the first process, they also transformed the meaning of poverty from a
personal shame to a national responsibility; they shifted welfare from
an insult to a right. And it is poor people's expanded sense of entitlement
and dignity that the New Right has targeted as much as benefits and
services. In its cultural war on the poor, the Right is attempting to
re-establish poverty as a mark of sin, a character flaw.

Cultural assumptions, as well as political-economic structures,
block the poor from claiming their rights and their humanity. The

* The authors developed many of the ideas in this essay in conversation with Paula
Ebron, Fran White, and Ann Withorn. Ann Holder and Ann Withorn provided moral
support and made the essay more readable.

battle for poor women's empowerment, then, must also take place on the uncharted terrain of culture, as well as on the more familiar ground of economic policy analysis.

Culture and Poverty

The focus here is on women and how cultural norms of womanhood are used to explain the causes and meaning of women's poverty, as well as to dehumanize poor women and push them to the margins of society.

When the authors speak of "culture" in this chapter we refer to habits of mind and feeling, "ways of seeing" that underlie the way people impart meaning to daily life and to the social world they inhabit. We are interested in the consciousness and ideology that surround questions of poverty and the welfare state. For us "consciousness" includes not only the explicit beliefs and values that people hold but also the psychological dimension: the unconscious commitments that affect how people act, that determine what disturbs, paralyzes, or mobilizes them.

A dominant culture (such as that of the contemporary United States) is a set of prescriptions and norms for living that anchor existing social and economic arrangements. It is important to expose and challenge the dominant culture. Whether one embraces it or not, this culture undermines alternative ways of living, loving, and seeing. Cultural norms accomplish this opposition, however, not only when they succeed in determining behavior. More deeply, their power comes from establishing the meaning attached to "deviating," or living outside the norms of society.

During the 1930s, for example, many mothers worked while unemployed fathers stayed home. Children reared in such families did not experience this departure from prescribed sex roles as an alternative to dominant values but as a shame or stigma. As parents themselves in the 1950s, such children were quick to re-establish "normal families."[2] Today the "traditional" family of father as breadwinner, mother as homemaker, and the children is no longer an empirical norm. Yet its power as a model of right living haunts and often punishes those who live outside it.

The women's movement has exposed the ways in which cultural norms—definitions of "proper" family, "appropriate" sex roles, "normal" sexuality, "good" mothering—circumscribe women's lives.

When women try to claim power over their lives, they must confront all the power of these cultural expectations, within themselves as well as in the broader society. But poor women must also confront the state's power to enforce those norms at will.

As black feminists have insisted, questions of racial identity have been crucial to the construction of gender in the United States. For example, the rules that separate "good women" from "bad women" have had a racial dimension.[3] Black women must prove themselves to be good; white women are always in danger of being seen as bad. In order to understand current welfare policy and the popular hostility to the welfare state, then, concerned citizens need to consider the ways in which poor women both challenge and embody cultural and racial norms.

Politics and Poverty

Feminists and other advocates for the poor have concentrated on proving the existence and extent of women's poverty. They have stressed the numbers and the hard data on benefits, as though ignorance of "facts" were the obstacle to women's poverty being recognized and addressed. The Right has provided most of the recent discussion of the cultural aspects of poverty, to reinforce and rigidify the dominant culture, not to challenge it.

On the one hand, conservative analysts invoke the dominant culture against those outside the mainstream. They locate the causes of poverty in poor people themselves, blaming them for their "inadequacies," lack of initiative, or "acceptance of dependency." Poverty is treated as a scourge, poor people as parasites on the majority. Poverty becomes not a circumstance but an attribute of a type of person.[4] The poor are presented as culturally different from the majority, a "pathological" subculture or, more recently, a permanent "underclass" prone to illegitimacy, crime, and debasement of the community. When poverty can be viewed as a function of race, the danger of cultural isolation for the poor becomes even greater.

On the other hand, liberals are willing to say that the culture of poverty is not immutable. Yet, in their failure to question the dominant culture, they link themselves to conservative critiques, even though their policy recommendations differ. While conservatives move to diminish welfare or deepen the stigma attached to it, liberals would keep economic supports but attempt to instill the work ethic and middle-class values in the poor. Both agree on the superiority of middle-class values, as well as on the assumption that lack of them causes poverty. They simply disagree about how best to force them on the poor—by threats and punishments or by "retraining" and "clinical intervention."

A quote from Hans Mayer begins this chapter because he provides an alternative framework to that of liberals and conservatives. Mayer asks how it is that those designated as "outsider" become dehumanized, objects of contempt for those who "play by the rules." For the purposes of this chapter the question becomes: How is it that those who bear the burden of poverty are blamed for their situation and seen as undeserving of genuine social support?

To answer this question, Mayer shifts the usual explanations. Rather than focus on deviance, the culture of the poor, he views adherence to the dominant culture as the problem. He reminds us how difficult it is to behave according to the rules. The specter of "outsider" status (or the effort to overcome it) strengthens the power of the rules; it keeps people behaving well. Moreover, the difficulty of adhering to the rules provokes resentment toward those who don't or can't.

Mayer's framework is especially illuminating today, when people perceive themselves to be losing ground. A television talk show that explored feelings about Medicaid abortions produced a telling response from one woman: "Why should we have to pay for someone else's pleasure?" This reaction, a familiar one, points out how economic realities become fused with moral issues to shape a potentially authoritarian response against welfare recipients.

The present economy makes personal sacrifice less meaningful as a means of guaranteeing present or future rewards. Such a situation allows people to turn against alternatives that seem to allow others the right to relief from the constraints and vulnerabilities of the marketplace. Only when people understand the fragile dignity that comes from playing by the rules, even if they lose, can they understand the popular passions that envelop the hopes of poor women.

When advocates of welfare rights sidestep a confrontation with cultural judgments about "proper" families, approved sexuality, and norms of right living, they eliminate the question of why it is so difficult to mobilize a movement in defense of an expanded welfare state. It is not enough, for example, to show how lack of decent jobs, not lack of husbands or "proper" values, creates women's poverty.

Popular attitudes, as well as policymakers, have shown themselves to be remarkably resistant to such "rational" interpretations. Nor have appeals to self-interest succeeded in winning support for welfare rights: The logic of spending money on poor children to prevent more expensive social costs later is simply not convincing to those who want to punish teenage mothers.

Such narrow, "common sense" analyses neglect the power of the morality and values that regulate private life and sustain the structure of work and family life. When self-interest is invoked to win popular support for the defense of welfare rights, we forget that self-interest can't be reduced to economics, that people's sense of worth is bound up with behaving well. When other people fail to "live by the rules" and go unpunished, then the sacrifices involved in "behaving well" are rendered meaningless.

Opposition to Medicaid-funded abortions is a good example of the failure of appeals to self-interest as a means of changing popular attitudes. In defense of Medicaid abortion, liberals argued that it was cheaper to fund them than to pay for expanding Aid to Families with Dependent Children (AFDC) rolls. Indeed, it does seem logical that conservatives who oppose the expansion of AFDC should be willing to pay the smaller cost of Medicaid-funded abortions. However, another logic, a cultural logic not addressed in the liberal defense, ties these two positions together.

Punishing both poor women who want abortions and AFDC mothers preserves the meaningfulness of the distinction between "good" and "bad" women, a distinction in which the racial dimension is seldom absent. "Good" women don't have abortions (not at least without feeling bad about them), and they don't have babies "out of wedlock." "Normal" women have breadwinners to support them, so it is more difficult to control their behavior from outside the family. Thus society punishes "bad" poor women who become pregnant without wanting a baby; it eliminates state funding for abortion. At the same time, it must also punish single mothers for failing to keep a man, so welfare benefits must be low enough to deny a dignified livelihood.

Following this argument, if the cultural assumptions about female sexuality, "normal" families, proper relations between men and women, and "good" mothering are not challenged, any defense of welfare rights will be inadequate. It will fail to break into the liberal-conservative continuum that requires punishing or pitying those outside the norms of "proper" living. Yet, in the current climate, so haunted by the New Right, this challenge is seldom raised.

Even those who most ardently advocate the welfare state are not immune from the impact of the Right. When the Right moved in to re-establish its standards regarding relations between men and women, female sexuality, definitions of the family, and homosexuality, it put liberals, progressives, and even feminists on the defensive. Those who advocate abortion, aid for teenage mothers, or gay rights fear they will be cast as antifamily, in favor of promiscuity—that is, that they will also be labeled "deviant." Many responded by trying to defuse these issues. They consider abortion and gay rights, for example, as "privacy issues," backing off from a defense of sexual freedom and female autonomy. Yet, such defenses deny what people know is at stake.

All the Women are White, All the Blacks are Men

The dangers of avoiding deeper cultural challenges can be illustrated by turning to two recent efforts to rethink poverty. First we examine the renewed discussion within the black community in response to the seeming intractability, and worsening, of poverty among black people. Second, we turn to feminists who have developed an analysis of poverty as a women's issue. We want to show how the absence of a critical perspective on the interaction of race and gender limits both analyses. The result is that both discussions treat as marginal the experience, needs, and insights of black women and other women of color. There is a particularly cruel irony here, since women of color have borne so much of the burden of poverty and of popular hostility to the poor.

The devastating impact of the Reagan years along with the emergence of black conservative analyses proposing "self-help" rather than public programs, have provoked a re-examination of the causes of poverty.[5] While black liberals continue to call for public programs, they have joined black conservatives in linking the persistence of poverty among blacks to the "crisis" of the black family.

The 'disintegrating' African-American family is the most important and alarming demographic development in our time," according to Pierre Devise of the Chicago Urban League.[6] And Salim Muwakkill, a black journalist writing in a socialist newspaper, gives the following as evidence of the deep crisis confronting the African-American community: "Black children are five times as likely [as white children] to be murdered as teenagers, four times as likely to be incarcerated between 15 and 19 and four times as likely to live in a female-headed household."[7] The casual equation of incarceration and murder with growing up in female-headed families is remarkable. The horror of such families and the exclusive concern with the fate of black males recalls the 1965 Moynihan Report, which many thought was dead and buried. Some blacks now argue that Moynihan should be reconsidered, that his analysis was too quickly and too defensively discarded. We think it is important to recall in some detail the assertions of the document and contemporary responses to it so that its revival will not turn the argument against black women.

Moynihan Revisited

In his notorious 1965 article, "The Negro Family: The Case for National Action," Daniel Moynihan tried to explain the persistence of poverty and unemployment in black America at a time when liberals thought systemic poverty would be cured through Keynesian economic policies.[8] In effect, Moynihan reduced racism and structural unemployment to a cultural failing of the black underclass. The "legacy of slavery" he argued, had resulted in a black American (male) population with structurally unemployable attributes and underclass values, such as lack of work orientation or interest in acquiring education and job skills.

"At the heart of the deterioration of the Negro community," he wrote in his most quoted line, "is the deterioration of the Negro family." According to Moynihan, slavery had left black people with a "matriarchal" pattern in which boys raised by mothers lacked the proper character structure to compete in the economic marketplace. Delinquency, poor educational achievement, the inability to delay gratification—all were presented as the products of "fatherless homes."

All this is well enough known. What is important is that the Moynihan report generated extensive controversy and opposition that have implications for today, in terms of what was and was not debated.

The black community and its allies vehemently denounced the Moynihan Report.[9] Indeed, it became the generative example for "blaming the victim"—for naming a black "culture of poverty" instead of racism as the cause of poverty. Lest we forget, it appeared at a time when the black liberation movement was exposing the structures of institutional racism as the barriers to black advancement. The Moynihan Report was a response to black demands, an argument for an expanded welfare state, a key document of the liberal "war on poverty." Yet by steering the discussion away from basic social and economic structures, Moynihan could call for reforming the poor rather than transforming society. It is worth looking at the contested issues, since they reappear in the current discussion as well.

Moynihan's arguments about the "broken" Negro family were countered by historians and sociologists who showed the existence of more complex, extended-family patterns within the black community.[10] The assumption of a white middle-class norm of what a "proper" family is, they argued, blocked Moynihan and other writers from seeing these alternative traditions. Against the assumption that nuclear families provided an ideal setting for childrearing, African-American culture was seen as embodying a tradition in which, as the novelist Toni Morrison expressed it, "It takes a village to raise a child, not one parent or two, but a whole village."[11]

What is striking, though, after 15 years of black feminist analysis, is how this early criticism responded, and did not respond, to the sexist character of the Moynihan Report, to its interpretation of the role of women in African-American history and its prescriptions for black women's future.

While some of Moynihan's critics recognized the attack on black women, they responded by defending the women's strengths in resisting a history of racist assaults on the community. Although this perspective has been and remains crucial, it stopped short of exposing or challenging the underlying assumptions about proper relationships between men and women that led Moynihan to blame black women in the first place.

A closer look reveals that Moynihan was concerned not about poverty in the black community but about the poverty of black men. Moreover, his evidence for black men's weakness in employment and education was not primarily in comparison with whites (men or women) but with black women. The implication throughout is that the employment and education of black women is denigrating to black men, perpetuating the "reversed" roles of husband and wife, which Moynihan said characterized the black family.

Moynihan's assumption that black women's education and employment status make them powerful, indeed too powerful, in relation to black men is key. It is an assumption that, as early black feminists pointed out, was often shared by black men (and women), indeed one that became embodied in the sexual politics of black cultural nationalism. Thus the racist aspects of Moynihan's "black matriarchy" thesis were underlined, but its sexist implications were unrecognized.

To take a striking example, when Moynihan proposed the army as an alternative source of discipline and character building for black men, the racist character of using blacks as cannon fodder in Vietnam was immediately obvious. Less emphasized was Moynihan's elegy to the army as a world of men, a world away from black women, a relief from "the strains of the disorganized and matrifocal family life in which so many Negro youth come of age."

More generally, the model of "traditional" family structure was upheld as the goal for the black community, as the solution to black poverty. It was not only a white middle-class model but, crucially for Moynihan, a male-dominated one. As he wrote: "Ours is a society which presumes male leadership in private and public affairs. The arrangements of society facilitate such leadership and reward it. A subculture, such as that of the Negro-American, in which this is not the pattern is placed at a distinct disadvantage." The defense against Moynihan was to accept the presumption of male leadership, and argue that it was intact in the black community.

Twenty years later the failure to challenge Moynihan's sexism comes back to haunt black women—indeed, all women. Now there are "legitimate" black as well as white conservatives to take up the call to reassert male authority. Now both black and white liberals are reviving the notion that it is female-headed black families that somehow cause poverty. And once again the concern is for the (male) children who must be "abnormally" socialized in female-dominated worlds.

At least this time black women have entered the debate to turn the emphasis around, by focusing on the burden that unsupported female-headed families place upon women and not on the "problem" of female-headed families for males. As Eleanor Holmes Norton puts it, "It is simply too much to ask what amounts to an increasing number of black women to raise the children of the black nation."[12] For Dorothy Height, writing in *Ebony*, the problem is the increasing isolation of teenage female-headed families from the once stronger extended family network, which "has fallen victim to the hardships of urban community life and the antifamily policies of public assistance agencies."[13] In her view, it's not the fact that families are female-headed that is the problem, rather that such families are "breaking down into smaller poorer units."

If the needs of poor black women are to avoid being pushed to the margins of society by the new debate about poverty, the sexism voiced by Moynihan must be exposed. Today, black women have begun to draw on traditions within the black experience to challenge the "normal," white, nuclear-family model, which is being posed as a backlash against the women's movements. As Moynihan realized, "normal" presumes male leadership, and "proper" socialization requires a child-centered, self-denying mother. By posing alternative models of family life, drawn from black history, black women are making the dominant culture itself contested terrain.

Good Women and Bad Women

It is in this context that the most popularized "feminization of poverty" discussion were disappointing.[14] The writings of Barbara Ehrenreich, Karin Stallard, and Holly Sklar attempted to debunk the myth that a "culture of dependence," attributed to women of color, was the root cause of poverty. They tried to show how unpredictable poverty is by highlighting the experience of Avis Parke, "with her handsome New England features and hearty outgoing manner...not the kind of person you would expect to catch paying for her groceries with food stamps." Her story—she was "a virgin when she married thirty years ago"—was presented as typical of the "new poor"and as a means of breaking the traditional isolation of poor women. By exposing how poverty haunts all women, the authors hoped to dislodge divisive stereotypes of poor women. Middle-class women can see themselves in Avis Parke; thus such examples help build cross-class identification among women.

Yet the very device intended to create unity serves to reinforce cultural stereotypes of who poor women are: promiscuous women, women of color, and unwed teenage mothers. For many readers, Avis Parke was simply presented as not "one of them." In fact, the term "displaced homemaker" used to characterize women like Avis Parke, who "played by the rules," comes to rescue such women from the stigma attached to being on welfare. By highlighting the "fall" of white, middle-class, once-married women into poverty, the historical poverty among women of color and young women is taken as a norm.

The dominant U.S. culture often views black women's poverty as due to promiscuity, having children "out of wedlock." The poor black woman is a type of person, whereas the poverty of a good woman, such as Avis Parke, is situational. By casting the new female poor as good women who have fallen on hard times, the authors appealed to, rather than challenged, the good woman-bad woman dichotomy. Black feminists have shown how casting black women as immoral is crucial to the construction of white womanhood, how the purity of white women is a mark of raclal superiority.[15] When Ehrenreich and others root for poor (white) women's claim to recognition in their "goodness," they left black women undefended. They also reinforced the values of self-sacrifice and sexual purity that imprison "good" women. They evoked sympathy for poor women as victims, blocking the ways in which rebellion against dependence on individual men may also be part of the reason for women's poverty.

What would have been the effect if Avis Parke had kicked out her husband, perhaps in order to come out as a lesbian? In choosing to build bridges to white women by avoiding racial issues, instead of reaching out to black women by addressing them, feminists will fail to create the alliances needed to protect all poor women from increasing stigmatization.

Beyond the Nuclear Family

In the 1980s, a series of developments occurred in our home state, "liberal" Massachusetts, that provide a dramatic "case study" for examining how these central issues related to cultural norms play themselves out in the making of social policy.

In May 1985, the liberal governor of Massachusetts reacted to press accounts decrying the placement of two young boys in the home of a gay couple for foster care. Although the Department of Social Services had spent a year investigating the two men, the governor removed the children from their care.

This precipitous move created a climate of permission for legislative New Rightists, who quickly introduced a resolution that would bar gays from foster care, guardianship, adoption, and family day-care—because of the "physical and psychological danger" their sexual preference represents to the well-being of children. The resolution passed overwhelmingly, 112 to 28.

Two weeks after the removal of the boys from the home, a new policy was issued. The new regulations invoked the "traditional" family structure—working father, mother at home with children of their own—as the model childrearing situation for foster-care placement. Except for relatives of the foster children, the policy made it very difficult for any "nontraditional" family to be considered for giving foster care. If society truly considers the well-being of children from already disrupted families, the policymakers argued, then it should not further "burden" them by placing them in nontraditional settings.

The *Boston Globe* editorial that anticipated the policy announcement made the stakes clear. Entitled "A Normal Setting," the editorial upheld what some called the "Ozzie and Harriet" or "Father Knows Best" image of family life. Families with working mothers, single parents, or gay or lesbian couples were clearly deviant, undesirable, and abnormal. Nowhere was there mention of the decreasing numbers of "normal" families, much less that such families have been the site of most battering and sexual abuse of women and children. And, of course, nothing was said about the inequality between men and women that lies at the core of what is "normal" about traditional families—just as Moynihan noted 20 years ago.

Amazingly, many of the liberal centers of power—even those that support women's and gay rights—showed strong commitment to this myth of the happy, traditional family. The *Boston Globe* and most politicians gave consistent support to the governor's stance. One New Right state representative exposed the profound conservative-liberal continuum that was operating here when he proclaimed that he was delighted to see the liberal governor taking time away from Reagan-bashing to uphold the value of the traditional family. Only the liberal social work and psychological professionals broke ranks and questioned the logic.

More important, the blatant way that the policy attempted to enforce cultural norms of right living through welfare policies was recognized and opposed by a wide variety of groups. The primary target of the foster-care policy was lesbians and gay men, who continued to lead the fight against it. However, the policy also triggered the historical memories of other constituencies. For some it recalled the Nazi separation of Jew from non-Jew. For others, it recalled Moynihan's punitive hierarchy of normal and deviant families. Leaders of the progressive black community denounced the racist implications of upholding the model of "traditional" family life. One black activist noted: "The traditional family enslaved my ancestors," thereby giving one more rejoinder to those who forget how central notions of proper family life are to those who believe in white racial superiority in the United States.

Finally, opponents of the policy emphasized how it does more than "regulate" the behavior of the poor and others directly subject to state control. It forced social workers into being "culture cops." Like so many other welfare-state policies, it was also about establishing a way of life, consistent with existing social and economic arrangements. The suppression of alternatives was integral to its goals.

This is a chapter whose political conclusion is still in the making. The authors cannot end with "solutions" to women's poverty or even with specific social-policy recommendations. Rather we have tried to explore the cultural environment within which social policy is formulated. As the discussion proceeds about the pervasiveness and seeming intractability of women's poverty, we suggest that substantive change will not occur without dislodging the cultural norms that keep some people behaving "well" and that force others to the margins of society.

Reforms that obviously helped to relieve the burden of poverty have been dismantled. Efforts to reassert them have been blocked, or never even started. Even as homelessness and hunger show the situation of the poor to be even more desperate, hostility to reforms intensifies, assuming ever more "irrational" overtones. We suggest that such hostility cannot be countered with appeals to economic self-interest. Instead, poor women and their advocates must find ways to counter the moral authority of cultural norms that both create blindness to growing impoverishment and provide a rationale for turning against the poor, the deviant, the "outsider."

Epilogue: Looking Back and Looking Forward

In 1986 when we wrote this chapter, we were alarmed at what we saw as the danger of the "cultural isolation of the poor," the construction of poor people in popular political discourse as a separate species of (barely) human beings, cast out from the charmed circle of the "right living." We turned our critical aim on the market, the harsh toll and uncertain rewards of "playing by the rules" that we suggested led people to turn against alternatives that allowed others relief from the constraints and vulnerabilities of the marketplace. We noted the apparent consensus across the political spectrum between liberals and conservatives the lack of values and lack of husbands (not lack of jobs and social support) caused women's poverty. We also recognized that black women were especially demonized in discussions of persistent poverty, which was attributed by almost everyone in a neo-Moynihan revival to the "crisis of the black family," or more directly to pathologized female-headed households. We challenged feminist discussions of the "feminization of poverty" for attempting to build alliances among women while bypassing or disavowing the issue of race that blocked those alliances. And, finally, we looked to an emerging struggle in Massachusetts over an anti-gay foster care family policy to broaden the argument about how social policy underwrites norms of right living, of proper families, establishing such arrangements as the circuits through which material benefits flow.

In all of this, we were brought the question of how poor women, welfare recipients, were culturally represented to the center of the debate over welfare policy and to explanations for the apparent growing popular willingness to dismantle welfare programs. The point was then and continues to be that relating the "facts" of who is on AFDC, for how long, and at what cost in terms of overall government spending, is an ineffective response to the onslaught. Our argument 10 years ago was less focused on challenging specific welfare policy initiatives than on charting a shifting ideological climate, whose consolidation we still hoped to unsettle. Along with Roz Petchesky, Zillah Eisenstein, Linda Gordon, Allen Hunter, and others writing at the time, we believed and tried to show how anti-feminist politics were critical to the agenda of the New Right, to legitimating the transition from the liberal to the neoconservative state.[16] What we argued was that the "pro-family backlash" fueled not only right-wing anti-abortion, anti-gay, anti-ERA initiatives, but was also central to the growing attack on "welfare rights," on entitlement, that we see in retrospect as a key wedge in the dramatic drive toward the privatization of everything.[17] As Petchesky and Gordon came to argue explicitly, we were proposing that welfare state policy not only regulates labor (disciplining all workers by making survival outside the labor market onerous and virtually impossible) but also disciplines women's behavior, enforcing the categories of good/bad womanhood, punishing those women who live outside the boundaries of the traditional family.[18] In this, we were part of the emerging feminist scholarship on the welfare state that was challenging the failure to recognize the gendered character of welfare provision and of hostility to the welfare state.

We were sketching out the lines of the ideological assault that preceded and made possible the full scale material assault that we have witnessed since the 1994 election. We were charting the resurgence of cultural and moral explanations for (maternal) poverty as they were taking shape in the early-mid Reagan years. In retrospect we would single out the rewriting of the culture of poverty as a "culture of dependence"[19] and the consolidation of notions of an "underclass"[20] as the critical ideological developments. We anticipated that welfare policy would become ever more harassing, insulting, and punitive, and that grants would be increasingly inadequate. (Piven and Cloward document, for example, that by 1984 there were about 1 million more rejections of AFDC applications nationwide than in 1972 due to increasingly Byzantine application procedures.) What we didn't anticipate was the ideological consensus that has emerged around workfare as the remedy for "dependence," that underlies broad public support for "ending welfare as we know it," that is, as an entitlement for poor mothers and their children. If anything, we underestimated the extent to which welfare policy would become a purely ideological and disciplinary instrument driven more by moral than economic considerations. A November 1995 Focus Group Report by Public Agenda for the Kaiser Family Foundation on "Public Attitudes Toward Welfare and Welfare Reform"[21] provides a disturbing confirmation of some of the trends in popular sentiment we discerned 10 years ago. The report notes that (overwhelmingly white) focus group participants seem to approach welfare with a "singular sense of moral outrage," and are "more concerned with the moral under- pinnings of the welfare system than with the costs they incur as taxpayers. The welfare system [is] viewed... [as] an affront to their own commitment to hard work and willingness to play by the rules." The authors noted further that whether welfare recipients felt shame seemed to determine whether participants felt empathy or disdain toward them. Finally, the report identified a recurrent combination of moral vehemence yoked to personal anecdotes. In every group someone had a story about a welfare recipient in front of them on the grocery check out line, and many of the more intense comments at the focus group sessions were grounded in observations of friends, family or neighbors who were on welfare. The niece of my mother's best friend knows someone on welfare who "drives a Lexus, piles steaks into her grocery cart, buys her kids $60-sneakers, has a fridge overflowing with food, turns $100 in food stamps into $20 of drugs on the street, etc."

Some of the issues we broached have emerged with even starker clarity 10 years later. Following Dorothy Roberts, today we would underline that a critical reason for the failure of public support for welfare is that the public views this support as benefiting black mothers, who are seen as inherently unfit, their children as inherently useless. Black mothers' work as mothers is devalued, their legacy to their children viewed as a legacy of pathology. Payment to mothers who don't work is actually bad for their children, since it teaches them dependency.[22] Lucie White a feminist poverty lawyer and theorist has sharpened our thinking on the failure of a broad feminist mobilization in response to the dismantling of the welfare state, a singular achievement of women's politics in the United States. She argues that while the women's movement has lost the feminist critique of work, working women nonetheless suffer the stress and misery of attempting to combine work and parenting, building resentment that often turns against welfare recipients.[23] Again the Kaiser Foundation Report supports this insight "I didn't get to stay home with my children, I had to give that up. So why should I pay so she can stay home with hers?" "I'm glad I worked because I want my daughter to see that and learn that, so she'll have some pride and dignity also."

There is a certain irony in turning to gay politics 10 years after we suggested links between the ways that the ideology of the normal family pathologized single mothers and gays and lesbians, similarly bound up in a "tangle of pathology," that could be their (our) only legacy to children. With "family values" rhetoric on the ascendance in the election season, with anti-divorce crusades from all sides, the attempt to route parenting rights through (stable, monogamous) marriage is stronger than ever. Lesbian/gay politics, meanwhile, is caught up in one track struggle for gay marriage, the prospect of including gays and lesbians among the "right living."

Looking back and looking forward, we have come to view the current discourses of welfare reform as discourses of abjection, a violent exclusion based on bad behavior. We are drawn to the language of abjection because it captures some of the violent intensity of current rituals of social purification, efforts to purge the body politic of "waste" and "excess." We view this as part of an attempt to articulate a new basis for our collective national existence, a "new America," a "Post Welfare State America," as a recent Republican Party memo put it, that will displace the 60 year hold of the New Deal on the American political imaginary. How to resist this consolidating cultural and political hegemony seems to us the paramount question that should engage feminist and other progressive forces. We conclude with a reminder that viewing the welfare state as the result of the largess of big government is only possible because of the lost memory of the social movements from labor to welfare rights that extracted a measure of collective responsibility and social provision. How desperately we need a revival of social movement, of collective action that might move some of the radical critiques of the rhetoric and representation of poverty, welfare, and dependence that have been produced in the last 10 years into political demands. It is only when the objects of representation become political subjects that the critique of representation finds its aim.

Notes

1. Hans Mayer, *Outsiders: A Study in Life and Letters* (Cambridge, Mass.: MIT Press, 1984).

2. This example is borrowed from Judy Housman, "Mothering, the Unconscious, and Feminism," *Radical America* 16, no. 6 (November-December 1982).

3. See Angela Davis, *Women, Race, and Class* (New York: Random House, 1981); E. Frances White, "Listening to the Voices of Black Feminism," *Radical America* 18, nos. 2, 3 (1984); Hortense Spillers, "Interstices: A Small Drama of Words," in *Pleasure and Danger: Exploring Female Sexuality*, ed. Carole S. Vance (Boston: Routledge and Kegan Paul, 1984).

4. We draw on some ideas of Michel Foucault, who has analyzed the significance of the historical shift of focus from crime to "the criminal" as a type of person, from madness to "the madman," and from sexual perversion to the "pervert." See *Discipline and Punishment* (New York: Vintage, 1969); *Madness and Civilization* (New York: Vintage, 1972), *The History of Sexuality* (New York: Vintage, 1980).

5. See, for example, Carlyle C. Douglas, "Urban League to Debate U.S. Aid and Self-Help," *New York Times*, 21 July 1985.

6. Quoted in Salim Muwakkill, "Black Family's Ills Provoke New Concern," *In These Times*, 12 June 1985, p. 5.

7. Salim Muwakkill, "Civil Rights Leaders Shift Course Inward," *In These Times*, 7 August 1985, p. 5.

8. Daniel P. Moynihan, "The Negro Family: The Case for National Action," prepared for the U.S. Department of Labor, Office of Policy Planning and Research (Washington D.C.: Government Printing Office, 1965). It is one of the dark ironies of our time that Moynihan, now Senator from New York, has become one of the most visible and diligent critics of current "welfare reform"—the dismantling of AFDC; and one of the most passionate congressional advocates for poor children. Throughout his career, Moynihan has been consistent in his support of an expanded welfare state, which was indeed the conclusion of the 1965 Moynihan Report. What came home to roost, however, were his views on the pathologies of the black family, specifically the inadequacy of black mothers. This view has been abstracted from his framework and turned into a spectacle to mobilize a racist base for the dismantling of entitlements.

    Moynihan's trajectory perhaps reveals most starkly the contradiction in the strategy of advocating for poor children while bypassing, indeed contributing to cultural and political discourses that denigrate their mothers. AFDC is after all premised on recognizing the social value of women's work. As long as the work of black mothers is devalued, as long as their legacy to their children is understood as a legacy of pathology, then the ground for public support to them is seriously eroded. Moreover, born into a "tangle of pathology," how can their children be recognized as socially valuable, as members of the community, rather than alien and dangerous (rather then endangered) outsiders? A dark logic extends from the Moynihan Report to Gingrich's redemptive image of orphanages, "Boys Towns".

9. See Robert Staples, *The Black Family, Essays and Studies*, rev. ed. (Belmont, Calif.: Wadsworth, 1978); Lee Rainwater and William Yancey, *The Moynihan Report and the Politics of Controversy*, (Cambridge, Mass.: M.I.T. Press, 1967); Charles Vert Willie, *A New Look at Black Families*, 2nd ed.(Bayside, N. Y.: General Hall, 1981).

10. See, for example, Herbert Gutman, *The Black Family in Slavery and in Freedom* (New York: Pantheon, 1976); Carol Stack, *All Our Kin: Strategies for Survival in a Black Community* (New York: Harper and Row, 1974).

11. Quoted in Louise Meriwether, "To Be Young, Black, and Pregnant," *Essence*, April 1984, p. 68.

12. E.H. Norton, "An Open Letter From a Black Woman to a Black Man," speech to the National Convention of the Urban League, July 1975 quoted in *The Underclass*, Ken Auletta (New York: Vintage Books, 1983), p. 263.

13. Dorothy Height, "What Must Be Done About Our Children Having Children?" *Ebony*, May 1985, p. 101.

14. See Barbara Ehrenreich and Karin Stallard, "The Nouveau Poor," *Ms.*,

July-August 1982, pp. 217-24; and Karin Stallard, Barbara Ehrenreich, and Holly Sklar, *Poverty in the American Dream: Women and Children First* (Boston: South End Press, 1983). The quotations that follow are all from "The Nouveau Poor".

15. For an elaboration of this point, see E. Frances White, *Listening to the Voices*, and Jacqueline Dowd Hall, *Revolt Against Chivalry* (New York: Columbia University Press, 1983).

16. This formulation is Rosalind Petchesky's, *Abortion and Woman's Choice, The State, Sexuality and Reproductive Freedom*, (Boston: Northeastern, 1984, 1990), p. 243.

17. For a fuller discussion of the connections between antifeminism, and the attacks on liberalism and social welfare see Petchesky.

18. See debate between Linda Gordon and Frances Fox Piven, "What Does Welfare Regulate," *Social Research*, vol. 55, no.4 (Winter 1988).

19. See Linda Gordon and Nancy Fraser, "The Geneology of Dependence: Tracing a Keyword in the U.S. Welfare State," pp. 235-68 in this volume, reprinted from *Signs,* vol. 19. no. 21, (1994) .

20. See Adolph Reid, "The Underclass as Myth and Symbol," R*adical America*, vol. 24, no.1 (January 1992).

21. Report no. 1094

22. See Dorothy Roberts, "The Value of Black Mothers' Work," in *Connecticut Law Review,* vol. 26, 871-8; and revised in *Radical America*, vol. 26 , no. 1.

23. See Lucie White, "Where Are the Women's Voices," in *Connecticut Law Review*, Vol 26, 871-8; and revised in *Radical America*, vol. 26, no. 1.

BEARING WITNESS TO TEEN MOTHERHOOD
The Politics of Violations of Girlhood
*Robin A. Robinson**

It's like my mother told me, "Don't get pregnant while you're young cause people talk about you. People point their fingers. They say you're no good. They call you all this stuff. And I had that in my head. So I was so embarrassed to go to the doctor...I refused to go to the doctor...I think I was eight months when I first went to the doctor...I was eight months, I think, when I first went to get it checked out...I used to think...to this day, two people will be sitting, talking, and I'd be paranoid they're gonna talk about me. What is wrong? Is my hair messed up? Cause my mother said I have to be perfect. I have to be what I'm not.

> "Tania," 17-year-old mother who abandoned her 2-year-old son

My mother is mad at me because my daughter doesn't even know her, because I don't live with her and she doesn't want me to tell my daughter, well, you didn't help me much...My daughter doesn't really like the juice but I try to give it to her cause her iron level's really low.

> "Ashley," 15-year-old mother, who lives in a foster home

Did I ever have sex with anyone but my boyfriend [age 28]? You mean willingly? Besides that stuff with my father? No, just (my boyfriend). When (my boyfriend) and I would fight, social services would get on his case about statutory rape, and he would say "how do you know I was the only one?" And he always made me look bad. But he was the only guy I was with.

> "Melina," 15-year-old sent to foster care at age 12 for one year when charges of sexual abuse by her father were substantiated.

* This article was written by Robin A. Robinson in her private capacity. No official support or endorsement by the Department of Health and Human Services is intended or should be inferred.

IN THIS CHAPTER, I BEAR WITNESS TO TEEN MOTHERHOOD. I tell you, from personal and professional perspectives both, how some teen mothers perceive the social world in which they live, and how the social world perceives them. I offer an introductory sociopolitical analysis of responses to teen mothers, of the helping professionals who advocate services and assistance, and the welfare reform crusaders who insist upon measures of deterrence and bootstrapping. I conclude with a vision of prevention and care, a proposal for assessment of needs of adolescent girls, and an example of what can be achieved in the larger political context. To begin, I offer you a true story of a personal encounter with an architect of current social policy regarding teen mothers in the United States.

A Story

A well-regarded economist in the area of welfare reform was on the faculty of the graduate school where I did my doctoral work in social welfare policy during the Reagan administration (he has since left). He had received a prestigious national award for a set of principles he had formulated, based on the wealth of aggregate studies he and others had conducted, on the subject of teenage mothers using welfare as an income support. His platform was to substitute his principles of Workfare, child support enforcement, and minimum wage subsidies for AFDC income supports; these principles have since become legion. But here's the story. After receiving the award, he gave a colloquium at the school on the subject of his work: teenage mothers using welfare as income support. Now this was a subject with which I was quite familiar—I had been a teen mother using welfare and ancillary services as my income support. After the economist's talk, he asked me what I had thought of the principles he put forth, (I had challenged him in the question-and-answer period following his talk, asking him where the teen mothers were supposed to leave their children when they went off to work, childcare being a radical notion at the time in this context.) I told him that in the context of my life experience, his proposed remedies were problematic at best and irrelevant at worst, and they troubled me, whereupon he told me that I (that is, my experience) didn't count. I asked him to explain.

"Well," he said, "first of all, you are white." I replied that statistics showed that the majority of teen mothers in the United States are white. "Well," he said, "you are intelligent." "Did he have evidence to suggest that most teen mothers are stupid?" I queried. "Well", he said,"you got married." I pointed out that a major recent study (at that time) had suggested that teen mothers who marry achieve less in terms of educational achievement and income than their unmarried counterparts who remain at home. "Well," he said, "you're attractive." "Let me see if I have this straight," I said. "Your profile of teen mothers, upon which you base your considerable influence on policy at the national level, rests on assumptions that we teen mothers are poor, black, dumb, and ugly?" He argued that to address the social problems of teen motherhood, we had to use those assumptions. So I didn't count.

An absurd story, clearly. I do count—my story counts—along with all the other stories of all the different types of women who have been teen mothers. Twenty-five years of direct service experience, formal research, and other scholarly enterprise with and about girls in the social margins tell me that every teen mother's story counts, and that the principal impediments to translation of these stories into constructive social policy are a rash of racist, classist, and sexist stereotypes that pervade popular and political culture.

An Analysis

I had been an honor student all my young life, active in school and community services, a volunteer counselor at a camp for developmentally disabled children, a Girl Scout, a volunteer to collect food for poor people. The eldest child and grandchild of a working-class family, I had been the one designated to change the family's status, to go to college, to achieve in my early life the family's transition from working class to professional identity. Upon the discovery of my pregnancy at age 16, the dream was dashed. My family and community of friends, teachers, and other respected adults decided that now I would be nothing, achieve nothing, do nothing. The message from my immediate world and the larger social sphere was clear: Stigma and adversity would prevail over talent, determination, and ambition.

The quotes that introduce this chapter, from qualitative research I have done about such girls, are testament to the struggles they face in the personal and social realms. Each quote represents several aspects of teen pregnancy and motherhood that policymakers, authorities, and providers must understand in the formulation of responsible and constructive social policy and services for this population.

Stigmatization and Betrayal

The mantle of stigmatization on girls in this culture and polity is a heavy one; girls are tempted and instructed by the popular culture—television, films, music—to place their sexuality at the forefront of the identity they are developing as they approach adulthood. The concurrent message—in school curricula, religious institutions, messages from political and social leaders, and also the media, through public service announcements and special programming—is that teenage sexuality is dangerous, wrong-headed, morally and socially unacceptable. Add to this confusing formulation the statistics of child sexual abuse and sexual assault: studies, through many methodologies, reveal 1) that one third to one half of all females in this country suffer some form of sexual molestation before the age of eighteen; 2) that one half to three quarters of teen mothers endure some form of child sexual maltreatment; 3) that three-quarters or more of delinquent girls were sexually abused as children; and 4) that two thirds or more female prostitutes were sexually abused as children and prior to prostitution. The model that this compendium of sexual teaching begins to suggest is that sexual attractiveness is desirable, sexual intercourse is wrong, sexual involvement is likely to be involuntary, hurtful, shameful.

Let us focus on teen mothers. Tania's quote of her mother's admonition not to get pregnant while she was young tells a story of the stigma of teen pregnancy. Tania is African American, a good student from a modest home in her early life, sexually abused by a family member and raped as a preadolescent by several acquaintances. Whatever internal messages she had absorbed about avoiding teenage sex and pregnancy had been thwarted by external events; her remark about not being perfect speaks to the self-perception that resulted from her experiences, because perfect girls do not have sex. The stigmatization process had begun, from her own definitions and those of the outside world. She became pregnant at 14, ran away from home, gave birth to a son at 15, abandoned the child—left him at the home of the child's father and his mother, and never told her own mother that she had had a child—and then attempted suicide several times, the last time nearly succeeding. After committing several petty larcenies—according to her a cry for help—she was committed to juvenile corrections. She had experienced betrayal—a traumatic dynamic of child sexual abuse—by those who purportedly loved her, and by the state, whose response to her anguish was to treat her as a criminal. My last knowledge of her was that she was living on the streets, committing petty larceny when she was desperate for a rest from her street life, and trying to convince the youth authorities to let her live as a foster child with her aunt. Tania had fulfilled the social prophecy for African-American girls.

Tania's story raises another effect of stigmatization regarding the plight of teen mothers: her fear of seeking health care during her pregnancy. Her self-described embarrassment, her refusal to see a doctor, boded ill for her own health and that of her child. Studies of adolescent mothers and their children show several conditions of high-risk pregnancies, low birth weights for their babies, prenatal distress, and higher infant mortality. Avoidable prenatal and perinatal problems can lead to later health issues for mothers and children, as well as learning disabilities among the children. But young mothers in crisis either do not know or do not (or cannot) respond to warnings about such matters. These conditions pose challenges of considerable social, moral, and fiscal expense to the larger social realm.

Melina's story tells another story of teenage sexuality and pregnancy. Melina, a bright Caucasian girl from a working-class family—an honor student "when I go to school"—endured six years of forced sexual intercourse by her father, followed by her removal from her family home by social services when she was 12. Thus, her initial sexual identity was created by the experience of an older man forcing himself on her, and her sense of powerlessness to prevent either the violence or the sex. During her one-year stay in a foster home, she continued the only sexual behavior she had known—sex with an older man who controlled the relationship—with a boyfriend 12 years older than she, who used violence to control her. When she became pregnant at 13, her boyfriend pushed her down a flight of stairs in anger. She miscarried. She stayed with the same boyfriend, in fear and in love, for the next two years—turbulent years—during which social services occasionally threatened the boyfriend with statutory rape charges for having sex with a designated Child in Need of Services, the label Melina had gained from her sexual history. When

I last spoke with her, she was still grieving the child that would have been two years old, and had been left in her father's care while her mother was ill in the hospital, although her father was under court order not to come within a mile of his daughter.

Melina's formation of sexual identity was that of a precocious awareness of sexuality as the result of early sexual trauma, resulting in a confused understanding of what it means to be sexual, or loved; the act of sex alone is confused for love and caring, and elements of betrayal and powerlessness are strong concurrent effects. Melina's story, like Tania's, is illustrative of the betrayal by social protections that label and punish the unwanted sex the girls experience, as well as their powerlessness to cope with their abusers, their personal crises, and the state's mechanisms to attempt to control their sexual activity.

Another important point to be underscored by Melina's story is the finding of several studies that show that the fathers of the children of teenage girls are mostly older men, the majority over the age of 20. Disturbingly, the younger the teen mother, the more consistent this finding is in terms of years difference between the mother's and father's ages. Thus, the suggestion of trauma and powerlessness holds, and education and publicity campaigns to get adolescent boys and girls to just say "no" are undermined.

Responsibility and Determination

One of the principal complaints characteristic of welfare reform rhetoric is the lack of responsibility that teen mothers demonstrate for themselves and their children: financial, emotional, practical. Over years of interviews with girls and women at the social margins, most of whom have had teen pregnancies and/or become teen mothers, a question I have explored with them is, "What makes you feel grownup, or, another way, when does a girl become a woman?" The answers are consistent: "Not sex." "Responsibility" is the most common answer, by far, and responsibility is defined foremost by a devotion to the needs of the child. Teen mothers mourn their lost girlhood and teen social life and fight depression as they speak freely and energetically about their need to continue their education, find a decent place to live, find and keep jobs, find birth control that works. The message of the popular culture that they receive is that they are *de facto* irresponsible because they became pregnant; they struggle to challenge that assumption in what is often the chaos and neediness of their daily lives.

I quoted from Ashley's story at the beginning of this chapter. Ashley, a 15-year-old mother who lived with her 10-month-old daughter in a foster home when I interviewed her, was a shy, soft-spoken girl from a large Italian middle-class family. The woman who fostered Ashley and her baby in her home was an administrator at a local community college, and Ashley was taking classes there toward an Associate's degree, rather than pursue what she considered an inferior course for a General Equivalency Diploma. Ashley had been sexually abused by her grandfather for several years in early childhood, as had her mother, aunt, and sister by the same man. She ran away from home when her father and mother divorced, and her mother and sisters went to live with the sexually abusive grandfather. Ashley eventually picked up charges that led to her commitment to juvenile corrections, and spent time in a residential treatment facility for girls. During that time, she did well in her studies wherever she was, when she could go to school. She ran away again after discharge from the treatment facility to avoid going back to her grandfather's house. When she became pregnant, she went to the foster home.

Determinedly, Ashley avoided bringing her child into the house of the grandfather who had abused her and her female relatives. She told of her responsibility to protect her daughter from harm, even at the expense of alienating her mother and other family throughout her pregnancy. Her isolation during pregnancy is more common than not in the stories of teen mothers, as babies' fathers abandon their pregnant girlfriends, other friends continue with their own adolescent joys and concerns, and parents—sometimes well-meaning and sometimes not—throw up their hands in symbolic despair at how to cope with their wayward daughters. Many teen mothers are the daughters of teen mothers, and the recapitulation of the burden to mother and daughter is daunting, often, to both. The isolation of pregnant teens and teen mothers is the product of such tension and shame.

Still, most of the teen mothers with whom I have spoken have or find the moral strength and determination to care for their babies as best they can. For better or worse, they do what they can to navigate the social welfare system for food, housing, transportation, childcare, medical care and medicine, and other services. Ashley's comment about the need to feed nutrient-rich juice to her anemic daughter, even though her daughter pushes it away, reveals her understanding of the medical necessity of the nutrients as well as her commitment to care for and guide the development of her daughter. Perhaps this is the salient metaphor to carry into a vision of what the social and political structure can and should do for teen mothers and their babies.

A Vision

In a recent group interview with teen mothers in a prenatal/post-partum clinic, in response to their question to me of what I could do to help them, I asked the girls if they were registered to vote. Only four of many who were 18 or older were registered. The rest looked at me with bewilderment. They did not understand the relationship between the power of their vote—and the power of their need—and the process of policy and law. They did not understand the origins in government, by elected officials, of Medicaid and food stamps and Aid to Families with Dependent Children (AFDC) and Women, Infants, and Children (WIC) nutrition programs and Section Eight housing. They had some vague notion of proposed cutbacks, and a clear understanding of what executed cutbacks had done to their ability to survive. But they did not perceive themselves as citizens with rights and obligations. Often, teen mothers' inexperience with any kind of contact with government or agencies leaves them wanting for basic human needs. Often, young mothers are at odds with a sometimes menacing infrastructure of welfare programs and staff who punish the girls' behaviors by controlling benefits.

Why can't or won't girls just obey the public admonition to abstain from sexual intercourse? Instruction in acceptable social values regarding adolescent sexuality is often a corollary to punishment by scant or withheld benefits, but alien to girls whose life experiences belie the concept of choice, and want for a cohesive, healthy public model of sexuality. The absence of such a model may explain the overall failure of campaigns to promote sexual abstinence among adolescents. I have found that most teen mothers are trying to be responsible about birth control. They are often confused by their experiences with sexuality, with public and private messages. Many babies of teen mothers I have interviewed were the result of birth control failures, or sheer ignorance of family planning methods. Much has been made in the media, in politics, and in social research of a "subculture" of teen mothers who have babies "to get on welfare." My research and that of many others does not support this contention. More likely, it is the case that for many girls, social and political realities fail to provide the protection, nurture, and care they need to pass through adolescence without fear or experience of sexual assault, economic deprivation, educational and vocational unmet needs, and pregnancy.

The Needs of Teen Mothers

In any case, most adolescent girls who become mothers, whether the pregnancy was intentional or unintentional, quickly develop a mother's sense of the primary need to protect and to provide for their infants. The messages they receive from the larger world are not without impact, however. Such messages of fear, of contempt, of imposed shame, of futility, are not lost on adolescents who are still forming their adult identities. Young mothers still need basic human needs of housing, food, clothing, education, social support, medical care, and legal protection. They need love and kindness. They need respect as human beings and as citizens of the social world in which they live.

Principal areas of welfare reform include the elimination of AFDC, the decrease or elimination of Medicaid, and the decrease or elimination of other supports such as food stamps, WIC, housing, daycare, and education subsidies. The elimination of each of these supports brings young mothers closer to thresholds of desperation. Generous support in the polity for provision of these needs, as teen mothers move toward adulthood and full assumption of adult obligations, will contribute to the general health and productivity of young mothers and their children.

Ironically, the more headway women have made into the labor force, the more stigmatizing AFDC has become. Apparently the social value of women at home rearing their children has all but vanished. But has it? The same political factions that decry the waste and immorality of AFDC tout family values as their prescription for a greater society. Many young mothers with whom I've spoken want to spend some part of their babies' early childhood at home with them, and then resume their education and/or vocational training to become economically self-sufficient. Most have absorbed that notion of family values. Somewhere in this maelstrom of irony are issues of race and class, of privilege and punishment. I submit that the stereotype of poor, minority, dumb, and ugly teen mothers drives the debate in this area of policy more than does clear analysis of the realities.

Most teen mothers with whom I've spoken have an understanding of the responsibility they have for their children's well-being, and hold their education and the attainment of fulfilling work at a living wage as high priorities. With this value, they recognize childcare as an integral part of any plan for them to work or attend school. Even the concept of workfare by conservative proponents of welfare reform has rightly led to the understanding in many segments of the political world that in order to work, mothers need childcare. Whether working for welfare benefits or working for wages, safe, reliable, and available childcare is a necessity. Since so many teen mothers have experienced some form of childhood maltreatment, they fear for the safety of their children, and are reluctant to leave them in the care of others. Policymakers who wish to support teen mothers' move to social and economic self-sufficiency must recognize the need for and provide safe care for the children of teen mothers.

Teen mothers face basic life needs as developing adolescents and as mothers providing for their children. Political rhetoric often focuses only on the needs of teen mothers in terms of services that cost taxpayers money; such rhetoric suggests that there is little but money to address the problems of teen mothers. A larger vision of supporting the needs of teen mothers toward healthy, productive adulthood includes an examination of what a healthy, productive society provides for its citizens.

The Need for Social Protection

"Social protection" is a term often used in the social sciences for the formal systems that constitute economic well-being for citizens of a polity. I will use the term here as a more general concept of the social obligation of the polity to provide all manner of protection for its citizens, including children. First among the principles of social protection is equality, in its most general and accessible sense. Is it not the equal right of every child born among us to claim the provisions of our social contract regarding basic human needs? Is it not further the equal right of every child born among us to claim equal opportunity regarding human worth, work, and achievement, another tenet of our social contract? Agreement on these two basic principles of social protection suggests the following greater vision for teen mothers and their children.

First, we must provide social protection as a context in which children can grow safely. This means that children, including teen mothers, must be equally protected by laws that forbid the abuse or neglect of children under the age of 18, whether that abuse or neglect is perpetrated by a family member, a community, or the policymakers who craft and control services for children and families. To neglect the basic human needs of teen mothers, whatever the social definitions of their sexual deviance or immorality, is still to neglect the basic human needs of children. Further, children must be equally protected by laws that forbid sexual assault and abuse. Child sexual abuse and molestation laws are on the books, but they are prosecuted capriciously, and statistics on this form of violence suggest that enforcement of laws forbidding it is wanting. Since the prevalence of sexual violation in the lives of teen mothers is so great, as mentioned earlier, this concept creates a necessary transition from teen motherhood as a child problem to teen motherhood as an adult problem.

Children, including teen mothers, must be full beneficiaries of a social contract of equal opportunity, so that they may achieve equally in accordance with the effort they are willing to put forth in any life enterprise, while protected in their status as children as described above. A model of education, job training, safe and affordable housing, adequate food, health care, and protection provides opportunity for economic and social self-sufficiency in exchange for children's, including teen mothers', acceptance as they reach adulthood of the responsibilities of the adult society that has nurtured them. These principles are so very basic, but they are missing in current social practice and proposed remedies to the scourge of teen motherhood.

Why does the political agenda identify teen mothers as a threat to the health of society? What is it about teen mothers that people fear? Research has dispelled myths about teen motherhood as principal causes of poverty, delinquency, welfare use, out-of-wedlock births, and other socially unacceptable behaviors. The majority of teen mothers come from the dominant racial group in this country. We must ask ourselves what misinformation or deeply held prejudices are driving social policy to the detriment of children. Moreover, we must ask ourselves what we are doing to teen mothers and their children while the misconceptions and fears persist.

The Needs of Teen Mothers: A Method of Inquiry

As I write this, during the Clinton administration, I am heartened by an opportunity to create a clearer understanding of the needs of teen mothers in the context of the federal government. Since 1982, the federal government has funded care and prevention programs in the area of adolescent pregnancy and parenting through its Adolescent Family Life (AFL) Program, located within the Public Health Service of the Department of Health and Human Services. Perceived by some in the field of adolescent pregnancy as conservative in its approaches, the Office of Adolescent Pregnancy Programs has funded, since its inception, demonstration programs throughout the country that provide health care and ancillary services to pregnant and parenting teens, and that teach pregnancy prevention through abstinence-based curricula that are medically accurate, free of religious content, and neutral on the subject of abortion, in accordance with a related Supreme Court settlement. Within this governmental context, I am directing an evaluation of AFL programs from the perspective of the clients, that is, the adolescents who participated in teen pregnancy care and prevention demonstration programs. This national evaluation is founded methodologically in the traditions of ethnography and phenomenology; by direct observation, by face-to-face intensive interviewing, by seeking the self-perceived meanings of adolescents' life events and program experiences, their stories can emerge in their own voices. Using such stories, we can report to policymakers, in the broadest sense, the needs of adolescent mothers and their children. Using such stories, policymakers can respond with programs that are more closely tailored to those needs, in the name of efficiency and humanity.

So many children lead such hard lives. I have told of some of the hardships they face. In an interview with "Cynthia," a teen mother, I came upon a startling reality. I interviewed Cynthia in her comfortable townhouse in a modest suburb of a major city. She lives there with her husband and her baby daughter. She grew up in a loving family in a comfortable home and reported no abuse or neglect of any kind. She and her husband both finished high school, and have full-time jobs at salaries that place them in the lower part of middle-income

America. They have had the love and support of their families in building this life. As I asked Cynthia if she had any lost dreams, she began to cry. Of all the teen mothers I have interviewed, she is the only one to cry so uncontrollably. I asked about her tears. "I have no choices now," she sobbed. I later realized that she is the only teen mother I have interviewed who had real dreams and choices.

Perhaps this social world, the United States in the 1990s, blames teen mothers and holds them in contempt because we are afraid that we created these desperate children, and we don't know what to do about them now. Perhaps we are afraid our children will become them. Perhaps we are afraid because we do not know, as adults, how to make it all better, and that is difficult to admit. We cling to myths rather than seek new truths. Perhaps in listening to the stories of teen mothers in their own voices, we can hear their needs and dreams, and answer them with care and choices.

FAMILY MATTERS, WORK MATTERS?
Poverty Among Women of Color and White Women
*Lisa Catanzarite and Vilma Ortiz**

WOMEN'S POVERTY IS AT THE CENTER OF THE CURRENT welfare reform debate. women and their children do make up an increasing proportion of the population of poor people in the United States, and female-headed families are on the rise. The ample attention is also because of suspicion among some public policymakers that the welfare system itself may have exacerbated these trends (and this emphasis is consistent with the increasing popularity of "less government"). As a result, much of the discussion of policy innovations focuses on getting poor mothers off Aid to Families with Dependent Children (AFDC) and into the labor force. Additionally, a great deal of rhetoric has been devoted to "family values." Poor women (and perhaps women in general) are targeted with messages meant to reform behavior deemed inappropriate. The word is: Get married or stay married; moreover, if you aren't married or won't stay married, then *do not* have children.

Female poverty, however, is complex. African-American and Latina women are more likely to be poor than are white women, and are likely to stay poor for longer stretches of time than are whites. Poverty policy will thus have a potentially greater effect on minority women and their children than on white women. In order to

* This piece is an extension and revision of a more technical article, "Racial/Ethnic Differences in the Impact of Work and Family on Women's Poverty." *Research in Politics and Society.* 1995 (5): 217-237.

adequately design public policies that will help all poor women, we need a better understanding of the differences that are most important for poverty reduction and prevention. The key questions we address in this chapter are: Do work and family matter in the same way for different ethnic groups? Are working white women less likely to be poor than working Latinas with similar backgrounds? Does marriage reduce the likelihood of poverty more for white women than for comparable African Americans? How can public policy successfully address the critical issues that poor and working poor women face?

Family Composition, Poverty, and Race/Ethnicity

A number of factors are important in understanding poverty conditions among black, Latina, and white women. For example, minority women are more likely to have *grown up* poor than are whites. Lower socioeconomic backgrounds have a number of ramifications for upward mobility, such as depressed levels of educational attainment and (relatedly, in these days of rising college costs) fewer resources of the extended family network. Further, among some groups, particularly Latina immigrants, larger families are liable to contribute to higher poverty rates. Collective differences in poverty backgrounds of differing racial/ethnic groups result in part from underlying disparities in class background, family composition, English proficiency, and other characteristics. In order to get a clear understanding of racial and ethnic differences in poverty risk, we need to compare individuals of different ethnic groups who are otherwise similar. That is, we need to understand better whether racial and ethnic differences are due solely to factors such as education levels, work behavior, and the like, or whether such differences persist, without these factors. Moreover, we must ask whether certain key poverty "prevention" strategies are more effective for whites than for women of color.

One reason commonly thought to explain higher poverty rates for minority women is their marital status and family composition, particularly their higher rates of family dissolution and female headship. Yet marital disruption is most significant in causing poverty for white women. Marital breakups are less likely to *cause* poverty for minority than for white women, since the women of color are more likely to be poor *within* marriages. Bane (1986) demonstrates that, among women who were impoverished after a transition from a male-headed to a female-headed household, only 24 percent of whites were indigent prior to the transition vs. a full 62 percent of African Americans. Leaving marriages is less of an economic disaster for black women than for white women because black women's economic status within marriages is already relatively poor. This is due in part to the lower average material resources of black than white men. While we expect that the same is true for Latinas, this has not been examined empirically. We expect that being married (vs. single) is less economically advantageous to African-American and Latina women than to whites. Conversely, being in a disrupted family (vs. being married) should be more harmful for whites than for minority women.

The discussion of black women's poverty has focused largely on the decline of nuclear families in the African-American community. A number of prominent authors have cited the rise in marital dissolution and female-headed families and connected these increases with the problem of minority male joblessness (Moynihan, 1965; Garfinkel and McLanahan, 1986) and the scarcity of "marriageable men" (Wilson and Neckerman, 1986; Wilson, 1987). Minority male joblessness and underemployment certainly contribute to indigence among minority women. Improving the employment opportunities of minority men will help to reduce women's poverty, but only indirectly, by providing women with better marriage prospects and male family heads. The underlying assumptions of these prescriptions are clearly patriarchal in nature. If women could only attach themselves to well-paid men, women's (and children's) poverty would be reduced. The reality, however, is that women, especially minority women, increasingly head families. And, they do so for a variety of reasons, only one of which is the employment status of minority men. Individual women may or may not prefer to be married. Rather than prescribing what should be the ideal family (as in recent Republican platforms) or lamenting changing patterns of family composition, discussion and policy concerning women's poverty should shift focus.

Work, Poverty and Race/Ethnicity

Given the reality of female-headed families, as well as the importance of women's earnings in poor two-parent and other families, we need greater attention to the conditions of women's employment—in particular, their jobs and wages. Certainly, much of the current debate about welfare—but not poverty—centers on forcing women to work more and receive lower AFDC benefits (see, Mead, 1986; more recently, California Governor Pete Wilson's 1996 State of the State address and proposed budget). But this policy, without a concomitant commitment to improving women's labor market locations and earnings, will not alleviate poverty, even if it does reduce welfare. In fact, it would surely worsen poverty for most recipients, as many women and children would be forced to forego medical insurance and scramble for childcare. Both welfare policy and labor market policy must recognize the increasing extent to which many women, especially lower-class women, have become critically important and often the primary economic providers for their families. Moreover, policymakers must begin to address the fact that women continue to be at a severe labor market disadvantage, their vital economic role notwithstanding.

Women's employment and earnings are critically important, both for married and unmarried women. The male "family wage" is no longer a reality (despite the fact that men's wages continue to be much higher than women's). With economic restructuring and the decline in real wages that began in the 1970s, most men now do not earn a wage sufficient to support a wife and children. For this and other reasons, the majority of married women, even those with infants under the age of one, are in the labor force.[1] Further, because of the rise in female-headed families, and the abysmal levels of child support payments, women are increasingly responsible not only for their own support, but also for that of their children. The problems of such families are heightened, as women face much worse prospects than men of securing a "family wage." Of course, this is even more important for African-American women than whites, since black women are much less likely to be married, and when married, contribute a higher proportion of family income than do white women.

Female and feminist scholars have argued that women's wages and labor market locations are critical to reducing poverty among female-headed families (see Smith, 1984; Pearce, 1987; Peterson, 1987). A number of such authors have cited the problem of occupational segregation as a contributor to women's poverty (see Ehrenreich, 1986; Pearce, 1986; Amott and Matthaei, 1986). And, while women in general are disadvantaged in the labor market, the disadvantage is more severe for minority women. However, the extent to which work effort has a greater impact on reducing indigence for white as opposed to minority women has not received sufficient attention. If a minority woman and a white woman (who "look" alike in every way except ethnicity) work the same number of hours, do they have the same chances of staying out of poverty? Further, the impact of occupational segregation on individual poverty has not been tested. If women work in low-level occupations with an overrepresentation of minority women, do they earn less than similar women in other occupations?

Certainly, work effort—working longer hours—improves earnings, and therefore lowers the likelihood of poverty. But, we expect that minority women get a lower payoff for their efforts than do white women. Wilson (1987) has argued that large scale economic changes have lessened opportunities for some segments of the minority population, particularly inner-city blacks. While traditional sociological theory predicts a direct relationship between level of work and economic status, we expect that this relationship is weaker among black and Latina than among white women. More specifically, since minority women are likely to receive lower hourly wages than are white women with similar individual characteristics (for example, education and work experience), working longer hours will have a smaller payoff for minority than for white women as a poverty prevention strategy.

In addition, we think that minority women's heavier concentration than white women in marginal, female-dominated occupations contributes to their disadvantage at work.[2] Earnings tend to be lowest in occupations where minority women, particularly black, Latina, and Native American women, prevail (Dill, Cannon, and Vanneman, 1987). Indeed, Dill (1987) demonstrate that the wage disadvantages, relative to workers' education and experience, are greater in occupations with a large contingent of minority women than in white-female dominated occupations. Thus, concentration in poorly paid occupations contributes to the labor market disadvantage that minority women face. We expect that, among similar workers (those with similar hours, education, etc.), being in an occupation with a heavy concentration of minority women carries an increased risk of poverty, primarily because of low remuneration in such occupations.

Overview

In order to investigate these questions, we analyzed the incidence of poverty for black, Mexican-origin, "other" Latina, and white women in the Los Angeles metropolitan area using the 1980 census.[3] We focused only on women with 12 years of education or less because this is the population most at risk of impoverishment. The analysis had two main parts. First, we examined racial and ethnic differences in the impact of work and marital status on the probability of being needy. Then we looked only at employed women and asked whether or not working in a low-level, minority female occupation increases the likelihood of poverty. We looked for *net effects*; that is, we took account of other individual and occupational characteristics in estimating the effects of marital status, work effort, and occupational segregation.

We began with four hypotheses:

First, we suggested that *minority women are more likely to be poor than are white women in similar circumstances*. We thought that the set of disadvantages that women of color face could not be adequately captured by looking at such factors as immigrant status, ability to speak English, level of education, work experience, age, number of children, number of adults other than the husband in the family, percentage of other adults who are not working, marital status, and hours worked. The special disadvantages more likely to face women of color than whites include discrimination in employment or housing, residence in economically depressed neighborhoods, attendance at poor-quality schools, or the financial demands of helping to support relatives outside of the current household.

Second, because of the lesser economic resources of minority than white husbands, we suggested that, among similar women: *Being married carries less financial benefit for minority women than for white women*. If it is true that women of color are less well-off inside of marriages than are whites, we suggested the converse as our third hypothesis: *Being in a disrupted family is not as economically devastating to minority women as it is to white women*.

Fourth, we predicted that white women's time spent working (hours worked) is better rewarded than minority women's: *Work effort is more beneficial to white than minority women as a poverty prevention strategy*. We expected we would find that among women who are similar in terms of educational status, age, immigration/language status, prior work experience, and family composition, that work effort would be more effective in reducing poverty among white than minority women.

Finally, we argued that the low-level jobs in which minority women tend to be concentrated carry an elevated risk of poverty. While poorly educated white women are certainly concentrated in low-paying, female-dominated occupations, they are less likely to be in *marginal* female-dominated occupations where minority women predominate, and where wages tend to be lowest. *Hence, we expected that minority female occupations would carry a greater disadvantage than the occupational locations of white women.*

The regional focus on the Los Angeles metropolitan area had several key advantages. Perhaps most important, greater Los Angeles has not only a substantial African-American population, but also a large and growing Latino population—made up of Mexicans and, increasingly was Central American and other Latinos. This diversity was crucial for our comparative analyses.

Results

Table 1 provides selected statistics describing our sample of African-American, Mexican-origin, other Latina, and white women. In this table, data on Mexicans and other Latinas is presented separately for those who immigrated between 1965 and 1980 vs. the combined group of earlier immigrants and native-born women.

We present figures for the percentage of women in each ethnic/immigrant group who were poor (both by our measure and according to the official poverty line). In addition, we provide information on other background characteristics that are related to poverty: the percentage of women with less than 12th grade education; the breakdown of women who were not working, working part-time, and working full-time; the percentage who were under 40; percent married; and average number of children.

As is apparent from the first row of the table, privation is much more prevalent among African-American women and recent immigrant Latinas (both Mexican and "other") than among whites and earlier-immigrant native Latinas. In our sample, black women and recent immigrant Latinas had poverty rates of 42-45 percent, while 15 percent of white women were impoverished. Earlier-immigrant native Latinas had poverty levels that fell between these two extremes

Table 1

Descriptive Statistics on Poverty and Individual Characteristics, By Race/Ethnic Group and Nativity, for Women, ages 20-64, with Education of 12th Grade or less, Los Angeles, 1980

Percentage or Mean (with standard deviation)

Variable	Blacks	Mexicans Immigrated '65-'80	Mexicans Native pre-'65	Other Latinas Immigrated '65-'80	Other Latinas Native pre-'65	Whites
% Poor*	42	45	28	42	24	15
% Under Poverty Line	27	25	17	24	15	8
Education <12	40	87	58	70	44	26
% Not Working	44	49	44	37	38	37
% Part-time	33	33	35	40	37	37
% Full-time	23	18	21	23	25	26
% Ages 20-39	55	81	56	69	51	46
% Married	41	71	65	59	62	67
Mean # Kids	1.13	2.01	1.43	1.21	1.13	.74
	(1.35)	(1.68)	(1.47)	(1.28)	(1.29)	(1.08)
N =	9,147	9,830	14,314	3,128	2,842	59,635

* Our definition of Poor is 1.5 times the official Poverty Line.

(28 percent of Mexicans and 24 percent of other Latinas were poor). Hence, black women were almost 3 times as likely to be poor as whites; Mexicans had poverty rates between 2 and 3 times those for white women: and other Latinas had rates of impoverishment that were approximately 1.5 to 3 times higher than for whites.[4] (The second row of the table, which contains the percentage of women below the official poverty line, shows essentially the same trend.)

These differences in poverty rates among women of different groups are due, in part, to divergences in other characteristics (for example, lower educational levels, more children among minority than white women). The succeeding rows of Table 1 provide detail on a number of relevant factors.

The third row of the table gives the percentage of women in our sample who had completed less than 12 years of education. (Recall that the sample includes only those with the equivalent of a high school education or less.) Recent immigrant Latinas had a large educational disadvantage. Not having completed high school was most common for these women (Mexicans; 87 percent, other Latinas; 70 percent). Native-born, earlier-immigrant Latinas did somewhat better (58 percent of Mexicans and 44 percent of other Latinas) than recent immigrants. Whites had far and away the highest rates of high school completion: only 26 percent had less than 12 years of education. And, black women were a distant second, with 40 percent (of those with twelve years of education or less) being high school dropouts.

Most women were in the labor force, and this was true for all groups. Not working was most common among Mexicans (49 percent of recent immigrants and 44 percent of other Mexicans were not in the labor force) and blacks (44 percent didn't work); staying out of the labor force was least common for other Latinas and white women (37-38 percent). The pattern of full-time work was the converse of this: Rates of full-time work were lowest for Mexicans (18 percent among recent immigrants and 21 percent for natives/earlier-immigrants), then blacks (23 percent), other Latinas (23-25 percent), and whites (26 percent). So, while working was the norm among these less-educated women, full-time employment was uncommon. Even among white women, only about one-fourth worked full-time.

The youngest group in the sample was Mexicans, followed by recent immigrant other Latinas, African Americans, earlier-immigrant native other Latinas, and, finally, whites. The population of recent immigrant Mexican women was overwhelmingly under 40 years old (81 percent), while just under half of white women (46 percent) were in this younger age group.[5]

African Americans were, by far, the least likely to be married—less than half of black women in our sample were wed (41 percent). Among all other groups, being married was the norm. For other Latinas, the prevalence of marriage was 59-62 percent (lower for recent immigrants); among whites, two-thirds were married; among Mexicans, 65 percent of earlier-immigrants/natives and 71 percent of recent immigrants were married. In conjunction with high marriage rates, Mexican women had the highest number of children (an average of 2 for recent immigrants, 1.4 among other Mexicans); next were other Latinas and blacks (just over 1 child), then whites (with an average of 0.7 children).

These descriptive statistics show large variations by ethnic/immigrant group. With respect to most characteristics thought to contribute to keeping women out of poverty, white women appear to enjoy an advantage. (The only exception is that marriage rates are higher among one group—recent immigrant Mexicans—than among whites.) Given these differences in background characteristics, it is perhaps no surprise that white women show lower rates of poverty than do minority women. But, are the racial and ethnic differences in poverty due solely to these differences, or are women of color still more likely to be impoverished? We now turn to the following questions:

1. Among women with similar characteristics (education, etc.), are minority women more likely to be poor than white women?

2. Do white women obtain greater economic benefits from marriage than do similarly situated minority women? Conversely, is marital disruption more economically damaging to whites than to women of color?

3. Do white women derive greater economic gains from work than do similarly situated minority women?

4. Among working women, does location in an occupation identified as minority, female contribute to poverty?

Figure 1 provides findings regarding net effects of race/ethnicity on poverty. The bars represent the probability of indigence for women of each minority group relative to the probability for whites *with similar characteristics.*

Figure 1

Net Effect of Poverty on Race/Ethnicity

Women, ages 20-64 with Education of 12th Grade or less, Los Angeles, 1980

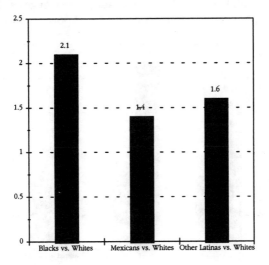

The bars represent the probability of poverty for minority women divided by the probability for white women. Probability of poverty is net of other factors (i.e., immigration, language, age, education, marital status and household composition, and hours worked.

Black women were just over twice as likely to be poor as were similarly situated white women. Mexicans were 1.4 times as likely to live in poverty as their white counterparts, and other Latinas had indigence rates that were 1.6 times those for comparable whites. As expected, white women were considerably less likely to be impoverished than minority women with similar backgrounds, family composition, and work effort.

The findings on the relation of poverty to marital status for whites versus women of color are provided in Figure 2. In this chart, effects are contrasted for unmarried vs. married women. The figures represent the factor by which poverty rates are higher for unmarried than married women.

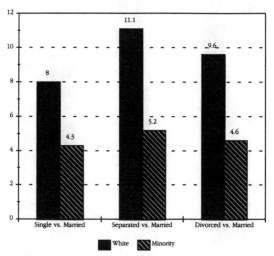

Figure 2

Net Effects of Poverty on Being Unmarried vs. Married among White & Minority Women

Age 20-64, with Education less than Grade 12, Los Angeles, 1980
Ratio of **unmarried** to **married** predicted poverty rates

The bars represent the probability of poverty for unmarried women divided by the probability for married women. For example, single white women are 8 times more likely to be poor than are married white women, while single minority women are just over 4 times more likely to be poor than are married minority women. Probability of poverty is net of other factors (i.e., immigration, language, age, education, household composition, and hours worked).

The first pair of bars in Figure 2 shows that single white women had poverty rates 8 times as high as their married counterparts, while single minority women were (only) 4 times as likely to be poor as married minorities. So getting married offered greater financial benefits for whites than for comparable African Americans and Latinas, as predicted.

Poverty risk was highest for separated women, and the divergence between whites and minorities was greatest for this group. White women who were separated had predicted poverty rates 11 times the rates for married whites; the contrast for minorities is a factor of 5.

The same pattern holds, but is less pronounced, for divorced women. As we posited, the economic disadvantage that comes with a disrupted marriage is much greater for whites than for black or Latina women. This is presumably because the difference in family income resulting from a marital breakup is greater for whites than for women of color. The literature on the feminization of poverty has emphasized the devastating impact of separation and divorce on women's poverty. Our findings clearly suggest that this phenomenon is more pronounced for white than minority women.

In order to examine the differential effects of employment for whites and minorities, we show the contrasts between full-time workers and others in Figure 3. The bars give the probability of poverty for women who worked less than full time versus the probability for full-time workers.

White women who were out of the labor force were 11 times more likely to live in poverty than whites who worked full-time, while relative risk for minorities was only 5 times that of their full-time counterparts. While the risk of poverty was strongly related to employment for both whites and minorities, the effect of working less than full-time (vs. full-time) was always higher for white women than for minorities. As predicted, white women's work effort had a greater impact on reducing the risk of poverty than was true for African-American and Latina women.

In results not shown here, we also found that, among working women, the likelihood of being poor was higher for women in occupations with a prevalence of African-American women, without these factors. Additionally, women employed in occupations that are white-female-dominated were *less likely* to be needy than other, similarly situated women. So, our prediction that the risk of privation would be higher in occupations with a prevalence of minority women than in those with high white female representation was borne out.

Summary

Neither the marriage market nor the labor market offers the same rewards to women of color as to white women. While family and work clearly matter a great deal for women's poverty, they matter *differently* for black and Latina women than for whites. In point of fact, they matter *less.* Minority women are more likely to be poor than are comparable whites of the same marital status and at every level of work effort.

Figure 3

Net Effects on Poverty of Working Less than Full-time to Full-time Work Among White & Minority Women

Age 20-64, with Education less than Grade 12, Los Angeles, 1980
Ratio of less than Full-time to Full-time predicted poverty rates

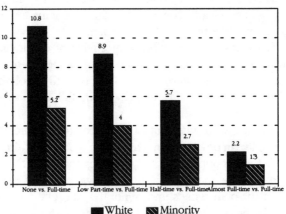

White   Minority

The bars represent the probability of poverty for women working less than full-time divided by the probability for women working full-time. For example, white women who are not working are 11 times more likely to be poor than are white women who work full-time, while minority women who do not work are just over 5 times more likely to be poor than are minority women who work full-time. Probability of poverty is net of other factors (i.e., immigration, language, age, education, household composition, and marital status).

We found, as predicted, that marital status had less relevance in determining whether or not minority women were poor than was true for similar whites. Being married (vs. single) reduces indigence less for women of color than for white women. The smaller advantage of being married for blacks and Latinas is doubtlessly due largely to the fact that the earnings of minority husbands are generally lower than white men's pay. Similarly, because the change in family income resulting from a marital breakup tends to be less pronounced for minority than white women, we found, as expected, that being separated or divorced (vs. being married) was less financially damaging for African-American and Latina women.

In addition to these differences in the relative advantages of marriage, we found that work effort was more effective in reducing the risk of privation for white women than for similar women of color, as predicted. The benefits of time spent working were clearly greater for white than minority women at every level of work effort.

Above and beyond individual-level factors, the occupational locations of different groups of women contributed to racial and ethnic differences in poverty risk. Working in an occupation with a large percentage of black women increased the likelihood of impoverishment, while being in a white female dominated occupation lowered this risk.

Conclusions

The two major routes out of poverty for women are work and marriage. Should it come as a surprise that the labor market is not a "level playing field" for women of color and white women? We think not. And, though we may not often conceptualize the *marriage* market in these terms, it appears that this market also is not a level field for women of different racial/ethnic groups.

Our findings underscore the importance of these differences. While marital status is related to privation for all women, the emphasis on marriage in discussions of women's poverty is less relevant to black women and Latinas than to white women. Accordingly, as a poverty prevention "strategy," getting married is less beneficial for African-American and Latina women than for whites. Further, popular claims that every woman is "just a divorce away" from penury are particularly misplaced for minority women, who experience relatively high rates of poverty even within marriages, and whose risk of indigence increases less dramatically with a family breakup than is true for whites.

Perhaps of greater importance, given the heavy emphasis on women's work in the current welfare reform debate, are our results regarding work effort: We find that minority women profit less from hours expended at work than do white women. Further, the occupational locations of women contribute to differences in poverty: Women who work in heavily black female occupations have a higher risk of indigence than do similar women in comparable occupations. Occupational segregation contributes to minority women's disadvantage (in addition to lower returns to work effort for minorities). The fact that remuneration varies across occupations and tends to be depressed in low-level, minority female occupations highlights our contention that occupational segregation is a significant *poverty* issue for less-educated women.

Although seemingly paradoxical, working is of monumental importance to the economic standing of women of color—despite the fact that minorities derive less gain from time spent working than whites. This is precisely because *marriage* offers less monetary benefit to women of color than to white women. Particularly for less-educated African-American women—who are relatively unlikely to be married—work is a critical poverty prevention strategy.

Attention to the conditions of women's work is of utmost significance, particularly in the current environment, where pundits across the political spectrum emphasize work as the panacea for women's poverty. Our results strongly suggest that public policymakers concerned with indigence among working-age women and their children cannot simply focus on pushing women into the labor market and reducing dependency on public assistance. By doing so, they would simply replace an inadequate *welfare* check with an inadequate *pay* check. This would be further compounded by increased responsibility for medical insurance and childcare, whose costs are prohibitive for at risk women. Clearly, any antipoverty policy that has women's work as its cornerstone must give attention to adequate childcare and affordable health care.

First and foremost, however, in order to be efficacious, an antipoverty strategy grounded on female employment should focus on *making women's work pay.* In the current climate, where the future of affirmative action is uncertain and employment discrimination legislation is being redefined and narrowed, we must not lose sight of the employment disadvantages encountered by women, particularly women of color. In order to effectively reduce poverty, it is essential that policymakers direct their attention to the labor market. Pivotal to the success of antipoverty efforts will be policies that: break down occupational segregation; increase the minimum wage; reduce the financial penalty in marginal, female-dominated occupations; and increase women's—especially minority women's—access to jobs that offer better pay in return for women's work effort.

Notes

1. By 1988, labor force participation (LFP) rates of married women with children under one were already 50.5 percent for whites and 71.5 percent for blacks (51.9 percent overall) (*Statistical Abstract of the United States,* 1990, p. 385). In light of recent data on the rising trend in LFP for this group (the latest historically to enter the labor force), rates are certainly higher now. Working has become the norm.

2. The heavy concentration of black women in female-dominated occupations is discussed in Malveaux and Wallace (1987) and Malveaux (1985). Catanzarite's (1990) analysis of national data for the 1970s suggests that Latinas may have occupied an intermediate position between black and white women in occupational segregation; that is, they appear to have been concentrated in better jobs than black women, but worse positions than whites. The relative positions of blacks and Latinas may have flipped with the recent increase in immigration.

3. The area includes Los Angeles, Orange, Riverside, San Bernardino, and Ventura counties. The Census file is the 5 percent Public Use Microdata Sample. The sample is comprised of 98,896 women, ages 20-64.

4. These figures are obtained by dividing minority women's poverty rates by those for white women.

5. Recall that the sample is limited to working-age women: 20 to 64 year-olds.

References

Amott, Teresa, and Julie Matthaei. 1986. "Comparable Worth, Incomparable Pay" in Rochelle Lefkowitz and Ann Withorn (eds.), *For Crying Out Loud: Women and Poverty in the United States.* New York: Pilgrim Press, pp. 314-23.

Bane, Mary Jo. 1986. "Household Composition and Poverty" in Sheldon Danziger and Daniel Weinberg (eds.), *Fighting Poverty: What Works and What Doesn't.* Cambridge: Harvard University Press, pp. 209-31.

Catanzarite, Lisa. 1990. *Job Characteristics and Occupational Segregation by Gender and Race/Ethnicity.* Ph.D. Dissertation, Department of Sociology, Stanford University, Stanford, California.

Catanzarite, Lisa, and Vilma Ortiz. 1995. "Racial/Ethnic Differences in the Impact of Work and Family on Women's Poverty." *Research in Politics and Society.* vol. 5, pp. 217-37.

Dill, Bonnie Thornton, Lynn Weber Cannon, and Reeve Vanneman. 1987. "Race and Gender in Occupational Segregation" in "National Committee on Pay Equity," *Pay Equity: An Issue of Race, Ethnicity and Sex.* Washington, D.C.: National Committee on Pay Equity, pp. 11-70.

Ehrenreich, Barbara. 1986. "What Makes Women Poor?" in Rochelle Lefkowitz and Ann Withorn (eds.), *For Crying Out Loud: Women and*

Poverty in the United States. New York: Pilgrim Press, pp. 18-28.

Garfinkel, Irwin, and Sara S. McLanahan. 1986. *Single Mothers and their Children: A New American Dilemma*. Washington, D.C.: The Urban Institute.

Malveaux, Julianne. 1985. "The Economic Interests of Black and White Women: Are They Similar?" *Review of Black Political Economy*. vol.14 (Summer): pp. 5-28.

Malveaux, Julianne, and Phyllis Wallace. 1987. "Minority Women in the Workplace," in Karen S. Koziara, Michael H. Moskow and Lucretia D. Tanner (eds.), *Working Women: Past, Present and Future*. Washington, D.C.: Bureau of National Affairs, IRRA Series.

Moynihan, Daniel P. 1965. *The Negro Family: The Case for National Action*. Washington, D.C.: U.S. Department of Labor, Office of Policy Planning and Research.

Mead, Lawrence. 1986. *Beyond Entitlement: The Social Obligations of Citizenship*. New York: Free Press.

Pearce, Diana. 1986. "The Feminization of Poverty: Women, Work, and Welfare" in Rochelle Lefkowitz and Ann Withorn (eds.), *For Crying Out Loud: Women and Poverty in the United States*. New York: Pilgrim Press, pp. 29-46.

Pearce, Diana. 1987. "On the Edge: Marginal Women Workers and Employment Policy" in Christine Bose and Glenna Spitze (eds.), *Ingredients for Women's Employment Policy*. Albany: State University of New York Press, pp. 197-210.

Petersen, Trond. 1985, "A Comment on Presenting Results from Logit and Probit Models." *American Sociological Review*. vol. 509 (1): pp. 130-131.

Peterson, Janice. 1987. "The Feminization of Poverty" *Journal of Economic Issues*. vol. 21(1): pp. 329-37.

Security Pacific National Bank, 1979. *The Sixty Mile Circle*. Los Angeles: Security Pacific National Bank.

Smith, Joan. 1984. "The Paradox of Women's Poverty: Wage-Earning Women and Economic Transformation." *Signs* (special issue on Women and Poverty) vol. 10 (2): pp. 291-310.

Tienda, Marta and Jennifer Glass. 1985. "Household Structure and Labor Force Participation of Black, Hispanic and White Mothers." *Demography* 22(3): 381-94.

Tienda, Marta and Lief Jensen. 1988. "Poverty and Minorities: A Quarter-Century Profile of Color and Socioeconomic Disadvantage" in Gary Sandefur and Marta Tienda (eds.), *Divided Opportunities and Minorities, Poverty, and Social Policy*. New York: Plenum.

Wilson, William Julius, and Kathryn M. Neckerman. 1986. "Poverty and Family Structure: The Widening Gap Between Evidence and Public Policy Issues" in Sheldon Danziger and Daniel Weinberg (eds.), *Fighting Poverty: What Works and What Doesn't*. Cambridge: Harvard University

Press, pp. 232-259.

Wilson, William Julius. 1987. *The Truly Disadvantaged: The Inner City, The Underclass, and Public Policy*. Chicago: University of Chicago Press.

WORKING IN AMERICA
The Female Immigrant Experience
Fong Yee Lee

We are Mexican, Cambodian, Cuban, Polish, Somali, Haitian, Vietnamese, Iranian, Irish, Canadian, Armenian, Afghan, and Japanese. We are young, middle aged, elderly, single, married, divorced, separated, widowed. We are not formally educated; we are college graduates. We come from a rural area; we come from metropolitan areas. We speak English; we are illiterate even in our own language. We left our country for new opportunities; we left to accompany or join other family members; we left to escape war and persecution. We have children; we are childless. We are immigrant women in America.[1]

HISTORICALLY, WOMEN DID NOT IMMIGRATE TO THE UNITED States in the same numbers as men. In 1900, only 30 percent of all immigrants were women. One reason was that migration to a foreign country was seen as a very risky venture, and men were judged better prepared to undertake its hazards than women. Moreover, a number of U.S. immigration laws specifically discriminated against women. For example, the Chinese Exclusion Act of 1882 and the National Origins Act of 1924 prohibited women from China and Japan from entering the United States.

One of the most problematic immigration laws affecting women is the 1986 Immigration Marriage Fraud Amendments Act. Aimed at reducing "marriage fraud," the law provides conditional residency of two years to spouses of green card holders. To convert the conditional residency to permanent residency, a joint petition must be filed by both spouses before the end of the two-year period. A divorce or failure to file this joint petition makes the conditional resident spouse deportable. By investing the power of deportation in the hands of the green card holder, the law gives the green card holder tremendous control over the other spouse. Immigrant women who are married to abusive spouses are particularly vulnerable under this act because they are faced with the choice of either staying in abusive relationships or risking deportation. The act's impact was softened in 1990 by an amendment supported by a coalition of immigrant advocates and women's groups. The amendment allows the Immigration and Naturalization Service (INS) to waive the joint petition in cases where the conditional resident spouse can demonstrate domestic abuse by her partner.

In spite of these legislative limitations, the numbers of women immigrants have begun to climb steadily since the 1970s when national origin quota restrictions were lifted. By 1990, over 47 percent of all immigrants were women. In fact, the Philippines, Korea, Mainland China, Taiwan, the Dominican Republic, and Jamaica send slightly more working-age women to the United States than men. There is every reason to believe that many women immigrate because they perceive relatively progressive views on gender equality in the United States. Many women from Korea and the Philippines are also qualified for employment-based visas as nurses or in other medical fields. Marriages between women and U.S. servicemen in these countries also contribute to a larger share of immigrant women.

Just as it is true for immigrant men, the vast majority of immigrant women who came to the United States during the 1970s and 1980s were from Asia and Latin America. Nearly two-thirds of Asian-American women and one-third Hispanic-American women in the United States are foreign-born, compared with just 4 percent of non-Hispanic white and African-American women. Consequently, one in seven girls or women over age four now speak a language other than English at home. Almost four million women live in linguistic isolation, defined by the Census Bureau as households where no one over age 13 speaks English fluently.

According to the Urban Institute analysis based on 1990 census data, immigrant women who arrived during the past decade have a lower level of educational attainment than native-born women. Slightly more than 37 percent of immigrant women do not have a high school diploma, compared to 17 percent for native-born women. Immigrant women also have a lower labor force participation rate than native-born women, 63 percent versus 70 percent. Almost 60 percent of immigrant women work in jobs classified as service, clerical, operator, and laborer. Low-wage employment enclaves, such as garment factories and electronics assembly plants, are dominated by Asian and Latina women. Interestingly enough, the wage differential between native-born and immigrant women is not significant. In 1989, the average weekly wage of immigrant women was 99 percent of the average weekly wage of native-born women—$345 compared to $347. One explanation for this modest wage disparity between the two groups despite differences in educational levels and labor force participation is that immigrant women frequently work more than one job. It is not uncommon to hear stories of immigrant women who hold second and third jobs, or operate small home businesses to earn extra income. In comparison, the wage disparity between immigrant men and native-born men is higher. In 1989, wages earned by immigrant men were 91 percent of wages earned by native-born men—$508 compared to $562. American women, whether foreign or native-born, continue to earn much less than American men—62 cents for every dollar. This data suggests that, overall, gender has a greater negative impact on earnings of foreign-born women than immigration status.

Immigrant Women and Poverty

Almost 18 percent of all immigrant women live below the poverty level, compared to 12 percent native-born women, according to the Urban Institute analysis. Among women who arrived during the past 10 years, the poverty rate is almost 25 percent.

An analysis of this poverty rate reveals that among foreign-born women, there exists a direct correlation between their income and their immigration status. Employer sanctions and fear of deportation have relegated undocumented women to the underground economy where low wages, poor benefits, and poor conditions are the norm. Refugee women, those who come to the United States with little income or assets, limited English, and suffering from the trauma of war or persecution, earn more than undocumented women but less than other immigrant women. Legal immigrant women, who come to this country to work or to be reunited with other family members, have the highest earnings of the three groups.

Interestingly enough, census data also shows that the longer a woman is in the United States, the higher her income. As a matter of fact, the incomes of legal immigrant women (excluding refugees) who arrived to the United States during 1970-1979 are slightly higher than those of native-born women. There is compelling evidence that the hard work of the first-generation immigrants pays off. Studies have found that earnings of all immigrants grow more rapidly than those of comparable native-born Americans. Within a decade or so after entry into the United States, the average immigrant earns as much as the average native. After 30 years, the average immigrant earns more than the average native.

Barriers to Self-Sufficiency

While immigrant and native-born women are both disadvantaged when compared to native-born men, immigrant women face some special barriers in achieving economic support and self-sufficiency.

A principal barrier is, of course, language. Participation in almost every aspect of society—schools, health facilities, landlords, employers, police, emergency services—requires some degree of proficiency in English. The ability to communicate with the mainstream also contributes to an immigrant woman's sense of identity and belonging in this country. However, in many immigrant families, women are not encouraged to participate in English language training (ELT or ESL) or other services because of their childcare or family responsibilities. Sometimes, intergenerational conflicts arise in immigrant families because of different rates of language acquisition among family members. Parents or grandparents may suffer from loss of self-esteem because they must rely on children for translation and explanation of routine chores. Immigrant women who are caretakers of elderly parents and young children are often caught in the middle of this conflict.

Lack of family support for language acquisition by women is exacerbated by the limited number of publicly funded English language training programs. The current crusade for English as the official language is based on the argument that immigrants are unwilling to learn English, and that language segregation will turn the United States into a poly-lingual Tower of Babel. English Only groups believe that people should learn English and, therefore, there should be no bilingual services. However, this argument discounts the fact that many immigrants are unable to learn English because of the lack of affordable ELT programs. For example, because of the lack of funding, the waiting list to get into such an ELT program in a community center in Boston's Chinatown is two years and longer!

Immigrant women also face cultural conflicts that affect adjustment to life in the United States. In their countries of origin, women often live with members of their extended family. Childrearing is often shared with older members, such as grandparents. In many immigrant cultures, the individual's behavior and choices are guided by strong religious or philosophical traditions, such as Islam or Confucian. When parents need guidance that their own families cannot provide, they seek out religious leaders or other elders in the community for help or support. In the United States, however, immigrant women are frequently cut off from these valuable resources without adequate substitutes. When immigrant women are faced with problems that they are unable to solve, they frequently do not know where to go for help.

Many immigrant women also live by the cultural value systems that limit their choices as individuals. In some cases, a daughter's education is sacrificed or delayed to finance the education of a son. Without family support, immigrant women may not be able to pursue post secondary education.

There are two groups of immigrant women who are particularly at risk—refugee and elderly women. The refugee women's flight from the home country and eventual resettlement in the United States are often acute, traumatic experiences. They might have witnessed the torture or murder of loved ones, experienced rape or imprisonment, survived dangerous escape from their home countries, and endured months or years in refugee camps. By the time they are finally resettled in the United States, they are frequently ill-prepared for employment. In addition, mental health services are scarce for refugee women. Since mental health services are foreign to many refugee cultures, women seldom seek counseling or therapy for themselves to cope with post-traumatic stress disorders. These problems frequently go unidentified for years while refugee women suffer in silence.

Elderly immigrant women also face particular isolation. They are often less adaptable to life in the United States than younger women. The positions of high esteem which they traditionally held within the family and the community are frequently eroded in this country. Oftentimes, they are widows whose children have grown and left the home. Some elderly immigrant women may have skills that can be transferred to the U.S. workplace, or they may be interested in learning new careers. However, elderly women generally do not receive priority for most ELT or employment training services. Consequently, they are at risk of becoming inactive or unproductive members of their families or communities.

The conflicts generated within immigrant families and communities by the adjustment process have in turn yielded a new area of concern. According to many immigrant women as well as service providers working with this group, domestic violence has become a growing problem in many immigrant ethnic groups. Since domestic violence is historically a taboo subject in many immigrant cultures, many communities deny that the problem exists. When immigrant women began researching the existence of domestic violence within their communities, they found that culturally appropriate materials or information addressing this subject did not exist. Information about available resources, such as counseling or shelters, were not disseminated in native languages. Shelters organized for native-born women frequently do not have bilingual or bicultural staff, particularly in immigrant languages other than Spanish. Training for immigrant men and women to prevent domestic violence is almost nonexistent. As awareness of domestic violence has become more widespread, a number of immigrant women's advocacy groups have begun organizing around this issue. In Boston, for example, the Asian Shelter and Advocacy Project (ASAP) established a shelter to provide services to Asian immigrant women, and to educate the Asian communities about this growing problem.

Immigrant women also face a number of legal or systemic barriers in their efforts to get out of poverty. Undocumented women are barred from working legally in the United States under the 1986 Immigration Reform and Control Act (IRCA), which makes it a crime for employers to knowingly hire aliens who are not authorized by the INS to work in the United States. This prohibition, known as employer sanctions, has proven difficult to enforce because employers are not familiar with the complexities of U.S. immigration laws, and because of the proliferation of documents which could be used to prove work authorization. According to studies conducted by the U.S. General Accounting Office as well as immigrant rights organizations, IRCA has caused employers to discriminate against job applicants who appear "foreign" or speak with an accent because of the fear that these job applicants are not "Americans."

Immigrants who are indigent are also unable to participate in many federally funded cash and related support programs, such as AFDC, SSI, Medicaid, Medicare, and Food Stamps. Except for emergency medical care, undocumented aliens are completely barred from receiving assistance under these programs. Legal immigrants are generally determined ineligible for the first three to five years after their arrival to this country if they have sponsors, since the income and assets of the sponsor are deemed by law to be available to the immigrant. Legal immigrants are also subject to deportation for "public charge" if they receive federally subsidized benefits. The only group that has access to these benefits in the same manner as U.S. citizens are refugees, based on the recognition that their experiences with persecution and flight from their home countries make adjustment to life in this country more difficult.

Immigrants are also considered a low priority for services in many mainstream programs. Many service systems do not consider the immigrant women's language or cultural needs when planning their programs or priorities. For example, the JOBS program, which provides an array of self-sufficiency services for AFDC recipients, targets services to the more typical welfare recipient who is white, English speaking, and has some high school education. Low-income immigrant women do not fit this profile. Many service providers also find immigrant women difficult and more costly to serve because of their need for additional language and cultural support. Since many providers are reimbursed by funders for performance outcomes (that is, the number of persons who are successfully placed into jobs), native-born women who are more job-ready are frequently served before immigrant women.

On August 1, 1996, Congress passed the historic "Personal Responsibility and Work Opportunity Reconciliation Act (H.R. 3734), which was then signed into law by President Clinton. In addition to ending a 60 year old national commitment to provide cash assistance to the poor as an entitlement, the law denies benefits to certain U.S. residents who are foreign born. Undocumented and other "non-qualified" aliens are banned from receiving almost all publicly funded benefits, with the exception of emergency medical; short-term and communicable diseases; nonprofit, in-kind community services such as shelters and soup kitchens; certain housing programs; and school lunches if the child is eligible for a free public education.

Most legal immigrants, both current and future, are banned from receiving cash assistance, Food Stamps and SSI until citizenship. They are banned from participation in Medicaid, AFDC, Title XX Social Services, and state-funded assistance. Exemptions are provided for refugees and asylees for the first five years in the country, veterans, and individuals with 40 quarters of Social Security earnings. Future immigrants entering the United States after the enactment will be banned for five years from most federal means-tested programs, including Medicaid. New verification requirements are imposed on virtually all federal, state, and local programs in order to deny benefits to non-qualified aliens.

While indicating his willingness prior to signing this bill, President Clinton stated his intention to seek legislation that will mitigate the negative impact of this law on legal immigrants. This law is punitive and mean-spirited, reflecting the anti-immigrant climate that is spreading throughout this country. Even Human Services Secretary Donna Shalala says, these laws represent a "race to the bottom" as lawmakers vie each other to see who can be the toughest on welfare recipients and toughest on immigrants. In the absence of far-reaching systemic reforms, we can expect that immigrant women will be forced to continue battling low wages, poor benefits, unsafe working conditions, and lack of affordable health care and childcare. Yet empowerment cannot be accomplished by simply providing language services within existing institutions. There must be simultaneous efforts to strengthen the connections between immigrant and native-born women so that both groups can come together to advocate for common interests. Organizing among limited English-speaking women is extremely difficult for obvious reasons. While there are many shared concerns among native-born and immigrant women, priorities may differ because of differences in socioeconomic status. For example, while tax credits for childcare may be important for professional women, immigrant women may be more concerned with safe, affordable childcare. While sexual orientation, sexual harassment, redistribution of household labor, and reproductive choices are important issues for professional women, limited English-speaking women in low-wage jobs may be concerned more with wages, benefits, and working conditions.

Despite persistent obstacles, immigrant women from diverse backgrounds have historically refused to act as victims of history and circumstances. This is particularly apparent in ethnic community leadership and advocacy. Many immigrant women have become leaders in grassroots organizations because of their talent and tenacity. A high proportion of directorships in these organizations that protect the welfare of the communities in areas such as civil rights, jobs, child care, legal assistance and health services are occupied by immigrant women. Clearly, the leadership of these women needs support and encouragement, particularly in light of government's retreat from supporting services for low-income women.

Notes

1. Nancy Iris. 1994. "Refugee Resettlement." In *U.S. Report on the Status of Women, 1985-1994.* U.S. Department of State Bureau of International Organization Affairs, Office of Economic and Social Affairs.

References

Fix, Michael and Wendy Zimmerman. 1993. *After Arrival: An Overview of Federal Immigration Policy in the United States.* Washington, D.C.: The Urban Institute.

Iris, Nancy. 1994. "Refugee Resettlement." In *U.S. Report on the Status of Women, 1985-1994.* U.S. Department of State Bureau of International Organization Affairs, Office of Economic and Social Affairs.

U.S. Office of Refugee Resettlement, Administration for Children and Families. 1993. *Mission Refocus: Focus on Women.* Washington, D.C.

Zimmerman, Wendy. 1995. *Demographic Data on Immigrant Women.* (A report in progress). Washington, D.C.: The Urban Institute.

WORKING YOUR FINGERS TO THE BONE

*Marion Graham**

I WAS BORN IN BOSTON, THE YOUNGEST OF A FOUR-GIRL family. When I was 13, my father's firm went bankrupt and he found himself out of a job. My family were so ashamed they wouldn't tell their friends that they had to move from the suburbs to a three-decker in Boston, even though they weren't really poor. Now I know a lot of people who would love to move out of the projects into a three-decker.

In 1960 I got married. I left my good job with the telephone company when I was pregnant with my first child, in 1961. I really looked forward to being home with my children. Nobody worked that I knew. During the '60s I was always pregnant when everybody was out rebelling against everything. I was too pregnant to rebel, so I have to rebel now! I have five kids. They are now 35, 32, 31, 30, and 27.

When I saw how my marriage was disintegrating, I did work at home for marketing research companies, and I did typing for college students, just to try to make money. I had planned for two or three years to get a divorce before I did. But I never had the money to do it. I knew I had to have a job in order to save the money to go to a lawyer. I couldn't leave the kids; there was no daycare. Finally, I had to go on welfare because my husband did not pay enough support, and sometimes he did not pay at all.

When I started working full-time again, I thought it was going to be wonderful, that I wasn't going to be poor anymore. I was going

---

* Marion Graham was originally interviewed by Jean Humez and Melissa Shook in 1984. Ann Withorn updated, edited and expanded the interview.

to be away from the bureaucracy; they couldn't call me in anytime they wanted to. Even then, though, I still earned so little that I was eligible for a housing subsidy, Medicaid, and food stamps. I remember at the time being ashamed to let people where I worked know that I was poor enough for food stamps. And I hated that.

About three years ago they came out with some new "poverty line," that's what they called it, and they decided I earned too much for most of those other benefits. I only grossed something like $8,600 at the time, but it was still too much for them, so they cut me off. I still had the same needs I had before, but suddenly I was no longer poor. I guess I was supposed to be proud.

Since then I got a raise, so I thought things would be O.K., but then I lost my housing subsidy because I earned too much. I ended up having to take an apartment that cost exactly seven times what I had paid with a subsidy. My rent came to half of my net pay. Just the rent. After that sometimes I would get to work but not be able to pay for lunch. I had my subway tokens, but no money to eat. Every week they take something different out of my salary. Life insurance, disability insurance, union dues, retirement benefits are all good, but you don't get much to live on. Now, finally, I can buy *Woman's Day* and *Family Circle* magazines—that used to be my dream.

How you dress for work, the hours and flexibility, transportation, whether you can bring a lunch—all these nitty-gritty things make a big difference in how you can live on a low salary. You just cannot afford to take some jobs even if they sound interesting because you have to spend too much money on clothes or transportation. It's sad. I couldn't afford to work at a place where I had to dress up, for instance. You can't "dress for success" on a secretarial salary. It's an invisible poverty.

You think you're not poor because you are working, so you don't even ask for the information about benefits you need. And nobody tells you that you might be eligible, because they think you are working and all set. Also, it is even harder to ask for things from your family, because if you are working you should have the money. I feel bad, though, that I don't have more chance to help my family. I can't afford it, even though I'm working.

The average pay in my union of clerical and hospital workers is not much above poverty for a woman who is trying to raise a family. When people need childcare they have to pay for it, and they can't afford it. I don't need childcare, but the health insurance, which I had to wait two years for, costs a lot. And I couldn't get it for my son, who has suffered from juvenile diabetes since he was very young.

Not having money affects everything about how you feel. I used to feel lousy about myself. I thought I was supposed to be set, to have slice of the American pie. Now I was a big person and I worked and everything, and I was supposed to get there. But instead I found myself just with a job and no money. When I reached 40 I was so depressed.

Now I have learned that I am not alone, that it is not my fault. The average secretary around here is just over the line for many benefits, but we still have expenses we can't meet. That makes some women, who don't understand how it works, take it out on women on welfare. They blame them for getting something they can't have, instead of blaming the rules, which keep them from getting anything. Some secretaries may think, "I am better off than they are," instead of seeing how we have similar problems. But they are afraid of the label that would be put on them if they identified with welfare. I don't do that because I have been there and I know both, and I know that none of it is good. It's bad to be on welfare, and it is bad to be working and have no money.

As secretaries here we have worked hard to do things together so that we can know each other as people, because at work we are all separated in our individual little offices. We go on picnics together, or to dinner, just to get to know each other. Although they don't pay us much, they act like we can never be absent or the world will fall apart, so we have to cover for each other, and we can't do that if we don't know each other. I keep saying, "If we are so important, why don't they pay us more?" But they don't, so we have to help each other.

'BUKED AND SCORNED'
Beyond "Ending Welfare as We Know It"

> I've been 'buked and I've been scorned'. I've been talked about as sure as you are born.

PAY THE GAS BILL AND THEY'LL SHUT OFF THE PHONE. DO THE laundry and the car fare to the dentist is gone. Buy the baby's diapers—and tell your older girl she'll have to skip her class trip because you can't give her bus money and she won't let you ask for even more extra help from the school. For women on welfare, everyday life is a series of small Sophie's Choices, a painful, bitter, humiliating juggling act. To be poor in the United States today is to live between a rock and a hard place, day in and day out.

But if that isn't tough enough, society seems to insist on adding insult to injury. A fly on the wall in an unemployment line or a social security office would still hear very different tones and innuendoes. Social security may be confusing, and unemployment may make you feel bad, but a woman who uses welfare to support her family must endure questions about her sex life, risk being fingerprinted (as a fraud prevention measure), and must grit her teeth and smile when they tell her that her benefits will soon be "transitional" whether her needs are or not, and that she must give up her dreams of the higher education, which she knows is her only hope. And if she turns on the radio, likely as not she will hear welfare mothers insulted and find out about yet another threat to her family's stability.

How did it get so bad? How has welfare become popularly viewed as, not just the stepchild program it began as in 1935, but as itself the source of the misbehaviors of an "underclass" who are utterly outside the norm of acceptable society?

Background

In the heat of federal and state anti-welfare fever, people often don't remember that popular opposition to providing public assistance for poor families was as present in New Deal and Great Society efforts to rescue the economy from itself as it was in the heydays of triumphant capitalism in the 1920s, 1950s and 1980s. But, underneath all the rhetorical heat, programs emerged and endured that, while still demeaning and compromised, also allowed some small measure of economic security for all families when the "realities" of the labor market and parental behavior left them stranded. The American people might not like "welfare," it was something to be avoided, but they accepted it as necessary for basic social security for those least fortunate.[1]

What we call "welfare" is part of the 1935 Social Security Act that launched the modern welfare state in the U.S. by shifting social welfare responsibilities from the states to the federal government. The Social Security system, however, always perpetuated the class distinctions that the welfare state was officially supposed to mute. Middle- and lower-income people who are employed, form two-parent families, and otherwise "play by the rules" are defined as "deserving" of aid and rewarded with access to the more generous, less stigmatized social insurance programs, such as old age pensions ("Social Security"), Unemployment Insurance and Worker's Compensation. The system's less adequate, unpopular and means-tested program, now Aid to Families with Dependent Children (AFDC, originally ADC), was targeted for the "undeserving" poor: namely, single mothers who have historically been regarded as violating society's most basic rules by seeking assistance for their children as single mothers, abandoned wives and women whose male partner does not provide adequate support.

From the start, Congress provided lower benefits for AFDC than the other public assistance programs created by the Social Security Act, not even including funds for the mother until the 1950s. Many states implemented AFDC reluctantly. In the 1930s and 1940s, some states refused aid to black women to keep them working as field and domestic help. In the 1950s and 1960s, they denied aid to many single mothers and women of color using "suitable home," "man in the house" and "midnight raid" policies, which equated unwed motherhood with unfit motherhood.

In the late 1960s, mandatory work programs, such as the Work Incentive Program (WIN), were created because poor women (the most highly employed sector of women in the society) had to be "forced to work." Despite an intensification in the 1970s, these work programs—forerunners of today's workfare—never met their own goals, due to child care shortages, labor market barriers, and lack of funds to implement needed employment training and social services. But their coerciveness sent a message about what happens to poor women: not only will income support be less than poverty level, but they will be forced to meet unattainable employment goals. In the 1980s, Reagan's first welfare cuts served not to help women become employed but also to eliminate backup welfare assistance for many women who were "working poor." The goal was to isolate AFDC recipients by assuring that few low-wage workers would think of welfare as a benefit to help them with their increasingly precarious situation—instead it became something that "others" got and they didn't.

Although the proponents of mid-1990s "welfare reform" wished to present their finally triumphant initiatives as "new", the most recent round of reforms is essentially an extension of the logic initiated by the 1988 Family Support Act (FSA), with the added twist of making all "welfare" programs into a block grant, no longer even part of sacrosanct "Social Security". The FSA was the first of the new bipartisan initiatives—which Mimi Abramovitz calls "the new paternalism"— that allow government dollars to dictate work, maternal, childbearing, and parental behavior with little pretense of cushioning the effects of poverty, or even of cutting federal spending. AFDC was transformed from a program that allowed women to stay home with their children (but with increasing pressures to become employed) into a mandatory work program. It's centerpiece, the Job Opportunity and Basic Security (JOBS) program—or workfare—required women on welfare to go to work, to enroll in school or to enter training programs, and expected states to provide support services and stricter collection of child support payments. Welfare mothers who were not otherwise exempt and who refused to participate, faced the reduction or loss of benefits, but states were not sanctioned for failure to provide adequate services.

JOBS only whetted the appetite of some for more punitive measures when it, predictably, "failed" to reduce use of welfare in the economic downturn of the early 1990s. There were only modest income and employment gains, if any, and slight if any lowering of the welfare rolls. The emotional costs of the additional threats, pressures and paperwork went unrecorded.

Today's "Personal Responsibility and Work Opportunity" Act (welfare reform) further institutionalizes the false hope that income support is available only as a brief respite from unemployment and as a path to immediate employment for all. Denied is welfare's real function—as a way for under-employed, unemployed, or never-employed mothers to provide minimally for their families when they can't find "affordable employment," that will provide adequate wages, benefits, and time for family care. The idea that families have "rights" to welfare when in economic need is simply forgotten. Even education and training are suspect because they don't produce guaranteed, quick, cheap results. Welfare must be available only as the absolute worst option, and always justified simply as a temporary, "transitional benefit." Indeed, there has been little partisan dispute. The fights in Congress and in the states have been, with some honorable exceptions, only about how much to cut, how thoroughly to punish, and how totally to limit eligibility for respite from the workplace.

Workfare and employment mandates are but the first side of the bipartisan assault. The flipside is a series of state initiatives designed to control the marital, childbearing and parenting behavior of women on welfare. New Jersey first introduced the idea of a family cap, that would deny benefits to children born after their mothers were on welfare. Other states, including Massachusetts, have followed, and the "Contract with America" included it, despite strong opposition from Catholic anti-abortion forces. Other states have considered cash rewards ("wedfare") for welfare recipients who marry anyone but the father of their children. Recipients who accept Norplant are rewarded, but, in some states, Medicaid will pay only to implant it, will not cover removing it unless medically necessary.

Such measures reflect a host of pernicious assumptions about women and welfare: That using welfare is a sure sign of a character-threatening "dependency;" that it causes family breakup; that women have babies to increase their welfare check; that single mothers are promiscuous and sexually irresponsible; and that marriage is an effective antipoverty strategy. These ideas are becoming law despite their cruelty and 20 years of research that has yet to find links between welfare use and a women's marital or childbearing decisions. Whether or not states fully implement wedfare and family cap provisions, the proposals and debates cause poor women to live in even greater fear of the very state they have turned to for help as a last resort.

The federal welfare reform legislation passed in July 1996 is especially dangerous because it allows the punitive mandates of state experiments to join with an abdication of federal entitlement. It turns AFDC into a block grant program, ending federal review of untested initiatives and a guarantee of federal standards. Lifetime time limits are imposed and almost all direct aid to unmarried teen mothers and legal immigrants is eliminated. Despite strong public opposition from some brave Democrats, such "welfare reform" embodies a major loss of "social security" for low-income families, and has important consequences for all of us, regardless of whether sometime in the future a few of the most undesirable aspects are fixed, as President Bill Clinton blithely promises unhappy liberals in the heat of the election year courting ritual.

Exploring the Issues

Since the 1980s, historians and sociologists—like Linda Gordon, Mimi Abramovitz, and Theda Skocpol—have provided much more depth to our understanding of the consistent contradictions built into the U.S. welfare system. They have shown us how early 20th century Mother's Pensions were fought for as ways to allow single mothers to keep their children, rather than losing them to orphanages and agricultural work programs. Most importantly, they have helped us understand that AFDC was the product of various compromises and assumptions that women and men reformers made in their efforts to create what we now see as a "social state" —a national government that assumed responsibility for the basic well-being of children and their single parents.

In *Pitied but Not Entitled*, Linda Gordon especially showed how white middle-class women reformers were not willing to fight for a program that both supplemented women in low-wage employment and allowed them to stay home with their children. Although African-American reformers tried to present such a program as the only thing that made sense for black women, white reformers feared that women's ability to stay home with their children would be lost if AFDC subsidized women's work.

In a sense, today we can see that both groups were right. Since it replaced the earlier Jeffersonian myth of the yeoman farmer, the deep ethic that accepted wage labor as the only source of social legitimacy has defined this culture. One was either a worker, independent even if poor, or a pauper, dependent and devoid of any social rights. Women's options were to attach themselves to a male worker, share his wages and benefits, raise the kids and hope he provided for her retirement or to place herself in a discriminatory job market while meeting her own and her children's needs as an "individual problem."

Despite all its flaws since its inception, AFDC has evolved into something like a third way option for single mothers. At the cost of great social stigma and personal humiliation, "welfare" offered women the option of receiving below poverty level benefits in order to care for her children at home. It did not allow her easily to combine employment with welfare (a major flaw that African-American women had noted) but it at least served as the base from which a largely African-American welfare rights movement could demand a "guaranteed income" as they were inspired by the civil rights movement of the 1960s.

In this movement, and through today's descendant, the National Welfare Rights Union, women saw AFDC as a floor that should help families move out of poverty and sustain them when employment was not available, or did not allow them to meet their children's needs. They also saw it as a logical stepping stone for achieving the real goal—a guaranteed minimal income for all.

The articles in this section explore the question of why welfare is so hated and how women can get what they need now that, as President Clinton promises, we have "ended welfare as we know it." Claire Cummings and Betty Reid Mandell begin with the story of how the welfare rights newspaper, *Survival News*, operates. They examine the frustration, vitality and energy that women on welfare bring to the task of "telling their story" and fighting for their children and themselves. Diane Dujon helps us to see that the most difficult issue is the same one we got wrong in the 1930s: How women who are single mothers can be provided *both* access to meaningful employment that is "affordable," *and* the unquestioned option to devote full attention to their children when they so choose. For, just as African-American women leaders understood then, women suffer if they are forced to endure the workplace without a back-up system tailored to their needs as parents. But, they also must, as the feminist reformers argued, always be able to claim the primacy of their mothering role, to declare their rights to support for their children when they deem that to be best. No matter how the opponents of women might see this dual demand as "having our cake and eating it too," the welfare rights movement of today has taken up the argument, insisting that caring for one's children is legitimate work, which must be valued by society for itself.

Sandy Felder and Nancy Rose explore different dimensions of the work/welfare question. Mimi Abramovitz, Frances Fox Piven, Nancy Fraser and Linda Gordon stretch us to understand the deeper reasons why "dependence" on the state is such a complicated issue in welfare reform debates. Ann Withorn reminds us that the women who work in the welfare state have a role to play also in helping to make the state something that can provide real relief. Noemy Vides and Victoria Steinitz show the critical role that education has come to play as a path out of poverty while women rely on the income welfare affords. All the chapters suggest that single mothers will always be in great jeopardy unless women across many levels can stop fearing dependence and instead come to claim the existence of a "dependable" state as their right.

Finally, the point of this section is to help us remember what welfare is not. Most important, welfare is not and should not be the absolutely worst thing that can happen to a poor woman. Living with a batterer is worse; a job that leaves a woman paralyzed with fear because childcare arrangements are not secure or it does not provide adequate health benefits is worse; being so destabilized from lack of income and bureaucratic harassment that you lose yourself in drugs or prostitution is worse. Indeed, all the authors here assume that welfare has to be seen as a precious right that has been neglected and mismanaged, but is an essential building block for a democratic and secure society.

Notes

1. Mimi Abramovitz and Ann Withorn once wrote an article together for an anthology that was never published. This summary of welfare history emerged from that article. Who knows what words belong to whom.

SURVIVAL NEWS

A Revised National Security Shopping List:

Affordable Housing
Health Care
Child Care
Education
Jobs
Living Wage
Pensions
Non-Toxic Environment

INDEX

Movers and Shakers

Do you want to change the system? Join us!

WEJ—ARMS—LISS—CBHN—MCH

WOMEN FOR ECONOMIC JUSTICE, 145 Tremont St., Rm. 607, Boston, MA 02111, 617-426-9734

ADVOCACY FOR RESOURCES FOR MODERN SURVIVAL (ARMS Student Center, Downtown Center, U-Mass/Boston, 617-956-1036

LOW-INCOME STUDENTS FOR SURVIVAL, 73A Magazine St., Cambridge, MA 02139, 617-547-0497

THE COALITION FOR BASIC HUMAN NEEDS, 64 Essex St., Cambridge, MA 02139, 617-497-0126

MASSACHUSETTS COALITION FOR THE HOMELESS, 34 1/2 Beacon St., Boston, MA 02115, 617-523-6400

Survival News
102 Anawan Ave.
W. Roxbury, MA 02132
617-327-4217

Non-Profit Org.
Bulk Rate
U.S. Postage Paid
Boston MA
Permit No. 55555

Test Your Welfare I.Q.

by Nancy Amidei
Reprinted from Towards Self Sufficiency

We encourage you to take this test*, learn from it, and share it with your neighbors, family, and coworkers. We need to become "myth-busters."

1. Programs for poor people (all cash welfare, food stamps, Medicaid, subsidized housing, education, etc.) take up what portion of federal spending?

Less than 10% ____ 1/3 ____ Over 1/2 ____

2. What portion of the poor get one or more subsidized in-kind benefits (e.g. food stamps, Medicaid, housing)?

100% ____ 60% ____ 40% ____ 25% ____

3. How many poor households have earnings, and pay taxes?

All ____ 2/3 ____ 1/3 ____ None ____

*Questions and answers continued on any page of *Survival News*

FINDING VOICE
Building Community at Survival News
Claire Cummings and Betty Reid Mandell

THE MAINSTREAM MEDIA LIES ABOUT WELFARE MOTHERS. THEY feature stories about mothers who neglect and abuse their children, mothers who have large broods of children, mothers who take drugs, and third generations of welfare mothers. They imply that these are typical welfare recipients, thereby feeding the prejudice that already exists in the public mind. By planting these prejudices in people's minds, they ensure that there will be no large-scale resistance to the current assaults on welfare.

What can we do to resist the media attack on welfare mothers? One thing we can do is to create our own alternative media where the voices of the poor can be heard. Some of us did that when we created *Survival News*, a lively activist welfare rights paper that focuses on Aid to Families with Dependent Children (AFDC), but also covers news about survival issues for all low-income people—Social Security Insurance (SSI), Social Security Disability Insurance (SSDI), nutrition programs, housing, health, childcare, social services, and General Relief.[1] Most important, it features the stories of the survivors of poverty themselves.

Survival News is unique in another way—it unites low-income and middle-income people in a sustained cooperative working relationship, while leaving majority control in the hands of low-income people. It got its start at the University of Massachusetts at Boston (U-Mass/Boston), in the office of Advocacy for Resources for Modern Survival (ARMS). ARMS is a welfare rights group made up of students who are current or former welfare recipients. It is a chapter of the Coalition for Basic Human Needs (CBHN), a statewide welfare group composed of welfare mothers.

Our Beginnings

Betty Reid Mandell, a social work professor at Bridgewater State College, was writing a welfare rights manual and needed to find out how welfare mothers themselves experienced the system. Her friend Ann Withorn, a professor at U-Mass/Boston, suggested that she talk with members of ARMS. They were glad to help, and together they wrote and published the booklet *You Can Apply*.

The ARMS members who helped Betty write the booklet were Dottie Stevens, Diane Dujon, Judy Gradford, Jeanne Dever, Diana Moon, and Hope Habtemariam. CBHN and the Massachusetts Chapter of the National Association of Social Workers (NASW) joined with ARMS in sponsoring the booklet, and funds were provided by The Haymarket Foundation, NASW, and the City Missionary Society. After the booklet was published and 1,000 copies were distributed, the welfare department agreed to pay $3,000 for a second printing to distribute at welfare offices. Some time after it was printed and delivered to the welfare department, we received a call from one of their functionaries saying that something went wrong with the sprinkler system in the room where the booklets were stored, and they were drowned! We asked whether their employment and training manuals also drowned in the flood, but that was apparently considered an impertinent question and remained unanswered. They never asked for more booklets. The trouble with a welfare rights manual is that it is outdated almost as soon as it is published, since welfare regulations change so fast. One of the ARMS members, Louise Rhodes, suggested that we really need a newspaper, to keep us updated on benefits. And that's where it began. Betty, joined by ARMS members in 1987, agreed to start a newspaper. There was newspaper ink in Betty's veins, since she had worked on her college newspaper and had an unrequited longing to be a newswoman. But newspapers are laid out by computers now, so Betty bought a Mac Plus and the PageMaker desktop publishing program and took classes at the Boston Computer Society to learn how to use them. With the help of Caitlin Andrews, a Bridgewater student who worked on the college newspaper, Betty learned layout skills, and the first three issues of the paper were laid out in the *Comment* office at Bridgewater and printed by the same commercial printer that printed the *Comment*.

Members of ARMS joined with Betty and some of her friends and

Bridgewater students—Claire Cummings, Mary Jo Hetzel, Joan Ecklein, Jackie King, Caitlin Andrews, Claire Lapointe, Cheryl Lees, Kris Brackett, and Julia Wood—to form a board. In 1988, we incorporated as Survivors, Inc. and became a nonprofit 501(c)(3) organization. Jack Backman, a lawyer and retired state senator, gave us free legal help with this. Jack advised us to find a name other than the name of the newspaper in case we wanted to do more things than publish a newspaper some time down the road. How far-sighted he was! We are truly not just a newspaper any more, and as we have taken on more projects, we have begun to call ourselves by our legal name, Survivors, Inc.

Survival News continues to be sponsored by ARMS, but board membership is open to anyone interested in working on the paper. More ARMS members joined as we went along, including Flo Osborne, Emma Jean Culbert, and Diane Kelley. We cooperated with other groups on various projects, and people from those groups joined the board: Florence Miller from WINGS (Women's Institute for New Growth and Support); Barbara Raines and Janet Pontes from UCAP (the United Community Advocacy Project of the Church of the United Community); Karen Rock, Liz Fenton and Laura Walker from CBHN; Laurie Taymor-Berry from the Massachusetts Welfare Rights Union. Board members brought along others, including Sylvia Palmer, Stacey Hill, Michael Page, Juanita McKoy, and Susan Wilkins. And sometimes people wandered in to our meetings at the ARMS office and found themselves members of the group. Our structure was loose.

Dottie Stevens, who signed the incorporation papers, was our first president. At the time, she was president of CBHN, a Massachusetts statewide welfare rights organization of welfare recipients. She kept us informed and involved in CBHN activities, including their "Up and Out of Poverty Campaign" and their fights to raise the grants and to win a clothing allowance for recipients. Later she became the president of the Massachusetts chapter of the National Welfare Rights Union (NWRU), and when she proposed to the NWRU board that *Survival News* be the official paper of the NWRU, the board voted in favor.

Diane Dujon, another of our founders, was at the time a member of ARMS, which was a chapter of the CBHN. Diane is a former welfare recipient who is now codirector of the Assessment Program at the College of Public and Community Service at U-Mass/Boston. Here are Diane's thoughts on the origins of the welfare rights booklet *You*

Can Apply and its successor, *Survival News*:

> We saw a need and wanted to be able to teach the skills that we were learning to other welfare mothers back in the community. We learned to know our rights, to know what documents we had to bring to the welfare office in order to obtain benefits. One woman whose house burned down had nowhere to go for days because her social worker had no idea how to expedite finding emergency shelter. We were able to educate the worker about which forms she needed to have filled out and the available resources for families who were homeless due to fire. We were learning that we had rights and were entitled to many services which were not publicized, such as educational grants and loans. We wanted to pass on to other desperate women how to avoid the barriers to achieving education. We wanted to use our education to help other welfare women get on their feet.

Betty has firm convictions about uniting theory with practice, and believes that academics should work as equals with the people they teach about. She wanted *Survival News* to unite theory and practice, and she wanted her teaching to be informed by low-income people, who have so much to contribute in real-life experience, expertise in organizing, and ideas about what policies would help them. She invited many of the welfare mothers on the board to speak to her Bridgewater classes. Diane and Dottie's first experiences in academia in front of Betty's classroom had a tremendous impact on them, as Diane remembers:

> …because Betty had validated our knowledge by inviting us to her class and letting us speak in our own words in talking about the issues we felt were important. Knowing Betty helped us to bridge the gap!

Dottie, Diane and Betty were contradicting deeply entrenched class patterns. Betty, in bringing welfare mothers into academia as experts in their own right, was going against training as an academic that, as Carmen Luke and Jennifer Gore argue:

> taught us that our public speech…must confine itself to the measured discourse befitting academic protocol. We are taught to maintain a scholarly separation of academic knowledge from the actual people who are engaged in the production of such knowledge.[2]

Our Purpose, Funding, and Reputation

Survival News states its purpose as follows:

> "We are low/no income people and their allies who are working together for change in the social welfare system; to provide information about benefits and rights; to provide a forum for the voices of low/no income

people and their allies to be heard; and to educate people and develop theory about social welfare issues. We are helping to build a national network of people who work for change in the social welfare system."

Since our founding, Betty's search for grants has been successful enough to fund two issues of the paper a year, make a video, buy three computers, and run three writing groups, a publishing group, and two consecutive groups that bring together welfare workers and recipients. Not many foundations fund organizing. Few fund women's groups. Even fewer fund organizing around welfare issues. But there are some alternative funds.[3]

We don't have an office and we've never had a full-time staff member, but true to our name, we survive. More than that—we thrive! We have been cited by *Social Policy* as one of the nation's outstanding alternative newspapers. We received a citation for outstanding work in progressive computing by Computers for Social Change in New York City. The Bertha Capen Reynolds Society, an organization of progressive social workers, sends a copy to each new member.

By now we have achieved some recognition nationwide as a major player in the field of welfare rights. In May 1995, the staff director of the American Civil Liberties Union (ACLU) Reproductive Freedom Project in New York City called us to see if we could help them find a welfare mother in Arkansas who would be willing to sue the state on that state's recently implemented child-exclusion law.[4] And a reporter from a major Toronto newspaper called to ask our opinion about workfare, which was being proposed by a member of Parliament for the province of Ontario.

Our Structure

We are a diverse board. Our board is made up of 41 people; 38 of them are women. Thirty-two are low-income, either because their wages are low or because they receive some form of public assistance: 17 receive AFDC assistance; five receive SSI; three receive OASDHI (Social Security); and seven are living on wages that are below or close to the poverty level. Of the low-income people, 11 are currently attending an undergraduate or graduate college program and 13 are college graduates. The rest of the board is comprised of middle-class women, deeply involved in welfare rights work: One (a former AFDC recipient) is the social service director of a Head Start agency; one is a writer and mother; four are college professors, one of them *emeritus*; and one (a former AFDC recipient) is the director of a program at a university. One of the professors is a former AFDC recipient.

We are also racially diverse (nine of us are African American and two are Latina) and we have a wide age range (four of us , the children of board members, are under 17 and three members are over 60). Additionally, four have declared themselves to be lesbian or bisexual.

Meetings are held monthly, and more often as publication dates draw near. Once a year we go the Imperial Restaurant in Chinatown for a dim sum lunch. And we find other occasions to eat and party, as when Rachel Martin, our writing teacher, left town, and again when she returned for a visit.

Our Advisory Board members (who give us specialized help from time to time) include two professors, a lawyer who was a former state senator, a writing teacher, a graphic artist, and a computer consultant.

About two-thirds of the subscribers are welfare recipients, and the remainder are their advocates and allies—including college professors, women's centers, feminists, and welfare rights activists from all around the country and the world. Eight thousand copies of the paper are distributed by mail subscription and by drop-off to various places where low-income people gather, such as shelters for the homeless, shelters for battered women, welfare offices, health clinics, daycare agencies, public housing developments, and state and community colleges and universities. Bundles of *Survival News* travel all over the country with board members attending welfare summit meetings; regional and National Women's Studies conferences; conferences of activists, social workers, unionists, anthropologists, and psychologists; the Socialist Scholars Conference; and welfare rights demonstrations.

Contributors of articles range from welfare mothers, welfare organizers, and poor and middle-class children on the "Youth Page" to theoretical pieces and reviews by such leading feminist scholars as Mimi Abramovitz, Mary Jo Hetzel, Guida West, and Ann Withorn.

One of our most dramatic stories by a contributor was provided by a 15-year-old Nigerian girl of the Ibo tribe. Her mother, the director of a women's center, had previously submitted an article to *Survival News* that we had published. Some months later, the daughter wrote us to ask for help. Her mother had life-threatening asthma and needed to go to Lagos for treatment, but didn't have the money. The members of the women's center had urged her to take $500 of the center's funds to finance her trip, but her mother didn't think it was fair to the other women to use those funds for her personal use. The daughter asked if we could persuade her mother that it was all right to use those funds. Her life, and the happiness of her five children, depended on it.

Betty's husband has asthma, and he mailed some of his medicine to the mother. We received a letter from the daughter thanking us and saying it had relieved her mother's suffering. Later, we received another letter saying that one of our subscribers, who had not given his or her name, had sent $500 to pay for her mother's treatment, and her mother was in a Lagos hospital "under the watchful eye of an Indian doctor."

Betty's home address and phone number in West Roxbury, Massachusetts, serves as the official address. Meetings have been held in various places—first at the NASW office, then at the ARMS office at the downtown campus of the College of Public and Community Service (CPCS) of U-Mass/Boston. When CPCS moved to the Harbor Campus of U-Mass, board meetings then rotated between the Harbor Campus, members' homes, and the WINGS office in Roxbury.[5] We meet wherever it seems most convenient for the most people.

We are keenly aware of the stress and pressures that poor people face, especially single parents with children who are struggling to survive. We gratefully accept any level of commitment that people can give. There are tasks, such as mailing the paper, that do not demand more than a few hours work but provide an occasion for high-spirited collective effort. And of course, we always eat on such occasions.

Learning Computer Skills

In the beginning, much of the typing and all of the computer layout work was done by Betty, who owned the only computer. However, we needed to help low-income women develop the necessary skills to publish the paper themselves. We sponsored some computer training courses at Curry College, where Betty's husband taught. But we soon learned that without a computer at home to practice on, people cannot develop their skills, particularly on a complex program such as PageMaker. So we set about buying computers for people to have in their homes, and have so far bought three computers, printers, and modems. Other board members have acquired their own computers. We have bought an organizational membership in the Boston Computer Society's Non-Profit Assistance Program (NPAP) which entitles our members to free consultation and reduced fees for classes. They have donated two Macintosh computers, one with a hard drive and one without. Our consultant, Peter Miller, from the NPAP is always there for us when we get stuck.

One of our computers is in the home of Claire Lapointe, our part-time staff person who began working for us in 1993 as a work-study student when she was working on a Master's degree in Adult Programming at U-Mass/Boston. Not only does she do *Survival News* business on the computer, but she also did her course work, and her twin nine-year-old daughters have delighted in it. Another computer is in the home of Barbara Raines, who types articles for us and does her course work for a Master's program in Community Planning at New Hampshire College for Human Service. Dottie Stevens uses the third computer and is excited about the potential of the Internet for organizing. Diane Dujon joins Dottie at her home in their joint forays on the information superhighway. So far, four of our members have laid out the paper with the PageMaker program— Claire Cummings, Claire Lapointe, Betty Reid Mandell, and Laurie Taymor-Berry. Others plan to learn it. We are well on the way to becoming a truly collective work group.

Group Projects

We have sponsored six collaborative group projects. The first group, in 1991-1992, was composed of 12 women in a five-month-long writing workshop. They published their articles in a special issue of the paper which they named Everybody's News. The same women formed another group in 1992-1993 called the "Advanced Publishing Group." The aim of this group was to teach computer skills, grantwriting skills, and business and advertising skills.

Another writing group of 10 women (most of them from the previous group) was formed in 1993. They published their articles in a special issue of Survival News. All three of these projects were taught by Rachel Martin.

In 1994, we sponsored the Jericho Project: Dialogue for a Change. Thirteen women (eight past/current welfare recipients and five workers from the Department of Welfare and Department of Social

Services) met for 10 meetings at U-Mass/Boston to discuss welfare issues and what it's like on the other side of the "great divide." They worked with Barbara Neeley, the facilitator, and Barbara Neumann, a writing specialist, to produce a special section of *Survival News*. In addition to discussing and writing powerful articles about their personal experiences, the participants developed a set of recommendations for the training of social workers and produced a design for a pamphlet of information for new welfare clients. They also developed policy recommendations regarding personal treatment, communication, coordination, and quality of services. Their recommendations reflected the concerns of both clients and social workers for guidelines based on mutual respect and dignity.

Everyone in the Jericho Project felt that it was important to continue the project for at least another year, in order to complete the pamphlet for new welfare clients and to build a solid foundation for a worker/client alliance within the welfare department that could continue to work for change, even after the Jericho project ended. Diane Dujon led the second phase of the project in 1995, and Laura Walker (another board member) was the coordinator.

In 1995 we launched another writing group, facilitated by Barbara Raines and a writing teacher, Susan Wilkins, who also joined our board. Called "A New Vision for Women in Recovery," this brought together 11 women who were either in recovery from substance abuse or had relatives who were in recovery. By this time, WINGS had completed rehabilitation of its house in Roxbury for seven women in recovery (most of them mothers whose children were living away from them—some with relatives, and some in DSS foster care). The women needed skills and leadership training workshops, and all of them willingly joined our writing workshop, along with four women from the *Survival News* board. They met biweekly at WINGS and published their articles in a special issue of *Survival News*. Barbara Raines used her leadership role in this group as a Master's project in her studies, using the articles produced by the group to organize around substance abuse issues.

Survival News Video

In 1994, Claire Lapointe produced a 12-minute video about *Survival News* as a class project in her Master's program at U-Mass/Boston. With the help of her instructor, Claire was able to create a polished, professional video complete with music. It features interviews with board members and shows the board at work—in the newspaper office of *Sojourner*, a monthly feminist journal, doing paste-up and layout, delivering the paper, and completing a mailing at Betty's home. Produced at a time when welfare bashing was the norm, the video highlights positive images of welfare mothers, which differ from the prevailing view and have created a demand for the video. The video was shown on Brockton cable television, then shown on the "City Life" program of WCVB (a commercial television station) along with interviews with Claire and Diane Dujon. As a result of that television program, Diane Dujon was invited to return for the next week's program to debate a welfare official and a legislator on the issues of welfare reform.

The video was one of the finalist entries in a nationwide video contest, and was submitted by Claire's instructor in still another contest. We have used it at teach-ins and conferences, as well as in workshops and classes to spread the word in a lively way about *Survival News.*

Learning to Share the Work

The writing and publishing groups aimed to strengthen the group's skills in publishing the paper and in fund-raising. The participants enjoyed the groups and gained a great deal from them. But the groups' success in strengthening the work of publishing the paper was mixed. The people who owned computers learned word processing and typed articles. PageMaker skills take longer to develop, and this has limited the number of people who can contribute in this way. Only Dottie Stevens continued to use the skills she learned to solicit advertising. Originally, Betty wrote all the grants except the one done by the Advanced Publishing Group, although other board members joined her in attending interviews with funding agencies. During the summer of 1995, however, Claire Lapointe, our part-time staff person, took the initiative to work with other low-income board members to write a proposal for the Presbyterian Committee on Self-Development. This has been the model for subsequent grant proposals.

Claire Lapointe also used her skills in adult programming to develop a committee structure that helps people to share responsibilities. Claire's skilled and cheerful leadership and dedication to our work inspired us and gave us all a lift. She has given a new stability and cohesiveness to our efforts and helped us to function more like a collective.

People have carved out roles for themselves. Dottie Stevens wrote the "Dear Blabbie" column and now has her own page, "Which Way Welfare Rights?" Both Dottie and Diane Dujon write about their organizing activities with the NWRU, and other organizing efforts in which they participate. Claire Cummings edits and lays out the "Profile" and "Voice of the People" sections. Florence Miller is in charge of the "Social Security Solidarity Page." Mary Jo Hetzel, Jackie King, and Betty Reid Mandell write theoretical pieces and Dottie Stevens, Jackie King, Betty Reid Mandell, and Ann Withorn do book reviews. Betty writes the "Repression" and "Resistance" columns, current welfare news, and "Updates on Benefits." Lisa Dujon and Jessica Berry edit the "Youth Page." We all review the articles and graphics that people submit. Progress toward doing the work collectively is slow, but there is progress. In our beginning years it was often hard to convince some board members to share in the work. One member expressed her resistance this way: "Let Betty do it. It's her baby." We doubt that anyone would make such a statement now. Some of the founding members have been deeply loyal from the beginning. Dottie Stevens has often said, "I *love* this paper!"

Yet, no matter how loyal the board is, most of them are busy with full-time jobs, childcare and organizing work. They simply don't have the time to do all the work that we need to do. The next step in our growth seems to be to find the money to hire a full-time staff member who can do some of the grantwriting, coordinate our projects, and help the board to function more efficiently.

Organizing to Change the System

The Jericho Project was an organizing project that aimed to help change the welfare system. Now we are going further in our efforts to change the system. We have launched two additional projects—organizing low-income students in state and community colleges and universities, and establishing a speakers' bureau.

We hope to mobilize a strong statewide organization of students that includes both the welfare poor and the working poor, and any other students who are interested in the issues. Combining welfare recipients with the working poor helps to defuse some of the hostility that working people feel toward welfare recipients.

The organization deals with survival issues that students face, including fighting the cutbacks in student aid that are proposed by House Republicans, and fighting to make it possible for AFDC recipients to complete a college education. It also deals with rising tuition and fees, the difficulty of buying books, and finding or creating affordable childcare. It informs students about benefits that are available to them such as scholarships, the Earned Income Tax Credit, Food Stamps, and WIC.

ARMS serves as the model for this organization. Diane Dujon has also helped to organize a chapter of ARMS at Bristol Community College, working with Professor Dan Gilbarg. Betty helped to organize a chapter of ARMS at Bridgewater State College before her retirement.

Our speakers' bureau on welfare works in cooperation with a group of Boston-area academics called the "Academic Working Group on Poverty," along with CBHN, and the Massachusetts Human Services Coalition. Each team of speakers includes a welfare recipient and an academic. If there is an honorarium, board members of Survivors, Inc. donate it to the organization; low-income speakers keep their honoraria.

The speakers' bureau merely formalizes what many welfare recipients and academics have been doing for years. We have been speaking at conferences, women's centers, social work schools, high schools and colleges, study groups, church groups—wherever anyone would listen to us.

Race and Class

In the beginning, most of our members were white. Of the founding ARMS members, only Diane Dujon was black, and we had no Latina members. Later two black women in ARMS joined. We needed to become more ethnically diverse. We reached out to four organizations of low-income people in the community with a more diverse membership and developed collaborative projects with them. My Sister's Place, sponsored by the American Friends Service Committee, served homeless women, most of them black. WINGS was founded by Black women who are in recovery from substance abuse. The United Community Advocacy Project of the Church of the United Community is located in Roxbury and has a multiracial but majority black congregation. Mujeres Unidas en Acción does education and advocacy for a mostly Latina population. We have been relatively successful in recruiting more black members, but less successful in recruiting Latina members. The Latina women in the writing groups participated enthusiastically in the groups because the teacher, Rachel Martin, is bilingual and very sensitive to multicultural issues. However, they seldom came to board meetings, perhaps because they were not fluent in English and the other board members did not speak Spanish. Some of us have tried to learn Spanish, but are far from fluent. Now we have two Latina board members: one from Puerto Rico and one from Nicaragua. They were both Betty's students and speak fluent English.

The authors of this article are both white and so may not be aware of all the racial dynamics of the group. However, it seems to us that our board is comfortable in dealing with race. We are all keenly sensitive to issues of prejudice and discrimination and united in our struggle against racism. We can discuss cultural differences seriously, and we can also joke about them. For example, one Black woman, when having trouble manipulating the mouse of a Macintosh computer, complained, "This mouse is racist!" When we were having a dim sum lunch, another Black woman said, "Where are the chitterlings?"

Social class differences are trickier. The welfare rights movement carries a long history of suspicion of middle-class people. In her history of the National Welfare Rights Organization (NWRO) of the 1960s and 1970s, Guida West[6] talks of the tendency of middle-class people to take over decisionmaking from the welfare mothers, and says that the tension between middle-class advocates and welfare mothers was never fully resolved. Guida formed a "Friends of Welfare" group, separate from the NWRO, to mobilize the advocates to share their resources with the movement but avoid decisionmaking. In her article "Know-How," Ellen Messer-Davidow[7] cites bell hooks', comments on the tendency of middle-class women to think they know better than low-income women: "Although academic feminists' probably know less about grassroots organizing than many poor and working class women, they were certain of their leadership ability, as well as confident that theirs should be the dominant role in shaping theory and praxis.'" In her book, *Tyranny of Kindness*, Theresa Funiciello[8] vents her fury on condescending welfare advocates and middle-class poverty pimps. When low-income people read her book, it strikes a responsive chord and often brings hostility to the fore that they had been stifling.

NWRO membership was open only to welfare recipients, although many of the leaders and staff members were middle class. The NWRU is somewhat more inclusive, accepting some tried- and-true advocates into their ranks, but they are still wary of the middle class. In Massachusetts, CBHN accepts only welfare recipients as members. A welfare rights group in Wisconsin called Welfare Warriors accepts only welfare mothers as members. They publish a welfare rights paper called *Welfare Mothers Voice*, which is exclusively by welfare mothers.

So we are somewhat unique in the welfare rights field in our attempt to combine welfare recipients and middle-class advocates in the same group. Since we are committed to the principle that people who are being served by an organization should control that organization's policies, we have a policy that majority control of the board should be in the hands of low-income people, and in fact two-thirds of our board members are low-income.[9]

Some of the middle-class members who were feminist academics were from poor and working-class backgrounds, or were former welfare recipients themselves. They were conscious and forthcoming regarding their internal identity split. The consideration of class differences (as well as the other differences of race, sexual preference, ethnicity, and level of commitment to and experience with political activism) grounded the decisions the board made. The ways these differences played out in group decisionmaking is a study in love and tolerance reminiscent of Norma Alarcón's admonition to "be patient to the point of tears" when listening to women from the "margins."[10] We all knew to one degree or another that we could not ignore our differences for it would "rob each other's energy and creative insight," as Audre Lorde points out.[11]

While the memories of poverty persist and help us to identify with the poor, it has been a long time for some of us since we didn't have enough money to open a checking account, or when we finally did have a checking account, we postdated checks. Those memories tend to fade when we for many years, have been able to wander through the supermarket aisles and buy whatever takes our fancy, without counting the cost. So, for example, when Betty asked a welfare recipient if she would come to an interview with a funding agency and offered to write a check to pay for the taxi, another welfare recipient said to the woman, "Will you be able to cash it?" The answer was "No," so Betty dug in her pocketbook for the cash. Stipends are paid in cash to the low-income participants of our groups. The welfare workers get their stipends in checks.

Middle-class biases sometimes come out unconsciously in subtle ways. For example, when Betty was explaining the proposal to make up teams of speakers for our speakers' bureau with "one middle-class advocate and one welfare recipient," a welfare recipient protested that welfare recipients are also advocates. She added, "I need all the affirmation I can get." Betty had not meant to imply that welfare recipients were not advocates, but the way she phrased it came across as elitist. At that moment, we all realized how far we had come and how much further we had to go in overcoming class bias.

We believe that the main thing that poor people need is money, and we are committed to give as much of our money as possible to low-income members. We pay low-income members a stipend for participating in our groups. We also reimburse them for childcare and transportation when they attend meetings. Some organizations require a receipt or a voucher before they will reimburse people for expenses, but one of our welfare mothers pointed out how demeaning and mistrustful this practice is, and how reminiscent of welfare department practice. So we put some cash in an envelope, and tell people to take out whatever they need. We pay low-income people $25 for each article, poem, or graphic that we publish, and $10 an hour for typing articles and laying out the paper.[12]

The middle-class people on the board feel it a privilege to be able to share their resources with low-income people, as they are keenly aware that the differences in our class positions are due to tricks of fate and historical position, not to any inherent differences. They feel that sharing those resources helps to even out the deep inequalities of this society, if only on a small scale, and helps to relieve their complicity in being part of such inequality. Often, the people with cars give rides to the people without. But figuring out how to share these resources can sometimes be awkward. In the beginning, when we went out to dinner after a board meeting, the middle-class members would foot the bill for the low-income members. Later, we made a policy to use organizational funds for our post-meeting communal meals, as we decided that was an important and legitimate expense and it eliminated the need for low-income members to feel grateful, an insidious requirement of relationships where one person is in the giving position. Wherever we can substitute institutional funds for personal gifts, we do so. There are times when this is impossible, as we are not a service agency and have no budget to meet the many personal crises that low-income people face. We have considered the possibility of setting up a revolving loan fund, either by ourselves or with other organizations, but so far have not had the money to do that.

The excruciating realization that we could not solve each other's economic problems, take in the homeless, nor support the poverty-stricken in our midst with the limited resources of the paper was uncomfortable and painful for a group dedicated to ending the horrors of poverty. The middle-class women fought their guilt, we all fought against stereotyping each other, we recognized our differences and we spoke to them truthfully. We took turns being leaders, we shared responsibility, we shared our jobs and sorrows as women, we allowed no marginality. These struggles created a newspaper where poor and working-class women now write a great deal of the articles and are the majority of the subscribers. Most inspiring are the testimonials from welfare mothers who never thought they could write at all. They are thrilled and proud of their accomplishments, as are the middle-class board members.

Social class issues arose around the struggle to decide what flavor or "voice" the paper should have in terms of the writing and the articles. Some of the welfare women wanted no-nonsense prose, short, with no "big words." The academics wanted that too, but also wanted the paper to be a forum for developing theory as well as for descriptive articles of women's own lives. They wanted to appeal to their fellow academics as well as to low-income people.

Footnotes and academic degrees were dropped as being elitist and unwieldy. The contention over this issue can also be viewed in class terms. The welfare women felt that using degrees after names was elitist and made their unattributed work look less worthy and created too much of a "class divided" look. Some of the middle-class academics agreed, and suggested a solution, reminiscent of early feminist "rags" like *Womankind*, the journal of the Chicago Women's Liberation Union, to leave out names from articles. However, some *Survival News* board members, particularly those who were former recipients or working poor, felt that this was not a good idea, since the academics had the satisfaction of being published elsewhere.

Also since welfare and working-class women have been totally invisible in academic feminism, it was important to them that their work be attributed.

This solution won the day; academics yielded to the view that poor women had been made invisible for too long. The poor women also agreed that they needed to deal with the fears which sometimes kept them in the background and allowed the middle-class academics, whom they perceived as more articulate, to be more visible in terms of writing. We agreed that everyone would be attributed equally and for any work they did with their full name only.

In soliciting subscriptions, we appealed not only to low-income people but also to their potential advocates, including academics, social workers, religious workers, and activists, particularly in feminist groups. We wanted to reach and organize both into a united struggle against the violence against women of poverty as well as all other forms of violence and discrimination against women. We wanted to link theory with practice and people's daily experience. We believed that we "cannot afford to privilege experience at the expense of theory, the local at the expense of the global."[13]

Bridging the class divisions in the welfare client/social worker/academic relationships that existed within our board became the model and symbol of our endeavor to make crossing class boundaries our centerpiece. As we dealt with our own class differences, and as we struggled with the community/academy split within our own group, we recognized that the pattern of class conflict we were witnessing and experiencing was a great opportunity as well as a "great divide." *Survival News* has created and is giving voice to a new feminist discourse with poor, working- and middle-class relations and identity at the center. As we gathered and published the painful experiences of hundreds of others' interclass contacts, we responded to those differences, together with our own differences, first in a column called "The Great Divide," which dealt with bridging the class division in the client/worker relationship, and then in the "Jericho Project."

We are excited by and proud of our influence on the wider women's movement and on academics. Because of our testimony at Senate hearings on poverty and welfare reform in Washington, D.C., at the "Who Speaks for the Poor" conference, and through meetings and discussions, Diane Dujon, Dottie Stevens, Laurie Taymor-Berry, and Betty Reid Mandell, with the support of other board members and *Survival News* coverage, helped to convince the National Organization for Women (NOW) to make poverty issues and welfare reform its top-priority commitment for the next two years. In addition, Ann Withorn, an advisory board member, helped to organize the "Academic Working Group on Poverty." In addition to the speakers' bureau mentioned before, members of the group are committed to working on and organizing around poverty issues. Plans include teach-ins on poverty and welfare at colleges and universities, exploring linkages with women's studies associations to gain access to women's groups and women's issues, working on research and writing that will make a difference, and working on media images of poverty and welfare.

Our yearly budget is about $40,000, which seems like luxury compared to our beginning years when our budget was under $10,000. As we look back on our accomplishments, it feels like we have done a tremendous amount with very modest resources. But we have been rich in our love for each other, and by bridging many divisions that society has erected, we have built a caring community together.

Notes

1. The program has different names in different states. In Massachusetts, the name has been changed from General Relief to Emergency Assistance to the Elderly, Disabled, and Children (EAEDC).

2. Carmen Luke and Jennifer Gore. "Women in the Academy: Strategy, Struggle, Survival," in Carmen Luke and Jennifer Gore. (eds.), *Feminisms and Critical Pedagogy*. (New York: Routledge, 1992) p. 195.

3. And we have successfully tapped many of them—Haymarket People's Fund, Boston Women's Fund, Boston Foundation, Resist, New England War Tax Resisters, Boston-Cambridge Ministry in Higher Education, Ben and Jerry's, Unitarian/Universalist Fund. The Lotus Foundation perhaps could not be described as alternative, but they have been regular and generous contributors. The Massachusetts Cultural Council supported a writing group. The Hyams Foundation funded a collaborative project with CBHN. One loyal, anonymous friend gives $3,000 a year every December. Subscriptions bring in about $1,000 a year, and a few people give donations. Some academics donate their honoraria when they give speeches on welfare.

4. The child exclusion law (often called the Family Cap) would deny

additional AFDC grant money to any child born after a mother receives AFDC.

5. WINGS is the acronym for the Women's Institute for New Growth and Support, an organization dedicated to the empowerment, education and political awareness of recovering women substance abusers. *Survival News* has a close relationship with WINGS through the sharing of some board members.

6. Guida West, *The National Welfare Rights Movement: The Social Protest of Poor Women.* (New York: Praeger, 1981)

7. In Joan E. Hartman and Ellen Messer-Davidow, (eds.), *En Gendering Knowledge: Feminists in Academe.* (Knoxville: The University of Tennessee Press, 1991) pp. 300-01.

8. Theresa Funiciello, *Tyranny of Kindness* (New York: The Atlantic Monthly Press, 1993)

9. An advocacy organization of low-income people in Springfield, Massachusetts called ARISE has a rule that two-thirds of their board should have incomes lower than 200% of the poverty line.

10. Norma Alarcón, "Doing Theory," in *Making Face, Making Soul/Haciendo Caras/Creative and Critical Perspectives by Feminists of Color.* (ed.), Gloria Ansaldúa. (San Francisco: Aunt Lute Books, 1990) p. 363.

11. Audre Lorde. *Sister Outsider.* (Freedom, California: Crossing Press, 1984)

12. Welfare Warriors do not pay for articles, although they do pay women for the work they do on the paper.

13. Carmen Luke. "Feminist Politics in Radical Pedagogy," in Carmen Luke and Jennifer Gore. *Feminisms and Critical Pedagogy.* (New York: Routledge, 1992) p. 49.

WOMEN AND THE STATE
Ideology, Power, and Welfare
*Frances Fox Piven**

MUCH OF THE FEMINIST LITERATURE OVER THE YEARS EVINCES an almost categorical antipathy to the state. Among socialist feminists, the antipathy is signaled by the use of such terms as "social patriarchy" or "public patriarchy" to describe state policies that bear on the lives of women.[1] And among cultural feminists, it takes form in the nostalgic evocation of the private world of women in an era before state programs intruded on the family.[2]

There is some irony in this situation. While women intellectuals characterize relationships with the state as "dependence," women activists turn increasingly to the state as the arena for political organization and influence. At least as important, the intellectual animus toward the state flies in the face of the attitudes of the mass of American women evident in survey data. Although the data show that most women are opposed to a defense build-up and presumably, therefore, are hostile to the military aspects of state power, in areas of domestic policy they evidently believe in a large measure of state responsibility for economic and social well-being, suggesting a belief in the strong and interventionist state that some feminist intellectuals abjure.[3]

Of course, activist women may be erring "liberals," and popular attitudes, including the attitudes of women, can be wrong. But in this instance, I think it is an undiscriminating antipathy to the state that

---

* An earlier version of this essay was prepared for the Research Planning Group on Women and the Welfare State, sponsored by the Council for European studies. The author would like to thank Richard A. Cloward, Barbara Ehrenreich, Temma Kaplan, Evelyn Fox Keller, Joel Rogers, and Alice Rossi for their comments.

is wrong, for it is based on belief in a series of misleading and simplistic alternatives. On the one hand, there is somehow the possibility of women's power and autonomy; on the other, dependence on a controlling state. But these polarities are unreal: All social relationships involve elements of social control, and yet there is no possibility for power except in social relationships. In fact, I think the main opportunities for women to exercise power today inhere precisely in their "dependent" relationships with the state, and in this chapter I explain why.

Before I turn directly to this issue, I want to consider the shift in the political beliefs signaled by the gender gap, for I think it important as well as evidence of my main contentions about power. Of course, everyone agrees the gender gap is important as well as being evidence of something. The media have bombarded us with information on the gap and also have given us the main explanation for it, attributing the new cleavage of opinion and voting behavior between men and women to the policies of the Reagan and Bush administrations.[4] This explanation is not wrong, for the Reagan administration policies may well have had a catalytic effect on the expression of women's political attitudes. The organized women's movement has also been given credit for generating the gap; despite the poor match between the largely middle-class constituency of the movement and the cross class constituency of the gap, and between the issues emphasized by the movement and the issues that highlight the gap, this explanation is probably not entirely wrong either.[5] Nevertheless, I think a development of this magnitude is likely to have deeper roots than have heretofore been proposed. I will conclude that those roots are in the expanding relationships women have developed with the state and in the new possibilities for power yielded by those relationships. But because the connection between beliefs and this new institutional relationship is not simple and direct, I want first to evaluate and give due weight to other influences on the shift in political opinion that has occurred among women.

Rather than showing the imprint of the women's movement, with its clearly modernizing tendencies, the emphasis on peace, economic equality, and social needs associated with the women's side of the gender gap suggests the imprint of what are usually taken as traditional female values. This oft-made observation suggests that the gender gap is not a fleeting response to particular current events but has deep and authentic roots. At the same time, traditional values of themselves cannot account for this development. The care-giving values held by women are old, but the sharp divergence between women and men is entirely new. Much tradition, however, may color the politics of women. The fact that traditional values associated with the family are now being asserted as public values is a large transformation. Or, as Kathy Wilson told a reporter on the occasion of the convening of the National Women's Political Caucus in 1983, "Women are recognizing that their private values are good enough to be their public values." More than that, the beliefs associated with the gender gap are specifically about the obligations of government to protect these values. Women are asserting that the state should represent women, on their terms.

All of this suggests the possibility that a major transformation of consciousness is occurring on a scale that implies powerful historical forces at work, whatever the precipitating role of Reagan administration policies. Although the comparisons may seem at first glance too grand, I think the public articulation and politicization of formerly insular female values may even be comparable to such historic developments as the emergence of the idea of personal freedom among a bonded European peasantry or the spread of the idea of democratic rights among the small farmers of the American colonies and the preindustrial workers of England and France or the emergence of the conviction among industrial workers at different times and places of their right to organize and strike. Each of these ideological developments reflected the interplay of traditional and transforming influences. And each brought enormous political consequences in its wake.

Change in the Objective Circumstances of Women

The gender gap simultaneously reflects the influence of women's traditional beliefs and the transformation of those beliefs in response to radical changes in the objective circumstances of American women. I want now to consider those objective circumstances the changes in the family, changes in the labor market, and the state have altered the opportunities and constraints that confront women as political actors. If ideologies are, as I contend, forged in the crucible of memory and experience, then the scale of these institutional shifts lends weight to my opening contention that a major ideological transformation is at work.

One large change is in the family. Rising rates of divorce and separation, combined with growing numbers of women who bear children but do not marry, mean that fewer and fewer women are in situations that even outwardly resemble the traditional family. Moreover, even those women who remain within traditional families now confront the possibility, if not the probability, of desertion or divorce and the near-certainty of a long widowhood. Even within those shrinking numbers of apparently traditional families, relations have been altered by the fact that many women no longer rely exclusively on the wages earned by men.

Even taken by itself, one should expect this large change in circumstance to have consequences for the politics of women. The firm contours of the insular and patriarchal family narrowly limited the options for action available to women, but they also created options for action, for exercising power in family relations, no matter how convoluted the ways. Now these options are contracting. They do not exist in families in which men are not present. And even when men are, the old forms of female power have almost surely been weakened if, as Barbara Ehrenreich argues, men in general are increasingly "liberated" from their obligations under the moral economy of domesticity and, thus, wield the threat of desertion or divorce.[6]

But if relations in the traditional family gave women some limited options for action, in the larger sense these relations made women dependent on men and, therefore, subject to them, even for access to the public world. It should not be surprising, therefore, that in the past the political opinions of women followed those of men so closely. The family was indeed an institution of social control, as of course all institutions are.

The shredding of marital bonds, together with the inability of families to maintain themselves on the wages earned by men, meant that more and more women were forced to enter the labor market. Women became wage workers on a mass scale. Whatever this change actually meant in the lives of women, it clearly meant that they had entered the mainstream of ideas about power simply because most of those ideas are about power in the marketplace. There are few analysts indeed who do not think that the economic resources and opportunities for organization generated by market relations are critical resources for power. In this very broad sense, the tradition of the political Left is not different. For nearly a century, leftist intellectuals have looked almost exclusively to production relations as the arena in which popular power could be organized and exercised. Production, by bringing people together as workers in mass-production industries, generated the solidarities that made collective action possible. And, once organized, workers in the mass-production industries also gained leverage over capital.

But the prospects for women generated by their mass entry into the labor market are neither so simple nor so happy. The situation is, of course, different for different women. For those who are better educated and perhaps younger, liberation from the constraints of the family has meant an opportunity to move into and upward in the realms of the labor market and politics. These women, among whom I count myself, have tried to shake themselves free of the old moral economy of domesticity and in its place have developed new ideas to name their new opportunities and aspirations. These ideas include the women's movement, liberation, modernization, and market success. The women's movement not only took advantage of burgeoning opportunities for women in government, business, law, and medicine, but it also helped create those opportunities.[7] In this sense, changes in objective circumstances and ideology were interactive, as I think they always are. If new ideas reflect new conditions, new ideas in turn may well lead people to act in ways that help shape those conditions.

But most women did not become lawyers, nor will they. Most women, forced to sell their labor, sold it in the expanding low-wage service sector as fast-food workers, hospital workers, or office cleaning women. In these jobs, perhaps as a result of the influx of vulnerable women workers, wages and working conditions have actually deteriorated over the last decade.[8] The relative stability of the ratio of female earnings to male earnings, despite the large gains made by some women, is striking evidence of the weak position of these workers.[9] They are located in industries in which unionization has always been difficult; those unions that did form realized few gains because widely scattered work sites made organization difficult and a ready supply of unemployed workers weakened the power to strike. The prospect of long-term, high levels of unemployment in the U.S. economy makes it less likely than ever that these structural barriers, which prevented unionization and the use of the strike power in the past, can now be overcome.

Nor is it likely that women will gradually enter the manufacturing industries in which workers did succeed in unionizing, if only because these industries are shrinking. New jobs are being created not in steel, autos, or rubber, but in fast foods, data processing, and health care. Of course, even if this were not so, even if women were likely to enter the smokestack industries in large numbers, it would be too late, for international competition and robotization have combined to crush the historic power of mass-production workers. In fact, the broad shifts in the U.S. economy from manufacturing to services and from skilled work to unskilled work, combined with the likelihood of continuing high levels of unemployment, mean that the possibilities for the exercise of popular power in the workplace are eroding for both men and women.

Women are thus losing their old rights and their limited forms of power within the family. In the marketplace, their position is weak, and prospects for improvement through individual mobility or the development of collective power are grim. These circumstances have combined to lead women to turn to the state, especially to the expanding programs of the welfare state. Income supports, social services, and government employment partly offset the deteriorating position of women in the family and the economy and have even given women a measure of protection, and therefore power, in these areas. In these ways, the state is turning out to be the main recourse for women.

Women in Relation to the Welfare State

The relationship of women to the welfare state hardly needs documenting. Women with children are the overwhelming majority among the beneficiaries of the main "means-tested" income maintenance programs, such as Aid to Families with Dependent Children (AFDC), food stamps, and Medicaid.[10] Moreover, the numbers of women affected by these programs are far greater than the numbers of beneficiaries at any one time, for women in the low-wage service and clerical sectors of the labor force turn to welfare-state programs to tide them over during family emergencies or their frequent bouts of unemployment. Older women, for their part, depend on Social Security and Medicare benefits, without which most would be very poor. However inadequately, all of these programs moderate the extremes of poverty and insecurity among women.

More than that, the programs that make women a little less insecure also make them a little less powerless. The availability of benefits and services reduces the dependence of younger women with children on male breadwinners, as it reduces the dependence of older women on adult children. The same holds in the relations of working women with employers. Most women work in situations without unions or effective work rules to shield them from the raw power of their bosses. Social welfare programs provide some shield, for the availability of benefits reduces the fear that they and their children will go hungry and homeless if they are fired.

Women have also developed a large and important relationship to the welfare state as the employees of these programs. The proportion of such jobs held by women has actually increased, even as the total number of social welfare jobs has greatly expanded. By 1980, fully 70 percent of the 17.3 million social service jobs in all levels of government, including education, were held by women, accounting for about one-third of all female nonagricultural employment and the larger part of all female job gain since 1960.[11] In these several ways, the welfare state has become critical in determining the lives and livelihood of women. Women's belief in the desirability of a responsible state, more widespread than men's belief, is partly a reflection of this institutional reality.

But will this new institutional context yield women the resources to participate in the creation of their own lives as historical actors? Can it, in a word, yield them power?

Women and Political Power

Very little that has been written about the relationship of women to the state suggests looking there for sources of power. On the contrary, the state is chiefly characterized as exercising social control over women, supplanting the eroding patriarchal relations of the family with a patriarchal relationship with the state. In my opinion, the determination to affirm this conclusion is generally much stronger than the evidence for it. Even in the 19th century, state policies had a more complicated bearing on the situation of women. Thus, although it is clearly true that changes in family law that granted women some rights as individuals, including the right to own property, did not alter their subordination to men, that is hardly evidence that the state by these actions was somehow moving "toward a new construction of male domination."[12]

This kind of argument is even more strongly made with regard to welfare-state programs. From widows' pensions and laws regulating female labor in the nineteenth century to AFDC today, state programs that provide income to women and children, or that regulate their treatment in the marketplace, are condemned as new forms of patriarchal social control. True, there is surely reason for not celebrating widows' pensions, or AFDC either, as emancipation. These programs never reached all of the women who needed support (widows' pensions reached hardly any), the benefits they provided were meager, and those who received them were made to pay a heavy price in loss of pride. Similarly, government regulation of family and market relations never overcame economic and social discrimination and in some instances reinforced it. But perhaps because some income would seem to be better than none, and even weak regulations can be a beginning, the definitive argument of the social-control perspective is not that the welfare state is weak and insufficient but that involvement with government exacts the price of dependence, somehow robbing women of their capacities for political action. It seems to follow that the massive expansion of these government programs in the past two decades and the massive involvement of women and their children in them are cause for great pessimism about the prospects for women exerting power, and surely for pessimism about the prospects for women exerting power over the state.

In general, I think this mode of argument is a reflection of the eagerness with which U.S. society has embraced a simplistic social-control perspective on institutional life, straining to discover how every institutional change helps maintain a system of hierarchical relations and, therefore, is evidence of the power of ruling groups. Of course, ruling groups have power, they do try to exercise social control, and they usually succeed, at least for a time. But they are not all-powerful. They do not rule entirely on their terms, and they do not exercise social control without some accommodation to other forces. Even then, the institutional arrangements that achieve social control are never entirely secure, for people discover new resources and evolve new ideas, and sometimes these resources and ideas are generated by the very arrangements that, for a time, seemed to ensure their acquiescence.

The critique of the welfare state developed by radical feminists was surely strongly influenced by the major leftist analyses of these programs. Overall, and despite the complexities in some of their arguments, the Left disparaged social welfare programs not for maintaining patriarchy but for maintaining capitalism. Where in other arenas leftists were sometimes ready to see that institutional arrangements had been shaped by class conflict, and even to see a continuing capacity for class struggle, in the arena of social welfare they saw chiefly arrangements for social control. In part, this outlook reflected the view, almost axiomatic among many on the Left, that the only authentic popular power is working-class power arising out of relations to the means of production. It was at least consistent with this view to conclude that welfare-state programs weakened popular political capacities, and weakened them in several ways. The complicated array of programs and categories of beneficiaries, combined with regressive taxation, fragmented working-class solidarity. The programs provided puny benefits but considerable opportunities for coopting popular leaders and absorbing popular energies; and the very existence of social welfare programs distracted working people from the main political issue, which, of course, was the control of capital. In this view, the welfare state was mainly understood as an imposition of power from above.

The Role of the State

But I do not think the evolution of the U.S. welfare state can be understood as the result only, or mainly, of a politics of domination. Rather it was the result of complex institutional and ideological changes that occurred in U.S. society and of the complex and conflictual politics associated with these changes. Over the course of the last century, the role of government (particularly the federal government) in U.S. economic life progressively increased. This development was largely a reflection of the demands of business in an increasingly complex economy. But it had other consequences beyond creating the framework for industrial growth. As government penetration of the economy became more pervasive and more obvious, laissez-faire doctrine lost much of its vigor, although it still echoed strongly in the rhetoric of politicians. Few analysts dispute the significance of the doctrine in U.S. history. It was not that the actual role of government in the economy was so restricted, for the record in that respect is complicated. Rather, the doctrine of limited government was important because it restricted the spheres in which democratic political rights had bearing. Eventually, however, the doctrine became untenable. The political ideas of Americans, like the ideas of European peasants, gradually changed as they reflected changing reality. An economy increasingly penetrated by government gave rise to the wide recognition of the active role of the state in the economy and gradually to the idea of the fusion of economic rights and political rights.[13]

This shift in belief is evident in a wealth of survey data that show that Americans think government is responsible for reducing economic inequality, for coping with unemployment, for supporting the needy, for, in short, the economic well-being of its citizens. It is also evident in electoral politics, as E.R. Tufte's 1978 analyses of the efforts of political leaders to coordinate the business cycle with the election cycle make evident, as do exit poll data on the popular concerns that generated electoral shifts in the 1980 election.[14]

Ideas undergird political action. The emerging recognition that government played a major role in the economy, and that the democratic right to participate in government extended to economic demands, increasingly shaped the character of political movements. Beginning with the protests of the unemployed, the aged, and industrial workers in the Great Depression and continuing in the movements of blacks, women, and environmentalists in the 1960s and 1970s, government became the target of protest, and government action to redress grievances arising in economic spheres became the program. The gradually expanding U.S. welfare state was mainly a response to these movements. However, it is not by any means that these movements were the only force in shaping the welfare state. On the one hand, the success of the protesters was owed to the growing legitimacy of their demands in the eyes of a broader public and the threat they therefore wielded of precipitating electoral defections if government failed to respond. On the other hand, the programs that responded to protest demands were limited and modified by other powerful interests, mainly by business groups who resisted the programs or worked to shape them to their own ends. Nevertheless, popular movements were a critical force in creating and expanding the welfare state.[15]

If the welfare state was not an imposition from the top of society, if it was forged at least in part by politics from below, what then will be its consequences in the longer run for the continued exercise of political force from below? This, of course, is the main question raised by the social-control thesis, and it is of enormous significance for women, given their extensive involvement with the welfare state. Thus far, that involvement is not generating acquiescence. On the contrary, the differing male and female expectations of government revealed by the gender gap, as well as the indignation and activism of women's organizations in reaction to the policies of the Reagan administration, were not the attitudes of people who felt themselves helpless. Rather, they suggest that women thought they had rights vis-a-vis the state and some power to realize those rights. If, however, the wide involvement of women in the welfare state as beneficiaries and workers erodes their capacities for political action, then what society has witnessed was a deluded flurry of activity that will soon pass.

Women and the Welfare State

But perhaps not. Perhaps this is the beginning of women's politics that draws both ideological strength and political resources from the existence of the welfare state. One sense in which this may be so is that the welfare state provides some objective institutional affirmation of women's political convictions. I said earlier that the welfare state was in large part a response to the demands of popular political movements of both men and women. These movements, in turn, had been made possible by changes in the relationship of government to the economy that had encouraged the idea that democratic rights included at least some economic rights. Once in existence, the social programs strengthen the conviction that economic issues belong in political spheres and that democratic rights include economic rights. In particular, the existence of the social programs is, for all the flaws of such programs, an objective and public affirmation of the values of economic security and nurturance that connect the moral economy of domesticity to the gender gap in political values and behavior.

This kind of affirmation may well strengthen women for political action. To use a phrase suggested by Jane Jensen in connection with the rise of the French women's movement, the "universe of political discourse" helps determine the likelihood and success of political mobilizations.[16] One can see the critical importance of the universe of political discourse or ideological context in determining not only the success but the scale of past expressions of oppositional politics among women. The participation of women in the food riots of the 18th and 19th centuries reflected the centrality of nurturance for women (as well as their access to the markets where collective action could take place). But perhaps women were able to act as they did on so large a scale because their distinctive values as women were reinforced by the traditional belief, held by men and women alike, that the local poor had a prior claim on the local food supply. By contrast, when middle-class women reformers in the 19-century United States tried to "bring homelike nurturing into public life," they were pitted against the still very vigorous doctrines of American laissez-faire economics.[17] Not only were their causes largely lost, but their movement remained small, failing to secure much popular support even from women. The situation is vastly different today. The women reformers who are mobilizing now in defense of social welfare programs are not isolated voices challenging a dominant doctrine. The existence of the welfare state has contributed to the creation of an ideological context that has given them substantial influence in Congress as well as mass support from women.

Women have also gained political resources from their relationship with the state. One critical resource appears to be of very long standing. It is, quite simply, the vote, and thus the potential electoral influence of women, given their large numbers. Of course, that resource is not new, and it is not owed to the welfare state. Women have been enfranchised for more than 60 years, but the promise of the franchise was never realized for the reason that women followed men in the voting booth as in much of their public life. Only today, with the emergence of the gender gap in politics, does the promise of women's electoral power seem real.

Part of the reason for the new significance of women's electoral power is in the institutional changes I have described. The "breakdown" of the family, although it stripped women of old resources for the exercise of power within the family, nevertheless freed them to use other resources. In fact, I think the breakdown of any institutional pattern of social control can generate resources for power. The disintegration of particular social relationships may well mean that people are released from subjugation to others and thus are freed to use resources that were previously effectively suppressed. The breakdown of the plantation system in the United States, for example, meant that rural blacks were removed from the virtually total power of the planter class, and only then was it possible for them to begin to use the infrastructure of the black Southern church as a focus for mobilization.

Similarly, only as women were at least partly liberated from the overweening power of men by the breakdown of the family has the possibility of their electoral power become real. The size of the gender gap and the fact that it persisted and widened in the face of the Reagan administration's ideological campaign suggest the enormous electoral potential of women. This, of course, was the media's preoccupation and was the preoccupation of contenders in the 1984 election as well. But its importance extends beyond 1984. Women have moved into the forefront of electoral calculations because they are an enormous constituency that is showing an unprecedented coherence and conviction about the key issues of the time, a coherence and conviction that, I have argued, is intertwined with the development of the welfare state. This electorate could change U.S. politics. In particular, it could change the politics of the welfare state, although not by itself.

The welfare state has generated other political resources that, it seems fair to say, are mainly women's resources. The expansion of social welfare programs has created a far-flung and complex infrastructure of agencies and organizations that are so far proving to be a resource in the defense of the welfare state and may have even larger potential. The historic involvement of women in social welfare and their concentration in social welfare employment have combined to make women preponderant in this infrastructure and to give them a large share of leadership positions as well.[18] The political potential of these organizations cannot be dismissed because they are part of the state apparatus. Such organizations, whether public or private, are part of the state, in the elementary sense that they owe their funding to government. Nevertheless, the byzantine complexity of welfare-state organization, reflecting the fragmented and decentralized character of U.S. government generally, as well as the historic bias in favor of private implementation of public programs, may afford the organizations a considerable degree of autonomy from the state. That so many of these organizations lobbied as hard as they did against the several rounds of Reagan budget cuts is testimony to this measure of autonomy. They did not win, of course. But mounting federal deficits are evidence they did not lose either, and that is something to wonder about.

There is another aspect of the politics generated by this organizational infrastructure that deserves note. The welfare state brings together millions of poor women who depend on its programs. These constituencies are not, as is often thought, simply atomized and, therefore, helpless people. Rather, the structure of the welfare state itself has helped to create new solidarities and has also generated the political issues that cement and galvanize these solidarities. One can see evidence of this in the welfare rights movements of the 1960s, where people were brought together in welfare waiting rooms, and where they acted together in terms of common grievances generated by welfare practices. One can see it again today, most dramatically in the mobilization of the aged to defend Social Security. The solidarities and issues generated by the welfare state are, of course, different from the solidarities and issues generated in the workplace. But that difference does not argue their insignificance as sources of power, as the Left often argues, and especially for women who have small hope of following the path of industrial workers.

The infrastructure of the welfare state also creates the basis for cross-class alliances among women. The infrastructure is dominated, of course, by better-educated and middle-class women. But these women are firmly linked by organizational self-interest to the poor women who depend on welfare state programs. It is poor women who give the welfare state its *raison d'etre* and who are ultimately its most reliable source of political support. Of course, the alliance between the organizational infrastructure and the beneficiaries of the welfare state is uneasy and difficult and sometimes overshadowed by antagonisms that are also natural. Nevertheless, the welfare state has generated powerful cross-class ties between the different groups of women who have stakes in protecting it.

The erosion of the traditional family and its deteriorating position on the labor market has concentrated women in the programs of the welfare state. The future of these women, workers and beneficiaries alike, hangs on the future of these programs. They need to defend the programs, expand them, and reform them. They need, in short, to exert political power. The determined and concerted opposition to welfare programs that has emerged among corporate leaders and their Republican allies and the weak defense offered by the Democratic Party suggest that the situation will require a formidable political mobilization by women. The programs of the welfare state were won when movements of mass protest, by raising issues that galvanized an electoral following, forced the hand of political leaders. The defense and reform of the welfare state is not likely to be accomplished by less. There is this difference, however. The electoral and organizational support needed to nourish and sustain the movements through which women can become a major force in American political life is potentially enormous.

Notes

1. See, for example, N.B. Barrett, "The Welfare System as State Paternalism," (paper presented to the conference on Women and Structural Transformation, Rutgers University, Institute for Research on Women, November 1983; E. Boris and P. Bardaglio, "The Transformation of Patriachy: The Historic Role of the State, in *Families, Politics, and Public Policy,* (ed.) I. Diamond (New York: Longman, Green, 1983), pp. 70-93; C. Brown, "Mothers, Fathers and Children: From Private to Public Patriachy, " in *Women and Revolution,* (ed.), L. Sargent (Boston: South End Press, 1980), pp. 239-67.

    See also Z. Eisenstein, The Radical Future of Liberal Feminism (New York: Longman, Green, 1981); Z. Eisenstein, "The State, the Patriachal Family and Working Mothers," in *Families, Politics and Public Policy,* (ed.), I. Daimond (New York, Longman, Green, 1983), pp. 41-58; M. McIntosh, "The State and the Oppression of Women" in *Feminism and Materialism,* (ed.), A. Kuhn and A. Wolpe (London: Routledge and Kegan Paul, 1978), pp. 254-89; J.G. Schirmer, *The Limits of Reform: Women, Capital and Welfare* (Cambridge, MA: Schenkman Publishing Co., 1982).

    Happily, however, some of the most recent work has begun to explore the political and ideological resources yielded by women in and through the welfare state. See, for example, L. Balbo, "Crazy Guilts: Rethinking the Welfare State Debate from a Woman's Perspective" (paper, 1981); and Balbo, Untitled (paper presented at the conference "The Transformation of the Welfare State: Dangers and Potentialities for Women," Bellagio, Italy, August 1983).

    See also A. Brochorst and B. Siim, "The Danish Welfare State: A Case for a Strong Social Patriachy; D. Dahlerup, "Feminism and the State: An Essay with a Scandinavian Perspective"; Y. Ergas, "The Disintegrative Revolution: Welfare Politics and Emergent Collective Identities"; H.M. Hernes, "Women and the Welfare State: The Transition from Private to

Public Dependence"; and J.G. Schirmer, "Cut Off at the Impasse: Women and the Welfare State in Denmark" (paper presented at the conference "The Transformation of the Welfare State: Dangers and Potentialities for Women," Bellagio, Italy, August 1983). See also A. S. Rossi, "Beyond the Gender Gap: Women's Bid for Political Power, *Social Science Quarterly* 64 (1983) pp. 718-33.

2. J.B. Elshtain, "Feminism, Family and Community," *Dissent*, Fall 1982, pp. 442-50; and J.B. Elshtain, "Antigone's Daughters: Reflections on Female Identity and the State," in *Families, Politics,and Public Policy*, (ed.), I. Diamond (New York, Longman, Green, 1983) pp. 298—309.

3. Attitudes towards defense spending accounted for a good part of the difference between male and female preferences in the 1980 election. This pattern persisted into 1982, when 40 percent of men favored increased defense spending but only 25 percent of the women did. However, by 1982 women had come to place concerns about defense second to their concerns about the economy. See A.H. Miller and O. Malanchuk, "The Gender Gap in the 1982 elections" and M. Schlichting and P. Tuckel, "Beyond the Gender Gap: Working Women and the 1982 Election (papers presented to the 38th Annual Conference of the American Association of Public Opinion Research, Buck Hills Falls, PA, May 19-22, 1983. for an examination of differences in the attitudes of married and unmarried, and employed and unemployed women; they conclude that the gender gap holds regardless of marital or labor-force status.

4. A.S. Rossi in "Beyond the Gender Gap" reviews studies that show the beginning of a gender gap as early as the 1950s. However, exit poll data after the 1980 election revealed an unprecedented 9 percent spread in the voting choices of men and women. In subsequent polls, the spread substantially widened to a 15 percent difference between men and women in response to the question of whether Ronald Reagan deserved re-election asked in a *New York Times* poll reported in December 1983. Moreover, while male ratings of the president rose with the upturn in economic indicators and the invasion of Grenada, the unfavorable ratings by women remained virtually unchanged.

5. Attitudes about the reproductive and legal rights of women, which have been the central issues of the movement, do not differentiate male and female respondents in the surveys. Single women, however, are much more likely than men to support the women's rights issues.

6. B. Ehrenreich, *The Hearts of Men* (New York, Anchor Books, 1983).

7. Where only 4 percent of the nation's lawyers and judges were women in 1971, women accounted for 14 percent in 1981. In the same period, the percentage of physicians who are women rose form 9 to 22, and the percentage of female engineers increased from 1 to 4.

8. L. Peattie and M. Rein, "Women's Claims: A Study in Political Economy"

(paper, 1981); and E. Rothschild, "Reagan and the Real America," *New York Review of Books*, 5 February 1981, p. 28.

9. See Peattie and Rein, "Women's Claims" for a review of data on women's participation in the labor force that shows the persistence of part-time and irregular employment as well as the concentration of women in low-paid jobs.

10. More than one-third of female-headed families, or 3.3 million, received Aid to Families with Dependent Children in 1979 (Census Bureau). An almost equal number received Medicaid, and 2.6 million were enrolled in the Food Stamp program. See S. P. Erie, M.Rein, M. and B. Wiget, "Women and the Reagan Revolution: Thermidor for the Social Welfare Economy, " in *Families, Politics, and Public Policy*, (ed.), I. Diamond (New York, Longman, Green, 1983) pp. 94-123.

11. *Ibid.*

12. Boris and Bardaglio, "The Transformation of Patriarchy," p. 75.

13. F.F. Piven and R.A. Cloward, *The New Class War: Reagan's Attack on the Welfare State and Its Consequences* (New York: Pantheon, 1982).

14. E. R. Tufte, *Political Control of the Economy* (Princeton, N.J.: Princeton University Press, 1978). See W.D. Burnham, "The 1980 Earthquake: Realignment, Reaction, or What?" in *The Hidden Election: Politics and Economics in the 1980 Presidential Campaign*, (ed.), T. Ferguson and J. Rogers (New York: Pantheon, 1981), pp. 98-140, for an excellent discussion of the issues that determined the outcome of the 1980 election. Burnham concludes that worry over unemployment was the critical issue leading voters who had supported Carter in 1978 to defect to Reagan in 1980.

15. F. F. Piven, and R.. A. Cloward, *Regulating the Poor: The Functions of Public Welfare* (New York, Pantheon, 1971); and F. F. Piven and R.A. Cloward, *Poor People's Movements: Why They Succeed, How They Fail* (New York: Pantheon, 1977).

16. J. Jenson, "'Success' Without Struggle? The Modern Women's Movement in France" (paper presented to a workshop at Cornell University, "The Women's Movement in Comparative Perspective: Resource Mobilization, Cycles of Protest, and Movement Success," May 6-8, 1983).

17. D. Hayden, *The Grand Domestic Revolution* (Cambridge, Mass.: The MIT Press, 1981), pp. 4-5.

18. A.S. Rossi in a 1982 analysis of the first National Women's Conference at Houston in 1977, reports that 72 percent of the delegates were employed either by government or by nonprofit social welfare organizations. See also Rossi, "Beyond the Gender Gap," for a discussion of "insider-outsider" coalitions made possible by government employment.

WE DON'T ALL AGREE THAT WELFARE HAS FAILED

*Ann Withorn**

ONE OF THE MOST CONFUSING EVOLUTIONS OF CONTEMPORARY welfare politics began around the time when Congress passed the Family Support Act in 1988 with bipartisan support. Mainstream politicians, writers, and policymakers created the great lie that, even though there are differences over what exactly to do next, still today:

- Everyone agrees that welfare, as we know it, has failed.

- All responsible (intelligent) people agree that welfare must end and be replaced with a program more in harmony with the "basic values of the American people."

The most clear example of this problem occurred during the Contract with America's Welfare Reform debate in March 1995. For once, many House Democrats rose up and protested long and hard about the need to retain a federal commitment to income maintenance, and against the cruelty of the Republican proposals. The next day, President Clinton chided House Democrats for being "too partisan." "After all, we all agree that welfare has failed," he intoned unctuously. "Let's tone down the rhetoric" (*Boston Globe*, 25 March 1995).

However, in the mid-1980s, Massachusetts welfare officials had made public speeches that agreed with welfare rights activists that the system was punitive and demeaning. When I make speeches, people consistently began their remarks with "We all agree...." I try to present a view that grapples with the complexities of the issue.

---

* The handouts that follow are ones that I give out before I speak. They are a quick summary of how different the arguments that "welfare has failed" are for welfare activists and for opponents of real reform. I also use the handouts to answer the question: "So what do we really agree on?

WHAT'S WRONG WITH WELFARE AS WE KNEW IT— EVEN BEFORE "WELFARE REFORM"

Here is the welfare rights perspective that builds on the arguments of the National Welfare Rights Organization, the National Welfare Rights Union, and local welfare rights organizations and activists in various places:

1. THE WELFARE SYSTEM FAILS TO RESPECT THE STRUCTURAL PROBLEMS WOMEN FACE IN TRYING TO FORM TWO-PARENT FAMI-LIES WITH MEN—when the men leave, or force the women to leave, women are often in situations where what they most need is time to heal themselves and care for their children. Women don't have to stay with men when the relationship hurts them, physically or otherwise. Taking care of children is a legitimate role, and mothers must feel able to choose it first, before they can make other choices. *Men as we know them fail single mothers.*

2. THE WELFARE SYSTEM FAILS TO ADMIT TO THE STRUCTURAL PROBLEMS WOMEN FACE IN THE WORKPLACE, ESPECIALLY IF THEY LACK EDUCATION AND ARE SINGLE PARENTS. Few jobs are available, and many of those that are available are not affordable (women can't afford the wages, inflexible time, lack of health and childcare). It is understandable that many single mothers cannot be employed, especially full-time and without wage subsidies. *Jobs as we know them fail single mothers.*

3. THE WELFARE SYSTEM FAILS TO PROTECT RIGHTS, as we see them, under the constitutional mandate to "promote the general welfare," and out of the logic of the Social Security Act, the federal government has an obligation to provide support so that children and families can have a minimal level of security, regardless of employment status, because abject poverty hurts all. In other words, some kind of welfare is a *right* that is not being well guarded by the government. *Women have a right to choose welfare if it makes the best sense for their families.*

4. WELFARE COSTS TOO LITTLE. AFDC GRANTS ARE SO LOW that they do not allow families any stability to plan how to get on with their lives when men and jobs fail them. At 60 percent of poverty level or less, a family is always behind on rent, can't travel, must borrow and is generally destabilized. This forces women to find additional resources somewhere,

so that *a woman on welfare must always be on edge out of fear that what they need to do to keep their families going will be labeled "fraud."*

5. THE WELFARE BUREAUCRACY CREATES CONSTANT STRESS by forcing women to constantly prove and reprove their situation, and by questioning their abilities as parents. Workers in the system often treat women badly. This stress further destabilizes family. A major reason this can happen is that the system is not democratic; it gives recipients no say in setting policies that affect their lives. *"Clients" are disempowered and disrespected.*

6. IT'S HARD FOR TWO-PARENT FAMILIES TO USE THE SYSTEM. The difficulty with getting on and off welfare, if another adult joins the family (either the father or a potentially helpful partner), becomes so bureaucratically crazy-making that mothers are afraid to tell the truth about their lives. This stress creates another source of destabilization and denial.

7. IT'S DIFFICULT TO COMBINE WORK WITH EXTRA SUPPORT. It is almost impossible to take either a part-time job or a low-wage "mother's hours" job, such as in the field of childcare, if you want to. Loss of benefits or fear of losing benefits makes it not worth seeking jobs that are really available.

8. AFDC DIVIDES WELFARE FAMILIES FROM EMPLOYED FAMILIES in ways that foster hostility: If transitional health or childcare benefits are available, they are not available to those working at low wages. Food stamps are harder for those with low wages to obtain. What few wage subsidies exist for welfare recipients are not available for all workers.

9. NOT ENOUGH TIME IS ALLOTTED FOR TRAINING AND EDUCATION PROGRAMS that are needed to reflect and respond to women's real abilities and desires. *Hope for the future is quenched.*

10. SOCIETAL STIGMA associated with getting what one needs to take care of one's family is intense and damaging to women and children. It has always been there, is deeply imbedded with racist stereotypes, and does severe damage to recipients and to those who need help but are too fearful of the stigma to apply.

WHAT'S REALLY NEEDED: A LOW-INCOME FAMILY SECURITY SYSTEM

A welfare rights-based proposal would look something like this:

1. FEDERAL GOVERNMENT WOULD HAVE THE MAJOR ROLE, as the source of basic income for poor families. The mandates of the Social Security Act, built upon the General Welfare clause in the Constitution, should be expanded, not diminished. Still, the welfare system will only be embraced when the current two-tier system is ended and replaced with a guaranteed income floor for all. *Recipients need a mandated role in setting policy and overseeing practice.*

2. ALL FAMILIES WITH CHILDREN EARNING LESS IN TOTAL THAN THE POVERTY LEVEL FOR FULL- OR PART-TIME WORK WOULD RECEIVE A FEDERAL INCOME SUBSIDY to bring them up to the poverty level or, if not employed at all, would receive the basic family allowance at some percentage of poverty level. Or as an alternative, all individuals, including children, would receive a basic income subsidy, which would be paid back in taxes as people earned money from wage work.

3. ALL FAMILIES WOULD RECEIVE CHILDCARE AND HEALTH CARE support until they are earning up to 150 percent of the poverty level or higher with demonstrated special needs. Or childcare and health care provided free to all, with families paying a sliding scale after earning certain levels of income. Education and training would be available for all.

4. A HIGHER MINIMUM WAGE AND FULL EMPLOYMENT should be guaranteed, with public or private sector jobs available for all seeking them.

5. CHILD SUPPORT SHOULD BE A RIGHT FOR ALL, not just for women on welfare; jobs and training must be available for fathers too.

6. SOCIAL SUPPORTS SHOULD BE AVAILABLE for treating substance abuse, stress, counseling, etc. These services would not be punitive, but allowed for all.

7. ALL PEOPLE DESERVE RESPECT, especially parents and children. Society needs to recognize that poverty is rooted in structural problems; individuals are not to blame, they often need support and assistance to get their lives together. Single parenting in poverty is the hardest work of society and should be recognized and appreciated.

WHAT'S WRONG WITH WELFARE, AS THE "WELFARE REFORMERS" KNOW IT

This is a summary of views of those who are politicians, academics, and policy types who see welfare as bad and having created many social problems. They cross the gamut from far Right politicians and writers, such as Newt Gingrich, Charles Murray, Marvin Olasky, or Lawrence Mead, to neoliberals like Bill Clinton and David Ellwood. All such critics draw on a long history of opposing income maintenance, which they see as either outdated or fundamentally wrongheaded.

1. AFDC IS BASED ON A BAD PRINCIPLE. For some who now oppose welfare, the very principle of a federal obligation to provide income maintenance is denied. They view federal aid as only emergencies, only temporary and only for children, not for their parents. This view is old, and has always been in the culture but has not been articulated for a very long time. For these folks—members of the John Birch Society, old anti-welfare people, the historically strong conservatives—it is a knee-jerk reaction to oppose welfare. Other critics such as Bill Clinton, Daniel Patrick Moynihan, and others, don't exactly deny the right; they just say that what we have been doing doesn't work, it degrades people, it promotes single parenthood, and it doesn't help women move on with their lives.

2. WELFARE GRANTS INEVITABLY HURT PEOPLE BY MAKING THEM DEPENDENT. This has been an increasingly widespread view since the mid-80s. Believers of this view hold that welfare programs hurt and weaken people who receive them because they give them an alternative to "independence," to supporting their families with wages that are always available if a family is willing to make hard choices. The economy has not failed single mothers; there are jobs; it's just that welfare makes people think they don't have to take them.

People must be taken off the welfare rolls, or forced into job programs—a dispute among the Right—and made to assume that there is no ongoing floor under unemployment insurance, that everyone has to be employed.

3. MOTHERHOOD IS NOT ENOUGH; parenting cannot be supported as an economic category of socially valued work. It must always be

combined with employment, unless the father is willing to pay for it by sharing his wages through child support.

Welfare encourages marriage break-up or lack of marriage by giving women alternatives. There are men to be with; women and men just have to take responsibilities for their children. Men are essential to a healthy family and are discouraged from being there by welfare. Paternity must be established and child support enforced.

No one should be able to expect public assistance for her child; it removes her from the job market and isolates her, and it saps her energy and keeps her from bettering herself. Especially if she is already on welfare, the expectation of support for additional children is not healthy.

4. SELF-DESTRUCTIVE BEHAVIOR HAS BEEN NURTURED AND FOSTERED BY AFDC—promiscuity, drug abuse, and lack of attention to the education of kids are caused by lack of employment and lack of a man in the home.

5. WELFARE SHOULD NO LONGER BE A CHOICE. Women always have other options, but they choose to be on welfare rather than work or stay married. Single motherhood and unemployment should not be rewarded nor should welfare really be available any longer now that women are expected to work.

6. NON-CITIZENS CAN PARTICIPATE. People who come to this country are admitted assuming they can support themselves. Their use of AFDC violates their terms of entry and promotes the wrong values.

7. WELFARE BUREAUCRATS have both coddled and abused recipients, which will naturally happen once a dependent relationship is established.

8. WELFARE COSTS TOO MUCH even though it is only 2% of federal budget, it still does not invest in the productive sector. So, any penny spent on welfare is a penny wasted.

9. RACISM IS NO LONGER A PROBLEM, so we don't have to consider how it affects chances or how we view women on welfare.

10. WELFARE HAS NO POLITICAL BASE OF SUPPORT and hurts other government efforts because it goes against "core values" that expect employment, traditional families, and sexual "responsibility" from everyone.

WHAT'S REALLY NEEDED: AN END TO WELFARE, AT LEAST, AND SUPPORT FOR EMPLOYMENT, AT MOST

1. ALL THAT SHOULD BE PROVIDED IS "TRANSITIONAL ASSISTANCE, with time limits (2 to 5 years), required work programs, and education only at the most basic levels. The goal is to prevent dependence by never raising expectations. The biggest agreement is on this:

* Most proposals will allow childcare, health care and even some subsidies to employers for hiring welfare recipients.
* Some proposals say no money, only vouchers and subsidies, with tight control.

2. THE NEW TRANSITIONAL PROGRAMS MUST REQUIRE PUNISH-MENTS and controls over the most destructive behaviors—teenage mothers must be at home, or in group settings with no money; family caps should be in place so that there is no reward for continued "breaking of the rules," also learnfare and shot fare, fingerprinting and identification cards. Sometimes, unmarried minors are denied benefits entirely, except for Medicaid.

3. THERE WILL BE AN END TO FEDERAL COMMITMENT. States will be given block grants with only punitive limits. There will be no guarantee of fair hearings, consistent standards, or even a mandate that states participate.

4. "WORKING POVERTY" IS ACCEPTABLE, but welfare poverty is not, and people who break this rule must be punished for the good of the social order.

5. NON-CITIZENS SHOULD NOT RECEIVE ANY ASSISTANCE. If they wish to come here, that may be O.K., but they must do it like other immigrants did, on their own, expecting no assistance.

WE'RE ALL WORKERS
Why Can't We Talk?
Diane Dujon

I HAVE WORKED ALL OF MY LIFE. SOMETIMES I GET PAID WHAT I'm worth, and sometimes I don't.But it's all hard work and I immerse myself totally—there is no detail that is beneath me. In fact, I am very obsessive about any work I do—to the point of jumping awake at night over some minor detail or unresolved problem. If my name or reputation is connected, I want whatever I do to be the best that I can muster. If I don't do well, I'll take the criticism and consequences; but I'll know it was the absolute best I could do. So, I recognize what work is.

Most work is not compensated for because it's not part of the labor market—but it is work! In fact, the poorer you are, the harder you work at everything (and the more you jump awake at night).

As a worker, I realize that it is work just to live! Whether I am in or out of the workplace, I know I am a member of the working class. Except for very few people who are independently wealthy and live off the interest their money earns, we are all dependent on outside resources to survive, whether it's a job or public assistance of some form. I get very dismayed when I hear one group of workers (those who are employed) criticize another group of workers (those who are unemployed) for the choices they make. They do not realize that they are all in the same boat. By not aligning themselves with the unemployed, employed workers have divided themselves from other workers. Don't they understand that sometimes it is your boss who decides that tomorrow you will apply for welfare? Whether we have jobs or not, we still need to eat, pay rent, and clothe our children.

When I first re-entered the workforce, the realization that we are all engaged in the same struggle became increasingly clear to me. The need to clarify it for others became one of my chief missions in life.

At first, annual salary increases were common and I was able to establish some credit and pay off some of my utility bills which had mounted while I was on welfare. For a little while, I thought I was finally going to be successful in climbing out of poverty.

Then, suddenly the raises stopped coming! For five years my salary remained fixed while all of my expenses increased. The state was cutting back and laying off workers at all levels. This resulted in all of us working harder and longer hours. I was thrown back into the insecurity I had known when I was on welfare.

I watched many of my colleagues who would not have related to me or my situation while I was on welfare, get scared. "What about my mortgage?" "I thought I had a good job and I never planned on doing anything else. This is my career!" "But my kids' education depends on this job, it's one of my benefits!" Recognizing that we were the only non-unionized (and, therefore, the most vulnerable) sector of the workforce on the campus, members of the professional staff organized a committee to investigate the possibility of joining a union. After two unsuccessful attempts, we unionized and I became an elected member of the Negotiation Team, which worked for 18 months to establish an initial contract would provide some measure of protection. What an experience! Public sector bargaining is supposed to be easier, and I do believe that's basically true, but I was astounded at the feelings of déjà vu that overtook me several times as we struggled to negotiate a reasonable contract with management. In some respects, management's attitude was similar to welfare policymakers' attitudes: "They're trying to get over on us," or "They're asking for too much!," or "That's a privilege only for the faculty (worthy)!" But we persevered and managed to elicit a surprisingly good contract, considering labor relations in the 90s.

My experiences in welfare rights organizing converted over to labor organizing very easily. I subsequently ran for and was elected to the decisionmaking committee for our chapter. I experienced the familiar exhilaration that comes with fighting the forces that seek to exploit. For me, many of the issues were similar to those I had advocated for when I was on welfare: universal fairness and inclusion of the disenfranchised in the decisionmaking process.

Both of my parents had been union members and constantly educated my sister and me about the struggles that workers had waged during the Labor Movement when they were young. As

African Americans, they were profoundly proud of the contributions of Asa Philip Randolph of the Brotherhood of Sleeping Care Porters, who became a vice-president of the AFL-CIO. They were, however, no less impressed with the valiant John Lewis of the Coal Miners' Union.

The Great Depression served to educate the suddenly unemployed working class to the fact that people are impoverished by outside forces that impact their lives. This universal understanding fostered a change in the debate, away from blaming and reforming the victim to thinking about how to change the structures of our society.

During the 1930s, the labor movement recognized that the bosses were the "enemy." To keep the bosses from being sovereign over their lives, workers organized into labor unions which fought for the eight-hour day, 40-hour week, sick time, vacation time, holidays, coffee breaks, and weekends off. These workers understood that all workers were vulnerable. They knew that employers exploited them by underpaying them and making them desperate. To promote their cause, these workers utilized the only weapon they had—they withheld their labor. They planned and executed various job actions, rallies, work slow-downs, sit-ins, and strikes. The bosses retaliated by instituting close-outs, firing discontented workers, and hiring armed guards and the police to enforce their authority. But the workers knew that desperate, unemployed workers could be used as scabs by employers whenever labor staged a work action.

When President Franklin Roosevelt ushered in the New Deal, he provided government support to the working class. Workers also advocated for the provision of a minimal level of benefits to the unemployed to reduce their vulnerability, which could be exploited by the bosses. Today, however, this feeling of solidarity between those in the workforce and those who are unemployed has evaporated.

When unions were strong, they continued to fight for better working conditions, increased benefits, and political power. However, little effort was spent to continue educating their membership on labor history, which could have strengthened the relationship between the employed and the unemployed.

In fact, some of the most vociferous opponents of the welfare state are low-wage workers. Even workers who belong to unions resent public assistance recipients. These glaring contradictions often put workers in extremely ironic situations. In recent years, unionized utility workers have staged strikes to protect their health benefits. Often management employs delaying tactics in an effort to weigh the workers down. Suddenly, these workers find themselves fighting to receive unemployment benefits to sustain them through the strike. Yet, somehow they never seem to realize that they themselves need the basic safety net that they so loudly condemn!

I hear workers denounce welfare recipients because of the few who commit fraud, mistreat their children, or abuse alcohol or drugs; yet, they defend union members who are often not the best workers. They seem to understand that if management can oppress those with substandard work habits, all workers are at risk. The same principle applies to welfare recipients. We must ensure that all people who need help are eligible to receive assistance, even if they are struggling with other problems.

Too many workers today are facing layoffs due to downsizing in the private sector and privatizing in the public sector. It does not matter how hard, how well, or how long they have worked; they are expendable. Although they have often given the best years of their lives to the company, there is little mutual sense of loyalty. As baby boomers reach age 50, they are increasingly finding themselves without jobs and with little hope of ever being employed with a similar feeling of security again. Many are told by prospective employers that they are too qualified or that their salary expectations are too high.

Some of these former workers engage in denial. After extensive, unsuccessful job searches, these workers have exhausted their unemployment benefits and depleted their savings and retirement plans, but they refuse to recognize that they are unemployed and opt to designate themselves as "self-employed." However, they find themselves working fewer hours with no benefits and little to show for their efforts except their newly printed business cards.

As workers, we all need to be concerned about the future. The battles our fore-parents fought so hard for and thought they won are being eroded. Company retirement plans were designed to be used *after* age 65 to augment the meager Social Security benefits that alone cannot sustain us, but many of today's workers are spending their retirement savings *before* they are even eligible for Social Security.

We need to be able to count on each other when all else fails—that's what a society is for. No one should have to rely on Divine Intervention for the basic necessities of life. By becoming educated about the issues and involved in the political processes, we can challenge the congressional and legislative *Ways to be Mean* Committees all across the nation that are enacting laws that will lower the standard of living for all of us.

As one who has lived on both sides of the paid labor force, I am determined to bridge the gap that exists between the two sides. As a member of both the National Welfare Rights Union and the Service Employees International Union, I am in the unique position of being able to *link up the struggles,* which is the motto of welfare rights!

WELFARE: THE BASEMENT OF THE WAGE SCALE
*Sandy Felder**

WE NEED TO ACKNOWLEDGE THAT THERE HAVE BEEN SOME conflicting values between welfare rights activists and paid workers over the question of work outside of the home. Union members and workers in general have pride in the fact that they work. Work by itself has value to them and to our work-oriented society. People are valued by the kind of work they do, and the importance of work is a basic premise of our society. Welfare rights activists have believed that society should support a woman's right to stay at home and raise her children and not require her to work outside of the home.

By itself, raising children should be considered a full-time job and should be valued and paid; however, this view does not hold with union members in general. There are a lot of workers— women workers—who raise children and work full-time jobs outside of the house. So when you talk to workers with families, you need to appreciate that they are saying, "I have children; I work; it's hard, but I manage." There is not a lot of sympathy for the argument that says welfare recipients should not have to work.

Instead, we need to remind workers about why welfare exists, and that in the long run, it is there for them in case they need it too. Unions have fought for good jobs, and when those jobs are lost, unions have fought for unemployment benefits to protect the laid-off worker. Welfare is the safety net when unemployment runs out.

So, understanding that workers feel proud that they work against all odds; that they are glad to have unemployment as an insurance in case they lose their jobs, workers need also to be helped to realize

---

* This piece was compiled from an interview conducted by Diane Dujon.

that welfare is an insurance when their jobs and unemployment dry up. However, the ultimate goal is that everyone should work.

The challenge is how to create a society where people can work and also care for their children. How can we create well-paid jobs, and also have health care and daycare? That is what unions fight for. Another reason to support welfare is to view it in economic terms for workers. We need to help workers understand that the welfare check is the basement of the wage scale. We need to think of the lowest wage in society—not being the minimum wage—but as being the welfare check. If we raise the welfare benefits, it allows for an increase in the minimum wage and ultimately the unionized wage. When we as workers allow welfare benefits to be cut, we are actually undermining our own wage base and our own standard of living. How low do we dig our basement? How low do we let the minimum wage stay? How low will we allow our own wages to stay?

We need to help workers see how welfare improves their interests in the long run. We need to talk to workers about their own stake in welfare's survival. I don't think we do it by simply gaining sympathy for the welfare recipient. We need to make the welfare recipients' interests workers' interests. In Massachusetts, Service Employees International Union (SEIU) Local 509 has been working within our own union, with the unions in the Massachusetts AFL-CIO, and on a national level to educate union members on these issues.

Another way that as a union we can help is to not only fight to protect welfare, but also to fight to create decent-paying jobs for all workers. The Mass. AFL-CIO has been leading a fight to increase the minimum wage. So far, so good. As of this interview, the state legislature has passed a dollar increase, raising the minimum wage to $5.25.

Welfare as a Gender Issue in Unions

Women are entering the workforce in increasing numbers. They are the "new" workforce. They also are still (for the most part) unorganized, but they are joining unions in higher numbers than men. However, the leaders of today's unions are overwhelmingly white men.

The majority of people that live in poverty in this country are women and children. Poverty has become defined as a women's issue. A gender gap exists within the labor movement. Issues like poverty, childcare, pay equity, and family and medical leave have been defined as women's issues. It's been the women coming into the labor movement who have been the voices on these issues.

There are some male union leaders who get it. Clearly, John Sweeney, formerly president of our national union, SEIU, understood these issues and made welfare reform an issue of our union at the national level. Part of his sensitivity to this was due to the fact that almost half of the members of SEIU are women and 30 percent are people of color. SEIU represents, and aggressively organizes, low-wage service workers.

I believe that welfare is not only a gender issue, but it is broader than that. The powers that be portray welfare recipients as the people who are stealing all the wealth of this nation and believe that our economy is shot because of these women who are abusing our tax dollars, despite the fact that welfare spending is less than 2 percent of the federal budget. There is no one powerful voice speaking about all the tax breaks that corporations and the wealthy are getting. It's really about keeping the rich, rich and everyone else struggling to get by. It's about social class and politics as well as being a gender issue. It's about who makes the laws, who controls the wealth in this country and keeping it that way.

What Union Members Think About Welfare

The middle class has been adversely impacted because of government service cutbacks and corporate tax give-aways. Yet, they have bought the line that their problems and loss of economic status are because of welfare recipients. They don't realize that it is the top 10 percent who own 90 percent of the wealth in this country, not welfare recipients. Union members are buying the right-wing rhetoric in this country. They are supporting the Newt Gingriches, Ross Perots, and the Christian Coalition.

In many ways, unions have lost the hearts of our members on the welfare question. Unions have not been able to speak to members in a way that helps them to define their real interests. However, because of the sweeping defeats in electing to office pro-labor candidates, organized labor leaders are realizing they have lost the hearts and minds of too many union members. They are beginning to rethink how to outreach to their members to educate them in a way that speaks to their interests. There are many workers today who have been laid off from their jobs, who never thought it could happen to them. But on a massive scale, we are not reaching American workers.

One of the major criticisms of the AFL-CIO has been its inability to speak effectively to, and on behalf of, today's workers. For the first time in history there was a challenge to the presidency of the AFL-CIO on these very questions. Newly-elected president John Sweeney was the leader in this effort.

Privatization and It's Impact on the Living Standard of Workers

Privatization—the public-sector equivalent to private-sector contracting out—has resulted in a deunionization of workers. In private industry, unionized companies, in order to get out from unionized wages and benefits, have turned to sub-contracting to nonunion companies work that was formerly performed by unionized workers. Privatization and contracting out are ways to undermine wage standards and avoid unions.

The public sector (government workers) has a much higher unionization rate than the private sector. Because of this, they enjoy decent wages, benefits, and job protections. Privatization has meant that workers lose their union and suffer a decline in their standard of living.

In Massachusetts, thousands of workers have lost their state jobs to privatization. In many cases, these same workers were offered their exact job back; but instead of working for the state, they were to be employed by a private corporation. In reality, it meant that they went to the same workplace, did the same work, but took home 30 percent less in wages and benefits and lost their union representation.

For the workers left behind in government jobs, bargaining with management has become much more difficult because the lower-wage private workforce makes it harder to hold on to and improve the economic conditions of the unionized workforce. In addition, public-sector workers are frightened of losing their jobs to privatization and are threatened regularly by their employers. SEIU Local 509 believes that it is in the interest of our existing membership to raise the standard of living for those publicly funded private-sector workers. In doing so, we raise the standard for our own members—a rising tide lifts all boats.

Our local union is undertaking an enormous effort, in partnership with our national union, to bring a union to thousands of publicly funded private-sector mental health and mental retardation workers in Massachusetts. We have rethought our view of public service and have moved from thinking that public sector means only work performed by government employees. We believe that the public workforce includes all workers funded by public dollars. We are moving to organize these workers. We are simply following our work!

Organizing this workforce is much harder than organizing traditional public-sector workers. One reason is that the wages of the privatized workers are so low that many are working two or three jobs. When we go to their homes on a house call, they are usually not at home and are at some other job. It is very difficult to find the workers. In addition, the turnover rate in these agencies averages about 66 percent per year, so it's hard to hold on to workers once they sign up. Their commitment to building a union is lessened because they don't see their work as a career as a lot of union members do. Private-sector labor laws are much stickier, as well. Fewer classifications of workers are allowed to join unions.

There is a lot of fear among unorganized workers about loss of their jobs if they engage in a union drive. One out of four workers leading a unionization drive at the workplace today end up losing their jobs for their efforts. Despite the illegality of this, by the time the court procedure is completed (anywhere from two to three years), the penalty to the employer is a slap on the hand and an order to hire the worker back with lost wages. If the worker has gotten another job, those wages are deducted from the total. Maybe it cost an employer a few thousand dollars to bring the worker back, but that's a pretty cheap price when an employer wants to beat a union. If you fire the worker, in essence you could kill the drive because few workers can afford to lose their jobs for the sake of a union. So, it's pretty cheap and has been a strategy of many bosses over time.

In the late 1950s, 37 percent of workers belonged to labor unions. Our economy was at an all-time high, and real wages for workers and their families, for the most part, were at a peak. Since that time, the real income for families has steadily declined. We have more families working multiple jobs. The value of the dollar, compared to the mid-'50s, has seriously declined. Today, only 16 percent of the workforce in the United States belongs to labor unions. The more workers don't have unions, the more the standard of living of those workers goes down, which ultimately leads to an increase of poverty in our country. Unless we organize at an unprecedented pace, workers will be falling faster and faster to the basement.

What Welfare Workers Can Do

As funding is cut from human service programs, welfare workers are being made to handle more and more cases. They are also put in the position of being the bad guy when it comes to denying benefits to people, by implementing policies that they did not create. The combination of these factors has led to demoralization and anger among welfare workers. Sometimes this gets acted out negatively on the recipients. I also think that a lot of problems for welfare workers come from the training they receive in their agency. They get trained to be paper bureaucrats and not social workers anymore.

Welfare workers, through their union, need to fight to reduce caseloads so that they actually have time to help people who come to them. They must fight for the right to do social work instead of clerical work. They should fight to ensure a level of services that allows people to get out of poverty and stay out.

The welfare worker's job should be not only to figure out how much money you have or don't have, or to determine whether you are eligible or ineligible for benefits. It should also involve helping you figure out a life plan and helping you to achieve it.

Welfare workers, and for that matter all workers, need to understand that workfare jobs are jobs that used to be fair-waged and -benefited jobs. Workfare erodes minimum-wage and higher-waged jobs by taking full-waged jobs out of the labor market. It threatens all workers. Often, workfare jobs are jobs for which the company previously hired fully waged workers. What company wouldn't want to get free labor? In Massachusetts, companies can pay $1 an hour while the state pays the rest in welfare benefits to get a workfare recipient for nine months. Although this is supposed to be time-limited, our concern is that they will not hire the worker into a real paid job and will just keep rotating nine-month workfare clients through the system. This reduces the number of real waged jobs overall. The Mass. AFL-CIO has gotten legislation passed to create a commission to oversee businesses and their commitment to hiring workfare recipients. We want to know how many companies are actually hiring workfare recipients into real jobs at real wages after the nine months.

I'm not optimistic that they are really going to hire those people; if they were, they could have done it already!

The Future for Poor People and Workers

I think the fight right now within the AFL-CIO, regarding who is going to lead the labor movement, is extremely important to the future of workers in this country. It's a battle over a change from business unionism, about organizing on a scale that has not been seen since the Thirties. It's about being much more militant and aggressive in fighting for workers rights, about being more politically active at a grassroots level.

When I reflect back on the campaigns and organizing efforts of the SEIU, we have a proud history of organizing low-waged workers. We represent janitors, nurses aides, and home-care workers, who are often, as a workforce, one step away from a welfare check themselves. We represent immigrant workers and undocumented workers. And we use aggressive tactics to win recognition for them. Our Justice for Janitors Campaign has used civil disobedience and international corporate campaigns to organize thousands of workers. Organizing the low-waged workforce, the service sector, is really important for the future. Raising the floor of the lowest-waged worker raises it for everyone.

Unions have an opportunity now to make a difference. We have a chance to change. The old way of cozying up to the politicians has not built power for working people. It has taken a while for those in the leadership of unions to realize this—not all do yet, but there is now a debate that is unprecedented.

Union leaders, at all levels, need to look like the members they represent and the workforce in general. They need to include women and people of color at the top as well as in the ranks. That is critical for the future of working people. For the first time in the history of the labor movement, there is a woman in the second highest position of the AFL-CIO. It's a start and a response to a recognition of the need for change.

Despite all the losses and turmoil, many of us are optimistic that if we begin to organize workers on a massive scale and if we begin to raise the kind of political consciousness that moves workers to action, then we can turn things around. I think workers and their unions are the people to do it.

WOMEN AND PUBLIC EMPLOYMENT PROGRAMS
What Has Worked, What Has Not, and What is Needed
Nancy Rose

DEBATES ABOUT WELFARE REFORM OVER THE PAST TWO DECADES have focused on putting poor women to work. Arguing that recipients have become "welfare dependent," politicians claim that they need to become "independent" by working for wages. Democrats have generally suggested a combination of "carrots" and "sticks"—some funds for childcare subsidies, education, and training, in addition to work requirements. Clinton's proposal of "two years and off" is the most severe of these work requirements, intended to put into practice his pledge to "end welfare as we know it." Republicans have skipped the "carrots" altogether, as their two-year maximum on AFDC would have few exemptions. Women would be forced to become "independent" and work—or they could get married.

But what jobs will be available? Years of plant closings, downsizing, and streamlining have eliminated millions of higher-wage jobs—both blue-collar in industries such as steel and autos, and white-collar in middle-management. The majority of jobs that have been created are low-wage, service sector jobs with no health benefits. They offer an unstable foundation for "independence" from working for wages.

This situation should lead to proposals for government job creation—programs similiar to the Works Progress Administration (WPA) in the 1930s and the Comprehensive Employment and Training Act (CETA) in the 1970s. Unlike workfare, these fair work programs were voluntary, based payments on market wages, and developed innovative and useful projects. But instead of recognizing the accomplishments and potential of public employment programs, they are usually seen as inefficient and unnecessary "make-work," and dismissed as failures. These assessments have some merit. However, the assessments followed from regulations that tried to prevent the programs from interfering with an economy based on production-for-profit. And the assessments need to be re-evaluated in this light.

There have been problems with fair work programs. The main one has been their lack of attention to women, as their main focus historically has been white, male heads-of-household. This was clearest during the 1930s, when three-fourths of the participants were white men. By the 1960s, the Civil Rights movement and urban ghetto riots led to an additional focus on African Americans, still predominantly men.

In this chapter, I examine past public employment and related education and training programs, including brief descriptions of the programs, how women have fared in them, and how criticisms followed from contradictory regulations. The conclusion outlines a public employment program and related policies that would be fundamentally designed for women, and suggests some responses to criticisms that are likely to arise at the mere mention of job creation programs.

A Brief History of Government Work Programs

Fair work programs are fundamentally different from the mandatory workfare programs that have been the norm since the early 1980s.Workfare is intended for people considered "undeserving," while fair work is designed for the "deserving" poor. Workfare is highly stigmatized, forcing poor women to work in order to prove they are not "lazy" and deserve aid, while fair work assumes that people want jobs. (And unpaid caretaking work in the home does not count as real work—unless you take care of someone else's children or do someone else's housework.) Workfare pushes people into low-wage jobs or requires them to "work off" their relief payments, while fair work bases payments on wage rates. Workfare pays little attention to the types of work done, while fair work has created a variety of useful projects. Workfare was historically developed for both women and men, although since the 1930s it has been aimed at women, disproportionately women of color, while fair work has mainly focused on men. And workfare supports the logic of capitalist production-for-profit, channeling welfare recipients into low-wage labor markets where their increased numbers help maintain low wages, while fair work programs expose a basic contradiction of capitalist economic systems: that production based on capitalists' profits rarely corresponds to production based on people's needs. As a result, workfare has been politically popular, widely supported by most of the population, who believe that it forces the poor to work, while fair work has been the target of intense criticisms.

Workfare

Workfare programs began during the 1600s in the northern American colonies. Workhouses, poor houses, and poor farms were established to make sure that the poor were not "lazy," and deserved to receive relief. Much of the work was "make-work"; for example, people were sometimes required to dig ditches and fill them up again or to move stones from one side of a workyard to the other. (It's curious that although job creation programs are often criticized as "make-work" this more accurately reflects workfare programs.) Aid was minimal—usually in-kind relief in the form of food, clothing, coal, and medical care. These "formal" workfare programs continued through the early 1900s, when the almshouses gradually became used as homes for the indigent aged. They were complemented by "informal" methods, as extremely low payments and often no payments at all, especially for people of color, were often used to force the poor into low-wage work.

The early programs were all set up by local governments. Federal programs began in 1962 with some small work and training programs for recipients of AFDC (Aid to Families with Dependent Children, the main form of welfare since the 1930s). They were made permanent in 1967 through the Work Incentive (WIN) program, which included an "income disregard" or "work incentive bonus," as a portion of earned income was not counted (i.e., disregarded) when computing a family's welfare payment. Throughout the '60s and '70s, the WIN program focused on education and training along with work, reflecting the importance in social welfare policy of "rehabilitation" and "human reclamation"—pulling the poor into the mainstream of society. Not surprisingly, during this period WIN focused disproportionately on men in two-parent AFDC families. The 1970s also saw the development of Community Work Experience Programs (CWEPs), in which recipients received no wages but only "worked off" their welfare payments.

Workfare mushroomed during the 1980s. An important component of the conservative attack on labor and the poor, welfare mothers became one of the scapegoats for economic stagnation. The 1981 Reagan administration welfare reform included mandates for states to develop WIN demonstration programs, experimental versions of WIN. These programs—from GAIN (Greater Avenues for Independence) in California to ET (Employment and Training) Choices in Massachusetts—had some helpful components. There was some basic adult education, skills training, and support for college education. In addition, "transitional" support services sometimes provided subsidies for childcare and extended Medicaid coverage for up to a year after women got off the AFDC rolls.

However, the emphasis was on rapid results. The programs stressed quickly getting recipients into the workforce in any job available, while education and training that provided skills which could help people obtain more secure jobs above the poverty line were minimized. (As a result, AFDC recipients attending college in California usually tried to avoid the work program for as long as possible since they would then be told they could remain in college for two years, sometimes extended to three, regardless of how many courses they needed for their degrees.)

These narrow objectives had consequences, however. Many women could not afford to work—after paying for childcare and health care—and went back on AFDC. The fact that many AFDC recipients also work for wages attests to their tenacity. Studies by the Institute for Women's Policy Research found that half of single mothers on AFDC combine AFDC and wage-work, either doing both at the same time, "cycling" between the two, or spending more time looking for work than in employment.

The 1990s have been even more troubling than the 1980s. Time limits on AFDC would force recipients off aid with no supports. They would thus be available for any job at any wage, or pushed into relationships that they would not otherwise choose.

Fair Work

Fair work programs have a very different history. They began in the late 1700s when rioting by unemployed workers led some cities to set up public works projects—for example, building culverts or repairing roads. As usual, protests brought results. Similar projects, meant to provide work for white, male heads-of-household, were developed by local governments during recessions and depressions during the 1800s and through the early 1930s. In addition, workrooms in which people sewed garments and rag rugs were sometimes set up for women and for men who were physically unable to do heavy labor.

The most extensive fair work programs were developed during the Great Depression of the 1930s. They included: the Federal Emergency Relief Administration (FERA), from May 1933 through December 1935, the first federal program for unemployment relief; the Civil Works Administration (CWA), from November 1933 through March 1934, quickly set up to put another two million men to work and to head off increased protest during the first winter of Franklin D. Roosevelt's New Deal; and the Works Progress Administration (WPA), the best-known of all the 1930s work programs, lasting from the fall of 1935 through June 1943, when mobilization for World War II substantially increased production and employment and finally brought the Depression to an end.

A great deal was accomplished in these programs. Between 1.4 and 3.3 million people were put to work each month—and 4.4 million at the height of the CWA in January 1934! Payments were based on wages in the private sector. And innovative and useful projects were developed. People built and repaired a million miles of roads and 200,000 public facilities, including schools, court-houses, parks, and airports. They created works of art, taught adults to read, and set up nursery schools. They sewed 383 million garments (coats, overalls, dresses, etc.) and more than one million mattresses for others on relief, and served over 1.2 billion school lunches to needy children.

The 1930s' programs attained these results in spite of the fact that they were targets of harsh criticisms and serious constraints, constraints that set the programs up to be seen as failures. They were supposed to provide useful work, and create as much work as possible with the allocated funds by using a maximum of labor and a minimum of machinery. At the same time, they were not supposed to replace workers who would normally be employed by the government or compete with the private sector. So, for example, workers on construction projects usually used simple tools, often picks and shovels, instead of grading and paving equipment. This made sense—it created more work. However, it meant that the projects were inefficient when compared to production in the private sector.

It also made sense to require the projects not to replace "normal government workers"—these people should have been hired through normal market channels and paid the going wage. However, this meant that projects were easily seen as unnecessary; it was assumed that the government would already be providing the services if they were really needed. And, in spite of the proscription, tax revenues were so depleted by years of the Depression that more than 1,000 government bodies went bankrupt, leading to the closure of schools in rural areas throughout the country. Many of these were reopened through the work programs, providing jobs for teachers and education for children.

Both in spite of and because of these constraints, the FERA, CWA, and WPA were the subjects of almost continual criticism. Complaints of inefficient and unnecessary "make-work" were most common. However, when projects were set up in which useful goods were produced in an efficient manner, they were quickly shut down. This was the case with the Ohio Plan, which combined idle workers with idle plant and equipment, as people on relief were put to work in factories that had been running at low capacity and were rented from their owners. And a mattress-making project—in which mattresses were sewn by hand using surplus cotton collected by the Agricultural Adjustment Administration (AAA)—was also ended prematurely.

Although the 1930s programs are models of what can be accomplished, there were also serious problems. Most important, the programs focused on white men, while women and people of color were marginalized. Women were allocated only one-sixth of the positions; they received lower wages than men; and they were assigned to work considered suitable—"women's work" in sewing, canning, and other goods production for blue-collar workers, and in service and arts projects for professional and clerical workers. Another set of problems was faced by people of color. It was widely assumed that they had a lower standard of living compared to whites, making it more difficult to establish eligibility; they were often restricted to racially segregated projects, making it more difficult to find placements; they were almost always classified as unskilled and consequently paid the lowest rates; and they were routinely removed from the programs altogether when they were needed as low-wage laborers, primarily in agriculture and also in domestic service. Women of color, who faced both gender and racial discrimination, fared worst of all.

The second major problem was that the programs never created enough jobs. Even though unemployment reached 25 percent of the total labor force, and 37 percent of the industrial labor force, at most the work programs created jobs for only one-third of the unemployed. Usually, it was less.

Although a few small defense training programs existed during the early 1940s, it wasn't until the 1960s that fair work education and training programs were developed on a larger scale. The 1962 Manpower Development and Training Act (MDTA) set up training programs that again focused primarily on white, male heads-of-household. These included classroom training (CT) as well as on-the-job training (OJT). In 1964 the Economic Opportunity Act ushered in the War on Poverty, as a myriad of programs were established for "human reclamation"—providing training, education, support services, and work experience intended to bring the poor into the mainstream of society. The urban ghetto riots that began in the mid-1960s led these programs to target young African-American men, broadening the focus from adult white males. These programs, too, only reached a fraction of the people who needed them, but provide examples of programs that do a far better job of meeting people's needs than the limited ones that have been the norm since 1981.

A particularly noteworthy program was developed for women. New Careers, which began in 1966 and was renamed Public Service Careers in 1970, offered paid employment as community workers to low-income women. They often worked in community action agencies, the multiservice neighborhood centers established through the Economic Opportunity Act which provided an institutional basis for community organizing. Thus, New Careers recognized some of the work that women were already doing in their communities, and paid them for it.

The sharp recession of 1969-1970 brought the return of job creation programs, first in the Public Employment Program (PEP) from 1970 to 1973, and then in Public Service Employment (PSE), which was part of the Comprehensive Employment and Training Act (CETA). CETA was passed in December 1973, and incorporated most of the programs authorized under the Economic Opportunity Act, the MDTA, as well as the PEP.) Yet PEP and PSE were far more constrained than their 1930s predecessors. They were much smaller than the earlier programs, reaching a maximum of only 742,000 positions in March 1978—in spite of the doubling of the labor force and the tremendous growth of the government in the intervening years. And, whereas the WPA put people to work in construction, production of consumer goods, and services, PEP and PSE were confined only to services. In spite of the limitations, a variety of socially useful work was done—for example, setting up screening programs in hospitals, providing additional personnel for law enforcement agencies, developing community programs in arts and recreation, helping staff battered women's shelters and childcare centers, weatherizing low-income homes, and helping fund activist community organizations.

As was true of the 1930s programs, PEP and especially PSE were targets of unremitting criticisms. As in the earlier programs, PEP and PSE were supposed to provide work that was apart from "normal government operations." And, as in the earlier programs, this left them vulnerable to charges of "make-work." First, service production is even more easily seen as inefficient than goods production since nothing tangible is produced. Second, it was easily assumed that if the services were necessary, the government would already have been providing them.

Additional criticisms plagued CETA. One was "fiscal substitution"—it was alleged that federal CETA funds simply replaced state and local funds so that no new jobs were created. However, the severe recession of 1973 through 1975, in conjunction with tax limitation initiatives in states such as Massachusetts and California, meant that tax revenues fell. Consequently, more and more government services would not have been provided without CETA funds. In addition, criticisms were also commonly made that wages were too high, attracting workers from private-sector jobs, an expression of the fear that CETA jobs were sometimes preferred over private-sector jobs. And charges that graft and corruption were common increased throughout the 1970s. Yet these are red herrings—little is done when these charges are made toward the military or other high-level agencies, but they are taken quite seriously when made toward social programs.

Public employment was one focus of CETA. Another was training programs. CT and OJT programs were continued from the 1960s, again primarily focusing on men. However, when CETA was reauthorized in 1978, some innovative training programs for women were developed. One was training in "nontraditional occupations," or NTOs. (Actually, these are nontraditional only because they are higher-wage, blue-collar jobs that have traditionally been closed to women, and are more correctly termed "male-dominated occupations," or MDOs.) Programs were also developed for teenage mothers and for "displaced homemakers," who had worked in the home much of their lives and suddenly found themselves in the labor force with no marketable skills. The latter programs included funding for support services, primarily childcare, as well as stipends, and were critically important in enabling the women to successfully participate.

In spite of the constraints on CETA, it came under attack by the Reagan administration. PSE was ended soon after Reagan became president in 1981, and the entire CETA program was allowed to expire the following year. All that remained of fair work programs was the Job Training Partnership Act (JTPA), which develops short-term training programs to quickly get people into jobs, often low-wage, service sector positions. The JTPA provided training for some welfare recipients in workfare programs during the 1980s and 1990s. But with minimal supports, and no stipends, many women were forced back on the rolls.

A Public Employment Program for Women

Instead of punitive programs that push women into low-wage jobs, we need a public employment program and related policies designed to meet women's needs. Several principles and policies are necessary.

First, work must be redefined—based most fundamentally on recognizing the value of unpaid caretaking work in the home, and women should be paid for this work. This could be done through a family allowance, as European countries have been doing for decades, in which all caretakers are compensated by the federal government. In conjunction with a progressive federal income tax, those who could afford to would repay this money. In addition to recognizing the value of work in the home, a family allowance would also recognize the importance of women's work in the community. In fact, women's work is vital as a kind of "social glue" in middle- and low-income neighborhoods.

Additional policies to boost wages and provide social supports are also needed to facilitate women's wage work, and to give both women and men choices about combining wage labor with work in the home. Labor market policies would include: raising the minimum wage and automatically indexing future increases to the rate of inflation; revitalizing affirmative action policies, and implementing a pay equity policy, to help close wage gaps between women and men and between people of color and whites; and providing protections for labor unions. Family policies would include: a paid family leave of at least six months to take care of a newborn or adopted child or a sick family member; flexible work hours; national health care; subsidized childcare; and an increased supply of low-cost housing.

The family policies should follow three guidelines. First, they should be universal so that everyone receives the benefits and poor people are not singled out. (This helps explain the relative resilience of Social Security while programs for the poor have been slashed.) Second, they should be federalized, i.e. provided by the federal government instead of individual states, which tend to do very little. Third, they should be paid by the government instead of by individual employers. This is contrary to the present system in which employers pay benefits (minimal as they are) for health care, often making it more profitable to require current employees to work longer hours rather than hiring additional workers.

At the heart of these policies would be a public employment program and related education and training. Examples from our history serve as models. Education and training programs from the 1960s and 1970s should be revived and expanded to meet women's needs. These should be seen as investments in the future of our society, not simply as expenses in the present. Both classroom training and on-the-job training should be expanded, and focused on providing skills that would help women obtain jobs paying wages above a realistically defined poverty line. Programs would include training for women in male-dominated occupations that have histori-cally paid higher wages. Further, if we are serious about facilitating wage labor for women, history shows and common sense tells us that long-term welfare recipients in particular need well-funded support services and stipends while they are in training pro-grams. This was clearly seen in the programs for "displaced homemakers" that were part of the 1978 CETA reauthorization, and could be accomplished, in part, through the broader family policies outlined above.

Education has become increasingly important. In fact, recent studies have shown that the most secure path out of poverty for women is a college degree. Instead of placing obstacles in the way of women attending college, they should receive societal supports.

As in the past, training without jobs makes little sense. We know from the programs of the 1930s that the federal government has the wherewithal to put millions of people to work. This time, however, instead of primarily targeting white males, the programs would focus on women. Women would no longer be confined to so-called "women's work," but would be encouraged to engage in higher-wage work that has traditionally been seen as the province of men. This would be particularly true of construction work. Indeed, given the lack of attention to public investment since the early 1980s, a great deal needs to be done—from repairing our crumbling bridges and roads to constructing public transportation systems and low-cost housing. Additional public investment is needed in education, also an increasingly, and shortsightedly, neglected area. Instead of building more and more prisons, we need programs to help young people stay in school. This, too, is an investment in our future.

Criticisms of public employment programs will undoubtedly arise. Reiterating charges from the past, they will probably be characterized as inefficient and unnecessary "make-work." They can be defended, in part, by arguments developed in this chapter—that past programs have been constrained by regulations designed to prevent their interference with the logic of production-for-profit. Additional, well-taken concerns that employment program workers may be used to replace normal government workers can be countered in part by requirements that program workers be paid the same amount as those already employed, and encouraged to join a union if one exists.

Furthermore, we should note that these programs make good economic sense. Since the early 1980s we have had supply-side economics, in which the rich have made out like bandits at the expense of everyone else. In addition to being patently unfair, this has further destabilized the economy. Capitalists produce goods and services only if they can be sold. However, much of the income going to the wealthy has been used for speculation—in land, junk bonds, art, etc. "Bubble up" economics is different—most of the money going into the hands of low- and middle-income people will quickly be spent on goods and services, increasing demand and leading capitalists to increase production and hire more workers. This is a much more stable foundation for economic growth than giving money to the rich and hoping they will use it for productive investment.

Decent jobs should become a right instead of a privilege. In conjunction with the family and labor market policies just outlined, this would give both women and men choices about work in a manner that accords a decent standard of living through a combination of pay and social supports. Policies based on blaming poor women for the ills of society would be replaced with policies that respect and value women's work.

THE GENEALOGY OF DEPENDENCY
Tracing A Keyword of the U.S. Welfare State
*Nancy Fraser and Linda Gordon**

DEPENDENCY HAS BECOME A KEYWORD OF U.S. POLITICS.
Politicians of diverse views regularly criticize what they term *welfare dependency*. Supreme Court Justice Clarence Thomas spoke for many conservatives in 1980 when he vilified his sister:

> She gets mad when the mailman is late with her welfare check. That's how dependent she is. What's worse is that now her kids feel entitled to the check, too. They have no motivation for doing better or getting out of that situation (quoted in Tumulty 1991).

Liberals usually blame the victim less, but they, too, decry welfare dependency. Democratic Senator Daniel P. Moynihan prefigured today's discourse when he began his 1973 book by claiming that

> the issue of welfare is the issue of dependency. It is different from poverty. To be poor is an objective condition; to be dependent, a subjective one as well...Being poor is often associated with considerable personal qualities; being dependent rarely so. [Dependency] is an incomplete state in life: normal in the child, abnormal in the adult. In a world where completed men and women stand on their own feet, persons who are dependent—as the buried imagery of the word denotes—hang (Moynihan 1973, 17).

Today, "policy experts" from both major parties agree:

> that [welfare] dependency is bad for people, that it undermines their motivation to support themselves, and isolates and stigmatizes welfare recipients in a way that over a long period feeds into and accentuates the underclass mindset and condition (Nathan 1986, 248).

---

* Reprinted without changes from *Signs: Journal of Women in Culture and Society*, vol. 19, no. 21 (1994). © 1994 by The University of Chicago. All rights reserved.

If we can step back from this discourse, however, we can interrogate some of its underlying presuppositions. Why are debates about poverty and inequality in the United States now being framed in terms of welfare dependency? How did the receipt of public assistance become associated with dependency, and why are the connotations of that word in this context so negative? What are the gender and racial subtexts of this discourse, and what tacit assumptions underlie it?

We propose to shed some light on these issues by examining welfare-related meanings of the word dependency.1 We will analyze dependency as a keyword of the U.S. welfare state and reconstruct its genealogy. By charting some major historical shifts in the usage of this term, we will excavate some of the tacit assumptions and connotations that it still carries today but that usually go without saying.

Our approach is inspired in part by the English cultural-materialist critic, Raymond Williams (1976). Following Williams and others, we assume that the terms that are used to describe social life are also active forces shaping it.2 A crucial element of politics, then, is the struggle to define social reality and to interpret people's inchoate aspirations and needs (Fraser 1990). Particular words and expressions often become focal points in such struggles, functioning as keywords, sites at which the meaning of social experience is negotiated and contested (Williams 1976). Keywords typically carry unspoken assumptions and connotations that can powerfully influence the discourses they permeate—in part by constituting a body of doxa, or taken-for-granted common sense belief that escapes critical scrutiny (Bourdieu 1977).

We seek to dispel the doxa surrounding current U.S. discussions of dependency by reconstructing that term's genealogy. Modifying an approach associated with Michael Foucault (1984), we will excavate broad historical shifts in linguistic usage that can rarely be attributed to specific agents. We do not present a causal analysis. Rather, by contrasting present meanings of dependency with past meanings, we aim to defamiliarize taken-for-granted beliefs in order to render them susceptible to critique and to illuminate present-day conflicts.

Our approach differs from Faucault's, however, in two crucial respects: we seek to contextualize discursive shifts in relation to broad institutional and social-structural shifts, and we welcome normative political reflection.3 Our article is a collaboration between a philosopher and a historian. We combine historical analysis of linguistic and social-structural changes with conceptual analysis of the discursive construction of social problems, and we leaven the mix with a feminist interest in envisioning emancipatory alternatives.

In what follows, then, we provide a genealogy of dependency. We sketch the history of this term and explicate the assumptions and connotations it carries today in U.S. debates about welfare—especially assumptions about human nature, gender roles, the causes of poverty, the nature of citizenship, the sources of entitlement, and what counts as work and as a contribution to society. We contend that unreflective uses of this keyword serve to enshrine certain interpretations of social life as authoritative and to delegitimate or obscure others, generally to the advantage of dominant groups in society and to the disadvantage of subordinate ones. All told, we provide a critique of ideology in the form of critical political semantics.

Dependency, we argue, is an ideological term. In current U.S. policy discourse it usually refers to the condition of poor women with children who maintain their families with neither a male breadwinner nor an adequate wage and who rely for economic support on a stingy and politically unpopular government program called Aid to Families with Dependent Children (AFDC). Participation in this highly stigmatized program may be demoralizing in many cases, even though it may enable women to leave abusive or unsatisfying relationships without having to give up their children. Still, naming the problems of poor, solo-mother families as dependency tends to make them appear to be individual problems, as much moral or psychological as economic. The term carries strong emotive and visual associations and a powerful pejorative charge. In current debates, the expression welfare dependency evokes the image of "the welfare mother," often figured as a young, unmarried black woman (perhaps even a teenager) of uncontrolled sexuality. The power of this image is overdetermined, we contend, since it condenses multiple and often contradictory meanings of dependency. Only by dis-aggregating those different strands, by unpacking the tacit assumptions and evaluative connotations that underlie them, can we begin to understand, and to dislodge, the force of the stereotype.

Registers of Meaning

In its root meaning, the verb *to depend* refers to a physical relationship in which one thing hangs from another. The more abstract meanings—social, economic, psychological, and political— were originally metaphorical. In current usage, we find four registers in which the meanings of dependency reverberate. The first is an economic register, in which one depends on some other person(s) or institution for subsistence. In a second register, the term denotes a socio-legal status, the lack of a separate legal or public identity, as in the status of married women created by coverture. The third register is political: Here dependency means subjection to an external ruling power and may be predicated of a colony or of a subject caste of noncitizen residents. The fourth register we call the moral/psychological: Dependency in this sense is an individual character trait such as lack of willpower or excessive emotional neediness.

To be sure, not every use of *dependency* fits neatly into one and only one of these registers. Still, by distinguishing them analytically we present a matrix on which to plot the historical adventures of the term. In what follows, we shall trace the shift from a patriarchal, preindustrial usage in which women, however subordinate, shared a condition of dependency with many men to a modern, industrial, male-supremacist usage that constructed a specifically feminine sense of dependency. That usage is now giving way, we contend, to a postindustrial usage in which growing numbers of relatively prosperous women claim the same kind of independence that men do while a more stigmatized but still feminized sense of dependency attaches to groups considered deviant and superfluous. Not just gender but also racializing practices play a major role in these shifts, as do changes in the organization and meaning of labor.

Preindustrial Dependency

In preindustrial English usage, the most common meaning of *dependency* was subordination. The economic, socio-legal, and political registers were relatively undifferentiated, reflecting the fusion of various forms of hierarchy in state and society, and the moral/psychological use of the term barely existed. The earliest social definition of the verb *to depend* (on) in the *Oxford English Dictionary (OED)* is "to be connected within a relation of subordination." A *dependent,* from at least 1588, was one "who depends on another for support, position, etc.; a retainer, attendant, subordinate, servant." A *dependency* was either a retinue or body of servants or a foreign territorial possession or colony. This family of terms applied widely in a hierarchical social context in which nearly everyone was subordinate to someone else but did not incur individual stigma thereby (Gundersen 1987).

We can appreciate just how common dependency was in preindustrial society by examining its opposite. The term *independence* at first applied primarily to aggregate entities, not to individuals; thus in the 17th century a nation or a church congregation could be independent. By the 18th century, however, an individual could be said to have an *independency,* meaning an ownership of property, a fortune that made it possible to live without laboring. (This sense of the term, which we would today call economic, survives in our expressions *to be independently wealthy and a person of independent means).* To be dependent, in contrast, was to gain one's livelihood by working for someone else. This, of course, was the condition of most people, of wage laborers as well as serfs and slaves, of most men as well as most women.[4]

Dependency, therefore, was a normal, as opposed to a deviant, condition, a social relation, as opposed to an individual trait. Thus, it did not carry any moral opprobrium. Neither English nor U.S. dictionaries report any pejorative uses of the term before the early 20th century. In fact, some leading preindustrial definitions were explicitly positive, implying trusting, relying on, counting on another, the predecessors of today's *dependable.*

Nevertheless, *dependency* did mean status inferiority and legal coverture, being a part of a unit headed by someone else who had legal standing. In a world of status hierarchies dominated by great landowners and their retainers, all members of a household other than its "head" were dependents, as were free or servile peasants on an estate. They were, as Peter Laslett put it, "caught up, so to speak, subsumed...into the personalities of their fathers and masters" (1971, 21).

Dependency also had what we would today call political consequences. While the term did not mean precisely *unfree,* its context was a social order in which subjection, not citizenship, was the norm. *Independence* connoted unusual privilege and superiority, as in freedom from labor. Thus, throughout most of the European development of representative government, independence in the sense of property ownership was a prerequisite for political rights. When dependents began to claim rights and liberty, they perforce became revolutionaries.

Dependency was not then applied uniquely to characterize the relation of a wife to her husband. Women's dependency, like children's, meant being on a lower rung in a long social ladder; their husbands and fathers were above them but below others. For the agrarian majority, moreover, there was no implication of unilateral economic dependency, because women's and children's labor was recognized as essential to the family economy; the women were economic dependents only in the sense that the men of their class were as well. In general, women's dependency in preindustrial society was less gender-specific than it later became; it was similar in kind to that of subordinate men, only multiplied. But so too, were the lives of children, servants, and the elderly overlaid with multiple layers of dependency.

In practice, of course, these preindustrial arrangements did not always bode satisfactorily for the poor. In the 14th century new, stronger states began to limit the freedom of movement of the destitute and to codify older informal distinctions between those worthy and unworthy of assistance. When the English Poor Law of 1601 confirmed this latter distinction, it was already shameful to ask for public help. But the culture neither disapproved of dependency nor valorized individual independence. Rather, the aim of the statutes was to return the mobile, uprooted, and excessively "independent" poor to their local parishes or communities and, hence, to enforce their traditional dependencies.

Nevertheless, dependency was not universally approved or uncontested. It was subject, rather, to principled challenges from at least the 17th century on, when liberal-individualist political arguments became common. The terms *dependence, and independence* often figured centrally in debates in this period as they did, for example, in the Putney Debates of the English Civil War. Sometimes they even became key signifiers of social crisis, as in the 17th century English controversy about "out-of-doors" servants, hired help who did not reside in the homes of their masters and who were not bound by indentures or similar legal understandings. In the discourse of the time, the anomalous similarity of the "independence" of these men served as a general figure for social disorder, a lightning rod focusing diffuse cultural anxieties—much as the, anomalous "dependence" of "welfare mothers" does today.

Industrial Dependency: The Worker and His Negatives

With the rise of industrial capitalism, the semantic geography of dependency shifted significantly. In the 18th and 19th centuries, *independence*, not dependence, figured centrally in political and economic discourse; and its meanings were radically democratized. But if we read the discourse about independence carefully, we see the shadow of a powerful anxiety about dependency.

What in preindustrial society had been a normal and unstigmatized condition became deviant and stigmatized. More precisely, certain dependencies became shameful while others were deemed natural and proper. In particular, as 18th and 19th century political culture intensified gender difference, new, specifically gendered senses of dependency appeared—states considered proper for women but degrading for men. Likewise, emergent racial constructions made some forms of dependency appropriate for the "dark races" but intolerable for "whites." Such differentiated valuations became possible as the term's preindustrial unity fractured. No longer designating only generalized subordination, *dependency* in the industrial era could be socio-legal or political or economic. With these distinctions came another major semantic shift: Now *dependency* need not always refer to a social relation; it could also designate an individual character trait. Thus, the moral/psychological register was born.

These redefinitions were greatly influenced by Radical Protestantism. It elaborated a new positive image of individual independence and a critique of socio-legal and political dependency. In the Catholic and the early Protestant traditions, dependence on a master had been modeled on dependence on God. In contrast, to the radicals of the English Civil War, or to Puritans, Quakers, and Congregationalists in the United States, rejecting dependence on a master was akin to rejecting blasphemy and false gods (Hill 1961). From this perspective, status hierarchies no longer appeared natural or just. Political subjection and socio-legal subsumption were offenses against human dignity, defensible only under special conditions, if supportable at all. These beliefs informed a variety of radical movements throughout the industrial era, including abolition, feminism, and labor organizing, with substantial successes. In the 19th century these movements abolished slavery and some of the legal disabilities of women. More thoroughgoing victories were won by white male workers who, in the eighteenth and nineteenth centuries, threw off their socio-legal and political dependency and won civil and electoral rights. In the age of democratic revolutions, the developing new concept of citizenship rested on independence; dependency was deemed antithetical to citizenship.

Changes in the civil and political landscape of dependence and independence were accompanied by even more dramatic changes in the economic register. When white working men demanded civil and electoral rights, they claimed to be independent. This entailed reinterpreting the meaning of wage labor so as to divest it of the association with dependency. That in turn required a shift in focus— from the experience or means of labor (e.g., ownership of tools or land, control of skills, and the organization of work) to its remuneration and how that was spent. Radical working men, who had earlier rejected wage labor as "wage slavery," claimed a new form of manly independence within it. Their collective pride drew on another aspect of Protestantism, its work ethic, that valorized discipline and labor. Workers sought to reclaim these values within the victorious wage-labor system; many of them—women as well as men—created and exercised a new kind of independence in their militance and boldness toward employers. Through their struggles, economic independence came eventually to encompass the ideal of earning a family wage, a wage sufficient to maintain a household and to support a dependent wife and children. Thus, working men expanded the meaning of economic independence to include a form of wage labor in addition to property ownership and self-employment.[5]

This shift in the meaning of independence also transformed the meanings of dependency. As wage labor became increasingly normative—and increasingly definitive of independence—it was precisely those excluded from wage labor who appeared to personify dependency. In the new industrial semantics, there emerged three principal icons of dependency, all effectively negatives of the dominant image of "the worker" and each embodying a different aspect of non-independence.

The first icon of industrial dependency was "the pauper," who lived not on wages but on poor relief.[6] In the strenuous new culture of emergent capitalism, the figure of the pauper was like a bad double of the upstanding working man, threatening the latter should he lag. The image of the pauper was elaborated largely in an emerging new register of dependency discourse—the moral/psychological register. Paupers were not simply poor but degraded, their character corrupted and their will sapped through reliance on charity. To be sure, the moral/psychological condition of pauperism was related to the economic condition of poverty, but the relationship was not simple, but complex. While 19th century charity experts acknowledged that poverty could contribute to pauperization, they also held that character defects could cause poverty (Gordon 1992). Toward the end of the century, as hereditarian (eugenic) thought caught on, the pauper's character defects were given a basis in biology. The pauper's dependency was figured as unlike the serf's in that it was wage-unilateral, not reciprocal. To be a pauper was not to be subordinate within a system of productive labor; it was to be outside such a system altogether.

A second icon of industrial dependency was embodied alternately in the figures of "the colonial native" and "the slave." They, of course, were very much inside the economic system, their labor often fundamental to the development of capital and industry. Whereas the pauper represented the characterological distillation of economic dependency, natives and slaves personified political subjection.[7] Their images as "savage," "child like," and "submissive" became salient as the old, territorial sense of dependency as a colony became intertwined with a new, racist discourse developed to justify colonialism and slavery.[8] There emerged a drift from an older sense of dependency as a relation of subjection imposed by an imperial power on an indigenous population to a newer sense of dependency as an inherent property or character trait of the people so subjected. In earlier usage, colonials were dependent because they had been conquered; in 19th-century imperialist culture, they were conquered because they were dependent. In this new conception, it was the intrinsic, essential dependency of natives and slaves that justified their colonization and enslavement.

The dependency of the native and the slave, like that of the pauper, was elaborated largely in the moral/psychological register. The character traits adduced to justify imperialism and slavery, however, arose less from individual temperament than from the supposed nature of human groups. Racialist thought was the linchpin for this reasoning. By licensing a view of "the Negro" as fundamentally *other*, it provided the extraordinary justificatory power required to rationalize subjection at a time when liberty and equality were being proclaimed inalienable "rights of man"— for example, in that classic reaction to colonial status, the United States' "Declaration of Independence." Thus racism helped transform dependency as political subjection into dependency as psychology and forged enduring links between the discourse of dependency and racial oppression.

Like the pauper, the native and the slave were excluded from wage labor and thus were negatives of the image of the worker. They shared that characteristic, if little else, with the third major icon of dependency in the industrial era: the newly invented figure of "the housewife." As we saw, the independence of the white working man presupposed the ideal of the family wage, a wage sufficient to maintain a household and to support a nonemployed wife and children. Thus, for wage labor to create (white male) independence, (white) female economic dependence was required. Women were thus transformed "from partners to parasites" (Land 1980, 57; Boydston 1991). But this transformation was by no means universal. In the United States, for example, the family wage ideal held greater sway among whites than among blacks and was at variance with actual practice for all of the poor and the working class. Moreover, both employed and nonemployed wives continued to perform work once considered crucial to a family economy. Since few husbands actually were able to support a family single-handedly, most families continued to depend on the labor of women and children. Nevertheless, the family wage norm commanded great loyalty in the United States, partly because it was used by the organized working class as an argument for higher wages (Hughes 1925; Breckinridge 1928; Pruette 1934; Gordon 1992).

Several different registers of dependency converged in the figure of the housewife. This figure melded woman's traditional socio-legal and political dependency with her more recent economic dependency in the industrial order. Continuing from preindustrial usage was the assumption that fathers headed households and that other household members were represented by them, as codified in the legal doctrine of coverture. The socio-legal and political dependency of wives enforced their new economic dependency, since under coverture even married women who were wage workers could not legally control their wages. But the connotations of female dependency were altered. Although erstwhile dependent white men gained political rights, most white women remained legally and politically dependent. The result was to feminize—and stigmatize—socio-legal and political dependency, making coverture appear increasingly obnoxious and stimulating agitation for the statutes and court decisions that eventually dismantled it.

Together, then, a series of new personifications of dependency combined to constitute the underside of the working man's independence. Henceforth, those who aspired to full membership in society would have to distinguish themselves from the pauper, the native, the slave, and the housewife in order to construct their independence and the social order in which wage labor was becoming hegemonic, it was possible to encapsulate all these distinctions simultaneously in the ideal of the family wage. On the one hand, and most overtly, the ideal of the family wage premised the white working man's independence on his wife's subordination and economic dependence. But on the other hand, it simultaneously contrasted with counter images of dependent men—first with degraded male paupers on poor relief and later with racist stereotypes of Negro men unable to dominate Negro women. The family wage, therefore, was a vehicle for elaborating meanings of dependence and independence that were deeply inflected by gender, race, and class.

In this new industrial semantics, white working men appeared to be economically independent, but their independence was largely illusory and ideological. Since few actually earned enough to support a family singlehandedly, most depended in fact—if not in word—on their wives' and children's contributions. Equally important, the language of wage labor in capitalism denied workers' dependence on their employers, thereby veiling their status as subordinates in a unit headed by someone else. Thus, hierarchy that had been relatively explicit and visible in the peasant-landlord relation was mystified in the relationship of factory operative to factory owner. There was a sense, then, in which the economic dependency of the white working man was spirited away through linguistic sleight of hand—somewhat like reducing the number of poor people by lowering the official poverty demarcating line.

By definition, then, economic inequality among white men no longer created dependency. But noneconomic hierarchy among white men was considered unacceptable in the United States. Thus, *dependency* was redefined to refer exclusively to those noneconomic relations of subordination deemed suitable only for people of color and for white women. The result was to differentiate dimensions of dependency that had been fused in preindustrial usage. Whereas all relations of subordination had previously counted as dependency relations, now capital-labor relations were exempted. Socio-legal and political hierarchy appeared to diverge from economic hierarchy, and only the former seemed incompatible with hegemonic views of society. It seemed to follow, moreover, that were socio-legal dependency and political dependency ever to be formally abolished, no social-structural dependency would remain. Any dependency that did persist could only be moral or psychological.

The Rise of American Welfare Dependency, 1890-1945

Informed by these general features of industrial-era semantics, a distinctive welfare-related use of *dependency* developed in the United States. Originating in the late 19th-century discourse of pauperism, modified in the Progressive Era, and stabilized in the period of the New Deal, this use of the term was fundamentally ambiguous, slipping easily, and repeatedly, from an economic meaning to a moral/psychological meaning.

The United States was especially hospitable to elaborating dependency as a defect of individual character. Because the country lacked a strong legacy of feudalism or aristocracy and thus a strong popular sense of reciprocal obligations between lord and man, the older, preindustrial meanings of dependency—as an ordinary, majority condition—were weak and the pejorative meanings were stronger. In the colonial period, dependency was seen mainly as a voluntary condition, as in indentured servitude. But the American Revolution so valorized independence that it stripped dependency of its voluntarism, emphasized its powerlessness, and imbued it with stigma. One result was to change the meaning of women's social and legal dependency, making it distinctly inferior (Gundersen 1987).

The long American love affair with independence was politically double-edged. On the one hand, it helped nurture powerful labor and women's movements. On the other hand, the absence of a hierarchical social tradition in which subordination was understood to be structural, not characterological, facilitated hostility to public support for the poor. Also influential was the very nature of the American state, weak and decentralized in comparison to European states throughout the 19th century. All told, the United States proved fertile soil for the moral/psychological discourse of dependency.

As discussed earlier, the most general definition of economic dependency in this era was simply non-wage-earning. By the end of the 19th century, however, that definition had divided into two: a "good," household dependency, predicated of children and wives, and an increasingly "bad" (or at least dubious) charity dependency, predicated of recipients of relief. Both senses had as their reference point the ideal of the family wage, and both were eventually incorporated into the discourse of the national state. The good, household sense was elaborated via the census (Folbre 1991) and by the Internal Revenue Service, which installed the category of dependent as the norm for wives. The already problematic charity sense became even more pejorative with the development of public assistance. The old distinction between the deserving and the undeserving poor intensified in the late 19th century's Gilded Age. Theoretically, the undeserving should not be receiving aid, but constant vigilance was required to ensure they did not slip in, disguising themselves as deserving. Dependence on assistance became increasingly stigmatized, and it was harder and harder to rely on relief without being branded a pauper. Ironically, reformers in the 1890s introduced the word *dependent* into relief discourse as a substitute for *pauper* precisely in order to destigmatize the receipt of help. They first applied the word to children, the paradigmatic "innocent" victims of poverty.[9] Then, in the early 20th century, Progressive Era reformers began to apply the term to adults, again to rid them of stigma. Only after World War II did *dependent* become the hegemonic word for a recipient of aid.[10] By then, however, the term's pejorative connotations were fixed.

The attempt to get rid of stigma by replacing *pauperism* with *dependency* failed. Talk about economic dependency repeatedly slid into condemnation of moral/psychological dependency. Even during the Depression of the 1930s, experts worried that receipt of relief would create "habits of dependence" or, as one charity leader put it, "a belligerent dependency, an attitude of having a right and title to relief" (Brandt 1932, 23-24; Gibbons 1933; Valle 1934, 26). Because the hard times lasted so long and created so many newly poor people, there was a slight improvement in the status of recipients of aid. But attacks on "chiseling" and "corruption" continued to embarrass those receiving assistance, and many of the neediest welfare beneficiaries accepted public aid only after much hesitation and with great shame, so strong was the stigma of dependency (Bakke 1940a, 1940b).

Most important, the New Deal intensified the dishonor of receiving help by consolidating a two-track welfare system. First-track programs like unemployment and old age insurance offered aid as an entitlement, without stigma or supervision and hence without dependency. Such programs were constructed to create the misleading appearance that beneficiaries merely got back what they put in. They constructed an honorable status for recipients and are not called welfare even today. Intended at least partially to replace the white working man's family wage, first-track programs excluded most minorities and white women. In contrast, second-track public assistance programs, among which Aid to Dependent Children (ADC), later Aid to Families with Dependent Children (AFDC), became the biggest and most well-known, continued the private charity tradition of searching out the deserving few among the many chiselers. Funded from general tax revenues instead of from earmarked wage deductions, these programs created the appearance that claimants were getting something for nothing (Fraser and Gordon 1992). They established entirely different conditions for receiving aid: means-testing, morals-testing, moral and household supervision, home visits, extremely low stipends—in short, all the conditions associated with welfare dependency today (Fraser 1987; Gordon 1990; Nelson 1990).[11]

The racial and sexual exclusions of the first-track programs were not accidental. They were designed to win the support of Southern legislators who wanted to keep blacks dependent in another sense, namely, on low wages or sharecropping (Quadagno 1988). Equally deliberate was the construction of the differential in legitimacy between the two tracks of the welfare system. The Social Security Board propagandized for Social Security Old Age Insurance (the program today called just "Social Security") precisely because, at first, it did not seem more earned or more dignified than public assistance. To make Social Security more acceptable, the board worked to stigmatize public assistance, even pressuring states to keep stipends low (Cates 1983).

Most Americans today still distinguish between "welfare" and "nonwelfare" forms of public provision and see only the former as creating dependency. The assumptions underlying these distinctions, however, had to be constructed politically. Old people became privileged (nonwelfare) recipients only through decades of militant organization and lobbying. All programs of public provision, whether they are called welfare or not, shore up some dependencies and discourage others. Social Security subverted adults' sense of responsibility for their parents, for example. Public assistance programs, by contrast, aimed to buttress the dependence of the poor on low-wage labor, of wives on husbands, of children on their parents.

The conditions of second-track assistance made recipients view their dependence on public assistance as inferior to the supposed independence of wage labor (Milwaukee County Welfare Rights Organization 1972; West 1981; Pope 1989, 73, 144). Wage labor, meanwhile, had become so naturalized that its own inherent supervision could be overlooked; thus one ADC recipient complained, "Welfare life is a difficult experience...When you work, you don't have to report to anyone" (Barnes 1987, vi). Yet the designers of ADC did not initially intend to drive white solo mothers into paid employment. Rather, they wanted to protect the norm of the family wage by making dependence on a male breadwinner continue to seem preferable to dependence on the state (Gordon 1992). Aid to Dependent Children occupied the strategic semantic space where the good, household sense of dependency and the bad, relief sense of dependency intersected. It enforced at once the positive connotations of the first and the negative connotations of the second.

Thus, the poor solo mother was enshrined as the quintessential *welfare dependent.*[12] That designation has thus become significant not only for what it includes but also for what it excludes and occludes. Although it appears to mean relying on the government for economic support, not all recipients of public funds are equally considered dependent. Hardly anyone today calls recipients of Social Security retirement insurance *dependents.* Similarly, persons receiving unemployment insurance, agricultural loans, and home mortgage assistance are excluded from that categorization, as indeed are defense contractors and the beneficiaries of corporate bailouts and regressive taxation.

Postindustrial Society and the Disappearance of "Good" Dependency

With the transition to a postindustrial phase of capitalism, the semantic map of dependency is being redrawn yet again. Whereas industrial usage had cast some forms of dependency as natural and proper, postindustrial usage figures all forms as avoidable and blameworthy. No longer moderated by any positive counter currents, the term's pejorative connotations are being strengthened. Industrial usage had recognized some forms of dependency to be rooted in relations of subordination; postindustrial usage, in contrast, focuses more intensely on the traits of individuals. The moral/psychological register is expanding, therefore, and its qualitative character is changing, with new psychological and therapeutic idioms displacing the explicitly racist and misogynous idioms of the industrial era. Yet dependency nonetheless remains feminized and racialized; the new psychological meanings have strong feminine associations, while currents once associated with the native and the slave are increasingly inflecting the discourse about welfare.

One major influence here is the formal abolition of much of the legal and political dependency that was endemic to industrial society. Housewives, paupers, natives, and the descendants of slaves are no longer formally excluded from most civil and political rights—neither their subsumption nor their subjection is viewed as legitimate. Thus, major forms of dependency deemed proper in industrial usage are now considered objectionable, and postindustrial uses of the term carry a stronger negative charge. A second major shift in the geography of postindustrial dependency is affecting the economic register. This is the decentering of the ideal of the family wage, which had been the gravitational center of industrial usage. The relative deindustrialization of the United States is restructuring the political economy, making the single-earner family far less viable. The loss of higher-paid "male" manufacturing jobs and the massive entry of women into low-wage service work is meanwhile altering the gender composition of employment (Smith 1984). At the same time, divorce is common and, thanks in large part to the feminist and gay and lesbian liberation movements, changing gender norms are helping to proliferate new family forms, making the male breadwinner/female homemaker model less attractive to many (Stacey 1987, 1990; Weston

1991). Thus, the family wage ideal is no longer hegemonic but competes with alternative gender norms, family forms, and economic arrangements. It no longer goes without saying that a woman should rely on a man for economic support, nor that mothers should not also be "workers." Thus, another major form of dependency that was positively inflected in industrial semantics has become contested, if not simply negative.

The combined result of these developments is to increase the stigma of dependency. With all legal and political dependency now illegitimate, and with wives' economic dependency now contested, there is no longer any self-evidently good adult dependency in postindustrial society. Rather, all dependency is suspect, and independence is enjoined upon everyone. Independence, however, remains identified with wage labor. That identification seems even to increase in a context where there is no longer any "good" adult personification of dependency who can be counterposed to "the worker." In this context, the worker tends to become the universal social subject: Everyone is expected to "work" and to be "self-supporting." Any adult not perceived as a worker shoulders a heavier burden of self-justification. Thus, a norm previously restricted to white working men applies increasingly to everyone. Yet this norm still carries a racial and gender subtext, as it supposes that the worker has access to a job paying a decent wage and is not also a primary parent.

If one result of these developments is an increase in dependency's negative connotations, another is its increased individualization. As we saw, talk of dependency as a character trait of individuals was already widespread in the industrial period, diminishing the preindustrial emphasis on relations of subordination. The importance of individualized dependency tends to be heightened, however, now that socio-legal and political dependency are officially ended. (Absent coverture and Jim Crow, it has become possible to claim that equality of opportunity exists and that individual merit determines outcomes.) As we saw, the groundwork for that view was laid by industrial usage, which redefined dependency so as to exclude capitalist relations of subordination. With capitalist economic dependency already abolished by definition and with legal and political dependency now abolished by law, postindustrial society appears to some conservatives and liberals to have eliminated every social-structural basis of dependency. Whatever dependency remains, therefore, can be interpreted as the fault of individuals. That interpretation does not go uncontested, to be sure, but the burden of argument has shifted. Now those who would deny that the fault lies in themselves must swim upstream against the prevailing semantic currents. Postindustrial dependency, thus, is increasingly individualized.

Welfare Dependency as Postindustrial Pathology

The worsening connotations of *welfare dependency* have been nourished by several streams from outside the field of welfare. New postindustrial medical and psychological discourses have associated dependency with pathology. In articles with titles such as "Pharmacist Involvement in a Chemical-Dependency Rehabilitation Program" (Haynes 1988), social scientists began in the 1980s to write about *chemical, alcohol, and drug dependency,* all euphemisms for addiction. Because welfare claimants are often—falsely—assumed to be addicts, the pathological connotations of *drug dependency* tend also to infect *welfare dependency,* increasing stigmatization.

A second important postindustrial current is the rise of new psychological meanings of dependency with very strong feminine associations. In the 1950s, social workers influenced by psychiatry began to diagnose dependence as a form of immaturity common among women, particularly among solo mothers (who were often, of course, welfare claimants). "Dependent, irresponsible, and unstable, they respond like small children to the immediate moment," declared the author of a 1954 discussion of out-of-wedlock pregnancy (Young 1954, 87). The problem was that women were supposed to be just dependent enough, and it was easy to tip over into excess in either direction. The norm, moreover, was racially marked, as white women were usually portrayed as erring on the side of excessive dependence, while black women were typically charged with excessive independence.

Psychologized dependency became the target of some of the earliest second-wave feminism. Betty Friedan's 1963 classic, *The Feminine Mystique,* provided a phenomenological account of the housewife's psychological dependency and drew from it a political critique of her social subordination. More recently, however, a burgeoning cultural-feminist, postfeminist, and antifeminist self-help and pop-psychology literature has obfuscated the link between the psychological and the political. In Colette Dowling's 1981 book, *The Cinderella Complex*, women's dependency was hypostatized as a depth-psychological gender structure: "women's hidden fear of independence" or the "wish to be saved." The late 1980s saw a spate of books about "codependency," a supposedly prototypically female syndrome of supporting or "enabling" the dependency of someone else. In a metaphor that reflects the drug hysteria of the period, dependency here, too, is an addiction. Apparently, even if a woman manages herself to escape her gender's predilection to dependency, she is liable to incur the blame for facilitating the dependency of her husband or children. This completes the vicious circle: The increased stigmatizing of dependency in the culture at large has also deepened contempt for those who care for dependents, reinforcing the traditionally low status of the female helping professions, such as nursing and social work (Sapiro 1990). The 1980s saw a cultural panic about dependency. In 1980, the American Psychiatric Association codified "Dependent Personality Disorder" (DPD) as an official psychopathology. According to the 1987 edition of the *Diagnostic and Statistical Manual of Mental Disorders (DSM-III* R),:

> The essential feature of this disorder is a pervasive pattern of dependent and submissive behavior beginning by early childhood...People with this disorder are unable to make everyday decisions without an excessive amount of advice and reassurance from others, and will even allow others to make most of their important decisions...The disorder is apparently common and is diagnosed more frequently in females. (American Psychiatric Association 1987, 353-54).

The codification of DPD as an official psychopathology represents a new stage in the history of the moral/psychological register. Here the social relations of dependency disappear entirely into the personality of the dependent. Overt moralism also disappears in the apparently neutral, scientific, medicalized formulation. Thus, although the defining traits of the dependent personality match point for point the traits traditionally ascribed to housewives, paupers, natives, and slaves, all links to subordination have vanished. The only remaining trace of those themes is the flat, categorical, and uninterpreted observation that DPD is "diagnosed more frequently in females."

If psychological discourse has further feminized and individualized dependency, other postindustrial developments have further racialized it. The increased stigmatization of welfare dependency followed a general increase in public provision in the United States, the removal of some discriminatory practices that had previously excluded minority women from participation in AFDC, especially in the South, and the transfer of many white women to first-track programs as social-insurance coverage expanded. By the 1970s the figure of the black solo mother had come to epitomize welfare dependency. As a result, the new discourse about welfare draws on older symbolic currents that linked dependency with racist ideologies.

The ground was laid by a long, somewhat contradictory stream of discourse about "the Black family," in which African-American gender and kinship relations were measured against white middle-class norms and deemed pathological. One supposedly pathological element was "the excessive independence" of black women, an ideologically distorted allusion to long traditions of wage work, educational achievement, and community activism. The 1960s and 1970s discourse about poverty recapitulated traditions of misogyny toward African-American women; in Daniel Moynihan's diagnosis, for example, "matriarchal" families had emasculated black men and created a "culture of poverty" based on a tangle of [family] pathology (Rainwater and Yancey 1967). This discourse placed black AFDC claimants in a double bind: They were pathologically independent with respect to men and pathologically dependent with respect to government.

By the 1980s, however, the racial imagery of dependency had shifted. The black welfare mother that haunted the white imagination ceased to be the powerful matriarch. Now the preeminent stereotype is the unmarried teenage mother caught in the "welfare trap" and rendered dronelike and passive. This new icon of welfare dependency is younger and weaker than the matriarch. She is often evoked in the phrase *children having children*, which can express feminist sympathy or antifeminist contempt, black appeals for parental control or white-racist eugenic anxieties. Many of these postindustrial discourses coalesced in early 1990s. Then-Vice President Dan Quayle brought together the pathologized, feminized, and racialized currents in his comment on the May 1992 Los Angeles riot: "Our inner cities are filled with children having children...with people who are dependent on drugs and on the narcotic of welfare" (Quayle 1992).

Thus, postindustrial culture has called up a new personification of dependency: the black, unmarried, teenaged, welfare-dependent mother. This image has usurped the symbolic space previously occupied by the housewife, the pauper, the native, and the slave, while absorbing and condensing their connotations. black, female, a pauper, not a worker, a housewife and mother, yet practically a child herself—the new stereotype partakes of virtually every quality that has been coded historically as antithetical to independence. Condensing multiple, often contradictory meanings of dependency, it is a powerful ideological stereotype that simultaneously organizes diffuse cultural anxieties and dissimulates their social bases.

Postindustrial Policy and the Politics of Dependency

Despite the worsening economic outlook for many Americans in the last few decades, there has been no cultural revaluation of welfare. Families working harder for less often resent those who appear to them not to be working at all. Apparently lost, at least for now, are the struggles of the 1960s that aimed to recast AFDC as an entitlement in order to promote recipients' independence. Instead, the honorific term *independent* remains firmly centered on wage labor, no matter how impoverished the worker. Welfare dependency, in contrast, has been inflated into a behavioral syndrome and made to seem more contemptible.

Contemporary policy discourse about welfare dependency is thoroughly inflected by these assumptions. It divides into two major streams. The first continues the rhetoric of pauperism and the culture of poverty. It is used in both conservative and liberal, victim-blaming and non-victim-blaming ways, depending on the causal structure of the argument. The contention is that poor, dependent people have something more than lack of money wrong with them. The flaws can be located in biology, psychology, upbringing, neighborhood influence; they can be cast as cause or as effect of poverty, or even as both simultaneously. Conservatives, such as George Gilder (1981) and Lawrence Mead (1986), argue that welfare causes moral/psychological dependency. Liberals, such as William Julius Wilson (1987) and Christopher Jencks (1992), blame social and economic influences but often agree that claimants' culture and behavior are problematic.

A second stream of thought begins from neoclassical economic premises. It assumes a "rational man" facing choices in which welfare and work are both options. For these policy analysts, the moral/psychological meanings of dependency are present but uninterrogated, assumed to be undesirable. Liberals of this school, such as many of the social scientists associated with the Institute for Research on Poverty at the University of Wisconsin, grant that welfare inevitably has some bad, dependency-creating effects but claim that these are outweighed by other, good effects like improved conditions for children, increased societal stability, and relief of suffering. Conservatives of this school, such as Charles Murray (1984), disagree. The two camps argue above all about the question of incentives. Do AFDC stipends encourage women to have more out-of-wedlock children? Do they discourage them from accepting jobs? Can reducing or withholding stipends serve as a stick to encourage recipients to stay in school, keep their children in school, get married?

Certainly, there are real and significant differences here, but there are also important similarities. Liberals and conservatives of both schools rarely situate the notion of dependency in its historical or economic context; nor do they interrogate its presuppositions. Neither group questions the assumption that independence is an unmitigated good nor its identification with wage labor. Many poverty and welfare analysts equivocate between an official position that *dependency* is a value-neutral term for receipt of (or need for) welfare and a usage that makes it a synonym for *pauperism*.

These assumptions permeate the public sphere. In the current round of alarms about welfare dependency, it is increasingly claimed that "welfare mothers ought to work," a usage that tacitly defines work as wage earning and childraising as nonwork. Here we run up against contradictions in the discourse of dependency: When the subject under consideration is teenage pregnancy, these mothers are cast as children; when the subject is welfare, they become adults who should be self-supporting. It is only in the last decade that welfare experts have reached a consensus on the view that AFDC recipients should be employed. The older view, which underlay the original passage of ADC, was that children need a mother at home—although in practice there was always a class double standard, since full-time maternal domesticity was a privilege that had to be purchased, not an entitlement poor women could claim. However, as wage work among mothers of young children has become more widespread and normative, the last defenders of a welfare program that permitted recipients to concentrate full-time on childraising were silenced.

None of the negative imagery about welfare dependency has gone uncontested, of course. From the 1950s through the 1970s, many of these presuppositions were challenged, most directly in the mid-1960s by an organization of women welfare claimants, the National Welfare Rights Organization (NWRO). The women of NWRO cast their relation with the welfare system as active rather than passive, a matter of claiming rights rather than receiving charity. They also insisted that their domestic labor was socially necessary and praiseworthy. Their perspective helped reconstruct the arguments for welfare, spurring poverty lawyers and radical intellectuals to develop a legal and political-theoretical basis for welfare as an entitlement and right. Edward Sparer, a legal strategist for the welfare rights movement, challenged the usual understanding of dependency:

> The charge of anti-welfare politicians is that welfare makes the recipient 'dependent.' What this means is that the recipient depends on the welfare check for his *[sic]* material subsistence rather than upon some other source...whether that is good or bad depends on whether a better source of income is available...The real problem...is something entirely different. The recipient and the applicant traditionally have been dependent on the whim of the caseworker (Sparer 1970-71, 71).

The cure for welfare dependency, then, was welfare rights. Had the NWRO not been greatly weakened by the late 1970s, the revived discourse of pauperism in the 1980s could not have become hegemonic.

Even in the absence of a powerful NWRO, many AFDC recipients maintained their own oppositional interpretation of welfare dependency. They complained not only of stingy allowances but also of infantilization due to supervision, loss of privacy, and a maze of bureaucratic rules that constrained their decisions about housing, jobs, and even (until the 1960s) sexual relations. In the claimants' view, welfare dependency is a social condition, not a psychological state, a condition they analyze in terms of power relations. It is what a left-wing English dictionary of social welfare calls *enforced dependency,* "the creation of a dependent class" as a result of "enforced reliance...for necessary psychological or material resources" (Timms and Timms 1982, 55-56).

This idea of enforced dependency was central to another, related challenge to the dominant discourse. During the period in which NWRO activism was at its height, New Left revisionist historians developed an interpretation of the welfare state as an apparatus of social control. They argued that what apologists portrayed as helping practices were actually modes of domination that created enforced dependency. The New Left critique bore some resemblance to the NWRO critique, but the overlap was only partial. The historians of social control told their story mainly from the perspective of the "helpers" and cast recipients as almost entirely passive. They thereby occluded the agency of actual or potential welfare claimants in articulating needs, demanding rights, and making claims.[13]

Still another contemporary challenge to mainstream uses of *dependency* arose from a New Left school of international political economy. The context was the realization, after the first heady days of postwar decolonization, that politically independent former colonies remained economically dependent. In *dependency theory,* radical theorists of "underdevelopment" used the concept of dependency to analyze the global neocolonial economic order from an antiracist and anti-imperialist perspective. In so doing, they resurrected the old preindustrial meaning of dependency as a subjected territory, seeking thereby to divest the term of its newer moral/psychological accretions and to retrieve the occluded dimensions of subjection and subordination. This usage remains strong in Latin America as well as in U.S. social-scientific literature, where we find articles such as "Institutionalizing Dependency: The Impact of Two Decades of Planned Agricultural Modernization" (Gates 1988).

What all these oppositional discourses share is a rejection of the dominant emphasis on dependency as an individual trait. They seek to shift the focus back to the social relations of subordination. But they do not have much impact on mainstream talk about welfare in the United States today. On the contrary, with economic dependency now a synonym for poverty, and with moral/psychological dependency now a personality disorder, talk of dependency as a social relation of subordination has become increasingly rare. Power and domination tend to disappear.[14]

Conclusion

Dependency, once a general-purpose term for all social relations of subordination, is now differentiated into several analytically distinct registers. In the economic register, its meaning has shifted from gaining one's livelihood by working for someone else to relying for support on charity or welfare; wage labor now confers independence. In the socio-legal register, the meaning of dependency as subsumption is unchanged, but its scope of reference and connotations have altered: Once a socially approved majority condition, it first became a group-based status deemed proper for some classes of persons but not others and then shifted again to designate (except in the case of children) an anomalous, highly stigmatized status of deviant and incompetent individuals. Likewise, in the political register, dependency's meaning as subjection to an external governing power has remained relatively constant, but its evaluative connotations worsened as individual political rights and national sovereignty became normative. Meanwhile, with the emergence of a newer moral/psychological register, properties once ascribed to social relations came to be posited instead as inherent character traits of individuals or groups, and the connotations here, too, have worsened. This last register now claims an increasingly large proportion of the discourse, as if the social relations of dependency were being absorbed into personality. Symptomatically, erstwhile relational understandings have been hypostatized in a veritable portrait gallery of dependent personalities: first, housewives, paupers, natives, and slaves; then poor, solo, black teenage mothers.

These shifts in the semantics of dependency reflect some major socio-historical developments. One is the progressive differentiation of the official economy—that which is counted in the domestic national product as a seemingly autonomous system that dominates social life. Before the rise of capitalism, all forms of work were woven into a net of dependencies, which constituted a single, continuous fabric of social hierarchies. The whole set of relations was constrained by moral understandings, as in the preindustrial idea of a moral economy. In the patriarchal families and communities that characterized the preindustrial period, women were subordinated and their labor often controlled by others, but their labor was visible, understood, and valued. With the emergence of religious and secular individualism, on the one hand, and of industrial capitalism, on the other, a sharp, new dichotomy was constructed in which economic dependency and economic independence were unalterably opposed to one another. A crucial corollary of this dependence/independence dichotomy, and of the hegemony of wage labor in general, was the occlusion and devaluation of women's unwaged domestic and parenting labor.

The genealogy of dependency also expresses the modern emphasis on individual personality. This is the deepest meaning of the spectacular rise of the moral/psychological register, which constructs yet another version of the independence/dependence dichotomy. In the moral/psychological version, social relations are hypostatized as properties of individuals or groups. Fear of dependency, both explicit and implicit, posits an ideal, independent personality in contrast to which those considered dependent are deviant. This contrast bears traces of a sexual division of labor that assigns men primary responsibility as providers or breadwinners and women primary responsibility as caretakers and nurturers and then treats the derivative personality patterns as fundamental. It is as if male breadwinners absorbed into their personalities the independence associated with their ideologically interpreted economic role, whereas the persons of female nurturers became saturated with the dependency of those for whom they care. In this way, the opposition between the independent personality and the dependent personality maps onto a whole series of hierarchical oppositions and dichotomies that are central in modern culture: masculine/feminine, public/private, work/care, success/love, individual/community, economy/family, and competitive/self-sacrificing.

A genealogy cannot tell us how to respond politically to today's discourse about welfare dependency. It does suggest, however, the limits of any response that presupposes rather than challenges the definition of the problem that is implicit in that expression. An adequate response would need to question our received valuations and definitions of dependence and independence in order to allow new, emancipatory social visions to emerge. Some contemporary welfare rights activists adopt this strategy, continuing the NWRO tradition. Pat Gowens, for example, elaborates a feminist reinterpretation of dependency:

The vast majority of mothers of *all classes and all educational levels* "depends" on another income. It may come from child support or from a husband who earns $20,000 while she averages $7,000. But "dependence" more accurately defines dads who count on women's unwaged labor to raise children and care for the home (Gowens 1991).

Surely, "dependence" doesn't define the single mom who does it all: childrearing, homemaking, and bringing in the money (one way or another). When caregiving is valued and paid, when dependence is not a dirty word, and interdependence is the norm—only then will we make a dent in poverty.

Acknowledgments

Nancy Fraser is grateful for research support from the Center for Urban Affairs, Northwestern University; the Newberry Library-National Endowment for the Humanities; and the American Council of Learned Societies. Linda Gordon thanks the University of Wisconsin Graduate School, Vilas Trust, and the Institute for Research on Poverty. We both thank the Rockefeller Foundation Research and Study Center, Bellagio, Italy. We are also grateful for helpful comments from Lisa Brush, Robert Entman, Joel Handler, Dirk Hartog, Barbara Hobson, Allen Hunter, Eva Kittay, Felicia Kornbluh, Jenny Mansbridge, Linda Nicholson, Erik Wright, Eli Zaretsky and the *Signs* reviewers and editors.

Notes

1. Another part of the story, of course, concerns the word welfare. In this article, our focus is U.S. political culture and thus North American English usage. Our findings should be of more general interest, however, as some other languages have similar meanings embedded in analogous words. In this article we have of necessity used British sources for the early stages of our genealogy, which spans the 16th and 17th centuries. We assume that these meanings of dependency were brought to "the New World" and were formative for the early stages of U.S. political culture.

2. This stress on the performative, as opposed to the representational, dimension of language is a hallmark of the pragmatics tradition in the philosophy of language. It has been fruitfully adapted for sociocultural analysis by several writers in addition to Williams. See, for example, Bourdieu 1977, 1990a, 1990b; Scott 1988; Fraser 1989, 1990, 1992; and Butler 1990.

3. The critical literature on Foucault is enormous. For feminist assessments, see

Butler 1987; Weedon 1987; the essays in Diamond and Quinby 1988; Alcoff 1990; and Hartsock 1990. For balanced discussions of Foucault's strengths and weaknesses, see Fraser 1989; McCarthy 1991; and Honneth 1992.

4. In preindustrial society, moreover, the reverse dependence of the master upon his men was widely recognized. The historian Christopher Hill evoked that understanding when he characterized the "essence" of feudal society as "the bond of loyalty and dependence between lord and man" (1972, 32). Here dependence means interdependence.

5. One might say that this redefinition foregrounded wage labor as a new form of property, namely, property in one's own labor power. This conception was premised on what Macpherson (1962) called "possessive individualism," the assumption of an individual's property in his [sic] own person. Leading to the construction of wages as an entitlement, this approach was overwhelmingly male. Allen Hunter (personal communication, 1992) describes it as a loss of systemic critique, a sense of independence gained by narrowing the focus to the individual worker and leaving behind aspirations for collective independence from capital.

6. In the 16th century the term pauper had meant simply a poor person and, in law, one who was allowed to sue or defend in a court without paying costs (OED). Two centuries later, it took on a more restricted definition, denoting a new class of persons who subsisted on poor relief instead of wages and who were held to be deviant and blameworthy.

7. Actually, there are many variants within the family of images that personify subjection in the industrial era. Among these are related but not identical stereotypes of the Russian serf, the Caribbean slave, the slave in the United States, and the American Indian. Moreover, there are distinct male and female stereotypes within each of those categories. We simplify here in order to highlight the features that are common to all these images, notably the idea of natural subjection rooted in race. We focus especially on stereotypes that portray African Americans as personifications of dependency because of their historic importance and contemporary resonance in the U.S. language of social welfare.

8. The evolution of the term *native* neatly encapsulates this process. Its original meaning in English, dating from about 1450, was tied to dependency: "one born in bondage; a born thrall," but without racial meaning. Two centuries later it carried the additional meaning of colored or black (OED).

9. For example, Warner (1894-1930) uses dependent only for children. The same is true of Abbott and Breckinridge (1921, 7) and National Conference of Charities and Correction (1890s-1920s). This usage produced some curious effects because of its intersection with the dependency produced by the normative family. For example, charity experts debated the propriety of "keeping dependent children in their own homes." The

children in question were considered dependent because their parent(s) could not support them; yet other children were deemed dependent precisely because their parents did support them.

10. Studies of welfare done in the 1940s still used the word dependents only in the sense of those supported by family heads; see, for example, Brown 1940; Howard 1943; Bruno 1948.

11. Starting in the 1960s increasing numbers of black women were able to claim AFDC, but prior to that they were largely excluded. At first, the language of the New Deal followed the precedent of earlier programs in applying the term dependent to children. De facto, however, the recipients of ADC were virtually exclusively solo mothers. Between the 1940s and 1960s the term's reference gradually shifted from the children to their mothers.

12. Men on "general relief" are sometimes also included in that designation; their treatment by the welfare system is usually as bad or worse.

13. For a fuller discussion of the social control critique, see Gordon 1990. On needs claims, see Fraser 1990 and Nelson 1990.

14 For an argument that Clinton's recent neoliberal discourse continues to individualize dependency, see Fraser 1993.

References

Abbott, Edith, and Sophonisba P. Breckinridge. 1921. *The Administration of the Aid-to-Mothers Law in Illinois.* Publication no.82. Washington, D.C.: U.S. Children's Bureau.

Alcoff, Linda. 1990. "Feminist Politics and Foucault: The Limits to a Collaboration." In Crisis *in Continental Philosophy,* ed. Arleen B. Dallery and Charles E. Scott, 69-96. Albany: SUNY Press.

American Psychiatric Association. 1987. *Diagnostic and Statistical Manual of Mental Disorders,* 3rd ed. revised. Washington, D.C.: American Psychiatric Association.

Bakke, E. Wight. 1940a. *Citizens Without Work: A Study of the Effects of Unemployment Upon Workers' Social Relations and Practices.* New Haven, Conn.: Yale University Press.

———. 1940b. *The Unemployed Worker: A Study of the Task of Making a Living Without a Job.* New Haven, Conn.: Yale University Press. Barnes, Annie S. 1987. *Single Parents in Black America: A Study in Culture and Legitimacy.* Bristol, Conn.: Wyndham Hall.

Bourdieu, Pierre. 1977. Outline of a Theory of Practice. Cambridge, England: Cambridge University Press.

———1990a. In Other Words, trans. Matthew Adamson. Oxford: Polity.

———1990b. *The Logic of Practice,* trans. Richard Nice. Stanford, Calif.: Stanford University Press.

Boydston, Jeanne. 1991. *Home and Work: Housework, Wages, and the*

Ideology of Labor in the Early Republic. New York: Oxford.

Brandt, Lillian. 1932. *An Impressionistic View of the Winter of 1930-31 in New York City.* New York: Welfare Council of New York City.

Breckinridge, Sophonisba P. 1928. "The House Responsibilities of Women Workers and the 'Equal Wage,'" *Journal of Political Economy* 31:521-43.

Brown, Josephine Chapin. 1940. *Public Relief, 1929-1939.* New York: Henry Holt.

Bruno, Frank J. 1948. *Trends in Social Work.* New York: Columbia University Press.

Butler, Judith. 1987. "Variations on Sex and Gender: Beauvoir, Wittig and Foucault." In *Feminism as Critique,* ed. Seyla Benhabib and Drucilla Cornell, 128-42. Minneapolis: University of Minnesota Press.

_____. 1990. *Gender Trouble: Feminism and the Subversion of Identity.* New York: Routledge.

Cates, Jerry R. 1983. *Insuring Inequality: Administrative Leadership in Social Security, 1935-1954.* Ann Arbor: University of Michigan Press.

Diamond, Irene, and Lee Quinby, eds. 1988. *Foucault and Feminism: Reflections on Resistance.* Boston: Northeastern University Press.

Dowling, Colette. 1981. *The Cinderella Complex: Women's Hidden Fear of Independence.* New York: Summit.

Folbre, Nancy. 1991. "The Unproductive Housewife: Her Evolution in Nineteenth-Century Economic Thought." *Signs: Journal of Women in Culture and Society* 16 (3):463-84.

Foucault, Michel. 1984. "Nietzsche, Genealogy, History." In the *Foucault Reader,* ed. Paul Rabinow, 76-100. New York: Pantheon.

Fraser, Nancy. 1987. "Women, Welfare, and the Politics of Need Interpretation." *Hypatia: A Journal of Feminist Philosophy* 2 (1):103-21.

_____. 1989. *Unruly Practices: Power, Discourse and Gender in Contemporary Social Theory.* Minneapolis: University of Minneapolis Press.

_____. 1992. "The Uses and Abuses of French Discourse Theories for Feminist Politics." In *Revaluing French Feminism: Critical Essays on Difference, Agency, and Culture,* ed. Nancy Fraser and Sandra Bartky, 177-94. Bloomington: Indiana University Press.

_____. 1993. "Clintonism, Welfare and the Antisocial Wage: The Emergence of a Neoliberal Political Imagery." *Rethinking Marxism* 6(1):1-15.

Fraser, Nancy, and Linda Gordon. 1992. "Contract Versus Charity: Why Is There No Social Citizenship in the United States?" *Socialist Review* 22(3):45-68.

Freidan, Betty. 1963. *The Feminine Mystique.* New York: Norton.

Gates, M. 1988. "Institutionalizing Dependency: The Impact of Two Decades of Planned Agricultural Modernization." *Journal of Developing Areas* 22(3):293-320.

Gibbons, Mary L. 1933. "Family Life Today and Tomorrow." *Proceedings, National Conference of Catholic Charities* 19:133-68.

Gilder, George. 1981. *Wealth and Poverty.* New York: Basic.

Gordon, Linda. 1990. "The New Feminist Scholarship on the Welfare State." In *Women, the State, and Welfare,* ed. Linda Gordon, 9-35. Madison: University of Wisconsin Press.

———.1992. "Social Insurance and Public Assistance: The Influence of Gender in Welfare Thought in the United States, 1890-1935." *American Historical Review* 97(1):19-54.

Gowens, Pat. 1991. "Welfare, Learnfare—Unfair! A Letter to My Governor." *Ms.* (September-October), 90-91.

Gundersen, Joan R. 1987. "Independence, Citizenship, and the American Revolution." *Signs* 13(1):59-77.

Hartsock, Nancy. 1990. "Foucault on Power: A Theory for Women?" In *Feminism/Postmodernism,* ed. Linda J. Nicholson, 157-75. New York: Routledge.

Haynes, M. 1988. "Pharmacist Involvement in a Chemical-Dependency Rehabilitation Program." *American Journal of Hospital Pharmacy* 45(10):2099-2101.

Hill, Christopher. 1972. *The World Turned Upside Down: Radical Ideas During the English Revolution.* New York: Viking.

Honneth, Axel. 1992. *The Critique of Power: Reflective Stages in a Critical Social Theory.* Cambridge, Mass.: M.I.T. Press.

Howard, Donald S. 1943. *The WPA and Federal Relief Policy.* NewYork: Russell Sage.

Hughes, Gwendolyn S. 1925. *Mothers in Industry.* New York: New Republic.

Jencks, Christopher. 1992. *Rethinking Social Policy: Race, Poverty, and the Underclass.* Cambridge, Mass.: Harvard University Press.

Land, Hilary. 1980. "The Family Wage." *Feminist Review* 6:55-77.

Laslett, Peter. 1971. *The World We Have Lost: England Before the Industrial Age.* New York: Scribner.

McCarthy, Thomas. 1991. *Ideals and Illusions: On Reconstruction and Deconstruction in Contemporary Critical Theory.* Cambridge, Mass.: M.I.T. Press.

Macpherson, C.B. 1962. *The Political Theory of Possessive Individualism: Hobbes to Locke.* Oxford: Oxford University Press.

Mead, Lawrence. 1986. *Beyond Entitlement: The Social Obligations of Citizenship.* New York: Free Press.

Milwaukee County Welfare Rights Organization. 1972. *Welfare Mothers Speak Out.* New York: Norton.

Moynihan, Daniel P. 1973. *The Politics of a Guaranteed Income: The Nixon Administration and the Family Assistance Plan.* New York: Random House.

Murray, Charles. 1984. Losing Ground: American Social Policy, 1950-1980. New York: Basic.

Nathan, Richard P. 1986. "The Underclass—Will It Always Be with Us?" Unpublished paper, quoted by William Julius Wilson, "Social Policy and

Minority Groups: What Might Have Been and What Might We See in the Future." In *Divided Opportunities: Minorities, Poverty, and Social Policy*, ed. Gary D. Sandefuyr and Marta Tienda, 231-52. New York: Plenum.

National Conference of Charities and Correction. 1890s-1920s. *Proceedings*.

Nelson, Barbara J. 1990. "The Origins of the Two-Channel Welfare State: Workmen's Compensation and Mothers' Aid." In *Women, the State, and Welfare*, ed. Linda Gordon, 123-51. Madison: University of Wisconsin Press.

Pope, Jacqueline. 1989. *Biting the Hand That Feeds Them: Organizing Women on Welfare at the Grass Roots Level*. New York: Praeger.

Pruette, Lorine, ed. 1934. *Women Workers through the Depression: A Study of White Collar Employment Made by the American Woman's Association*. New York: Macmillan.

Quadagno, Jill. 1988. "From Old-Age Assistance to Supplemental Social Security Income: The Political Economy of Relief in the South, 1935-1972." In *The Politics of Social Policy in the United States*, ed. Margaret Weir, Ann Shola Orloff, and Theda Skocpol, 235-63. Princeton, N.J.: Princeton University Press.

Quayle, Dan. 1992. "Excerpts from Vice President's Speech on Cities and Poverty." *New York Times*, 20 May 1992.

Rainwater, Lee, and William L. Yancy. 1967. *The Moynihan Report and the Politics of Controversy*. Cambridge, Mass.: M.I.T. Press.

Sapiro, Virginia. 1990. "The Gender Basis of American Social Policy." In *Women, the State, and Welfare*, ed. Linda Gordon, 36-54. Madison: University of Wisconsin Press.

Scott, Joan Wallach. 1988. *Gender and the Politics of History*. New York: Columbia University Press.

Smith, Joan. 1984. "The Paradox of Women's Poverty: Wage-earning Women and Economic Transformation." *Signs* 10(2):291-310.

Sparer, Edward V. 1971 (c.1970). "The Right to Welfare." In *The Rights of Americans: What They Are—What They Should Be*, ed. Norman Dorsen, 65-93. New York: Pantheon.

Stacey, Judith. 1987. "Sexism by a Subtler Name? Postindustrial Conditions and Postfeminist Consciousness in the Silicon Valley." *Socialist Review* 96:7-28.

____. 1990. *Brave New Families: Stories of Domestic Upheaval in Late Twentieth Century America*. New York: Basic.

Timms, Noel, and Rita Timms. 1982. *Dictionary of Social Welfare*. London: Routledge & Kegan Paul.

Tumulty, Karen. 1991. *Los Angeles Times*, 5 July 1991.

Vaile, Gertrude. 1934. "Public Relief." In *College Women and the Social Sciences*, ed. Herbert Elmer Mills, 19-40. New York: John Day.

Warner, Amos Griswold. 1894-1930. *American Charities and Social Work*. New York: Thomas Y. Crowell.

Weedon, Chris. 1987. *Feminist Practice and the Poststructuralist Theory*.

Oxford: Basil Blackwell.

West, Guida. 1981. *The National Welfare Rights Movement: The Social Protest of Poor Women*. New York: Praeger.

Weston, Kath. 1991. *Families We Choose: Lesbian, Gays, Kinship*. New York: Columbia University Press.

Williams, Raymond. 1976. *Keywords: A Vocabulary of Culture and Society*. Oxford: Oxford University Press.

Wilson, William Julius. 1987. *The Truly Disadvantaged: The Inner City, the Underclass, and Public Policy*. Chicago: University of Chicago Press.

Young, Leontine. 1954. *Out of Wedlock*. New York: McGraw Hill.

FOR BETTER AND FOR WORSE
Women Against Women in the Welfare State
Ann Withorn

I would rather have a man worker any day. They, at least, are more likely to listen to you and seem sympathetic. The women are meaner. They act like it's their money and you should work hard like they do.

—Boston welfare recipient

Our office was all women, including the director, and I'll tell you, it was enough to make you hate women. Everybody fought among themselves and hated the director, who was horrible. Then they brought in this nice young man and now everything is much better.

—Suburban service worker

What makes our clinic so wonderful is that it's for women, by women. There is none of that male medical bullshit. We all struggle together to work out better ways to do things. It's not easy, but it is so much nicer not to have men around, laying their ego trips on everything.

—Feminist health center nurse

I just want to be treated like a person, like someone who you think you could be. It makes me so mad when you are supposed to be my ally and you won't look at me, or really talk to me like an equal. Or when you say you will take our "leadership," but only when we agree with you.

—Welfare rights activist

MOST SOCIAL SERVICES TO POOR WOMEN ARE PROVIDED BY female service workers. Together these women most often discuss "problems" identified with women's traditional roles: family difficulties; childcare; "personal" problems with relatives or lovers or with the lack of health care, housing, and income. The help that women workers usually offer is traditional female "nurturing": listening, some general and specific suggestions, sympathy and, sometimes money and other resources. Both workers and recipients suffer from the low status of being involved with society's "dirty work." Even when clients and workers unite in activist coalitions, most of the people around the tables and on the streets are women. In such an environment, complex relationships often divide women—connections that could, instead, teach important lessons and foster powerful alliances.[1]

As a teacher of human service workers and welfare recipients, and as a feminist and an activist, I meet many women frustrated by the gap between their hopes for human services as a base for good relations among a variety of women and by the reality of hostility and distrust among women in the welfare state. Here I examine the relationships among women in the human service world in order to understand better what is so hard and to determine what hope exists for the welfare state as an arena for struggle and change among women from many backgrounds.

The Human Service Arena

Human service work takes place in a variety of settings, which together constitute much of the welfare state. There are the large state bureaucracies: welfare departments, child welfare agencies, state institutions for the mentally ill and retarded—where public employees act like what sociologist Michael Lipsky has called "street-level bureaucrats" by providing the gateway to such essentials as money, public housing, medical and mental health services, or "protective" services to people who are usually poor and are primarily women and their children.[2] Low-income women usually come unwillingly to such settings because they have few other "private" options, or even because they are mandated to do so by schools or courts.

Many other community-based agencies also provide human services, usually through contracts with the state supplemented by insurance, grants from private foundations, or donated funds. They offer such programs as daycare, counseling, homemaker and adult education services, residential care for retarded and mentally ill people, and rehabilitation services, in settings that often attempt to be more connected to neighborhood or constituency group needs. Finally, a few alternative programs such as battered women's shelters still offer services as a means for making social change. All these services, whether or not they are directly funded by public money, can be considered part of an expansive understanding of the "welfare state." And, for almost every area of service, advocacy coalitions of providers, recipients, and "advocates" exist which try to affect the funding and regulation of services.

It is difficult to generalize about so much activity. On the one hand, agencies differ in their degree of bureaucratization, the professionalization of their staff, and the punitiveness of their function. Both people who receive services and workers tend to view their environment differently across the spectrum from big bureaucracy to smaller agency.

On the other hand, human encounters within most agencies are quite similar, with the possibilities for positive and negative relations present almost everywhere. Even in the most punitive state agency, a woman can appreciate a service worker who "treats her like a human being"; and the most feminist battered women's shelter can foster hostile, untrusting relationships. And, surely, most services simultaneously offer women relief from some aspects of their traditional roles, while also stigmatizing and punishing them for their "neediness."

Since the 1980's, leftist and feminist writers have paid new attention to the welfare state. By now, the best writers have come to see the state as a complex arena for social legitimation and struggles over cultural, social and economic power. This is not the place to review the wide range of extremely stimulating (if often inaccessible) writing which has been both a direct response to the growing assault on the welfare state, and also has emerged especially from feminist historians' examination of the women who built the fundamental policies and programs of the welfare state. However, whether more positive in its presentation of the welfare state's role allowing women to escape the constraints of unfriendly labor markets and families, or more critical of the ways in which women have remained trapped by constrictive programs and policy assumptions, little of the literature has yet reached down to look at how women, as women, actually experience using or working in the services and activities that comprise the state.[3]

Yet we still need to recognize that, in the day-to-day experiences of women, many of the negative impacts of the welfare state can be thwarted by the self-conscious actions of workers, especially when coupled with well-placed demands by women recipients and advocates. And that even programs that were created based on the most "progressive" principles can become punitive and denying, if workers bring insensitive attitudes. After 25 years in this business, I do believe that it *is* possible for women to emerge from human service encounters more able to cope with their lives, perhaps even to understand and meet their personal and social needs. And the crucial dimension for the successful delivery of almost all human services is the establishment of a respectful relationship between workers and women who receive services. Because of the broader social functions of human service agencies, this relationship usually reinforces and solidifies class, racial, and cultural conflicts in society. But, because of the real nature of the needs women bring to agencies (and despite state efforts to disregard them), sometimes it is still possible for astute women service workers to help women obtain what they need and make new political alliances if they are neither naive about the difficulties nor cynical about the possibilities.

Workers vs. Clients

When service workers first develop an analysis of the potential of human service work, whether on the job or in school, they often decide it should be easy to "correct" things through their own behavior. The basic feminist insight that women can identify with and support one another, as women, seems overpowering. One young radical of the early 1980s expressed hopes similar to those heard at radical conferences from young social work students a decade later:

> I started out really naive. I thought that since I understood how we were all oppressed as women, and how the Welfare Department was out to screw us all, then it would be easy for me to work with clients, and with my fellow women unionists. Very quickly I found out that no one trusted me because of these ideas and, worse, that I was reproducing some of the very patterns of insensitivity that I criticized. (1981)
>
> I came to this conference because I wanted to make connections to other social workers and women on welfare. I know if we work together and understand each other better, we can make a difference in the agencies.(1995)

Of course, most service workers don't enter the workplace trying to alter things. Instead, they come with class backgrounds and/or professional training that already distance them from women who seek services from them, whether they recognize their limits or not.

They are likely to be influenced by all the stereotypes that abound in this society about their separateness from "people in need of service." Other pressures combine to create the complex dynamic which reduces the potential for positive relationships between low-income women and women service workers. First, the power relationships are direct, even in the most "community-based" agencies. Workers are paid to provide services, which clients may or may not even see as needed. In almost all service encounters, even in less punitive agencies, the direct-service worker is the "gatekeeper," the person who can deny or provide needed resources, lessen or intensify state harassment, and in myriad ways affect the quality of life for women who walk in the door seeking help. Clients always recognize the power differentials, even as some service workers may try to deny them. So a simple gender identification between women workers and clients is inadequate. The only way to build relationships is to start with this understanding.

Second, the class and race of many women service workers, as well as their functional roles, pose further objective barriers to solidarity with most low-income women. The classic image of "white, middle-class social workers," removed from their clients' lives and issues, may not be as true in community agencies, but then professional training may step in to reward workers for differentiating themselves from former neighbors. When built-in role conflicts interact with class and race differences, the results can be devastating, even in "alternative agencies":

> With us it's intense. All our staff are women of color. The women who come here sometimes expect us to be "sisters," and they get angry when we push them. And sometimes we may expect too much of them. It's better than other places, but the problems sure aren't solved.

Such basic tensions often seem to overshadow any hope for a "contradictory" nature to human service work; the power to hurt seems so much greater than the ability to help. Yet for women service workers honestly to assist other women, much less to build alliances based on recognition of mutual needs and common oppression, the powerful organizational barriers, coupled with class and race differences, must be recognized, examined, and understood.

Besides the material factors of power, class, and racial conflicts, however, there are many mechanisms by which women of all backgrounds have learned to distrust and disassociate themselves from each other. Despite 30 years of feminist inroads, many women service workers still try to reject any identification with women clients and thereby reinforce client distrust. The cumulative effect leads workers either consciously to reject equal relationships with clients or to act in ways that make such connections impossible, even when workers think they are desirable. As one woman student wrote in a paper examining her work in a homeless women's shelter:

> Try as I might, it is hard for me to see women letting themselves go so much. I just can't understand how they get so messed up they lose their children and their dignity. It was easier when I worked with battered women; they were standing up for themselves. It hurts me to see my women so self-destructive. I can't face it some days.

Personally, women service workers face the same structural and psychological constraints as other women workers. They are usually working two jobs—one unpaid as primary family caregiver, the other underpaid. And, while the woman service worker may have chosen her "second job" partly because it builds upon skills learned in her first, that very similarity can be overwhelming. As one child advocate observed:

> I love my work but sometimes it is too much. When my own kids are in trouble I often think, "What am I doing here helping someone else's children? I should be home with my own."

This "overdose of nurturance" can be extremely difficult to handle and may lead women service workers, like this counselor, to seem cold toward clients:

> Since I had my baby I just don't have as much to give. I used to listen to everyone and be really understanding. Now it's not just the time, although that's part of it. It is also that I don't have the same emotional energy to spare. I see myself getting more structured and bureaucratic, and it makes me sad, but I don't know how to stop.

Such comments are common even though many service workers also feel that, as women, they are more sensitive to the problems women clients face. Without an overly clinical discussion of the psychological needs service workers project on their clients, I suggest that there may be "a lot going on" in relationships between women service workers and the women they try to assist. Exactly because of the intensity of the issues and problems facing all women, it can be difficult for women service workers to accept differences in women's ways and means of coping.

I call the negative side of this the "who do you think you are?" phenomenon—the tendency of women service workers to judge their women clients more harshly than they would men. These judgments may be based on a sense of what's "realistic" for a woman to do in U.S. society and a fear of the repercussions for any woman who tries to break the rules. They may allow service workers to deny low-income women options that raise questions about the worker's own life choices. According to one feminist welfare recipient:

> I think many of my women workers are threatened by my choice to be on welfare, but they cannot admit it. I am saying that I don't want to work at a bad job in order to support my children in poverty, and that I don't want to live with a man to give me legitimacy. Many social workers are in bad, low-paying jobs or bad marriages, or both. I represent a threat to them and they can't admit it.

Or once, in a discussion on recent welfare reform proposals to a "sympathetic" audience of social work students, an earnest young woman queried:

> But I know I have to wait to have a baby. I would like to get pregnant but I know that I need to finish school, get a job for a few years and then have my children. It doesn't seem right that women on welfare shouldn't have to make the same choice.

Sexual dynamics may also be at play. Almost any good human service encounter involves highly personal sharing, even if only to determine eligibility. As many feminist service workers have discovered, once the barriers to mutuality are discarded, then sexual feelings can emerge, in both directions. If service relationships become too equal, the potential for more intensely personal, even sexual, interaction arises. While some male service workers may accept and even use this tension, many women service workers may not want to acknowledge their own sexual feelings toward any women, much less women clients. In our homophobic society, this becomes another reason for women in a human service relationship to fear each other.

All told, many service workers share their culture's moral sense about women's proper role. The assumption that women should care for themselves and their families in certain prescribed ways runs very deep in social work and may even stem from the profession's 19th-century feminist roots. The move of liberals toward more conservative notions of "family values" may even have served to reinforce this notion. Even Hillary Clinton now claims *not* to "believe in divorce." Since most service relationships consider questions of how a woman should perform her basic roles, women service workers may experience constant challenges to their own values. As one child-welfare worker put it:

> I know I should be nonjudgmental and I try. But I also care about the kids (that's why I do the job) and the effects on them of troubled mothers. I don't know how to be sympathetic to both mother and kids, even though I am a mother too and know how hard it is for me. So I often act strange with the mother because I feel guilty for her and I don't know what to do about it.

So women service workers may be under great personal pressure to deny the very commonalty essential to feminist consciousness. In addition, it can be difficult for them to achieve professional legitimacy within their agency unless they put extreme distance between themselves and their clients. Especially if they have management ambitions, women may find it extremely difficult, except in the most grassroots programs, to connect with clients, or even less "professional" staff.

Professional ideology makes the tensions even worse.[4] In the absence of a more political perspective, "professionalism" may offer service workers some theoretical justification for avoiding moral judgments, while at the same time setting standards. But overall, professionalism reinforces dominant class and race differences and disallows a politicized and personalized sense of one's work. Finally, a professional identity makes it harder to develop more egalitarian models of connecting. Even though recent approaches that stress the "assets" and strengths of clients are an improvement against older patterns, they all too often still allow professionals to remain as the judges of client's "coping strategies." Seldom are workers encouraged to transcend their "expertise" by simply working with women clients as they would with neighbors or relatives. Women on welfare often deeply resent being "managed" in these ways.

Similarly, standard bureaucratic procedures work against an egalitarian practice. Here many service workers are stuck again. The need to escape from the never-ending nurturance that seems to be their lot as both women and as service workers drives many women to seek limits and clarity in bureaucratic "efficiency." The result, however, can be a withholding, punitive environment, which finally negates the very nurturance that led many women to become service workers in the first place.

Even professional women advocates can fall into traps that distance them from hearing and relating directly to women on welfare whom they honestly believe to be "allies." When confronted with real anger from welfare recipients about their distance, they may psychologize the problem. They may, for example, analyze the tension away by claiming that "after all, in hard times, it is easier to turn on your friends than your enemies," rather than by examining where their own needs for control and authority are part of the problem. Many advocates still find themselves unable to defer to women on welfare about issues central to their lives, when it means that advocates might lost influence with legislators, professional constituencies, or the press. Left unchanged, such patterns defeat the real partnerships so strongly desired by all, and so necessary for change.

The results of all this are often intense and unspoken. Service workers try, consciously and unconsciously, to deal with strong feelings about what women clients can and should do, as well as to consider their own personal and professional options. Recipients feel judged and confused. This situation is surely worse in welfare and mental health agencies, but even contacts that are inherently less authoritarian present the problems one teenage mother expressed:

> I don't know what they want from me. At my baby's daycare center they are friendly enough, but then they always make these little remarks that sound like they think I am messing up. It's like they say they are my friends, but I really think they wish I didn't have the baby. So I don't really trust them.

Clients vs. Workers

No matter what the setting, the imbalance of power between women service workers and women clients makes it difficult to see the service encounter as an event in which both client and worker can have impact. But, if a healthy relationship allows for more mutual human services, then we must begin with an honest appraisal of the power of both parties to build such a relationship. So we need to consider the effects of anti-woman attitudes among the women who *seek* service, without minimizing the primary responsibility of service workers to change the human service environment.

First, there is always pressure for women clients to adopt a "client role," usually marked by subservient behavior, in exchange for "success" in the bureaucracy.[5] This pressure stems from the state's fundamentally patriarchal role toward women needing services; indeed, women are "ineligible" for most services if they have a man to support them. This built-in, intuitively obvious "male role" played by the state leads many women to behave quite rationally like "good clients" in the same way they behave like "good wives": they act submissively, manipulatively, or with ostentatious gratitude. One woman put it bluntly:

> I'm always playing a role when I go to the Welfare Department. It's like going on a date. I think about what I'm going to wear and how I'm going to act and what I need to do to please them with the least amount of honesty about who I really am.

In behaving this way, women recognize their subservient status and choose to act accordingly. They are often reinforced. In "job clubs," which are set up to help welfare recipients find jobs, members are taught how to "interview well," how to dress, and how to "act motivated" in order to please potential (presumably male) employers. "Good clients" may even find themselves trotted out at press conferences to declare how much they benefited from mandatory work programs. The individual woman who pleases the Welfare Department may even become "queen for a day," receiving media attention and trips to conferences to promote the benefits of compliance.

While such behavior may be a survival strategy for any individual in a specific situation, it is obviously not a model for healthy development nor for activist strategy. What's more, many women find it harder to be a "good client" when they face a woman service worker. On the one hand, sometimes women seem to resent having to play the same dependent role with another woman—"Who does she think she is?" again—and become personally angry with women service workers in ways they are not with "natural" male authorities. On the other hand, some women just expect all women will be allies and are confused and angry when women service workers do not "act differently" from men, without understanding the bureaucratic pressures on women workers. Other women clients may simply be irritated because they assume that it is men, not women, who have real power, and they feel cheated by having a worker who is less potentially useful. One older woman was clear:

> Oh, my last worker was nice enough, but she had no power. So why should I talk with her? If I'm going to have to deal with any of them, I would rather have it be someone who can do something for me.

When I talked with a group of politically active welfare recipients about their reactions to such feelings, they were torn, just as I was. All felt that women service workers had treated them badly. "They are even less likely to treat me like a person than most of the men are," was the unanimous complaint. Yet all felt somewhat uncomfortable with their bias against women workers. One member of the group expressed the issue quite self-consciously:

> I know it's like the old woman-hating stuff, where women don't trust other women. Sometimes I know I want a man worker so I can manipulate him in traditional sexist ways. But I haven't got much power here and I have to use what I've got. Having a woman worker may get in the way. Besides, many women workers seem to resent us, like we're not suffering hard the way they do.
>
> It's confusing. Sometimes I am prejudiced against them or have unreal expectations of them. And then again sometimes they are more difficult to deal with. One thing is true, though. When you get a good woman worker, that's usually the very best. She can really make you feel supported and able to get what you need.

Both recipients and service workers bring bad habits and attitudes as well as reasonable evaluations of power to the human service relationship. Creating a different dynamic requires altered expectations of how women should behave as "clients." Just as there is no obligation to accept racism among white clients toward minority service workers, so clients' anti-woman attitudes need to be challenged, even within the confines of the welfare state.

Relationships Among Women Service Workers

> How can you expect us to be concerned about how bad things are for the patients when we are so understaffed that it's dangerous for us? In conditions like these, all I want is to give them enough medications so they don't beat me up.

For female service workers to make alliances with women clients, they must also understand the power relationships that affect their own work. Otherwise, the demands of a system within which they have little power will preoccupy service workers' attention, push them into interminable disputes with each other, and block attention to possibilities for real change.

Many of the same pressures that make it difficult for women social workers to relate well to clients also impede their ability to see the need for aligning themselves with one another. The overload of nurturance, which they give both to family and to recipients, makes sympathy and support for fellow workers hard to muster. Add the pressures stemming from low pay and low status, and it becomes hard for service workers even to pay attention to one another without irritation, much less to form alliances for change in the quality of service. In addition, the varied and complicated reasons why women may become service workers can create very different expectations among the women in a workplace. One activist in a large private agency summed up the dynamics well:

> Here we have a real mix of women. There are a few of the "old guard" unmarried middle-class professionals who see saving kids as their life work and moral duty. Although they are dying out, their spirit judges the rest of us. Then there are the "new breed" of assertive women who see themselves on the way up into successful management positions. They seem almost embarrassed to admit that they are really still social workers. There are also a good many working- and middle-class women who see this as a good job that doesn't threaten their home and family life. And there are a few of us radicals, feminists, who want to talk about unions, or abortion, or alliances with clients, and we threaten everybody else.

Women who self-consciously seek support from other women within their agencies have a particularly difficult time coming to terms with the lack of easy solidarity among workers. They are often able to understand (and seek to change) the power and class divisions between service workers and clients. But they find themselves just impatient and judgmental about similar tensions in the workplace among different levels of staff or among staff of different ages or races. Or, if they start to build connections with fellow workers, they may find that it becomes more difficult to connect to women who come for service:

> We have a boss who is a real loser, so I am trying to work with other women staff here to get him out. One of the women working with us has been on staff forever and is key, so we are making headway. But she treats some of the mothers who come here really badly, and I am confused about being too close to her. She really shouldn't be in her job either.

The double standards for men in human services are especially hard to take. Women service workers, for example, may criticize female coworkers if they are unprofessionally "soft" and overly concerned about their clients and coworkers, while male workers are praised if they are ever warm and nurturing. Yet when men do play traditional authoritarian roles, they are seldom criticized, as women are, for being too "hard" or "difficult to work with," as women so often are.

Before women service workers as a group can expect much trust from the women who come seeking service, they must come to terms with differences among themselves. And, before they can hope to work together, in unions or in other ways just to improve their own work lives, they must also examine the power relationships, woman hating, and other pressures that seem to divide them as deeply from one another as they are divided from clients.

Can This Contradiction Be Saved?

As the possibility for providing really supportive services shrinks in the face of shrinking budgets and the public attack on the whole welfare state, politicized service workers and service recipients within the American welfare state wonder what to do. The need for unity among service workers and between clients and service workers seems obvious, but the possibility of achieving it seems utopian. Even worse, the daily struggle to improve things can lead to a deep "burnout" of creative energy and political purpose. Some progressive workers may even begin to "triage" their support for women on welfare: Maybe they can be of more help supporting just battered women, but give up on the losing battle of talking about how all welfare recipients need time and money.

In times like these, we need to remember the tensions that have long been understood by the Left and by feminists. Most human services agencies are created to control and reproduce existing social relations. Agencies quite naturally deliver services that continue oppressive patterns. Services reinforce reliance on men as well as solidifying women's role as society's primary nurturer. This is the nature of modern society. But the capitalist welfare state is also "contradictory." It has also, historically, helped women recipients *and* workers to break away slightly from traditional roles: by providing recipients with subsistence benefits and services for a life without men and by providing women workers with jobs with enough status and income so that they could gain personal and professional recognition. And, poor and punitive as they may be, its services offer institutional alternatives to some of the nurturing roles demanded so unconditionally of "good women." One woman expressed the tension with a powerful question:

> Why do they make it so hard? Lord knows I need the money and the services I get and I would like to be happier with them. But what I have to go through to get the little they give me makes me wish, most of the time, that I never heard of any of it.

Another woman, off welfare for only two years, asked:

> Why can't I remember that I really needed the help? All I think about now when I hear "DSS" is how they made me feel like such a bad mother. But I know that I *was* having problems, and that some of the services— the daycare and even the counseling—did help. But all I remember most of the time is how bad they made me feel about myself.

Statements like these remind us how important it is to change, but not end, the welfare state, as we know it.

For women service workers at all levels the complexity comes around full circle. As the nurturers hired, at inadequate pay, to provide the care that other women have "failed" to provide, they wonder: Should they reject such roles and become male-identified managers? Should they do their job with the self-sacrifice always demanded of women? Or can they foist some nurturing back on women clients? The problem becomes especially complex because, in my experience at least, most service workers and clients to not want to abandon their care-giving roles, on the job or in the home, but they do want recognition and support for performing them. And both need options besides nurturing in their lives, as well as relief from being seen only as caregivers. Again, while this mutual conundrum theoretically unites service workers and clients, it does not suggest the basis for any easy alliance.

Yet a few experiences suggest alternatives to the grim scenario: First, we need to return to the lessons learned when women have self-consciously tried to provide services to each other. Although now, in the mid-1990s, most of these programs are gone, except for battered women's shelters, there are books which discuss them and veterans who are around. We need to remember this record of struggle, because, no matter how they have faded, feminist services have demonstrated that women can provide effective services from a base of shared experience and feminist analysis. All suggest that fighting the hierarchy among service workers and between service workers and clients is worthwhile, however difficult. Most important, feminist services provide a model that shows how services can be something valuable in themselves, not merely as organizing tools or as palliatives to an unfair society. One 1970s feminist health activist put it this way:

> By working at the clinic I understand better both how bad things are and that there is hope for change. I see how women are hurt in so many ways by doctors, husbands, and lovers who don't understand their needs. I also see that, when we do things differently, when we act differently toward each other and toward women wanting service, things feel different. Maybe we don't have the new answers yet about what to do, but at least it feels like a more equal, more honest way to try.

Second, many women try to use their union or outside advocacy groups as support for engaging in advocacy *with* clients. There are also many progressives in human service unions, even in leadership positions. Some have tried openly to reduce the stresses on service workers so that they can be more sensitive to clients. The social workers' union in Massachusetts, SEIU 509, has established a "women's committee" for women service workers to discuss their work with one another and provide the support that work-place structures deny. Although the committee has not focused as much on relations with women clients as on other concerns, from the beginning members have tried to address common experiences and to fight some of the individualism and elitism fostered by professionalism. Diane Dujon has found that women workers often speak of the need to raise consciousness among women service workers before better relations can reasonably be expected with clients.

In Boston, the women of *Survival News* received funding for "the Jericho Project," which allowed welfare recipients and workers to talk together about their perceptions of each other and to explore policy changes that would allow service workers not to be hostile toward clients. This was a far cry from the days when recipient groups simply demanded that a particular bad worker be fired. The possibility of such discussions, however, depended upon a supportive union, and in bad times union members may vote out leaders who are seen as too "pro-recipient."

Another forum for learning new models may be the advocacy coalitions that have been built in many cities during the "welfare reform" struggles. These have given welfare mothers and social workers new opportunities to work together as equals. If both groups use such common activity as a way not only to fight cuts but also to explore their trusts and distances from each other, a lot might be accomplished. In the heat of the fray, it might be hard to pay so much attention to process, but my experience in Boston suggests that it is essential to creating mutual trust. Of course, the nature of much social service work means that welfare rights groups will remain frustrated with women service workers. But alliances with the progressive unions and advocates may sow the seeds of new relationships, as one welfare rights activist expressed:

> When we marched together to fight the [Welfare] office closing, workers and welfare mothers were walking along together, laughing and joking about the [Welfare D]epartment, the governor, and our lives. After that it will be a lot harder for workers to treat us like "cases," and for us to see all of them as "the enemy."

It will take such a two-pronged strategy to enable women service workers and clients to understand their intertwined situation. Women service workers, and even professional advocates, will need to overcome their fear of identification with clients, as women, while welfare recipients will need to begin demanding such identification as the starting point for a relationship. As one particularly strong woman expressed:

> I've worked hard to train my welfare worker. She now understands more about why I operate the way I do, because I saw my job as getting her to see where I was coming from. Now she calls *me* to ask what I think of new proposals. I guess she'll leave soon—they always do when they get too good—but I hope she'll take what I taught her on to the next office and I'll just have to start training the next one.

For better and for worse, then, the welfare state (and the human service agencies that comprise it) remains a setting centrally defined by women's roles and women's issues. Whether women come willingly as clients or not, whether they come seeking help to perform traditional roles or because they are being psychologically and materially punished for rejecting such roles, the special nature of women's place in society is the fundamental context for human service activity, for both service workers and clients. As long as the women there are unable to recognize and consider the implications of this shared reality, then women remain divided from one another, and "human services" remain associated with punitive, demeaning tasks. If they are able to acknowledge their shared situation, however, then whole new areas for feminist activity may open up. As one woman commented, when asked what she thought of my topic:

> I don't know what it means but it's got to matter that we're all women here, and we're always talking about women's problems. If we can figure this out, we may be able to change the way we think about what we ought to do.

Notes

1. This essay was originally published in *Radical America* magazine and has been revised based on 10 more years of activism and listening. The first version grew out of a series of ongoing discussions with and observations of feminist and other service workers in the Boston area. Some of the material used here has been published in my books: *The Circle Game: Services for the Poor in Massachusetts* (Amherst, MA: Univ. of Massachusetts Press, 1982) and *Serving the People: Social Services and Social Change* (New York: Columbia University Press, 1984). My work with progressive human service unionists and welfare recipient groups in the Boston area, and through the Bertha Capen Reynolds Society (a national organization of radical social workers) has also generated some of these observations.

2. See Michael Lipsky, *Street Level Bureaucracy* (New York: Basic Books, 1981). For a recent book that treats of these same issues, see, Michael Fabricant and Steve Burghardt, *Crisis in the Welfare State* (New York, 1993). Also Theresa Funiciello's book, *Tyranny of Kindness*, (Atlantic Monthly Press, 1993) offers an incredibly hard-hitting criticism of how workers and administrators manipulate and control recipients.

3. Linda Gordon's book, *Heroes of tTeir Own Lives* (New York: Viking, 1989) is a notable exception.

4. See Margali Larson, *The Rise of Professionalism* (Berkely: Univ. of California Press, 1977) and my book *Serving the People* for more critiques of professionalism.

5. See Funiciello for the most recent hard-hitting and perhaps unfair presentation of how clients view "well-meaning" advocates.

DEPENDENT ON THE KINDNESS OF STRANGERS
Issues Behind Welfare Reform
*Mimi Abramovitz**

FEW OF THE POLICY ISSUES INITIATED SINCE THE NOVEMBER 1994 election have been as controversial as those pertaining to children. The Contract with America, which has bipartisan support, is hell-bent on cutting programs set up to help the nation's families—and that means that children, especially, will be hurt. If enacted as originally proposed, the Contract's plan to balance the budget without raising taxes will throw some 10 million children off the welfare rolls. Other features will put still other children in harm's way. For this reason, many critics refer to the Republican plan as the Contract on America.

The current drive to dismantle the system of entitlements established by the Social Security Act of 1935 does not make sense. This act was designed to protect individuals and families against the normal risks of an industrial society, the life contingencies over which people often have little or no control. Over the years, Congress created programs such as retirement and unemployment insurance, Aid to Families with Dependent Children (AFDC), Medicaid, and Medicare to protect the American people against the risk of losing income due to old age, joblessness, illness, disability, and family dissolution. The oldest of these programs has been in effect for 60 years. Although their provisions are far from perfect and much less generous than those in other Western nations, they are all we have. Eliminating these programs will put personal and societal well-being at enormous risk.

---

* This piece is excerpted from an interview conducted by Jay Kaplan and published in *culturefront*, vol.4, no.2 (summer 1995).

The entitlement programs are particularly controversial—the word "entitlement" as connected to poor people is a very powerful tool for those who seek to dismantle these programs. The word carries several meanings. Technically, entitlement means the federal government must automatically give states federal dollars, for the specific use of allocating benefits to people. Current law requires the federal government to provide matching funds for entitlement programs. It guarantees the benefits of all who are eligible and apply under state rules governed by federal guidelines. In contrast, Congress sets the budgets of discretionary programs, increasing or decreasing them annually as it sees fit. The current Republican thinking is to strip programs such as AFDC (often called welfare), food stamps, school lunches, and veterans benefits of their entitlement status and turn them over to the states in the form of block grants.

But this isn't really a problem of definition, law, or ideology. It's a matter of principle, if you will, of what we used to call social responsibility. Deep poverty, lack of civil rights, and widespread discrimination based on race, sex, age, physical condition, and sexual orientation prompted the federal government to pass laws that made our nation more socially responsible. Today, some people think we have gone too far. We are hearing calls for more individual responsibility on the grounds that the nation's social problems stem from defective values and lax individual behaviors. These critics seem to blame mother-only families for drug dealers, drive-by shooters, and the deficit.

By guaranteeing federal dollars for safety-net programs, entitlements protect people from circumstances beyond their control such as illness or layoffs. If we end entitlements and turn the programs over to the states—which are having their own fiscal problems—many people in need will go unprotected. Without federal support, state governments could run out of money during recessions, when demand for benefits increases, or simply because of natural population growth. States with a more conservative approach to these matters could also decide to use block grant funds under conditions or for purposes other than those intended by Congress. This is already happening; some states now deny aid to children born to mothers already on welfare. Without entitlements, fewer people will be helped, and growing numbers will find themselves in waiting lines for public assistance. Many Americans might once again be as destitute as they were during the Great Depression, which would certainly offend our basic sense of decency and compassion.

Those who advocate social responsibility argue, instead, that social institutions have to work better. The inability of the market to provide work for all those looking for jobs, the deterioration of our schools, the lack of affordable medical services, and discrimination—all need to be corrected. Grinding poverty and exclusionary practices make it difficult, even impossible in some cases, for people to carry out their family and work responsibilities. While some people fall into poverty due to self-destructive behavior, can this really be the case for most of the 37 million people now living below the official poverty line?

Many people have never gotten enough help, financially or socially. There's not enough interest in preventing these problems in the first place or dealing with them effectively when they come up. How does it help a person who is self-destructive to lower her AFDC check? Won't this just add to the stress?

Much of the controversy about who "should" receive welfare is based on myths, not facts. Perhaps the principal myth is that there are long cycles of multigenerational dependency upon welfare payments—that a child born on welfare will remain on it as an adult. Research, however, indicates that, while some daughters of women on welfare receive AFDC when they grow up, most do not. Inter-generational dependency on AFDC is simply a myth, one that stereotypes all five million people on welfare. In fact, some 70 percent of the women leave the rolls within two years for work or marriage. Many come back when their marriages break up, or when they lose their jobs, often because they are fired for missing a day to meet with a teacher or for staying home with a sick child. Remember, women on AFDC are single parents, doing the job of two parents with fewer resources.

Most studies, moreover, have not separated the impact of poverty from that of welfare, which is a problem since everyone on welfare is poor. If poverty is considered separately, we might learn that inter-generational welfare dependency is more a consequence of how hard it is to escape poverty than of anything else. If there were enough jobs, fewer people would end up on welfare.

Other not-so-controversial programs, like Medicare, food stamps, and college loans are also falling under the ax. Nothing, it seems, is sacred, not even Social Security, which is at risk down the line. An important distinction which needs to be made is that some programs are for the poor only and others serve the non-poor as well. Some 50 percent of all U.S. households receive some kind of government benefit, be it AFDC, Social Security, or tax deductions for mortgage-interest payments. The middle class is no longer safe.

If the amendment to balance the budget eventually passes, the more popular and generous middle-class benefits will be hit hard. Since Congress has taken tax increases, military spending, debt interest payments, and Social Security off the "chopping block," domestic programs serving the middle class will have to be slashed. Only one-third of entitlement spending comes from programs for the poor, and cutting them will produce less than 10 percent of the $1.4 trillion needed to balance the budget.

What this means is that the budget ax is falling most heavily on the means-tested programs—those programs which serve those in greatest need. Congress is not even taking that distinction into account. Though this may end up to be even-handed, it could throw more and more people from all classes into deeper poverty and greater despair.

Another major controversy focuses on question of values. The notion of restoring "family values" drives the AFDC discussion, as if poor women on welfare lacked them. The discussion, in fact, represents a narrow view of family structure and does not take into account the growth of single-parent households. The stated purpose of the Republican welfare reform bill is to stigmatize "illegitimacy." Does the government have the right to use taxpayer dollars to impose a rigid, one-size-fits-all set of values on people just because they need public aid? It's horrendous that receiving an AFDC check is considered debilitating: The average payment nationwide is $377 a month. Few would say that a wife's reliance on her husband's income amounts to debilitating dependency, or that government-subsidized corporations are "welfare dependent."

Generalizations regarding teen mothers—the myth that they dominate the welfare rolls, or the notion that they become pregnant to obtain AFDC benefits—easily become hot topics. In fact, teen mothers head about 8 percent of AFDC cases nationwide. In fact, all the research shows that there is no relation between the size or availability of the AFDC grant and childbearing decisions. Further, for many people, especially young teenagers, having children is not a calculated decision. Even middle-class women have unintended pregnancies. Certainly, teenage pregnancy ought to be discouraged through prevention, not punishment. And since recent studies indicate that many young women are impregnated by men aged 20-50, pregnancy prevention programs need to address sexual abuse as well as birth control. Laws that seek to punish teens will not discourage teen pregnancy.

If we are going to question the need for society to provide minimal financial support to teenage parents, then we should also be asking why society should bail out mismanaged and corrupt banks, provide price supports to farmers, pay for illegal military actions, fund prisons that do not deter criminals, and so on. Society may have to pay for behaviors among its members that some do not like; the consequences of not doing so are simply too inhumane.

Job creation is a good idea, given the magnitude of the job losses due to business downsizing and outsourcing. With deindustrialization, the better-paying, union-protected jobs have given way to low-paid, often part-time work in the service sector. For welfare-to-work programs to be effective, we must create well-paying jobs. Generally, these programs produce only small income gains, sometimes just $200-$300 a year over AFDC payments.

At $4.25 an hour the federal minimum wage falls more than $2,300 below the poverty line for a family of three. Other than employers, whose profits go up when labor costs go down, who benefits? When it comes to forcing welfare mothers to work for poverty wages, shouldn't we ask about the value of taking care of children? The people who want to force poor women on welfare to work outside the home are the same people who oppose childcare and family leave for working-class and middle-class women. These women should, they argue, stay home and take care of their children, but poor women should not. This is a double standard.

If we want people to work, the economy must provide jobs and childcare. The data show that many women on welfare have a work record. More would stay on the job if they had long-term access to affordable childcare and adequate health coverage. When jobs do become available, the newspapers show hundreds of poor women and men lining up for hours to apply, even when they know that only a few people will be hired.

As for the taxpayer, no one has ever asked me if I am satisfied with the way the government spends my tax dollars. Why is it we only worry about taxpayer feelings with regard to programs for the poor? Moreover, public opinion polls consistently show popular support for government assistance to the poor, the hungry, or the homeless. The public reacts negatively when the pollsters link this assistance to highly stigmatized programs such as welfare and Medicaid. When the question is raised in terms of the government addressing basic human needs, however, there is considerable public support.

Politicians love to distinguish between the working poor and the welfare poor, when in fact there is an enormous overlap between the two. Both groups suffer staggering economic insecurity. The working poor might begin to blame their employers and the politicians, if policymakers did not serve up poor women on welfare as scapegoats for the sagging economy and the frayed social fabric.

Driving a wedge between two desperate groups only serves the interests of business leaders and politicians. It does nothing to soothe the concerns of what Secretary of Labor Robert Reich has called the anxious middle class. Like the welfare poor, the ever-expanding working poor need jobs with higher pay and union protection. In addition, women on welfare and the working poor would benefit from jobs with childcare and health insurance. Dividing women by class is convenient for politicians. If poor women joined forces with those in the working and middle classes—who, despite more resources and, in some cases, a partner who helps, are in the same boat—women as a group would be a formidable political force.

Cuts in social programs are not at all even-handed. Programs serving the poor are being hit hardest of all. One of the most hypocritical measures is the plan to deny aid to children born on welfare, while providing the middle class with a tax credit for additional children. It certainly costs money to raise children, and investing in them is worthwhile for the nation's future, but *all* children should be so favored.

It's dangerous for the government to be in the business of deciding who should and should not have babies. It's eugenics to discourage people from having babies just because they are poor, as the Republican Contract does by cutting off welfare to stop non-marital births, or as President Clinton does when he says that only people who can provide for children should have them.

Of course it is easier for families to thrive when they have resources. But the government should not be in a position to make judgments about reproduction. First, the above statement by Clinton implies that the poor should not have children, since to be poor means never having enough money. Second, it raises the question of who decides who should reproduce. The historical record is not encouraging. Once, we removed children from the homes of poor parents simply because middle-class officialdom did not like the lifestyle of the poor. We also sterilized people someone deemed unfit, frequently because they were foreign-born or poor. I fear these biases will surface again, especially in the current mean-spirited and divisive political climate.

As the gap between the rich and poor has grown in the United States, our society has become more polarized and less cohesive, which is a genuine concern. Some people blame the decline on the pressures of diversity, criminality, and antisocial behavior. While I do not place diversity and antisocial behavior in the same category, high crime rates have made people feel unsafe. Instead of supporting the crime-prevention programs recommended by many criminologists and law-enforcement officers, the nation's leaders implicate the poor and polarize society by telling us that stiffer sentences and more prisons will turn things around.

People are also worried and feel unsafe because their standard of living has fallen drastically. Instead of increasing the minimum wage, creating jobs, and fixing the economy, the nation's leaders have let the value of AFDC and unemployment insurance erode by 40 percent in 20 years, while calling the poor "lazy" and blaming "diversity" for our economic woes.

Out-of-wedlock children are also used to polarize the public. In this case, there seems to be a moral panic about widespread changes in the role of women and family structures that cut across class and race lines. Many people project their anxiety about these changes onto unwed, poor mothers and seek to punish them by denying them benefits and services. Policymakers know that lowering benefits will not change behavior. So these penalties are meant to cut program costs and, more importantly, to send a message to all women about deviating from their prescribed roles as wives and mothers.

The major beneficiaries of the tax cuts in the Contract *on* America are families earning more than $100,000. Tax cuts, of course, reduce government revenues and increase the deficit. Debt-interest payments are the third largest item in the federal budget. Reducing them would harm those who have made loans to the federal government: affluent individuals and major corporations. Our resources are finite, and refusing to collect taxes makes spending decisions harder and promotes balancing the budget on the backs of the poor. We have a revenue, not a budget problem. It seems to me that it's socially *irresponsible* to try to run a country without bringing in the needed revenue to do so.

Let's look for solutions from the "other" side. How can we, as a society, expect individuals to carry out their work and family responsibilities—which I think most people, rich and poor, desperately want to do—when the conditions for functioning responsibly (enough food, adequate shelter, accessible health care, not to mention a job with decent income) are disappearing? How can people respect the social order when politicians divide and degrade it, or change their minds every week just to win votes? Integrity and competence are sorely lacking at the top. Let's clean up that act first, and I'm sure the benefits will trickle down!

TOGETHER WE ARE GETTING FREEDOM

Noemy Vides and Vicky Steinitz

"IT'S VERY WEIRD. I DON'T KNOW HOW I GOT THE COURAGE. For three years I tried to hide it from everybody and here I am telling my story to this big audience." Noemy's decision to "come out" as a public assistance recipient at the U-Mass/Boston Welfare Teach-In was fueled by her anger at the labeling and mistreatment of student welfare recipients and her conviction that "those of us who know need to say it, shout it out, and teach and educate the rest, and also defend ourselves."

Planning the Teach-In

A U-Mass/Boston faculty member talked about the importance of having a Latina presence. We had discussed the invisibility of Latina students at the university before and wanted to make sure that this time their voices were heard. Noemy, with Miguelina Santiago, a fellow student, set out to talk with Latina women about their welfare experiences and to see if some would be willing to speak out:

> We decided to collect real-life stories or testimony and share it, including our own, despite our learned and imposed shame. Those of us who said "I'll talk" equipped ourselves with strength and courage to tell and defend our truth. The testimonies of the Latina students are unique and strong but also sorrowful, so much so that for some of them it was unbearable to share their own experiences with a big audience.
>
> I decided to open my identity with the audience and my fellow Latina students because we are seen as cheaters, intruders, and illiterates. As Latinas, we are victimized and punished over and over, for being deserted with our kids, for being foreigners, and for being unskilled in many ways. Not speaking the language, not having our families here to help us to take care of the kids, being poor and without enough education is too much to bear alone. We have been accused of coming to this country to

benefit ourselves with welfare benefits. But the real truth is that we come to the United States many times because of political problems in our countries to the extent of getting killed there. We do not come to take advantage of this help but end up asking for assistance mostly because we are deserted by our kids' fathers. So it is necessary to speak out and let the rest of the world know the real story.

In a series of autobiographical papers, conversations, and interviews, Noemy shared with Vicky her life experiences and reflections on those experiences. Together we selected critical passages from these tellings, probed for explanations of how and why her life has taken its particular turns, edited drafts of her life story, and reached agreement on a final version. While our aim is to portray Noemy's struggles and overcomings as fully as possible, we decided that some experiences were too painful to include.

Here is Noemy's testimony, organized according to critical transitions in her life. We are well aware it is not a unique tale, but rather emblematic, in many ways, of the Latina immigrant experience. In the final section, we reflect on common themes in the lives of immigrant Latina women that increase their vulnerability and make even more onerous the struggle to survive as poor women. We consider the pressures, within both their native and adopted countries, which generate shame and self-blame in women, and the liberating potential of education when it becomes, as it did for Noemy, the practice of freedom.

Noemy's Life Story, Growing up in Las Flores

I grew up in Las Flores, a small town in El Salvador. Growing up there is one of the sweetest and most satisfying memories at this point in my life. Las Flores was a beautiful town surrounded by trees, hills, and a cluster of houses. There were not many people so almost everybody knew each other. This town was so clean and safe, nothing bad ever happened to me. We had a river which took the place of a beach. We used to go and do our laundry there and have some fun in between, while the clothes dried. We swam, got a lot of tan, and had lunch there.

I knew most of the people there because my mother used to make sweet breads, cheese, and caramel popcorn and sent me to sell it house to house. My mother was a hard-working woman and very independent for that culture, town, and time. She wanted to make her own money and save it for future needs.

I was an obedient and loving girl. For me, my mother was the most important person in my life. I do not recall her treating me with any special love or care, but I could tell she loved us a lot and took good care of her children, and that was enough for me to love and appreciate her as much as I could. My father was an alcoholic and he would beat my mother when he drank. His behavior got chronic when we kids were getting older. When I was about 10 or 12 years old, I used to stand up to protect my mother from my father. I used to feel so sorry for her when these things happened. I was terrified when he did not come from work at a certain time, for we knew what was going to happen.

My family was a large family. My mother was overwhelmed by taking care of the 10 of us and the house responsibilities. My mother was constantly told by people to leave my father, but nobody offered her any money or shelter. She was constantly criticized by her family for having too many kids, but nobody told her how not to get pregnant. I used to ask her how she could live that kind of life with my father and getting pregnant every year, and her response was, "I had no other choice." That made me feel that no matter what I did to help her, it was never enough.

Being the oldest child and a girl, I had to take responsibility for my siblings at an early age and help my mother with the house chores. My social life in Las Flores was very limited. My outside contact was mostly school. Attending school was very rewarding for me because my teachers always treated me with respect and admiration for my hard-working approach. I studied a lot and wanted to be a student. I loved learning.

Getting Married

I got married in Las Flores at the age of 18 to a young man who came there to work as a policeman. My life started to change. His job took us away from there and later from El Salvador. I lost contact with my family and my community. Moving to another town after my marriage led me to feel isolated, lonely, and somewhat strange. I needed to learn how to adapt to these feelings, situations, and my new responsibilities as a wife.

In the midst of this change in my life, the political situation in my country forced us to move to the United States. My husband was in La Guardia Civil. He realized war was coming and resigned from the Guard because he didn't want to be in the war. But he knew he was going to be asked to join up, to fight for one side or the other. The only way out was to leave the country. He had family in Los Angeles and decided to go there. He left when I was five months pregnant.

At the time he left we were living in the place where he was born, in Morazan. There was a river there. After he left, I started reading the newspaper. Every day there were stories of people being killed and they became more and more terrible, bodies found without arms, without legs. I rented a small apartment with a small store. I was selling things to support myself and he used to send me some money each month. I was destroyed by my pregnancy with Maybel. I was sick the whole time. I lost so much weight I was hospitalized and given injections. Giving birth to a child by myself with no support was a nightmare. He stopped writing for a few months after Maybel was born. I started writing him, asking, "When are you going to send for me?" And, finally, he said, "Come." I had to leave my eight-month-old daughter in the care of my mother. I didn't see her again for three and a half years.

Becoming an Immigrant

Moving from El Salvador to the United States was not in my dreams, and it was not easy either. I was forced to do it because it was expected that I follow my husband wherever he went. I came with five other women. The trip took about 21 days, by bus through Mexico. We crossed the border in a station wagon with a "coyote." She told us to say we were coming to visit. In May 1979, I arrived in Los Angeles. This city shocked me with its huge population, its immensity, and its busy streets that I had never seen before. The culture and values of this new society where I was going to live scared me, starting with a strange language and with different people. Early, I learned that if a foreigner did not learn English, she could not communicate with many people. If one did not learn to communicate, one's world would be very limited.

Almost immediately, I became pregnant with my second child. I didn't want to get pregnant, but my kid's father insisted. At first, we lived with one of his sisters, who owned a store. She was a very critical, demanding person. When I was five months pregnant, he left me for another woman and I was left alone. My struggles started. I did not know where to go for help, medical or financial, where and how to look for English classes. I was lost in an alien world. But despite all, my second child, Edgar, was born. The father returned when the baby was three months old and tried to kidnap him while I was out looking for work. I found the baby and ran to ask a friend of my mother's from Las Flores for shelter. She let me stay in a small room and found me a factory job at night.

This is the part I hate myself for! I knew the baby's father was looking for him. One day his cousin gave me a ride and I told him he could tell the father he could come and see the boy. He arrived and looked like the victim, having traveled two hours by bus. I felt sorry for him and said I'd give him another chance. He tried to find a job in Los Angeles but couldn't. He called a cousin in Boston who was a supervisor in a clothing factory. He said, "Sure, I can find you a job." After six days on the bus, we arrived in Boston.

When the driver announced we were getting to Boston, I looked around and saw those brick houses, all close together. I got off this bus with so much sadness. The city looked so sad. Arriving in Boston and trying to get used to this city took me longer. It filled me with desolation, a feeling of being lost, of not knowing who I was anymore. While I was living through my struggles, Edgar got sick and had to be hospitalized for almost a month. The doctors were never able to find out what was the matter with him. I blamed it on the house we were living in because it did not have any heat and we had to sleep in a very cold living room.

Again the old movie repeated, and I found myself pregnant for the third time. By now I should have known better how not to get pregnant, but with all these moves from one place to another and in a new and strange country and culture, one is completely lost and out of space. I was working as a cleaner at a hospital, but I had to leave because I was pregnant and sick. Sammy was born.

At the end of '82, my parents and three of my siblings came with my daughter. The whole family moved to our own apartment in Chelsea. My mother, brothers, sister, and I all found cleaning jobs. We were managing, but my personal life was not OK.

Pursuing an Education

After six months in my cleaning job at Howard Johnson's, the supervisor began to trust me and told me I could be her assistant if I learned a little more English. Then, there was an accident at the hotel and I was told I would have to testify in court. On the way to court with my supervisor, the car was in an accident. I broke my nose and that was the end of my job. I had terrible headaches and couldn't work for a year. I took ESL classes at the YMCA for six months and then began working for a friend who had a cleaning business. Some of the ladies in these families were supportive. They told me I should study. My ESL teacher told me about the GED exam. She said I could study on my own and lent me the book. I took the exam and passed. I said to myself that after all three kids start school, I'll go to more advanced ESL classes. My husband didn't like this idea. He made me promise I'd continue to fulfill all my roles as wife, mother, etc.

I was a new parent with children in the Boston public schools. I started to feel frustrated. I did not know what to do when my children came home complaining that the teacher did not understand them, that the other children spoke different than them or called them names; and, other times, the way they said Spanish words was half English, half Spanish, or words that do not exist in the dictionary. One day, I took my kids to school and I saw a sign—SUBPAC meeting [SUBPAC stands for Subcommittee of Parents, Advisers, and Councils]. I went in right away and started listening. What a surprise! The meeting was in Spanish. There were parents with the same frustrations I had. They presented their worries and fears for their children's safety, education, and respect. I said to myself that this is what I need to help my kids.

I participated in this bilingual parents' advocacy group for five years, first as secretary and then as vice-president. I met with school administrators and teachers; I encouraged new parents and went to court to fight for our rights and needs. In 1987 I won an award as the most active mother of the year at the Winship School. That same year, I did a year's course in Early Childhood Education at Roxbury Community College. My grades were good and I decided I needed to find a job in an office. There was a volunteer position at ABCD for the summer. I was youth coordinator of recreational and educational programs. At the end of the summer they gave me a full-time

Employment and Training position.

Single Mother, Worker, and Student

Soon after I began work at ABCD, my kids' father got involved with another woman and left the home. I was crying all the time. I couldn't deal with it. I hid it from my coworkers and nobody could understand what was happening to me. A month or two later, I told my director and he said he couldn't believe it, I was such an attractive woman. A month or two after that, my director started sexually harassing me. Of course, then I didn't know it was called sexual harassment or that you could do anything about it. I felt uncomfortable; I started losing confidence; I thought it was my fault, something I had done. I began to look for another job.

My next job was as an intake worker with the East Boston WIC office. I worked 24-30 hours a week. One day I picked up a sheet of paper about CPCS [College of Public & Community Service at U-Mass/Boston]. At that time I wasn't thinking about more education. I was crying and thinking this man was going to take my kids away. The flyer said that adults will feel comfortable there, working experience is taken into account, program in human services, all the things I wanted. I called the next day. They told me they were having a workshop the same week. I went. I was the only Latina in the room. I felt, "Who am I to be here?" I didn't know what was going to happen but I felt I was doing the right thing. In '91 I became a student at U-Mass/Boston. The next year I moved to Cambridge WIC to be a nutrition assistant, not just an intake worker. I wanted to learn about food so I would know what to eat and feed my kids.

The kids' father was living with another woman. There was little communication and he was very aggressive. I had already filed for divorce and I had to go to the courts to get a restraining order because he was threatening to kill me. Once when he was going to take Edgar to New York for the weekend, he came to the house, he hit me, and he left. I moved out to my mother's house. The process started of going to court for mediation; he wouldn't show up. He was brainwashing my kids, telling them he left because I didn't love him and other things were more important to me, like working outside the home and going to school. He told them I would leave them too. He was making good money, but he paid child support for only one month.

As you can see, I endured many trials, not because I was stupid and did not know what a traitor my kids' father was, but because I was living in a cage with locked doors, with so many limitations and barriers to overcome. But harming my children, and me knowing it, was too much to take, and, without thinking twice, he had to go. Divorcing from him was the best thing I did because he was against my education and my independence.

Becoming a Public Assistance Recipient

After almost three years of separation, I realized that I was always short of money and could not provide for my family's basic needs, even though I was working. The kids were getting older and they were embarrassed by their appearance. I resisted the idea of going to the welfare office and asking for help. I used to tell myself I could make it, until I got to the point of not having food, or money to buy it, for a couple of days every week.

Then one day, I dressed up in a shell and went to the welfare office and applied for food stamps and Medicaid, because at the place I worked I could not afford to pay medical insurance. I brought to the welfare worker the tons of required information. It took three months, after traveling back and forth many times, to get Medicaid and food stamps. Then, the worst part came. I did not want my kids to know that I was receiving welfare. I tried to hide it for six months. I was very ashamed. When the kids found out that I was on welfare, they asked me, "Why Mommy, why? Why do you have to go on welfare? You are working. Why don't you make enough so you don't have to go to the welfare? Are we 'welfare kids?'" The first time they went to the grocery and paid with those stamps was O.K. Then, they did not want to go anymore. It has been a shame for them because their friends have been around. It is a shame still for me, so I do not blame them.

Graduating from the University

I started college because I thought I couldn't afford to live without being educated. But I was never able to visualize my graduation, me wearing the cap and gown. What I saw was barriers, struggles, limitations. I felt I was deserting my kids, like their father did, leaving them for so many hours to go to class. I constantly talked to them about this, daily, weekly, explaining why I was doing what I was doing, how I was trying to get a better education so we could survive. English was the main barrier I saw. Only I knew how hard it was, how much time it took me to finish one semester, reading articles four to five times to understand, writing papers over and over again. I remember Carla Johnston, who taught my first management course, which was very difficult for me, saying, after my first presentation, "Remember, none of us could give these presentations in another language." This gave me courage to continue doing my papers.

When I got to the point of having 30 competencies finished [more than halfway], I started to feel happy; my self-esteem was growing. Then I got to 42, and I knew if I had 42, I'd have 50. Graduation tasted sweet and I was full of hope and strength. I felt liberated in some ways. I learned that commitment is important and that if you have support you can do anything. Four years ago, I thought I'd be satisfied with a Bachelor's, but now I think one degree is not enough. There's so much I want to know. I want to do a Master's in Education. I know I can teach because I value education, but I haven't figured out yet whether I have the vocation to be a teacher. Also, I want to get an administrative position. I've applied to the East Boston WIC program where I used to work. It's a temporary position as Immunization Coordinator, working with pediatricians, nurses, and the WIC director. [While we were working on this chapter, Noemy was offered and accepted this position.]

Vulnerability, Shame, and Liberating Education

Noemy's work as a nutrition assistant in the WIC program and her study in college of the history of poverty and social welfare in the United States gave her the necessary information to challenge the wrong assumptions that welfare or federal aid is dirty, along with its recipients. Her excitement about the ideas of Brazilian educator Paolo Freire fired her conviction that education can be a tool against oppression and that "when we educate others and ourselves, together we are getting freedom." Still, it was not easy for her to speak out.

There are many reasons why it was so difficult. Noemy's testimony documents the vulnerabilities and heartbreaking losses faced by Latina immigrants: having to leave family and country under conditions of great uncertainty and danger; coming to an alien, incomprehensible land where fear is a constant companion; being dependent on an untrustworthy and manipulative husband; becoming pregnant, even though she wants desperately to avoid having more children; being abandoned, left with small children and no resources, and prey to the sexual advances of men primed to take advantage of women alone; being unable to earn enough money to support her family, no matter how hard she works; struggling to learn English to avoid the stereotypes about those who speak "broken English." Having learned that a woman's role is to follow her husband, to keep quiet and accept what befalls her, to hide her troubles and not ask for help, Noemy had to struggle against her socialization to find the strength to tell her own truth.

Early lessons about woman's place, the absence of choices, and the consequences of rebellion are strong inhibitors. Later discoveries of how alone one is, as a newcomer in a country where the shock of the system changes behavior and one can no longer rely on the solidarity of sisterhood, make immigrant women even more fearful. Experiencing the stigma of being a public assistance recipient is one more powerful silencing force.

The struggle to overcome these forces is made more difficult by the ease with which what should be anger against those who dominate and judge turns into anger against oneself and others like oneself. While Noemy knows it's not her fault that her husband deserted her, when she imagines people labeling her as she pays with food stamps, she can't help feeling ashamed and angry at herself: "Why wasn't I smarter to marry the right man?" Fear of being stigmatized leads Latinas to separate themselves from other women who may be even more devalued. Thus, long-term immigrants keep their distance from "naive" newcomers, and Latinas from more "developed" countries look down on the "ignorant peasants" from poorer countries. By accepting the dominant judgments, women suffer even more. Unable either to value their own struggles or to recognize their shared oppression, they remain silent and isolated.

Noemy believes her own transformation began when she moved to Boston and found helpful and understanding people who encouraged her to seek an education —"It is here I was born as a new woman with visions, dreams, hopes, opportunities, and fulfillment." In the years alone with her children, "I started to take charge of myself and my kids by not asking others what to do. I stopped being a follower." Becoming involved in her children's schooling fueled her determination to educate herself. At college, Noemy transformed her view of herself, and of the two cultures in which she lives, coming to understand El Salvador's "pain and struggles" and developing pride in being part of a "long-suffering people, but with tireless spirit." Noemy came to realize that she was accepting the oppressor's definitions when she felt ashamed of her inability to speak English perfectly and to be self-sufficient in a society where she was discriminated against and viewed as less than a complete human being. By talking and writing about her learned shame, she pursues her own liberation, replacing shame with autonomy and responsibility.

We agree that education is the key ingredient in women's struggles to survive. Without a college degree, women stand little chance of finding jobs that pay enough for them to support their families alone. What's more, educational progress builds self-worth; it provides concrete evidence that one has strengths and is a person of value. Beyond these economic and psychological benefits, a critical education that challenges dominant explanations can be transformative. Such an education provokes awareness that the labels—ignorant peasant, abandoned woman, broken-English speaker, welfare cheat—have nothing to do with who one really is, but serve to keep women subjugated and divided. A critical education gives women tools to understand the uses of power; it emboldens us to move beyond the imposed shame that silences, to speak out and join together in a common liberatory struggle.

WELFARE: WHAT IT'S NOT!
Diane Dujon

1. WELFARE IS NOT ENOUGH! Welfare recipients live on about 45 percent of the poverty line, and less than 30 percent of eligible recipients receive housing subsidies. Food stamps only last 10 days, no matter how frugal one is.

2. *Welfare is not* a planned, all-expense paid vacation to the Garden of Eden. Obtaining and maintaining welfare is hard work. Instead of governors talking about "two years and you're off," it would be nice to experience "30 days and you're on!"

3. *Welfare is not* "sitting at home waiting for the welfare check." You and your children will starve to death unless you are vigilant and adamant about your right to receive the benefits for which the Welfare Department has deemed you eligible. When there is no money, you spend large amounts of time at yard sales, bazaars, and thrift shops, and you work harder, cooking from scratch and performing household tasks the old-fashioned way.

4. *Welfare is not* an identity. We are all in and out of the workforce periodically for a variety of reasons (layoffs, quittings, firings, etc.). Sometimes, it's your boss who decides you apply for welfare tomorrow!

5. *Welfare is not* an aspiration, career goal, or a field of study in which to major. People who apply for welfare are desperate and would make other choices if they could. If the men in our lives were more dependable and less violent; or the job market were more reliable, flexible, and worker-friendly; or the government demonstrated that it valued families by providing universal health care, childcare and paid family medical leaves, we would all have more options.

6. *Welfare is not* an IQ score, a failing grade, or a shame. We know enough to feed, house, clothe, and educate our children, and that is our first job.

7. *Welfare is not* an inheritance to be handed down to our children. Our children are no more likely to receive welfare benefits as adults than anybody else's children; and if they do, it's often due to the "*isms*" (racism, sexism, classism) of society.

8. *Welfare is not* a membership to a sperm bank or fertility clinic. Welfare families have an average of two children, similar to all other families.

9. *Welfare is not* a sign of immorality, irresponsibility, or poor parenting skills. It's more likely a sign of paternal failure, employer failure, and/or societal failure.

10. *Welfare is not* a crime. Most welfare fraud is committed by doctors, pharmacists, and welfare workers. Recipients do not deserve to be fingerprinted.

11. *Welfare is not* an exemption from the IRS. Welfare recipients pay the same taxes that all other citizens do—meals taxes, sales taxes, liquor taxes, gas taxes, property taxes, etc.

12. A.F.D.C. are not Greek letters symbolizing an African-American sorority. More welfare recipients are white. It's ironic that the very attribute which was valued in a slave woman in the agrarian South (a high fertility rate) has become a target for disdain by the masters' descendants.

Welfare should be a societal "token of love." As a society, we need to practice unconditional love by being *dependable*. If we make a commitment to others, we ensure our own survival. We need to challenge injustice everywhere—not by raising Hell, but by lowering Heaven!

AND STILL I RISE
Visions of a New Movement to Abolish Poverty

> We must move past indecision to action...If we do not act we shall surely be dragged down the long dark shameful corridors of time...Now Let us begin. Now let us rededicate ourselves...the choice is ours, and though we might prefer it otherwise, we must choose...
>
> —Martin Luther King

SO WHAT'S A POOR GIRL TO DO?

The problems facing low-income women demand serious change, the kinds of big change that can only be made by broad radical movement—one that's *out there* for basic justice, for economic and social rights. As the opposition to welfare, and all poor people's programs has intensified and radicalized, we are less and less patient with strategies that end with lobbying to defend yet one more ineffective program. While this may still have to be done, for us the task is to educate, organize and mobilize a broader constituency that will make the connections between welfare cuts and the increasing risk of poverty, and then between poverty and the lack of security for all in this society.

When we think about the possibility of creating such a change, the best model we know of is the predecessor to the Civil Rights Movement, the Abolitionist Movement.

We love the Abolitionist Movement because it was big and brave, funky and disorganized and accomplished a lot. For probably the widest range of people in the history of this country there was a period of time when, if you felt "radical"—whatever that word meant to you—there was a connection. You could be a white person stuck in some little tiny town and think, "I am weird...I must be an abolitionist." Or you could be a free Northern black person who owned property and think, "well, I still must be some kind of abolitionist." Or you could be a clergy person who just couldn't read your Bible and avoid the issue; you could be one of all sorts of people whose association with issues of justice and change, of what needed to be done, would come under this huge big, radical umbrella of "abolitionist."

There were the people who defined their radicalism by helping with the Underground Railroad and people like John Brown who waged war and thousands of others who did very brave, militant things. But there were also radical women sitting in their kitchens making clothes for babies in slave families. There were people teaching runaway slaves; black and white people who would repair books and devise lesson plans; people who let their homes be used by visiting abolitionist speakers. A woman could begin by connecting abolitionist concerns with the meaning of justice to her own life. Working people started finding the base for their own demands in the metaphor of freedom—they would not be "wage slaves."

These themes and activities stressing slavery and freedom were important for mobilizing people. They mobilized exactly because there was always something you could do: whether it was write, read, speak out, or organize. Most people who thought of themselves as abolitionists simply knew there was a big job to be done, one which had to be done, about which anyone who cherished justice had to speak out and act, somehow. And while they waged the ideological battle, abolitionists also recognized the need to protect the victims of the system by providing them with shelter, food, transportation, jobs, and education.

This is what welfare mothers, immigrants, all of the designated victims of the Right need now: a broad set of allies who simply *must* organize and speak out with them for economic rights because they see their situation connected to *everyone's* ability to achieve justice from this society. And, just as the Underground Railroad provided sanctuary to those slaves who were both courageous and fortunate enough to find their way to a "station," so must today's activists find ways to offer relief and support as the pain of living on the margins intensifies. Our movement must be the same kind of broad-based movement for basic justice, a movement that sees the fate of all of us tied up with the fates of those who suffer most in society. Then it was slaves, today it is still the descendants of slaves and other people of color, as well as all women on welfare, poor people, and immigrants.

Building the Base

The authors in this final section help us to see how to sustain a new movement. Dottie Stevens and Marion Kramer show how organizing itself gives energy and strength, and how new visions arise out of the fray. We show how simple logic gets lost, and how words get used so that it can seem like welfare rights activists and conservatives are in agreement about "ending welfare." Education is still key both to changing popular attitudes and to providing activists and potential activists with skills for the future, as Ann Withorn and Erika Kates present. Change must have organizational support, so we include the resolutions and statements of the National Organization for Women and the Committee of One Hundred as examples that times are changing, that more people are hearing the strengths in women's voices, and finding new arenas to fight—even winning office themselves as Diane Wilkerson, State Senator from Roxbury, Massachusetts, has done.

We conclude by sharing what we have learned as we added our own voices to the chorus, to the conference platforms and to the meeting rooms. We end by trying to touch once again upon the many things we have to understand and do if we are going to build a broad-based movement to abolish the power of the Right and replace it with a more truly dependable, just and free society. We know we need our own expansive and shared sense of what justice means in our day: for abolitionists, it meant education and land for former slaves and respect for all free labor's right to organize; today, it means jobs, income, education, health care and child care. We know too that abolitionists could come together across a lot of differences, because they shared a sense of uniting against a common enemy. They knew the enemy was a system, not just individual slave owners. They called it "the Slave Power" and "King Cotton" and they educated themselves not only about how to fight it but as to who specifically the enemy was and the danger of the enemy's ideas and actions. By educating themselves in this way abolitionists came to understand their own goals, and the challenges they faced much more deeply.

Abolitionist tracts and slave narratives were about what it was like to live as a human being under the condition of slavery—how slavery debased people, both slaves and free whites, women, and children. People learned about how slavery was justified and structured, the international economics and the "ethical" arguments used to maintain and advance Slave Power.

Reading those stories today, we understand that part of telling them over and over was to keep people understanding *both* the need for justice *and* the existence and nature of forces that oppressed them. Because people act more clearly when they have a vision, know the stakes, and can see the tremendous costs of losing the battle—that's how the abolitionists inspired people to keep going. As more and more people began to realize that the whole nation, not only people who were slaves, was doomed if Slave Power were left unchallenged, the imperative for action spread.

So our final reason for writing this book is to proclaim that we *can* stop what is happening to welfare mothers, to urban youth, to immigrants, to all the most vulnerable people. But we can only do so if we find the where-with-all to build the kind of movement to abolish poverty the Abolitionist's created to end slavery. If we lose, everyone who is not now vulnerable becomes at risk for the future—for just as slavery needed to expand to survive—so the fuel that drives the power of the Right is the existence of people whose very needs and ways of living can be viewed as weakening the "good" society. We can only find the incredible energy we will need to win if we truly understand how serious the enemy really is, and if we speak out and think hard about how define a vision for change that drowns out their omnipresent voice of ignorance and fear. To accomplish the vision, and find the energy, we will lean on the wisdom, power and fury of those who have gone before:

> How, then, ought I to feel and speak and write, in view of a system which is red with innocent blood drawn from the bodies of millions of my countrymen?...My soul should be, as it is, on fire. I should thunder, I should lighten, I should blow the trumpet of alarm long and loud. I should use such language as is most descriptive of the crime.
>
> —William Lloyd Garrison

WELFARE RIGHTS ORGANIZING SAVED MY LIFE

Dottie Stevens

I GREW UP IN EAST BOSTON, MASSACHUSETTS, A NEIGHBORHOOD with a large Italian population (mostly immigrants). For me, they represented large families, strange accents, and wonderful smells from delicious mysterious foods. Wine was on the table for all meals, and even the young children were encouraged to sip it from fancy glasses. My street was a mixture of nationalities. We were also Irish, French, English, Native American, and Chinese, as well as many other mixtures we couldn't figure out. My own background was Irish and German.

On the other side of my street was a housing project that went on for four blocks. It became my playground and community. My own home was a two-family house. Nana lived on the first floor and my mother, two brothers, two sisters and I occupied the second floor. Mom was divorced and had to apply for welfare to keep us together. I don't remember seeing Mom much after she began to work under the table, because the welfare's cash benefits wouldn't cover all the bills.

I found that if I wanted attention or something to eat, I could go to any of my friends' homes on the street or in the projects and blend in with their families, and feel I belonged. I liked to stay at my friend Angela's house the best. She had a mother *and* father at home and they always had fresh, hot Italian bread to share with me. Angela had one brother, and many aunts and cousins, but what I was most impressed with were her four handsome uncles! They all communicated loudly, bellowing passionately to everyone in their space, arms and hands slicing through the air. To me, that noise and confusion represented what family was *supposed* to be.

I am a product of the system, so to speak. I was a child of five years old in a single-female-headed household with four siblings, and we were on welfare. Memories of everyday living were not too bad. We were used to having no heat until Thanksgiving, and we never had hot water in the summertime. We lived in our own home and envied the families living across the street from us in the projects. They *always* seemed to have heat and hot water all year round. Their electricity *never* got shut off. They received repairs if anything broke down and had their apartments painted every other year automatically. It seemed to me that living in the projects was *luxury!*

My mother was (and is) a proud woman and a very hard worker. As an adopted, only child of a doting, elderly, immigrant couple, she was ill-equipped to cope with five children in poverty and an ex-husband who never paid her any child support. But she did the best she could.

Mother did not like her social worker, Mrs. Brown, who always made her feel like a loser. She would come to our house unannounced and ask to look in closets and cabinets as if my Mother was hiding something or someone. To this day, I can see the tension and feel the anxiety this worker provoked in my mother's life.

We did not have a bad life; we did not really know we were poor. We did not own a car; we had no phone. But Mother managed, somehow, to get us all into parochial school. She always told us education was the key to success, although she had had very little education herself. My mother's influence lasted only until the eighth grade. After all, I was a teenager and my mother was the *last* person I listened to!

At 16 years old (after another fight with my mother) I eloped, thinking it was the way to a better life. (Wasn't the point to "at least get him to *marry* you"?) A son was born of this union, the only good part about it. Although I was madly in love, after my first child was born, reality set in and I knew my marriage wouldn't last. Two years later, we parted and my world fell apart. I was only 18 years old!

I loved my baby son, but alone with no income, I did not think I would be able to keep us together. So I went to Mom's house for help.

I divorced at 20, worked for several years at factory work and waitressing jobs, went to night school for a while, then married again. This marriage lasted six years. I had two more children and, when the fighting got real bad, this husband just disappeared, and we have not seen him since. At 28, I was divorced again!

I had just about given up on the love-and-marriage bit; I went back to night school and was set to stay a single parent, when husband #3 showed up on the scene. He was kind, affectionate, and took an interest in me and my children. I fell passionately in love and thought this was meant to be!

I had married this last time out of my culture, into one I could not understand. Things that seemed odd and uncommon to me, I chalked up as different ways, traditions, customs, and language. We were different! I went along with it: different dress, different conversations, recreations and working conditions. I just wanted to be a good wife and mother, to take care of the home, go to the PTA meetings, bake, shop, keep myself attractive, and be there for my man. But through day-to-day experiences, I eventually realized what was happening, and this was not the reality I had expected for my family!

What had happened to love? This was not what I thought it would be. Yes, he professed to love me and the children and showed compassion and kindness. Yes, he vowed to love and care for us forever. Yes, he could be sweet and gentle, but look out! *Emotionally, Freddy Kruger lived here.* I couldn't close my eyes for too long; if I slept, anything could happen in the dark.

I knew I would have to hide from him because he was not about to let us go. I was running, escaping for my life and my sanity! With my children (the baby in my arms and the three others in tow), I fled from an abyss of cruelty, deceit, and oppression that I had never known existed. I had been a romantic fool, brainwashed to believe in love.

I stayed in a battered women's shelter for a month. I finally managed to get him out and get our home back. When I looked toward the future, it seemed desperately bleak and uncertain. My self-esteem was nil and I had no money. My children and I had been physically, mentally, and emotionally battered for a long time and needed many years of therapy and counseling to be able to deal with it; and after two decades, we are still haunted by the abuse. When my youngest child went to school, I knew I needed to do something to better myself economically. We had been subsisting on welfare benefits that could not decently support a family, so I thought I should go back to school and earn a degree that would enable me to earn a breadwinner's wage. I had never gone to high school and was told

I needed a GED to get admitted to college at U-Mass/Boston, College of Public and Community Service (CPCS). When I was eventually admitted to CPCS, the first thing I did was buy four pairs of knee-socks and I was ready for a new start in my life!

In September 1979, I was finally on my way—to where or what, I had no idea, but I felt it would be O.K. I was getting educated! This college was not what I expected; it was comprised of adult working people and many single mothers on welfare trying to do the same thing as I. I had found my niche and I thrived!

In my second semester, I entered a class called "Basic Organizing." This class was made up of 13 welfare-recipient mothers and a few human service professionals. Ann Withorn was our instructor, and she made me feel as if I had come to the right place. Was I in for a surprise when I found out *my* life experience was really a valuable asset in her class! I had just ended my third marriage; and I was a former abused and battered wife of a substance abuser.

Some of the other student mothers were so smart, I thought I could not keep up, but we learned to become a self-help group and helped each other in many ways to earn credits by working together in groups. And what a dynamic group we were! We actually became a sisterhood—sort of a sorority of poor women—sharing our most intimate secrets, experiences, hopes, dreams, and disappointments. We developed a collective knowledge, which we were able to use to help each other fend off the Welfare Department. We adopted a principle to never go to the Welfare Department alone—we became each other's advocates at fair hearings. We exchanged clothing, shared childcare responsibilities when our childcare arrangements fell through, compiled lists of wealthy suburban communities' trash pick-up days, and organized furniture shopping sprees for the nights before trash collections. Individually, we were weak, but together we were formidable!

The "Basic Organizing" class began organizing on campus and developed into a Recognized Student Organization, which allowed us to obtain office space, a telephone, and a small budget with which to work. We voted on a name and were now called "Advocacy for Resources for Modern Survival" (ARMS). We voted to become a chapter of The Coalition for Basic Human Needs (CBHN), which was the state-wide welfare rights organization. Our priority was to advocate for welfare recipients' access to higher education. We began to serve on many advisory committees and on boards of directors of antipoverty agencies that affected our lives, such as daycare centers, health care providers, fuel assistance agencies, tenants' rights organizations, clothing and food distribution centers, etc.

Many of us felt intimidated and unable to even know what was being said at the meetings, but we took notes, came back to ARMS, and discussed all that we had heard and educated each other. This was a wonderful time getting closer to the other women and their children and beginning to trust each other. Working together, we were able to keep ourselves informed on several fronts at once. We were able to monitor proposed changes in the service delivery of a variety of agencies, assess their often conflicting policies, make holistic appraisals of their effects on our lives, develop recommendations, and, most importantly, significantly impact the final decisions. *We were making a difference!*

In this "Basic Organizing" class, the group decided to organize around welfare issues. The Aid to Families with Dependent Children program was very important to all of us because we derived our income and health benefits from it, but it was an inadequate, punitive system that harassed and demeaned us. We all decided to fight back using techniques that would enable us to earn our sheepskins. We started to research poverty issues going all the way back to the Elizabethan Poor Laws, and we found out that poor people *always* had it bad! There were the manors and the serfs, the Pharaohs and the slaves, the Old South and the Blacks, and now we had billionaire politicians and Workfare participants!

Learning the theories, history, and practice of organizing saved my life; actually, it brought me to life! I finally had something worthwhile to live for. I feel I was politicized through this course and found many other ways to earn credits around welfare issues in other classes.

Our first demonstration at the State House was a revelation to me. We had rehearsed a skit for weeks, obtained some props (for example, generic brand macaroni and cheese and toilet paper), and marched to the Hall of Flags inside the State House. Although there were 30 of us in our group, I was amazed to find a few hundred more folks already there.

There were many people from different cultures there, speaking and chanting. I was afraid that some of our own people would not understand our skit, which depicted the contrasting lifestyles of the wealthy and the poor. Some of them could not understand the English language; but when we held out the generic toilet paper, they understood that on a welfare budget toilet paper is a luxury item. One woman in our group was dressed as a lobster to signify the governor's proclivity for lobster lunches.

Then we tried to meet with Governor King and present him with a free ticket we had made out of a large poster board and magic marker inviting him to watch our performance entitled, "The Wild World of Humans, based on the television show, *The Wide World Of Animals*. We never did see the governor; but for me, I was hooked on actions! I was making a difference and earning credits for school at the same time.

I never took a summer off from U-Mass/Boston. I had not attended high school. I needed to learn what I had missed or I would not get my degree in Human Services. I knew something about this subject and I was interested in helping others, so this work totally engulfed my life.

My first advisory position was with Joe Kennedy's Citizens' Energy Committee, an antipoverty agency that distributes fuel for low-income households. There I learned to confront authority and demand the services for which we were eligible. I also sat for 15 years on the Board of Directors of Greater Boston Legal Services (GBLS), where I learned about the laws that governed our lives and how to go about changing them. This was really on-the-job-training!

My second year in college, I found out about student loans and work-study monies that could not be counted against our welfare grants, so I applied for both. Although it was not enough, it did help me keep a roof over our heads and food in our bellies.

My first work-study job was with CBHN, where I was also the ARMS representative on the board. I loved working with these women, who I saw as strong and courageous, doing a job that defied any kind of set description. Each chapter focused on the issues that were most important to its membership, but we were all working to combat the myths around welfare and to improve benefits. Some days, we would just meet and strategize for an action and then have to speak to the local paper or go on a television talk show. Other days, we would just show up at the office and a full television crew and cameras would be waiting for a story without any prior notice, and we never disappointed them!

While working on the Citizens' Energy Committee, I met the Reverend Graylan Ellis-Hagler and invited him to every action we were working on with welfare rights. He always showed up and would lead us in a prayer before we would start our action. He was always in the front lines going into the State House and would sing with his beautiful booming voice, "*We Shall Not Be Moved.*" If the Capitol Police got nasty with us, he was there to defend us. Reverend Graylan taught me a lot of different tactics and helped me learn Liberation Theology.

I could never have imagined what was in store for me. I found a way to fundraise for Rev. Graylan's Church of the United Community. Over time, I became an elder of the church and its welfare advocate in our United Community Advocacy Program (UCAP), working with others in the prison, substance abuse, youth, and poverty ministries.

Just about the time President Reagan was being inaugurated, Massachusetts' Governor King proposed implementing "Workfare," which meant that we would be pulled out of school and mandated to take the first minimum-wage job we could find. We were determined to fight back because we knew that for us, education was the key to our futures.

We fought back in several ways. First, we alerted the chancellor of U-Mass/Boston that if the governor's Workfare plan was adopted, the university would lose hundreds of students. This would put the University on the defense when questions about student/teacher ratios were raised. We got his attention! Working together, we established a very successful network with the university faculty, staff, and administrators that defended and advocated for the students on AFDC whenever they were threatened by their workers.

Another strategy we used was to produce a documentary on Workfare with the help of Mackie McLeod, a local disc-jockey and independent producer at a popular rock radio station. Mackie was interested in teaching ordinary citizens how to use the public air waves. This was just what we had dreamed of! He supplied the technical expertise, state-of-the-art equipment, and the studio (which we bootlegged for six months); and we supplied the issue!

Mackie taught us to think about our audience, determine the three most important points we wanted to make, and decide who would be the best people to make those points. Originally, we wanted to create an organizing tool—a radio documentary that would educate other welfare recipients about the proposed Workfare policies and the dire consequences that Workfare held for them. We also wanted to remind workers that welfare mothers are workers, too, and we wanted to inform women that welfare is a women's issue.

After we had our agenda, we conducted taped interviews with an economist, a director of a battered women's shelter, a mayor, union leaders, feminists, legal experts, sociology professors, welfare recipients, and each other. We researched the music library at the radio station, selected songs which were relevant to our message and interspersed them throughout the tape. Finally, we had produced our documentary, which was entitled, *"Workfare: Anatomy of a Policy."* It was grueling, hard work; but it was worth it! We were really proud of the result.

Later, six of us students went to Washington, DC, and received the Alice Award, which is granted to people in the film, tape, and/or print media whose work portrays women in the low-wage workforce. The Alice Award was named after a character on *Mel's Diner,* a television program which depicted a single mother working in the diner at minimum wage and always looking for ways to make additional income because her wages did not cover her expenses. Out of 300 professional media entrants, ARMS was the only nonprofessional group. We received the first-place honor for a radio documentary. This award was presented by The National Association of Working Women, which now recognized welfare mothers as working women! All that, and *more* credits for school—this was living!

ARMS continued to wage the battle against Workfare on several fronts. We were successful in agitating the Welfare Department to the point where they finally designated CPCS as an "approved training site" and basically left us alone. Of course, we then pushed for *all* of UMass to be classified as a training site. When this was won, we got them to recognize all institutions of higher learning as training options. (This victory is being lost today, as "welfare reform" takes away recipient rights to higher education.)

After reading several newspaper articles proclaiming that Governor King was a "good Catholic," we even met with the cardinal and the College of Bishops. We informed them that the Workfare plan was inconsistent with the recently released *Pope's Encyclicle on Work and Dignity,* which clearly stated that mothers should not be forced to work outside of the home and that caring for her children was a mother's first job. This meeting resulted in a Bishop's Letter which denounced the Workfare plan and was published in the local newspapers. The governor postponed the enactment of Workfare.

Several of us participated in influencing the political process preceding the gubernatorial election. And, we ultimately celebrated Governor King's defeat and the demise of the Workfare plan, temporary though it was!

In 1982, ARMS members Diane Dujon, Judy Gradford, and I decided to fund-raise in an effort to attend the National Conference Against Workfare in Chicago. We felt we needed to hear what was happening in other states and wanted to share our success in staving off Workfare in Massachusetts. The three of us showed up at the conference with video equipment to record this event.

There were about 200 people there, including welfare mothers and fathers, and professionals with their own agenda. What a baptism into national organizing this turned out to be! Different factions wanted to control the agenda, and an actual fist-fight broke out while I was behind the video camera. This resulted in a split in the welfare rights group, mostly along class lines. We were forced to make a decision on which group we would join. Judy and Diane chose the group that seemed the most sincere to them; I picked the group that prayed before their meetings because I knew that without God on our side we did not stand a chance. Luckily, we all chose the same group, which was my first introduction to Marian Kramer (the current president of the National Welfare Rights Union), from Highland Park, Michigan.

We returned from this adventure vowing to plan and implement at least two actions at our local level. ARMS received a $1,000 grant from our college to hold a two-day conference that we called "Survival in the Eighties: Situation Serious." Many poor people's groups attended this event, including CBHN and Women for Economic Justice (WEJ), as well as many student groups on campus. At this conference, we learned that the amount of the welfare grant was 40 percent below the poverty level! We thought there must be something illegal about that and decided to talk to our lawyers.

Soon afterwards, we did have another action at the State House. We rallied, spoke out, and marched to a hearing where then-Governor Dukakis was testifying on the AFDC budget. We had written on a scroll an "Economic Emancipation Proclamation" and demanded a redress to our grievances. We forced him to listen, but he really wasn't interested. He said he had two sick children at home and did not have time to do anything for us.

Next, we launched the "Up To Poverty Campaign." ARMS, CBHN, WEJ, and the Mass. Law Reform Institute thought the name of the campaign was a statement in itself. Ninety other women's groups endorsed it, and the campaign was on its way. The campaign was successful in getting welfare grants increased in the first three years: 10 percent the first year; 9 percent the second year; and 9 percent the following year. In the ensuing years, the campaign changed its name to "Up and Out of Poverty," and then again to "Up and Out of Poverty, Now!," but the campaign has not been successful since 1987 in getting another increase.

Sometime in 1986, ARMS launched another innovative initiative—the *Survival Newspaper*—a paper written for, by, and about low- and no-income people and their families. The paper helped women attain writing and computer skills and assisted them in publishing their work. *Survival News* is the official paper of the National Welfare Rights Union and is distributed in 38 states and six other countries.

In 1987, I attended a National Welfare Rights Union annual meeting in Columbus, Ohio, and brought the "Up and Out of Poverty Campaign" to the table, where it was voted on and adopted. Soon there were 33 states working to bring families up and out of poverty! I participated in several Survival Summits, sponsored by the National Welfare Rights Union, in various states. These summits had welfare recipients, unemployed, the underemployed, members of unions, the homeless, black-lung and white-lung survivors, academicians, clergy, activists, scholars, and Native Americans working together to plan a strategy that would help people survive in this economy. After attending hundreds of meetings all across this country, I came to the conclusion that it is all political.

One of the strategies resulting from the summits was the "Elect the Victims of Poverty Campaign," which educated and recruited poor people to run for public office at all political levels: city councils, state and local representatives, Congress, vice-president, and, yes, even president of the United States. We wanted to broaden our base and increase voter registration among the poor *and* run our *own* candidates! Subsequently, I attended a 500-mile poverty tour of southern California with the NWRU, where we spoke at 38 events in one week!

We participated in speak-outs at college campuses, soup kitchens, and churches; gave our stories to the press, and toured homeless shelters. We spoke through an interpreter with people who couldn't speak English. It was a successful event, although I needed to sleep for three days straight when I got back home.

During the poverty tour, I was approached by Marian Kramer, president of the NWRU, and Ethel Long-Scott, director of the Women's Economic Agenda Project (WEAP) in Oakland, California, who asked if I would consider running for governor of Massachusetts. I thought about it and decided that it was the thing to do. Even if we didn't win (though I was convinced that it was possible), we could light the spark of inspiration that as poor people we could change the political debate! We would win in many other ways by educating low- and no-income people of their right to run for office and the necessity of voting.

When I returned home and informed my friends and colleagues that I was going to run for governor, some of them were very skeptical. They were concerned for me because politics can be so ugly. But I informed them that I could not be hurt through smear campaigns because, "I am a welfare recipient; I am *below* reproach."

The "Elect the Victims of Poverty Campaign" established a national network of campaign candidates in several states. These candidates ran for a variety of offices in their local areas, and some even won! I think running for governor of Massachusetts was one of the best things I ever did. It was the best hands-on civics course anyone could take. After all, what is government, but the people? Who better to run for political office than the people who have to live under policies that are impacting their lives? It's our hope to control our own destinies and save our own lives. We don't need a Ph.D. or an uncle in the State House! All we need is common sense and a desire to serve. We would bring to office what most politicians don't have—our own experience.

We learned a lot during the campaign about how the entire political system is set up to discourage the poor from participating. We contacted the Democratic Party Committee to find out how to get my name on the ballot. They told us that we would have to obtain the names of all the delegates in the state, at a cost of $1,200! Of course, we did not have that kind of money available; but as poor people, we believed in the "dollar down and the chase is on" principle. We sent them $100 and promised them the rest.

After sending out thousands of cards to the delegates, asking for their support at the state convention, I was granted seven minutes to speak from the floor. Our diligence had paid off! However, we did not get enough votes on the floor and had to settle for a write-in campaign.

The campaign received substantial national press coverage, but not in Massachusetts! There were several gubernatorial debates, but I was not allowed to participate because I was not considered a "viable candidate." However, when I was on a national television program, it was not aired in Massachusetts because "the other candidates would be denied equal time"!

Campaigning included attending church and community meetings, college forums, block parties, neighborhood rallies, and demonstrations, as well as political events. Some of these public forums were grueling because people believe all the negative stereotypes they hear in the media about welfare recipients and respond with venomous personal attacks. For example, I was invited by a progressive community group to participate on a panel with other candidates who were running for various political offices. During my five-minute presentation, I talked about how living in substandard housing caused my son to be diagnosed with lead paint poisoning, which severely affected his behavior. Afterward, there was a reception where the media and the audience were encouraged to speak directly to the candidates. Just as I was being interviewed by a reporter on camera, the wife of the director of the local welfare office rudely interrupted the interview and accused me of poisoning my own child by "sitting around watching him eat lead paint"! I was mortified!

During the campaign, my constituents volunteered their time, their homes, their cars, and their meager resources to the effort. They had decided that it was time we took matters into our own hands. We knew what needed to be done. Because of my campaign, there were hundreds of people who registered and voted for the first time: welfare mothers, the homeless, alcoholics and drug abusers seeking treatment, and people who felt that neither the Democrats nor the Republicans would address their concerns. They wanted to participate in democracy in hopes of improving their lives. They understood that they were the disenfranchised of our society and that the politicians were not representing their interests.

On Election Day, hundreds of voters called my campaign head-quarters to inform us of their voting experiences. Many voters (including members of my campaign staff) reported that they had been told by poll workers that they could not vote for a write-in candidate or were told to write my name in the wrong space. My own mother was told that she could not vote for me! After the election, we never were able to receive an accurate count of votes because some polling places determined that there were not enough votes for me to count and threw them away!

Later, one of the most ambitious activities we ever staged was a week-long "Siege for Survival" which we held on the Boston Common. We modeled it after the seven-day Battle of Jericho, including a symbolic blowing of the horns which signaled the beginning of a People's Tribunal. We invited victims of poverty to bring criminal charges and testify against those who had committed injustices against the poor. The panel of judges included Howard Zinn, historian and author; Frances Fox Piven, professor and writer; Ellen Convisser, president of Mass. NOW; Leona Smith, president of National Union of the Homeless; and Marian Kramer, president of NWRU. We got a lot of attention from tourists and office workers on lunch break. For once, the press even came! But most important was the spiritual uplift we all received.

I did successfully complete my undergraduate education at UMass, although the school loans put me $36,000 into debt. I must say, however, that it was all worth it. My life took on a new meaning. Now, some of the other former members of ARMS and I fight for the women who come after us. We know from first-hand experience that higher education is one of the most successful routes out of poverty, especially for women. We cannot stand by and let politicians close the door on women struggling to provide a better life for their families.

I am still actively organizing poor people as the president of the Massachusetts Welfare Rights Union and first vice-president of the NWRU. Our latest strategy has been to utilize the Universal Declaration of Human Rights, which holds all governments accountable to a universally recognized standard of behavior in how they treat all people, including their own citizens.

In 1993, the Institute for Policy Studies honored the NWRU with the prestigious Letalier-Moffit Human Rights Award, for outstanding work on human rights in this country and around the world. Welfare rights has now been recognized as a fundamental human right.

RECOGNIZING MOTHER HEROES
Ann Withorn*

ONE WAY FOR ACADEMICS TO MAKE A DIFFERENCE, EVEN IN these times of institutional retreat in the face of spurious charges of "political correctness," is for us to challenge universities to take a lead in protecting welfare recipients who attend college. An important way to accomplish this, as women college presidents in Massachusetts and hundreds of other educators across the country are doing, is to lobby directly for programs that support women on welfare when they try to attend college, and to oppose any reform that doesn't allow women to go to college to earn whatever level of degree they can attain. When this happens, as it has in Massachusetts, the debate and policy outcomes are shifted. It is also possible to create state or citywide groups of academics to lobby, coordinate research efforts, and support each other in paying attention to the welfare issue. In Massachusetts we have done this by creating an Academics Working Group on Poverty. But, within universities, some of us can try to do more, just as Oberlin College and Wilberforce and other abolitionist colleges pushed others to oppose slavery a century and a half ago. So, when I speak at universities, I often suggest an academic way we could begin to change consciousness and build a movement at the same time: The Mother Hero Certificate.

Essentially, the Mother Hero Certificate is a serious proposal to universities to train students to value the lives and work of single mothers—and to understand fully and deeply how serious the implications of the assault on all women, all families, all people will

---

* This is a proposal for universities concerned about supporting single mothers. The author welcomes ideas for changing, expanding, or developing this certificate: Ann Withorn, 617-287-7365, College of Public and Community Service, Univ. of Massachusetts/Boston.

be, if attacks on single mothers keep succeeding. In short, it is a way to take more seriously the need to defend the rights of all women, all people, by defending single mothers.

I propose this certificate of study for students and academics to consider, revise, and expand as a way to help them, as faculty and students, understand the issues better and be more able to offer support and to work for serious change. It is a useful starting point for a discussion about the role of the academy. I was going to call it the Single Mother's Empowerment certificate, but I wanted to be empowered to stop talking about empowerment. So I tried to think about another way to support the heroic efforts of single mothers. I decided to build both upon Linda Gordon's concept that poor women needed to be "heroes of their own lives," and to graft it onto the ideas behind the "Mother Hero" awards they used to give in the Soviet Union.

Much as some of the certificate may seem rhetorical, I do believe that if we worked to use it as a base for a real program, and more students gained the knowledge and experience embodied in this certificate we would be doing the work of building a movement for change. In addition, more single mothers who try to attend college would not feel so alone, jumping from ice floe to ice floe. When a woman on welfare, or a struggling employed mother, met a graduate of the certificate she would not encounter suspicion and disregard. Instead, she would find at least one person who would say to her, "Wow, you are a single mother, doing the hardest work of this society all by yourself? You must be incredibly brave and strong, even to attempt that in this unsupportive society. How can I help? You are fantastic!"

Imagine what this would feel like...Just imagine.

The First
Mother Hero Award

In Recognition of the Outstanding Commitment, Dedication
and Hard Work done with and for:
Mothers Struggling Against Poverty

The Mother Hero Certificate

Purpose: To educate and train students (and faculty) to understand, legitimate, support, and defend the women who are responsible for their households as they strive to provide for themselves and their children.

Relationship to Existing Women's Studies Programs: Most of the literature and questions, especially for the first three areas, are often covered in women's studies courses; this certificate only reframes and regroups issues to provide a more focused way of recognizing and defending mother heroes and should be encouraged for all students, regardless of major.

Need for the Certificate: Because of the implications for all women of the full-scale attack on the legitimacy of women's turning to the state for assistance with income and other needs in the face of the profound hostility of the current family system and the existing job markets to women's mothering obligations.

Length of Time to Complete: Initial competence can be gained with one year of focused activity, but the required work of understanding the issues and helping to make change will last a lifetime.

Basic Curriculum Areas: All are required and all intersect. They are probably best presented in the order listed below. An action component is required in every area, along with the required Action Internship.

Mother Heroes 101—How Do You Spell Relief? Recognizing and Legitimizing the Required Work of Motherhood.

♦ Content: Focus on the issues for single mothers, but link the issues for all women. The unavoidable necessity of the work of mothering. Theory on the work of care; the discipline of mothering. The importance of time, flexibility, and responsiveness—analogy to agriculture (farming is more than a science, and must be changed given differing conditions). Costs of providing, costs of not providing effective mothering. Racial and class dynamics—whose mothering is valued and whose is not. The implications of doing the work alone—the role of supports from father, birth family, friends, community. Pressures and demands on children and their effects on mothers. Mothering a "special needs" child. Mothering when the streets are unsafe. Views of what constitutes "good mothering" and "bad" in context of basic gendered and cultural constructions. The opportunities made available by money and the barriers to "good" mothering posed by the lack of it. *Lesson: In this society all mothers are "single" mothers first—they need relief that accepts and does not judge their real situations.*

♦   Sources for learning: Sara Ruddick; the "care" writers; writers about the hours of women's work, especially cross-culturally. Many choices here. Films and fiction: especially good for gaining the cross-cultural dimensions. Outside speakers: different types of mothers describe their duties and obligations.

♦   Possible learning activities: Spend a day with a mother, or record your own activities—make videotape, interactive compact disc or keep a log. Observe and report on media images of mothers. Pairs of students interview each other about the work of mothering they observed in their lives. As a mother or if you were a mother, what would be your standards of "good enough"? Imagine a rainy, cold weekend with two kids in a three-room apartment on a budget of $100, $50, $25, $10, $2—assume minimum basic food in the house.

♦   Action goal: Collectively list the 10 things most mothers need to do their work better and possible ways to get each of them. You should pick one (i.e. more time, better workplace conditions, pay for caring work, changed status) as your focus for the certificate and design a personal action plan to be evaluated at the conclusion of the certificate—see below.

Mother Heroes 202. Work Your Fingers to the Bone: Paid Employment as a Source of Relief for Single Mothers.

♦   Content: Possibilities and constraints of jobs—wages, hours, working conditions, requirements, and eligibility analyzed in terms of the limits they pose for differing situations of mothering. Who is employed where, under what conditions? What is a "good job, an affordable job" for a single mother and who can get them? Jobs and "benefits": illusion of dignity without security vs. illusion of security without dignity. Jobs and time for mothering—the chicken pox test. The support networks needed to find, take, and keep jobs. Education and jobs. The appeal and trick of "home work." The one-job family in jeopardy. Jobs without wives. Racial and cultural dynamics in defining acceptable jobs and offering differing lessons. The changing expectations of "good mothers" as employees as well as mothers. Danger of drawing the line so sharply between wages and the supports needed to allow for employment. Danger of "super woman" myth. *Lesson: Waged employment "as we know it" has failed single mothers; it must change.*

♦ Sources for learning: Ammott and Matthaei, Albelda, Rose. A wide range of books and materials on the history of women's struggle to be in, and then survive the workplace are essential to understanding the profound contradictions of the workplace for women. Read about pay equity, mommy tracks, discrimination and sexual harassment in the workplace. Again, films, documentaries, novels, etc. Bring in single mothers who work in differing types of lower wage jobs to discuss how employment helps them mother, how it makes it difficult.

♦ Possible learning activities: Interview parents in the school's daycare center. Visit differing work sites and inquire as to standard working conditions, salary ranges; just observe. In pairs, discuss how you or your mother or close relative/friend manage work and home where the money goes, how much is enough. Make lists of costs and benefits of differing jobs in relation to the work of mothering: Design the ideal "mother friendly" job for someone without a high school degree, whose first language may not be English—compare to options at other educational levels.

♦ Action goal: Attend Coalition of Labor Union Women meetings. Work with, or form, Student Mothers group at your school. Work with others on campus to conduct a survey of how your school supports the mothering work of its women employees, and of how it welcomes and supports students who are mothers.

Mother Heroes 303. Intimate Injustices: Men as a Source of Relief for Single Mothers

♦ Content: How male roles have changed over time and are different in different cultures. How men help and hinder the work of mothering in U.S. families today. The amount of work most men do in the home; gendered roles. The numbers of divorced and never-married women why and what it means. Measures of male violence and dominance and their effects on families. The effects on women, and their ability to do the work of mothering, of male dominance, violence, and sexual abuse—effect on children of the same. How young girls are raised to submit. How men must change and how society hinders this. The financial meaning of divorce and child support. Mental health issues related to women's inequality in families. Racial and cultural differences are critical here. Economic functions of men; relationship between male poverty and women's options. Supporting men as fathers, without assuming the need to "head" families. Lesbian mothers; what happens without men in the home as an option? *Lesson: The traditional family, as we know it, has failed mothers; it must be changed.*

- ◆ Sources for learning: Stephanie Coontz, Linda Gordon, Nancy Folbeare, but again, there is much literature on the functions and failures
of the traditional family, but it is being forgotten in these times when
we are revaluing families as some people wish they were. See
especially the communitarian romanticism regarding family. In addition to all the standards, again films, fiction, poems may be most
useful. Speakers from battered women's shelters, divorced women,
lesbian mothers, women from different countries and cultures; AFDC
mothers talk about the men in their lives.

- ◆ *Possible learning activities:* family histories. Survey of men's and
women's work in students' birth families, or adult families. Interview
mothers and compare their own economic options to those of the
men in their lives—what would happen to each if the union broke
up; design a "relationship insurance" policy for mothers—how would
risk be calculated? How to set fair pay off rates?

- ◆ Action goal: Work on media campaign for local shelter. Provide girls'
empowerment workshops in schools. Prepare an exhibit of the
media's view of family life vs the statistics for the school or some
other public place.

Mother Heroes 404. Big Daddy: The State as a Source of Relief for Single Mothers

- ◆ Content: Theory of the role of the state in supporting existing
hierarchies of class, gender and race while at the same time offering
some amelioration. International comparisons are useful. The history
of state and societal efforts to help single mothers in U.S. cope has
always been a mixture of assistance and control—help when men
and job market failed but punished for seeking it and for *being alone.*
Early aid and the terms under which "good mothers" received it. What
happened to bad mothers. Always best to be widowed or to pretend
to be. Never enough money, always huge numbers of controls; women
of color were always "bad," AFDC has always been a small percentage
of all programs, but the continuing "illegitimate" program. AFDC vs. Social
Security. Other policies besides income policies have always been
confusing—force poor women to work, don't support middle-class
women with childcare, abortion confusions. The bureaucracy has always
been fragmented, extensive and intrusive—never a service. Always
punitive and increasingly so as two jobs were required, so more mothers
are employed and as too many "good mothers" took welfare because
they couldn't manage. What's happened to welfare since the failure

of welfare rights organizations to gain guaranteed income, and the removal of elderly and disabled from state-level "welfare." From the "feminization of poverty" to punitive welfare reform. The contradictions and politics of current welfare policy—ideological and fiscal meanings, history of welfare organizing. *Lesson: The welfare state, as we know it, has failed single mothers; it must be changed.*

♦   Sources for learning: much material in the past ten years on women, gender and the state. Especially Linda Gordon, Michael Katz, Mimi Abramovitz, Nancy Fraser, Ellwood and Bane, but many others. *For Crying Out Loud* has useful first-hand accounts; *Survival News* does too. There is a great deal of very specific material on AFDC and welfare mother's situations put out by the National Welfare Rights Union, Center for Welfare Policy and the Law, and by local advocacy and legal rights organizations. State welfare departments put out studies. It is always best to invite women who receive welfare to speak; it is good sometimes to invite welfare workers, too. In-class debates among students, or between local administrators and advocates, and highlight the issues.

♦   Possible learning activities: Interview family members about their history of receiving any government service. Get all the applicable regulations and try to design a life without breaking any of them. Live on a welfare budget for a month. Visit welfare office and apply for welfare, or just observe in welfare office. Borrow food stamps and buy someone's food.

♦   Action goal: Get involved at welfare rights group, or at local poverty program; help recruit student volunteers to help the groups. Create a participatory action research group to monitor and immediately reveal and protest the results and human rights abuses stemming from federal and state "welfare reform." Create a list of positive changes in public programs ("feasible" or not) that could help single mothers.

Mother Heroes 505. Knowing the Enemy: The Cultural and Political Assault upon, and Betrayal of, Single Mothers

♦   Content: Examine the numerous sources for the historic and intensified assault on single mothers—religious roots of sexual "morality"; capitalist anti-state opposition to government, especially government that appears to help poor people, women, people of color; misogynist fear of women without dependence on men alone; current labor market's need to have everyone with no option but low-wage jobs;

communitarian retreat into family values. Examine the particular roots of the recent ground swell of opposition and the punitive proposals put forward aimed especially at "illegitimacy," single and teen mothers. Cultural arguments as a closeted way to talk about race. Why is it so widespread? Why is welfare the one failing area out of three that is blamed? The differences between a Clinton (who wants working poor, not paupers,) and a Gingrich (who wants to punish and isolate one of the enemies of a "personally responsible" society, where no one has any legitimate claims fore social assistance). Need to reorder and reshape society and deny the pain most people are feeling by using scapegoats. Follow the intellectual arguments to their logical conclusions and build a more clearly authoritarian social state. Put in context of the rise of the Right and the abandonment of liberalism. Consider the popular, "intellectual" and political terms of the debate. *Lesson: Argument and action has to be taken to change the consensus to one where single mothers are valued for doing important societal work and recognized for having a hard time and deserving help.*

◆ Sources for learning: All of the materials used in Big Daddy class plus conservative sources from Charles Murray, Lawrence Mead, neoliberals such as Christopher Jencks, Mickey Kaus, William J. Wilson, and Bill Clinton, The Contract with America, Personal Responsibility Act, etc. Watching the talk shows and taping them is useful. Debates are helpful.

◆ Possible learning activities: Interview women on welfare, welfare workers, fellow students, family members, and compare views of why people are on welfare, why people are poor, what government should do. In class, work on arguments and information to answer specific questions. Conduct a television and newspaper media watch to keep track of the ongoing coverage of low-income issues. Word games with work, Workfare, welfare, dependency, underclass, intact family, etc.

◆ Action goal: Conduct a survey of attitudes on your campus: identify five strategies to affect them, carry out at least one.

Mother Heroes 606: Action Internships: Opportunities for Action Now and Over the Long Haul

◆ During the course of completing this certificate, all students will take part in a significant service/organizing internship with an organization that strives to offer better relief to single mothers in one area of life: employment; family functioning; public policy, and services. During this internship the student should keep a log and analyze what s/he is learning in regard to the issues raised in the certificate. S/he should assess how s/he is changing, the changes s/he sees occur because of the work of the organization, and of her/his own activity.

* At the conclusion of the internship, the student should submit the log, evaluate the experience, and submit an evaluation of the work from an on-site supervisor (along with her/his own evaluation of the evaluation). S/he should also submit a Future Action Plan for how she will apply the learning of the internship, and the certificate to her/his future personal, employment, and political choices, as well as a proposal for the standards by which s/he would choose to be evaluated.

This proposal is submitted to universities and colleges in the hope that individual students will consider adopting it as a personal curriculum for change and that schools themselves will review its current programs to decide where to house a Mother Hero Certificate and whether some programs might be changed in order to be more supportive to current and future Mother Heroes among us.

NOW IS THE TIME
Mainstream Feminism's Statements on Welfare Rights
Martha F. Davis

THE NATIONAL ORGANIZATION FOR WOMEN (NOW) IS THE largest and most enduring of the activist groups founded during the "second wave" of the women's movement. From the start, the issue of women's poverty was given a prominent place on NOW's agenda. At its first national conference in 1966, NOW stated that:

> We start with a concern for the plight of women who now live in poverty. The most serious victims of sex discrimination in this country are women at the bottom, including those who, unsupported, head a great percentage of the families in poverty; those women who work at low-paying, marginal jobs, or who cannot find work, and the seriously increasing numbers of high school dropouts who are girls. No adequate attention is being given to those women by any of the existing poverty programs.[1]

Indeed, "[a]iding women in poverty and expanding opportunity" was one of NOW's five targets for immediate action.[2]

Despite this rhetoric, many of NOW's early members lacked personal experience of poverty and brought little understanding to the issue. The strong commitment of a few activists within NOW to identify welfare as a women's issue was seldom translated into national NOW action.

With the latest round of "welfare reforms" in the 1990s, however, NOW members have mobilized at every level of the organization. This reflects a growing awareness of the need to bridge class and racial divides in order to sustain the women's movement beyond its early accomplishments, as well as a reaction to the overtly anti-women sentiment fueling the most punitive reforms.

Beginning in 1991, NOW President Patricia Ireland participated in a series of meetings with National Up and Out of Poverty Now, the National Welfare Rights Union, and other welfare rights groups to develop common agendas. NOW's 1992 national convention, held in Boston, Massachusetts, was devoted to poor women's issues. The centerpiece of the conference was a "Town Meeting," patterned on those held by Bill Clinton during his election campaign, with prominent participation by Marian Kramer of the National Welfare Rights Union and local welfare rights activists. Subsequent national conferences have continued to address these issues through workshops and strongly worded resolutions. In 1995, drawing attention to the need for a safety net in order to protect battered women, NOW's sister organization, NOW Legal Defense and Education Fund (a separate organization founded by NOW members), sponsored a national summit on "The Link Between Violence and Poverty in the Lives of Women and their Children." Between conferences, NOW activists have often been on the streets in front of the House of Representatives, the Senate, and the White House, protesting efforts to eliminate the safety net for women and their families.

Significantly, these national efforts have been replicated on the local level. For example, in 1993, the NOW Legal Defense and Education Fund initiated a lawsuit in federal court in New Jersey challenging that state's new policy of denying AFDC benefits to children born to women on welfare.[3] The local New Jersey NOW chapter joined the lawsuit as an amicus. In Nebraska, the local NOW chapter delivered testimony to the state legislature as it considered punitive welfare reforms, driving home the point that welfare is a women's issue. The New York NOW chapter addressed the relationship between violence and poverty in testimony before its state legislature, pointing out that welfare time limits and other punitive measures would work to trap poor women in abusive relationships.

NOW's commitment to sustain activism on both the national and local levels is perhaps best reflected in the 1994 resolution below:

ECONOMIC JUSTICE EDUCATION CAMPAIGN 1994

WHEREAS, the issue of economic justice for low-income women and children is a NOW priority; and

WHEREAS, ending welfare is the latest strategy being used by the right wing and the Clinton administration to attack low-income women, and ending welfare "as we know it" has the potential for being equally punitive to poor families; and

WHEREAS, major and continuing cutbacks by government and corporations are forcing more workers, especially women, out of jobs, especially good paying jobs; and

WHEREAS, this so-called welfare reform includes the use of false and misleading information and myths which demean and insult low-income women, and the passage of laws which give the state power and control over the lives and behavior of low-income women and which punish them and their children, such as child exclusion waivers; and

WHEREAS, the next six months to one year will be a watershed period in the welfare debate that will likely result in significant changes in the welfare system; and

WHEREAS, the National Organization for Women, along with our partners in the welfare rights movement, have both truth and solutions to counter the right-wing lies and punitive measures;

THEREFORE BE IT RESOLVED, that NOW institute an emergency national education and action campaign around the issue of feminist welfare reform, "as if women matter," to include:

1. creation and distribution of a brochure similar to Who Cares About Women's Rights-NOW Cares;

2. creation and distribution of a Welfare Rights Action Kit, to include an electoral strategy, for use by chapters and states (with one copy free-of-charge to each state);

3. assistance, where possible, in subsidizing the travel and related expenses of low-income welfare rights activists, so the NOW states, chapters and regions may involve these activists in workshops, teach-ins, speak-outs and advocacy, enabling the voices of poor women to be heard and included in our education and our action;

4. promotion and support of a grassroots Congressional campaign to influence welfare rights legislation which will develop decent-paying jobs in both government and private business and permit the women to rise up and out of poverty with dignity and provide skills for their future;

5. development of a media campaign to counter the myths and promote the true solutions for "ending poverty as we know it";

6. programs to educate the public and legislators that bearing and raising children is valuable in and of itself and should be fully supported should be included in all education and lobbying efforts.

Notes

1. Margaret H. Mason, "Poverty: A Feminist Issue" (undated), p. 24, NOW Papers, Schlesinger Library, Radcliffe College.
2. *Ibid.*
3. C.K. v. Shalala, Docket No. 95-5454 (3d Cir.), appeal pending.

COLLEGES CAN HELP WOMEN IN POVERTY
Erika Kates

OVER THE PAST 30 YEARS WELFARE POLICIES HAVE ATTEMPTED
to link benefits with employment. Efforts have usually included
longer-term approaches—the so-called "human capital" approach—
focusing on providing welfare recipients with education and job-
training, as well as short-term approaches focusing on finding
employment and providing "job-search skills." More recently we have
seen a shift in these trends as time-limited benefits and employment
become a condition of receiving AFDC benefits; recipients are now
either required to work immediately at "voluntary" jobs in the public
sector or to seek employment in the private sector. This switch in
policies is justified in terms of saving taxpayers money, helping
impoverished families, and introducing AFDC recipients to the work
ethic, thus helping them to move out of the "underclass" and into
mainstream America.

Those are the myths. The reality is that the participation of AFDC
recipients in welfare-to-work programs or welfare-for-work programs
have resulted, at best, in a small proportion achieving marginal, and
often temporary, financial gains.[1] Even when recipients find work,
many continue to experience repeated welfare "dependency"—either
cycling on and off welfare, or combining welfare with work because
their wage levels are so low they are still eligible for AFDC benefits.[2]
Moreover, these sweeping changes ignore the fact that many AFDC
recipients already have long employment histories, and about half
have high school diplomas or GEDs.

There are many negative consequences of such approaches; the
one I would like to discuss here is the deleterious effect on access to
higher education for low-income women. I argue that although past
policies offering postsecondary education access have been flawed,

they offer substantial promise for a large number of low-income women.[3] I suggest that we learn from those experiences and expand those options. I also suggest using institutions of higher education as allies in this effort and, using Massachusetts as an example, describe the efforts of a coalition of low-income women, educators, and community groups to restore the longer-term and more effective education and job-training options for welfare recipients.

Going to College: Learning from the JOBS Experience

The most recent sweeping federal welfare legislation, JOBS, (Job Opportunities and Basis Skills, Title II of the Family Support Act, 1988) required states to provide certain employment and training activities, and permitted states to offer others, such as enrollment in higher education. Among JOBS provisions were the requirements that eligible recipients develop employment plans with their caseworkers, and that states show that 75 percent of JOBS participants have an average participation rate of 20 hours of approved activities each week.

By 1992 all states had chosen the postsecondary education option, but, as my research into 32 states' JOBS policies toward higher education showed, effective participation was bounded by a variety of conditions. These limitations—including time, degree, and course restrictions; attendance requirements; and intrusive monitoring—were imposed by states' widely differing interpretations of JOBS regulations. Two-thirds of the states in the survey had imposed time limits on recipients' college attendance, with one-third of these states permitting two years participation (regardless of level of education pursued) and 9 percent permitting only Associate's degrees (in a quarter of states these restrictions were blamed on limited childcare funds). Although three states were considering time limits on higher education (four or six years) one-third of states, including Massachusetts, had not established any time limits.

States also interpreted the 20-hour participation rule very differently. Sixty percent required full-time college attendance, that is, 15-16 classroom hours per week, with a few states requiring participants to put in an extra 4-5 hours of work-study or volunteer work. However, 40 percent of states had more flexible policies, allowing time spent in library research, study groups, advising, laboratory work, and travel to college to be "counted" in the 20 hours. This meant that in these states a part-time course load of 6-8 course hours (the minimum needed to qualify for a Pell grant) fulfilled the 20-hour requirement, resulting in a much more realistic workload for single parents.[4]

There were also widespread variations in monitoring college attendance and student performance. Many JOBS offices, instead of being satisfied with general evidence of enrollment and satisfactory grade point averages (as required of all Pell grant recipients), also required each participant to have attendance sheets signed for each course by faculty or college administrators—on a monthly, weekly, or sometimes daily basis. One consequence of this monitoring was that for the first time, college personnel other than financial aid officers knew which students were "on welfare" (compromising the confidentiality of students' financial status).

Another limitation occurred in course choices. Recipients were required by caseworkers, who had little or no training in the relationship of higher education to the labor market, to declare their course of study prior to enrollment. Since JOBS regulations prevented participants from changing their employment plan (the "one-course-of-study-rule") and imposed penalties on those who did, this had severe consequences for recipients. There was also a lack of consistency in caseworkers' definitions of "employable areas of study"; some regarded any degree as assisting in recipients' future employability, while others vetoed certain subjects, such as religion, journalism, or art.

In spite of these obstacles, the survey showed that 80 percent of states' JOBS administrators reported that they were supportive of the postsecondary option because they thought it held better possibilities for long-term effectiveness, and utilized the skills and talents of recipients better than other available options. Thus, a contradictory picture emerges from the survey. While there appeared to be national support for access to higher education, in actuality both formal regulations and informal policies—together with the general "culture of compliancy"[5] of the Welfare Department—often inhibited such access.

Creating Supportive Educational Environments for Low-Income Women[6]

In contrast to the culture of the JOBS offices and public welfare agencies, the "culture of education" with its prevailing values of flexibility, informed choice, and confidentiality, is, broadly speaking, much more supportive. Students are encouraged to take time to decide their major course of study, to make appropriate course choices for their individual circumstances and talents (with informed one-on-one advising to help make those decisions), to pursue their studies at a reasonable pace, and to trust that their financial status and grades are kept private.

In addition to this general culture, though, a number of colleges provide additional kinds of supports to low-income women. Fifty-six colleges (located in the 32 states discussed above) were also surveyed, revealing that numerous colleges develop specific strategies to mitigate some of the difficulties created by JOBS:

♦ They provide resources that complement or act as a substitute for JOBS resources. By providing free or subsidized childcare, colleges can ameliorate a shortage of available JOBS resources. When these centers are on-campus "state-of-the art" facilities, have caring and supportive staff, and provide parent education meetings and suppers, they develop into genuine "two-generation" services. Some college counseling centers provide parenting education, time- and stress-management counseling, and support groups for single parents. Another important resource, provided by over 50 percent of colleges in the survey, is a women's center or lounge, providing a comfortable space where women can meet, eat lunch, relax, and study. Such a space also is conducive to reducing the sense of isolation experienced by many single parents, and encourages the development of an active support network. Numerous colleges also help provide food and clothing for low-income families; either by offering a fully stocked food pantry, or through clothing and book exchanges.

♦ They seek compromises and negotiate with JOBS personnel. By engaging in discussions with JOBS personnel, educational administrators and financial aid officers are able to work out "understandings" with JOBS personnel over the ratio of time spent in study and travel that will be counted in the 20-hour rule. Some also provide orientations to curriculum offerings so that specific courses of study are accepted for employment plans; some recruit students directly from JOBS offices; some have JOBS counselors with offices on the campus; and others work out convenient and respectful systems for monitoring attendance and performance.

♦ They form communication networks: between JOBS offices and colleges, within individual colleges, and among colleges. The most important effects of these networks are to reduce institutional isolation, and to encourage educators and administrators—and in some instances, caseworkers—to share information and strategies that will help students. When "blessed" with official sanction and the leadership of presidents and chancellors, such networks can be very effective: For example, in the early 1990s a group of women college presidents in Massachusetts lobbied state officials for more childcare and continued access to higher education for JOBS participants. But, even when networks are not officially sanctioned by upper-echelon college administrators, they can be very effective.

♦ They encourage the participation of community groups and businesses. Some colleges encourage business and community groups to take on projects to help students and their children. They contribute clothing, including "interview outfits," for mothers, food and holiday packages, sports equipment and camp scholarships for children, and direct financial support. These efforts not only aid individual families, but they also help to dispel the stereotypes of "welfare moms" as members of the public become more aware of how hard-working, intelligent, and determined many of these women are.

♦ They resist unacceptable JOBS policies. When JOBS policies are perceived as contradictory to the fundamental principles and values of educational institutions, administrators may refuse to comply with them. For example, in two states colleges administrators refused to establish study halls specifically for AFDC recipients so that their study hours could be monitored.

♦ They become advocates for policy changes. Each of the former strategies can be escalated when a college, or group of colleges, through its administrators or professional organizations advocate at the local, county, or state level for policy clarification or change. Helpful connections and discussions with state agencies (education, labor, housing, and welfare) were documented. In several states, legislators or governors took a personal interest in the progress of low-income women students.

While none of these strategies alone can resolve all the obstacles, they are important stop-gap measures in a policy environment that has proven to be highly ambivalent, at best, about supporting the idea of access to higher education for low-income women.

Applying These Lessons to Massachusetts

Having worked closely with low-income women in college for 10 years in Massachusetts, I have seen a number of colleges put into practice some of the above-mentioned strategies: Faculty have formed groups to fight against poverty; women college presidents have conducted research into AFDC recipients' experiences in their own institutions and advocated for better access; students have formed low-income student organizations, lobbied against benefit reductions and for more childcare, and participated in discussions shaping state financial aid policy.

While the strategies mentioned above may have been effective previously, such discrete and piecemeal efforts are unlikely to work in the prevailing climate of welfare "reform." A number of people—faculty; educational administrators; childcare, housing, and job-training professionals; current and former AFDC recipients; and members of community organizations—have formed the Welfare, Education, Training Access Coalition (WETAC). Many members of the coalition have personal experience of being a recipient-student or with working with recipients; about 40 percent of the members of the coalition are low-income women, and a small but noticeable proportion is composed of women who once were "on welfare."

The aim of our coalition is to improve access to postsecondary education and job-training options, and the strategies we adopt are campus organizing, education, advocacy, and lobbying. Our goals include changing the states' welfare policies to remove the 20-hour work requirement for women involved in higher education and job-training and to ensure that there are adequate time limits to complete educational programs, as well as adequate childcare to support those efforts. We are fueled by an immediate concern over the large numbers of women dropping out of colleges and job-training programs in anticipation of what they fear they will be forced to do. We have strong evidence that recipients are fearful of having the "rug pulled out from them" as options which they supported and which gave them some hope for the future are being withdrawn.

Conclusion

In spite of the legacy of failure of the earlier "Workfare" experiments, welfare reform policy in the mid-90s is still being driven by the goals of welfare-to-work or welfare-for-work. For decades, higher education was largely ignored by public policy makers and evaluators, and as a result student /AFDC recipients were "invisible." No data on their college attendance were routinely collected until the implementation of JOBS, and not until 1995, when the Government Accounting Office summarized data on a wide variety of JOBS-sanctioned activities, did it become clear that participation in college had become the most widely participated in of all JOBS activities.[7] Despite the millions of dollars spent on evaluating various welfare-to-work programs, no national data are available on the long-term effects and cost effectiveness of higher education and training options. Certainly, aggregate data linking education and income levels show clearly that postsecondary education makes a large overall difference to income levels. In addition, a small number of studies of AFDC recipients who have experienced postsecondary education, together with our personal experiences, provide compelling arguments to support our efforts.

While we are not naive about the difficulties of turning the welfare policy tide immediately, we think our concerns are warranted. Hopefully, the research discussed here, as well as WETAC's activities, will highlight the potential for a large group of AFDC-recipients women to reap benefits from postsecondary education (financial and otherwise). Equally important, we hope it will illuminate the benefits for their children—in the long term from improvements in their standard of living and expectations of education, and in the short term from the role-models their mothers provide.[8]

Notes

1. See for example, S. Harlan and R. Steinberg, eds., *Job Training for Women: The Promise and Limits of Public Policies* (Philadelphia: Temple University Press, 1989); and J. Gueron and E. Pauly, *From Welfare to Work* (New York: Russell Sage, 1991).
2. R. Spalter-Roth, H. Hartmann, and L. Andrews, *Combining Work and Welfare: An Alternative Anti-Poverty Strategy* (Washington, DC: Institute for Women's Policy Research, 1992).
3. Postsecondary education includes a wide range of educational activities: basic education, English as a Second Language (ESL), technical diplomas, certificates, Associate's and Bachelor's degrees.
4. College administrators and AFDC recipients often stated that different welfare offices within the same state interpret these policies differently,

and even that caseworkers within the same office interpret policies differently.

5. Term used by M.J. Bane and D. Ellwood, *Welfare Realities: From Rhetoric to Reform* (Cambridge: Harvard University Press,1994).

6. Many of the resources we discuss here are applicable to all women in poverty, whether they are AFDC recipients, or not.

7. Ninety-nine percent of JOBS offices offer postsecondary education, and the highest proportion of JOBS participants in any single activity is in postsecondary education (17 percent). General Accounting Office, *Welfare to Work: Participants' Characteristics and Services Provided in JOBS* (Washington, DC, May 1995).

8. Small-scale studies of individual institutions or single states have shown great improvement in the financial status and well-being of women who participated in higher education. See M. Gittell, J. Gross, and J. Holloway, *Building Human Capital: The Impact of Postsecondary Education on AFDC Recipients in Five States* (New York: Ford Foundation, 1993); and E. Kates, "After College, More Than Survival? A Follow-up Study of Low-Income Women Students," Proceedings of the Second Annual Women's Policy Research Conference (Washington, DC: Institute for Women's Policy Research, 1990).

WHY EVERY WOMAN IN AMERICA SHOULD BEWARE OF WELFARE CUTS

*Women's Committee of One Hundred**

Welfare is the ultimate security policy for every woman in America. Like accident or life insurance, you hope you'll never need it. But for yourself and your family, sisters, daughters, and friends, you need to know it's there. Without it, we have no real escape from brutal relationship or any protection in a job market hostile to women with children. Why is Congress trying to take it away?

Imagine the worst. You're laid off from your job. You lose your health insurance. Your marriage falls apart. Your young children need childcare. And you have no family close enough to help.

This is the kind of thing that "happens to someone else." Someone we like to think is "different." And to underline the difference, we usually figure the woman is somehow at fault. "Why did she have kids if she can't support them?" we ask. "What's the matter with her?"

But, at heart, we know how uncomfortably close we are, ourselves, to being without support, without savings. All it takes is a few strokes of hard luck. Hard luck so common, it strikes millions of women with children every year. Women with no job security in unstable or abusive relationships, with nowhere to turn but welfare.

Would you let your employer take away your health insurance? Would you let the government cancel your social security? Of course not. But the public program that benefits struggling women

---

* This piece comprises the text of a full page ad, placed in *The New York Times*, Tuesday, August 8, 1995. It was an attempt to get people involved and sway new legislation to end AFDC. In August 1996, Congress passed their Personal Responsibility legislation. A coupon/response form was a part of the original ad.

most—Aid to Families with Dependent Children (AFDC)—is now considered fair game in Washington. And women are supposed to be quiet about it.

What Myths Underlie the Attack on Welfare?

The welfare "reform" proposal in Congress is based on myths about women *and* about welfare. Even the phrase describing the bill—the "Personal Responsibility Act," taken from Newt Gingrich's Contract with America—exploits these myths. It implies that impoverished women with children, unlike people who get VA benefits or retirees on Social Security, are responsible for their own troubles and need a whack from a mortality paddle to get back in line.

This is not only insulting, but dangerous.

Those who want to cut welfare assume the American job market is hungry for untrained, unskilled workers. It's not. Mothers shoved off welfare will not find jobs waiting. And even if a mother finds a job available, chances are it won't pay a living wage that's enough to cover childcare, let alone include health insurance.

Everybody agrees that the current welfare system is flawed. But these reckless and irresponsible cuts do nothing to fix anything. They only make it harder for a woman raising her children to recover from life's hard knocks—which today's system, even with all its flaws, actually manages to do. That's why we say that welfare isn't supporting failure. In most cases, it's enabling success.

The fact that most women who resort to welfare find a way off within two years by their own efforts, while keeping their children fed and clothed, says a great deal about them. It certainly demonstrates their "personal responsibility." And it should make the rest of us ask why they're being maligned, threatened and lectured.

How Defending Poor Women Protects Us All

The assault on poor women aims to divide American women, leaving all of us more vulnerable than ever. Legislation now pending in Congress would end Aid to Families with Dependent Children and critical nutrition programs. It would free states to reduce their own level of support far below the poverty line.

Most inexcusable of all, it would allow the richest society on Earth to break its most fundamental pledge to women: that if the worst happens, a woman can keep her children with her, with food on the table and a roof over their heads.

These punitive provisions have no offsetting benefits. They won't save money, speed women into jobs, improve health care, or provide more childcare. They won't do anything but complete the humiliation of women who have no other choice and jeopardize the well-being of our poorest children.

No American woman has anything to gain from this so-called "welfare reform." Each one of us has everything to lose. That's why we ask you to act quickly.

President Clinton must stop this attack on women's security. Mail the coupon to us, and we'll speed it along with thousands of others to the White House. And call or write your Senators and Representatives today. This fight is for all of us. Make sure help is there when women need it most.

10 Facts Most Americans Don't Know About Welfare

1. Only 8% of welfare mothers are teenagers. Less than 3% of poor families are headed by women younger than 19.
2. The typical welfare family includes a mother and two children, about the same as the average American family.
3. Welfare mothers on average receive $367 a month. Even with food stamps worth $295, this is still 31% below the poverty line for a family of three. Benefits have lost about a third of their value since 1979.
4. Welfare to single mothers makes up just 1% of the federal budget—3% if food stamps are included.
5. Thirty-eight percent of AFDC parents are white, 37% are African-American, and 18% are Latino.
6. Over 70% of women applying for welfare receive benefits for less than two years; only 8% remain over eight years.
7. More than 60% of AFDC families have a child younger than six. Forty percent have a child younger than two.
8. Full-time, year-round work at minimum wage puts a woman and two children $3,000 below the poverty line—with no health care coverage.
9. Unemployment has steadily increased since World War II, while unemployment benefits have decreased.
10. Carefully conducted research has found that AFDC benefits do not influence a never-married mother's decision to have a child; nor do they influence mothers already on welfare to have additional children.

Does Welfare Support Failure or Enable Success? Two True Stories

JULIE SUE WESTWOOD, married for 20 years, had five kids, a house, a savings account. Then a serious car accident and divorce left her with nothing but a $498 check from AFDC and $250 a month in food stamps.

"I would wake up at 4 a.m., get up, get dressed, and pay whatever bills had to be paid, care for the children, go to school for eight hours, come home, do the laundry, meals, housekeeping, meet the kids' needs—and study late after they fell asleep. In spite of all the trauma, homelessness, and illness, I graduated with a B.A. this year.

"Things are going to change for us."

GLORIA WILSON raised her children on AFDC for two years until she could leave them with family and work two menial jobs to survive.

"The scariest part about getting off welfare was not having health insurance for the kids. I'd have to go to the emergency room an hour away and then we'd usually wait four hours more."

Working for the past 24 years, she remembers her AFDC experience vividly. "It infuriates me to hear the politicians talking about kicking mothers off welfare. Without skills, without education, without medical insurance, without family support, what are these women supposed to do?"

For further information please write or call:
Women's Committee of One Hundred
750 First Street, N.E., Washington, D.C. 20002
202-336-8345
The Committee of One Hundred represents a new mobilization of informed women—including prominent scholars, activists, elected officials, professionals and artists—pledged to defend women's security.

A war against poor women is a war against all women

Acknowledgments

This ad was cosponsored by 1199 National Health and Human Service Employees Union, National Association of Social Workers, Coalition of Labor Union Women, Catholics for Free Choice, American Postal Workers Union, AFL-CIO, Office and Professional Employees International Union, AFL-CIO, Welfare Reform Network of New York, Ms. Foundation for Women, Feminist Majority, Wider Opportunities for Women/Women and Poverty Project, Communications Workers of America, Democratic Socialists of America, Women's Action for New Directions (WAND), National Committee on Pay Equity, United Farm Workers of America, AFL-CIO, Center for Women Policy Studies, National Council for Research on Women, National Jobs for All Coalition, National Coalition for the Homeless, NOW Legal Defense and Education Fund.

SPEAKING FOR OURSELVES
A Lifetime of Welfare Rights Organizing
Marian Kramer

I HAVE BEEN IN THE MOVEMENT ALL OF MY LIFE, ATTENDING community meetings and rallies with my parents and grandparents as a youngster. I *really* became involved during the Civil Rights movement through my church while I was a student at Southern University in Baton Rouge, Louisiana. Even though my family was involved in the movement, they told me that I had been sent to school to get an education and I should not get involved. As soon as I got there, I got involved!

After receiving intensive training, I began working for the Congress of Racial Equality (CORE) as a full-time organizer on their voter registration campaign in the South. Many of the organizers were white students from the North—middle-class, ivy-leaguers—who brought many skills as well as political and economic analyses with them. We were trained to be eternally alert and to know the lay of the land, every little pathway and dirt road through the woods for miles around, so that we could get away in a chase. I *really* learned how to drive in some of those hollows and bottoms many nights, escaping from the Klan, the sheriff, or both.

The African Americans in the South were organizing against the tyranny and oppression they experienced every day. We wanted the right to vote and participate as full-fledged citizens. We were tired of the indignity foisted on us by laws that upheld segregation in restaurants, public transportation, hotels, hospitals, schools, and even cemeteries. I still remember going on long trips and packing all of our food, water, medicines, and other necessities so we could drive straight through because we were not able to go to restaurants or hotels (I *still* pack toilet paper whenever I travel).

Our goals coincided with the government's plan to eradicate Jim Crow laws and policies in order to facilitate the industrialization of the South, which was still primarily an agricultural society, with its chicken farms, cotton fields, and orange groves. The large manufacturers in the North, seeking to reduce labor costs, wanted to build factories in the South, but were limited by the segregation laws. They wanted to be free to hire whomever they wanted and did not want their executives and other employees to be saddled with the problems that segregation brought, including the retaliatory bombings that had become too commonplace.

Every society sets up an infra-structure to support its production. In the United States, production is the engine that drives the economic train. Slavery was established so the production force belonged to the producer. Laws were enacted making it legal for slave owners to abuse, rape, and even kill their slaves. The need for expansion and production served as the underlying cause of the Civil War. In this instance, the government was assisted by the revolutionary Abolitionists. At the end of the Civil War, the slaves were freed, but still enslaved—many became sharecroppers or itinerant farmers, working for slave wages that left them in debt at the end of the harvest season.

When the automatic cotton picker was invented, fewer pickers were needed in the cotton fields. Hundreds of thousands of farm workers migrated to the northern cities. Laws were enacted that protected the manufacturers, and unions forbade African Americans to join. Henry Ford recruited African Americans from the South to replace striking workers. Ultimately, unions got the message and began to open up to all workers.

Everything is still based on production. Union contracts, laws, courts, and schools are used to protect production. When President John Kennedy passed the Civil Rights Act with the approval of the "Big Six" (the major civil rights organizations), the new law was used to industrialize the South. It was no longer feasible to have Jim Crow laws which prohibited corporations from making money from all segments of our society. Once the Jim Crow laws were changed and the bombings stopped, Dow Chemical Company and other large corporations moved south.

To accommodate the needs of industry, streets and roads were built, sewage was improved, and better housing was constructed, which also benefited residents of the communities, including African

Americans. Southern cities began to expand, creating thousands of construction and other job opportunities.

Later, I moved to Detroit to get married. It was different in the North. As a Southerner, I was used to being on the front line, running from the Klan and losing folks either because they were killed or too terrorized to stay. I was paranoid because of my experiences in the South. It took a long time before I could stop looking over my shoulder. I had been led to believe that racism was a southern problem, but the covert racism of the North was a rude awakening!

We began fighting urban renewal in Detroit, which threatened the community, and formed an Alinsky-type organization. We learned a lot from Saul Alinsky, the founder of the Industrial Area Foundation, which had sponsored *The Back of the Yard Campaign* in Chicago during the mass migration of African Americans from the South. These workers, displaced from the farms in the South, arrived in Chicago with no money and camped out along the railroad lines in the rear of the slaughter houses while they hoped for work. The residents of the community felt invaded and wanted to stop the influx of the poor Southerners into their community. Saul Alinsky recruited students and advocates from outside of the community to organize the community to "be a part of the pie." These organizers would come into the community and break it down by religious denominations, church parishes, block clubs, and union affiliations to raise the funds needed to confront the city officials and save the community. Alinsky's model of organizing permitted him to move organizers in and out of the community as needed because they were not attached to the community, although they were paid *from* the community. In fact, when we pressed him about the racist attitudes that were behind *The Back of the Yard Campaign,* Alinsky told us that he could train us to organize to take over the campaign!

In January 1966, while we were fighting for the community against urban renewal, we were mobilizing *The Poor People's War Council on Poverty* to be held in Syracuse, New York. We took a bus load from Detroit, and there I met Beulah Sanders and National Welfare Rights Organization (NWRO) founder George Wiley. Those of us who had been trained in the Civil Rights movement were introduced to Frances Fox Piven and Richard Cloward, who were organizing poor people. They had researched the methods that poor people's organizations had used in the past to influence the government to capitulate to their demands and understood that poor people's power was in their numbers. They realized that the government consistently under-counted the poor and, therefore, was able to minimize the amount of funding needed to combat poverty. Frances' and Richard's strategy was to expand the welfare rolls by identifying the poor (who could mobilize to increase the demand) and force the government to increase funding to meet the people's needs. This strategy needed experienced civil rights organizers who had the trust of the people in the community and were able to mobilize them to action. These organizers came cheap, receiving a stipend of $44.89 every two weeks (if there was money in the budget).

George Wiley offered me an organizing position and called City-Wide (a Detroit welfare rights group) to be sure I was included in their meetings. I committed myself to organizing my community on the local level around welfare rights, but refused to get involved on the national level. The West Side Mothers group (which still exists) was a cofounder, along with CORE, of the Jeffrey Welfare Rights Organization. Jeffrey Welfare Rights became part of the City-Wide Welfare Rights Organization, which in turn became a chapter of the National Welfare Rights Organization (NWRO).

Before the NWRO, AFDC recipients were not represented by anyone. Welfare was a very unpopular issue and was treated as if it were a disease by most organizations. Women were increasingly becoming employed (by General Motors, Ford, Chrysler, etc.). Welfare eligibility was loosened, and recipients were not penalized for working because the corporations needed a large workforce.

The women from the community participated in the original meetings, and I worked to get them there. The movement was against poverty. The idea was to give the women the supports they needed to keep their families together and to offer education and training when they decided to re-enter the workforce. These goals forced the government to provide increased welfare benefits and to provide added services—housing subsidies, nutrition programs, adequate childcare, and supports to allow poor women to obtain education and training. The National Welfare Rights Organization was strong in the '60s, increasing its membership to more than 100,000 members in the United States, Guam, and Puerto Rico. We fought as a united organization across the nation. In addition to teaching the members their rights, the NWRO provided training on how to leaflet, how to conduct door-to-door organizing, and how to determine the appropriate tools for picketing, rallies, and demonstrations. We participated in workshops, developed during the Civil Rights movement, on how to plan and carry out nonviolent acts of civil disobedience and direct action.

We learned how to connect with the struggles of the Black Panthers, hotel and motel workers, as well as tenants fighting against slum lords and substandard living conditions. There were several confrontations—some so volatile that some of us even carried pistols in our bosoms.

In those days, the recipients were the main base. By going door-to-door, we were able to assess people's needs and lead people into applying for welfare. Rather than organizing block clubs the way Alinsky had, we began organizing in the local welfare offices. The women who were in welfare rights were a thorn in the side of the welfare commissioner and carried a lot of weight. They became involved in all aspects of the community—public housing, rent strikes, nutrition programs, etc. Before long, the women were taking over welfare offices and demanding respect, especially, the larger welfare offices with many recipients. We began getting victories, including the child allowance (a flat grant in some states) every September. Every time we won a victory, our membership increased. Whenever a governor wanted to try a new policy that was prohibited by federal law, he had to apply for a waiver. We were able to review the waivers and give our input *before* decisions were made. We were successful in impacting public policy to the point where clients, to have clout, told workers they were with welfare rights even if they were not.

Welfare rights was the key for creating programs designed for women. We taught lawyers that there was a need for legal expertise in poverty law, which eventually led to the establishment of Legal Services. We drafted the principles that the Food Stamp Program was built around. Through direct action and organizing, we pushed Sears Roebuck to give welfare recipients credit. We were able to convince educators that our children needed preschool learning and we helped to establish Head Start. We even picketed welfare offices in support of our welfare workers' need for caseload reduction before they unionized.

We spent every day and every night organizing and networking. During the day, I worked at the hotel workers' union as part of my community. Block clubs, unions, and churches participated in the union efforts. I organized the youth in the Dodge Revolutionary Union Movement (DRUM) and the Black Students United Front. I was also one of the founding members of the League of Revolutionary Black Women, remaining at the local level, but part of the national movement. In June 1967, although I had the respect of the membership, I was bothered by union racism which led to my quitting my organizing with the union. A month later, the Detroit rebellion exploded.

Soon after this time, my husband and I split up, and I was forced to apply for public assistance. I had been trained in welfare rights and refused to be exploited. I continued to advocate for myself and others. Whenever I went to the welfare office, the workers rushed to meet my needs to get me out of the office as soon as possible.

Meanwhile, Jeffrey Welfare Rights was beginning to feel tension building between them and the National and City-Wide Welfare Rights organizations, mostly along class lines. We sent in dues, but never got any reports and received little respect. Funding was controlled by the professional organizers and grant-writers. The leaders had never been on welfare, but wanted to control the members. The organizers were *leading* the welfare rights movement!

The organizers brought in students and experts who thought they had all the answers. They wanted the members to follow their leadership and allow them to choose which issues would be at the forefront of the struggle. Their form of organizing was based on the Alinsky model, but the recipients were becoming empowered and preferred the "Johnnie Tillmon Model" of organizing. Johnnie, a founding member of NWRO from Watts, believed that if you collected 50 cents from everyone on public assistance, you could have enough funding to keep the organization running. She also believed that the victims should be the leaders and speak for themselves because no one else knew the situation better than those who were affected. Citing the contributions that slaves and former slaves made to abolish slavery and the efforts that women made to the suffrage movement, Johnnie expressed her doubts that others could have been as successful: "(T)hose who benefit, if only slightly, from the economic status quo cannot successfully vanguard social change, no matter how good their intentions." She believed that the best organizers were those who were invested in the community because they had to live in the community. She often stated: "It's a proud thing to be spokespeople for the poor!"

Johnnie's concept of organizing was misunderstood by the organizers. As she explained it, her model did not negate the contributions of others. In fact, we needed their access to statistical data and research. We just wanted the organization to be run more democratically, like the unions were supposed to be.

Eventually, Jeffrey Welfare Rights pulled out of the City-Wide and the National Welfare Rights organizations. The issues around leadership led to the demise of City-Wide Welfare Rights, but groups still joined State-Wide Welfare Rights.

In 1975, with declining membership and no funds to pay the bills, NWRO disbanded; but each state chapter continued to organize around poverty issues: hunger, childcare, and the new issues of homelessness and Workfare. Many of us still communicated with each other on a regular basis. Quite a few of us got jobs as paralegals working with Legal Services, and we were able to meet with each other at conferences and meetings sponsored by Legal Services. There were two attempts to re-establish the NWRO, but the leadership would have been the same, bringing with them the same problems we had faced before. As a result, both attempts failed to garner the necessary support to reorganize on the national level.

In 1986, the National Anti-Hunger Coalition was experiencing some of the same difficulties between the victims and the advocates that had plagued the NWRO. The members who were living in poverty felt that the advocates were too passive and moved to expand the board to better reflect the movement. I was elected to serve on the Election Committee, whose charge was to recruit more Hispanics and other people of color. Some of the advocates were in opposition to this plan, fearing their loss of control. The members who were welfare recipients proposed a Hunger Action Conference, "Who Speaks for the Children?"

During the conference, the welfare recipients approached Annie Smart (Louisiana), Arena Edwards (Texas), and me and expressed the need to speak for themselves; they suggested building a new national welfare rights organization. They were deeply disturbed that most of the professional advocates were supporting the Family Support Act and its provision for mandating that the poor work for their welfare checks, which they saw as the legalization of slavery. Meeting together, we voted to pursue a National Welfare Rights Conference, which was held at Georgetown University in Washington, DC, in 1987.

At the National Welfare Rights Conference, the participants discussed the need to build unity between low-income workers and recipients by showing how capitalists were profiting at the expense of all of us. We discussed how things had changed since the NWRO's demise. We realized that now we have homelessness, death in the streets, and rising unemployment as technology replaces workers. To implement welfare reform, governors are requesting numerous waivers to the federal laws, and our input is not being sought, even when we ask. We decided we had to reunite as a national organization because most of the organizations we had previously relied on were broken due to their inability to address new issues. Funding for many of these organizations had dried up, and the people were forced to desert. We felt we needed to move from organizing to include lobbying. We also noted that there are lots of poor people who do not receive any type of assistance and they needed to be included in the struggle. We knew we needed to build unity among the unemployed, the low-income workers, and the homeless. Massachusetts' "Up and Out of Poverty Campaign" rekindled the fire to advocate for improved welfare benefits. We decided to model ourselves after unions because we wanted to build solidarity and have a more democratic organization than the NWRO had been. We formed the National Welfare Rights Union (NWRU) based on this membership-driven analysis.

There are several major differences between the '60s and the present. At least in the '60s people could eat; now there are more than 80 million people in the United States living in poverty. Before, women were struggling to get into the labor force with good wages and benefits. The welfare rights movement started among the poor, who were fighting to open up training programs to enable them to get jobs so that welfare wouldn't be needed. In the '60s, the recipient leaders were undereducated, but they *were* able to get jobs once they were off welfare. Today, lots of welfare activists have degrees, but there are no jobs! In Detroit, it used to take months to retool the auto factories between models and the employers used to lay off the workforce during retooling. The factories needed General Relief to tide the labor force over and to keep them healthy so that they could work when the retooling was complete. A worker could get fired from one plant and go down the street and get hired by another plant. Auto workers who were forced to move to different plant locations used to get relocation money to prevent disruption of the workforce. With the advent of technology, there is no delay between models on the assembly line. Robotization has replaced thousands of unionized workers. Corporations don't need us anymore, and they have to downsize to be able to compete. We now have a permanent army of unemployed—a new class of folks who aren't needed in the workforce. Corporations don't need programs to regulate the people anymore.

Now, there are no jobs paying a living wage. Our jobs are being eliminated and, simultaneously, the push is on to eliminate welfare. "Aid to Dependent Corporations" is more important. The funding is being taken from welfare to pay for the new technology in the plants. Increases in government appropriations that provided workers' salary increases have ceased.

On the one hand, we now have the ability to wipe out homelessness and hunger; on the other, just to get a job as a supervisor on the line, we need an engineering degree. To further complicate matters, drug testing is everywhere. We should be thinking ahead and deciding how to utilize the technology we have for the benefit of everybody. We need to build housing and feed people which creates jobs.

We're weak now because the majority of people don't understand welfare reform. The media and politicians have convinced people that they are doing what needs to be done, even though forty years of research attests to the fact that these reforms are based on myths. Few people know that there is a growing, vibrant movement that is mounting opposition to these punitive policies because the media refuses to report it. We need to break the media black-out and expose workers, the youth, and seniors to the realities of welfare reform and its potential impact on them. The older generation must teach the younger generation about our long history of struggle. The youth need to understand why we have public assistance programs and how our foreparents fought against oppression in the labor force and the ravages of poverty at home. We need to develop more collective leadership because mass movements work better as collectives. This will allow all members to be generals. Everyone will be able to contribute because all of our lives are affected. We also need to understand economics and the political picture because Clinton and the other politicians are using fascism to divide us. With the current trends, poverty is going to be phenomenal. Instead of providing affordable housing, legislation is being passed that makes homelessness illegal. We are constantly being arrested for taking over vacant housing for the homeless that we have paid for with our taxes. Meanwhile, the government is using foreign and domestic terrorism as an excuse for strengthening the FBI and the police state. We are fighting to thrive, not barely survive. If it takes a revolution, welfare rights is going to be a part of it!

Organizing is harder now because there is no funding for welfare rights organizing and activism. All of us have to work other jobs to be able to take part in the struggle. Although services are being severely cut, people still need help. Since most members of the NWRU are experienced veterans in the *war on the poor,* we are constantly challenged as we struggle to assist people in getting their needs met. We find ourselves filling in for Legal Services and Welfare Department workers. On top of our jobs and with little funding, it can be extremely overwhelming.

The government is engaging in propaganda to split us, but groups are coming together. Unity is dangerous to politicians because it brings people together and helps them to realize that their individual struggles are intertwined. This knowledge can lead to large voting blocs that can jeopardize politicians' careers. Jobs made people individualistic, but the expanding joblessness has provided a unifying force. We have a history of representative constituents, but we are now organized due to the economic plight. We must educate our communities and connect the two. This time, with opposition on all fronts, the growth of the movement should be faster than it was in the 1960s.

People think welfare rights activists are loud-mouthed know-nothings because that is how the media has portrayed us. We always have to fight our way in to meetings, conferences, and symposiums to express our concerns, but the professional organizations have had to come our way because there are no jobs for anyone.

Members of the NWRU are increasingly being invited to speak to groups who normally feel estranged from welfare. In ghost towns (such as Gary, Indiana, where the steel mills have closed down), unemployed workers are demanding to hear about welfare rights in their union meetings. Workers are stepping forward!

Faith Evans, who had been the only male recipient on the Executive Board of the NWRO, was hired by the National Organization for Women (NOW) to help them address the concerns of poor women. Faith made sure that we were included in NOW's agenda. We have been keynote speakers and participated in several workshops at NOW conferences. Patricia Ireland, president of NOW, was arrested with us when we confronted Congress on the punitive welfare reform policies.

In 1995, NOW's Legal Education and Defense Fund established the Women's Committee of One Hundred to help combat the political assault on women. They raised funds to publish a full-page ad in the *New York Times*, "Why Every Woman in America Should Beware of Welfare Cuts."

The Lawyer's Committee for Civil Rights Under the Law sponsored a national conference in Washington, DC, in 1995. For five months, we worked with them designing and planning the conference, which was entitled, "African-American Women in the Law: Exerting our Power—Reclaiming our Communities." They paid the entire costs for 15 African-American members of the NWRU to attend the conference. We were able to sharpen the focus of the workshops through our participation and make them more relevant. The Committee also sponsored several of us to be included in their delegation to the United Nation's Fourth Women's Conference in Beijing, China. We were able to significantly impact the direction and goals of the conference by contributing to the platform that was adopted. Women are stepping forward!

The two major newspapers in Detroit went on strike in July 1995. Although 2,000 workers were on strike, the union was unsuccessful in its attempts to get the managers to settle the strike. After more than six months, the NWRU and other community organizations began to get involved in the dispute. Bishops from various religious denominations, city councilors, and women's groups joined the picket lines and were arrested along with the reporters and photographers from the newspapers. Organized technicians are stepping forward!

Many students are working as a condition of receiving financial aid, fighting to get childcare, and are becoming homeless. Recent graduates have school loans that they can't pay back because they cannot find suitable employment. Dissatisfied with performing "community service" by working in the soup kitchens and shelters, hundreds of students are organizing across the country to end poverty and eliminate the need for these services. Students are stepping forward!

Politicians have tried to convince us that gang members are a problem. Subsequent to the 1991 rebellion in Los Angeles, members of NWRU approached the gang members, educated them on the issues, and changed their perspective. Now they have joined with us because they realize that our issues are the same. Gang members are stepping forward! *There's a movement taking place!*

Whenever we get arrested, we always ask for a jury trial. In this way, we are able to turn the courtroom into a schoolroom, educating the jury about the struggle for justice and why we must fight for our rights.

It's definitely not the same as it was in the '60s—then, we were dealing with industrialization. Now, cuts in education, housing, school loans, nutrition programs, and labor have made us all vulnerable.

There is so much to do. Welfare grants should be universal and raised at least to the poverty line and indexed to the annual cost of living allowance. We're all we've got! We have to stop waiting for leaders; we are the leaders history has molded. We need to find funds to enable us to get out and organize and educate through programs such as our Annie Smart Leadership Development Institute, where we train organizers, in order to back our organization. We need to increase the readership of our own publications, such as *Survival News, Sojourner,* and other grassroots media. We need to build and strengthen alliances with professional groups such as the Bertha Capen Reynolds Society and other leftist organizations—we're what history has left!

Advocates are now coming back saying that what the poor have been saying is true—we are all vulnerable, and revolutionary changes are needed. Welfare rights activists are more revolutionary than anybody. People who are not eligible for benefits have to learn why they need to be committed to the struggle for economic and social justice so that all of us can eat and get benefits.

Several Canadians came to our NWRU convention in August 1995. They became members because they are also witnessing their government's retreat from social responsibility. Now the global economic crisis has made it an *international* struggle!

APOLOGIES DON'T HELP
*Milwaukee Welfare Warriors**

THANK YOU FOR YOUR HELP IN PUBLISHING FACTS AND MYTHS about those of us who receive government child support. May we ask you to go one step further in your support of our families?

Popular lists of "facts" about welfare are defensive: We *only* have two children, *only* stay "on" welfare for two years, *only* receive $370 a month, *only* use up 1 percent of the federal budget, *only* need help temporarily to get us on our feet, would "*work*" if *only* we could afford childcare/health care or could find a job, are *mainly* white adults, not teens, and *mainly* children.

These apologetic "facts" present statistical truths about welfare. However, they omit two profound realities of welfare:

1. AFDC is a public child support program.

2. Most single-mother families on welfare are victims of abuse and/or abandonment.

No other moms are called *dependent* or made to feel like parasitical, apologetic criminals for receiving support for their children. Widowed moms, some divorced moms, married moms all expect and receive support—from both the government (tax deductions, Social Security) and the biological fathers. Neither they nor their children are accused of being social deviants or mentally defective (low self-esteem, etc.) because they receive economic support. Nor are they labeled "recipients"—an insulting, passive, one-dimensional label of the complex being a single mother on welfare is.

And what about those of us with three, four or five children, or those of us who are teen moms? What about the moms who can't

---

* This piece represents a letter written by Welfare Warriors in their fight for the lives of mothers and children: Welfare Warriors, 4504 N. 47 Street, Milwaukee, WI 53218.

both raise kids alone and work full-time? What about the women who aren't white? What about those of us who use the support for far more than two years? Most of all, what about the vast majority of us who will never get our families out of poverty with one woman's salary?

Apologetic statistics are not working to convince Americans that children and mothers have a right to share in our wealth. Apologies are not convincing taxpayers that children need support, even if mom is employed. Apologies are not stopping the violence and terrorism of welfare reform. Apologies are not stopping the government from taking children away from loving homes. Apologies are not stopping the government from giving the majority of our tax money to corporations and the Pentagon. Apologies are not creating living-wage jobs for moms (or dads). Apologies are not helping Americans understand the problem or the solutions. Apologies are not helping single mothers and children retain the strength needed to fight back.

It is time for our allies to do more than apologize for our existence. It is time to stand up for our right to public support for our children and our right to do paid work or get help from a partner without losing that support. It is time for our allies to state loud and clear that they will not tolerate systematic punishing of mothers and children for being victims of abandoning dads and a slave-wage work force.

IT IS TIME FOR OUR ALLIES TO FIGHT FOR US, NOT APOLO-GIZE FOR OUR EXISTENCE.

PUNISHING PEOPLE OUT OF POVERTY
Jobs, Welfare, and Community Change
Senator Dianne Wilkerson

I HAVE BEEN IN MASSACHUSETTS ALMOST ALL OF MY LIFE AND I remember spending short periods of time as a child living with my mother, who was a single woman with eight children, on AFDC in Massachusetts. I remember the anguish, although I never understood what it was. Also, I have had the experience as an adult of raising children on AFDC.

One of the most significant reasons I decided to run for the state legislature was because I knew during the 1992 campaign, that the then-sitting legislature had indicated that it was their intention to take up the welfare reform issue in the 1993-'94 legislative session. We had gone through "reforms" three or four times since I had been in Massachusetts, and it seemed to me that every time that our legislature had reformed our system, things got a little bit *worse!* I had always been of the opinion that the reason things have gotten so disorganized with our system is because we didn't have anybody who had actually lived through raising children on AFDC making the decisions and developing policy about what a *real* reformed system ought to look like to make it work for the people—the children—for whose benefit it was created, who would otherwise live in poverty in Massachusetts. I thought that running for the legislature would be a chance to be involved in an issue in a much more direct and personal way than I could ever do from the outside. After all, the welfare system was established by the government to meet the needs of poor women, so why are government officials blaming them for using it? It's been a very difficult time.

What I learned is that the state could not have chosen a worse time to make decisions on welfare reform. Our country was just coming off 12 years of in-your-face Republican politics—the meanness and the *me*-ness—about social policies. I also think that, more than anything else, for 12 years the Republican federal government administration had told the people that it was O.K. to be mean. That you didn't have any responsibility as an American, as a human being, for anyone else; that the people who didn't have the wherewithal (the money) to take care of themselves were at fault. Even if these people had children, then, the children had to take the lumps with their parents because they should *never* have been born in the first place.

With that overarching national discussion going on, it made it incredibly difficult to deal with an issue that was so personal to me in our state legislature. So, it was a fight. There was a *real* battle!

Referring to me as controversial is probably an understatement! First, I think people don't like to be challenged. I think that's the first fact and reality about life. Second, I think that another reality is that they don't like to be challenged by a *woman*. And then third, probably as significant as the first and the second, they certainly don't want to be challenged by an *African-American* woman who talks to them in more articulate English than *they* can speak—that was an additional frustration. People always ask, "How can you deal with it? How come you don't get angry and lose your cool?" And I say, "I do! I just don't do it at *them* because you have to be careful. If you want people to listen to what you say, then *how* you say it is incredibly important." If you have an opinion, you *do* have to be very careful how you say it.

I learned that this wasn't an issue that had much to do with party membership: It wasn't a Democratic/Republican issue. It was very much a class issue, very much a race issue, very much a gender issue, and very much a power issue. And all of those things coming together at once make for a dangerous combination. There's also the reality that all the *"isms"* that we deal with in this country, somehow, got wrapped up in our national discussion and state discussion about welfare reform. One of the things we heard constantly from legislators during campaign speeches (and even after) was, "The *people* want change!" "The *people* have spoken!" "The *people* want us to do this and we have to respond to the people!" "The *people* are tired!" "The *people* are fed up!" The only thing you can take from that is that they are not talking about *poor* people; they're not talking about *children*.

Some of the forces that are out there are good and some are not. The negative force that I experience is the legislature, itself. Many elected officials are running so scared that they respond by acting and doing things that they think their constituents want them to do and they invoke the name of their constituents as a move to justify their actions. That's probably some of the most negative.

So, there was a decision made that "*the people*" were more important than the "*other* people," and there was a major trade-off. I think we have a country that is in some very difficult economic times that no one wants to talk about! It's common practice that when there is a national crisis that we don't have an answer to, and particularly when the economy is the problem, there is this tendency to create arguments and impressions that the reason that we are in this bind is because of "*these* people" or "those *other* people." What it did was allow legislatures all over the country— and certainly Massachusetts is no exception—off the hook. They simply convinced people that the number-one problem in this country is that we have too many poor people on AFDC; although, in Massachusetts (which is not much different than most other states), it was all of 2 percent of the state's total $16 billion budget! The legislators actually did a very effective job of convincing people that was the reason why John Jones hadn't gotten a pay raise from his job in two or three years.

One of the biggest disappointments for me has been the number of female legislators who have gotten very comfortable and have jumped into the same *modus operandi* of some of the more ignorant male legislators, or the disillusioned, or the unenlightened. Some of the female elected officials I've witnessed, in their zeal to be accepted in the club, have decided that they have to be even tougher on women's and children's issues than the male legislators. This phenomenon has resulted in an even more effective coalition on the other side because male legislators are able to sit back and get what they want, which is, I think, an all-out effective attack on women (the poorer, the better for them) and have it done by someone else.

Oftentimes, that someone else (all across the country, and Massachusetts is no exception) is *women* legislators. It has been very disappointing. I don't think that's a sexist thing to say. There's nothing wrong with the notion that many people voted for and elected women officials because they believed that we *were* different. I would like to think that my agenda had a lot to do with my constituents' decision to vote for me, because they had five choices: There were four males that were running. I don't think it was a case of "I want a *woman* senator," but "*because* she's a woman, I believe that she may bring something different to this office," and some of that difference is a better understanding of social issues, women's issues, children's issues. I don't think that's anything to be embarrassed about. I would like to think I know a whole lot more about being a woman and what we deal with than some of my male colleagues.

To see women get elected for that reason and then hide and pretend that their being a woman had nothing to do with it, or to make such statements as, "I don't want to get pegged with *only* dealing with women's issues!" is very sickening and disheartening to me. I think that women's issues are life issues. I feel just as comfortable talking about daycare and AFDC as I do about banking or the environment, manufacturing, and public safety. You have to be secure in yourself, though, to understand that. If you are secure, then you don't need to run, to walk away, and to shy away, and to pretend that you don't want to have anything to do with the very issues that made you who you are! I think that's been one of the more difficult realities that this entire movement has had to deal with. Some certainly volunteered for the job, but the activity of some of the prominent women in this country is starting that *same* bigotry and nonsense, and *they* ought to know better!

I was amazed when I arrived at the State House to find that the black legislators don't really communicate with each other, but we need to. I think that's why we lost the welfare battle so badly. Everyone doesn't come with the same level of understanding about all issues. People assume that because an elected official is black he or she will understand all the issues of poverty. There was one black representative who kept in constant touch with me throughout the entire welfare reform debate because we set up the communication beforehand while working on other issues. We need more of that!

One of the things that we—as proponents of fairness and respect for motherhood and childrearing as work and, more important even, respect for the notion that children should not be punished because of what we may think about their mother or father—need to make understood is the notion that as a country, we have reason to be investing in children who are not our own because it is in *everybody's* interest to have a healthy, well-fed, well-housed, and well-educated citizenry, and that being poor ought not to take you totally out of that mix. I think that's part of what happened.

The people who are controlling the message, the media, the microphones, the televisions, and the newspapers did an *incredibly* effective job convincing the American people that poor people are a problem and that if we just put them in their place, we'll all be better off. Or that they are poor because they *want* to be, and *choose* to be, and the only way we can fix it is to *punish* them out of being poor. "Punish people out of poverty," is the way I characterize the message.

On the other hand, except for the recipients themselves and a small group of people that want to be labeled as liberals (we had a group of women in academia, including the Women College Presidents, come to the State House) and the advocates for the recipients, there wasn't a core group of people that would have to be involved in killing that message. That core group would have been and *should* have been middle-class America. I say that because most middle-class folks that I know are only one or two paychecks from being on welfare themselves. And then the other part is *women!* One of the most amazing things in this process was the total inaction and invisibility of middle-class women—the kinds and numbers of women that were out there 25 years ago and have continued to be out there, walking the streets and guaranteeing that the whole issue of women's choice is protected. I believe that the same principles that brought people out on those issues should have galvanized them around these issues. The women that I thought we would see, that *should* have been out there, were not. In fact, instead, they would show up at forums and be the first ones to ask questions such as, "Why should *I* pay for Jeannie to stay home and have children? I had a child and I had to go back to work and I didn't have a choice to stay home and take care of my child!" These attitudes prevented us from getting the constituency we absolutely had to have for us to have a fair fight. It wasn't a fair fight!

The poor children of this world are not equipped to fight Congress! The poor children are not equipped to fight the Rush Limbaughs of the world! Poor children cannot compete with these people, such as some of the talk show hosts, who make a *quarter of a million dollars* a year to spew hate, antagonism, and bigotry. And there was just no match. *No* match! It was a very hard lesson that we learned in the process. You'd like to think that people don't actually have to fall off a cliff to know that if you slip and fall, you're probably going to get hurt. I still believe that. I want to be optimistic about it. It is very difficult, though (in the context of the mean-spiritedness that seems to be ruling the day in this country), to continue to carry the message. I think that we have to *keep* saying it and, hopefully, we can get the message across to people before too much damage is done.

I think the answer to what is going on politically is a short answer, because I don't think it's that complicated. Our country was a farming country and, with higher technology, we moved into becoming manufacturers; and we did that for a long time. Twenty years ago, manufacturing jobs represented 50-60 percent of the income generated in this country; now we find it's down to about 20 percent and falling. Because of all the advanced technology, we are *never* going back to that day when we need that kind of human power to do the work that needs to be done. As a result of that, we have lost, without exaggeration, hundreds of thousands of jobs off shore (out of the United States) and it comes at a time when our state administrations and certainly our federal government are totally ill-equipped and inept to come up with a way to replace those jobs. So, there are two things that are happening.

The first is that we don't have a plan or a strategy, and there isn't any national discussion about creating a plan or a strategy to *really* up-start our economy. So, as a distraction, what we do is convince people that there is something else that's a bigger issue. In 1993 and '94, we used welfare. In 1995 and '96, it's affirmative action. We convince ourselves that the reason that our economy is bad is that there are hordes of black people, Hispanics, and women who are taking jobs from these nice, educated white men. So, the pattern continues, and unless we are all going to be there to stand loud to change it, we are just going to have a continuing misunderstanding that results, not only in misinformation, but in generating the kind of divisiveness that can destroy this country. So, what we have done was engage in a distraction that said, 'Our problem is not our economy; it's *welfare*.'"

The second thing we have done was convince people that poor people, *individually,* are the problem and that we just need to get tough on them. Myths, then, become the basis for the creation of policy to deal with it. And it's happening all over the country! We *could* deal with it by dealing with the *real* issue, and that is that our economy has changed and our talk has not changed with it. Our policy and our technology used to use our brains to figure out ways to create new employment opportunities.

The other big joke is that we don't have the kind of economy that could support employment for the people that we're talking about and on whose ability to work we are trying to condition our continuing support. And we're talking about *poor* people, many unskilled and uneducated, and we're saying that if you want us to continue to maintain you in poverty, you've got to *work* for it.

Serving My Constituents

Among my constituents, there are a lot of different emotions, probably as many emotions as there are diverse groups. There is some unconcern, some despair, some helplessness, and, I think, some optimism, as well. It's important to note that the diversity is representing many of the kinds of folks who would be most affected by the policies and social issues that we discuss. A majority of the population in my district is African American, but I also have a very large Hispanic constituency. I have the largest gay and lesbian voting population in the city in my senatorial district. We also have a substantial number of whites in the district and we have an enormous amount of children—the largest number of public school children in the entire Commonwealth of Massachusetts live in my district. So, issues around education are important. Some of the highest incidence of poverty in the state is in this district. In fact, a lot of the welfare families live in this district. There's a lot of contradiction, but I think, in general, the mood is one of real caution.

I think that the same kind of hopelessness and despair that the bulk of children seem to be experiencing (and actually are articulating as an explanation of why they are engaging in some of their more negative behaviors) can be seen in adults as well. They exhibit the notion that "you have to do whatever you're going to do in life quickly because you're not going to be around long," and "I'd better buy what I can buy *now* because things could turn and I could be out of work in a year or two." There's an *urgency* about life in our surroundings that seems to be on the minds of so many people.

In my district, it is very important for the voters to see their elected officials out in the community. I spend a lot of time attending community meetings, rallies, celebrations, and other events. Many people are not sure what we are doing inside the State House, but they are bothered if they do not see us at their functions. It is wonderful to meet so many of my constituents on their home turf and to be able to talk to them personally about the issues that are important to them.

The Political Solutions

Motor Voter is fine legislation, but we need more. I try to say it everywhere I go. We also need voter education and we need to make sure that people go out to vote.

I was fascinated to hear the governor from Puerto Rico say that in Puerto Rico, there is an 85 percent turn-out for elections. They have been conducting a study in all of the major cities (New York, Los Angeles, Holyoke, etc.) with large Puerto Rican populations to determine their voting record in the states. They have found a 60 to 70 percent *decrease* in the voting of Puerto Ricans. These are citizens, so there is no problem with culture, language, or color; yet when they come to the states, they don't participate in the way they used to. I don't think it's because they are less interested. I think it's because this government has no voter education and no incentive to establish any. We have work to do!

Change is possible because the legislature has already begun to re-think their earlier decisions around welfare reform. When you don't know what to do to improve the economy or solve some of the problems we have in this country, it's easier to blame a certain group. If you can convince people that it's the fault of someone else, it will look as though you've done something, even if you've done nothing.

The issues are and the most difficult task is to convince the legislature (statewide) and the federal government that it would cost us less in the long run to invest in people's health, education, and welfare now. That's the challenge! It's the most important and simplest way that I could use to characterize how we get out of this mess. That is the need to convince people that we get more benefit from, not only individuals, but our people—our citizenry—when they are healthy. It would cost incredibly less than it would otherwise. Since that's an issue for people, it's one that we ought to be dealing with, and there's some major resistance to doing that. But that's the message, and we've got to keep convincing them. We've got to use all of the allies that we have.

TALKING ACROSS THE TABLES
Moving Beyond Dialogue to Negotiation and Action

WHILE PREPARING THIS BOOK, WE BOTH GAVE TALKS TO LOTS of people. Diane spoke to national and local groups of students and activists: white, Latino and black. Among others, she spoke on platforms with Noam Chomsky, Frances Fox Piven, and Stanley Aronowitz. She debated Lawrence Mead at Columbia University and spoke to Welfare Rights Union members all over the country. Ann gave talks to social work schools, poverty program staff, and women's groups, even to progressive business groups in several states. Together, we spoke to unions, to groups of high school and college students, to churches. We have been on television, radio talk and call-in shows. Even though we spoke most often to generally friendly audiences, there were often people in the crowds who still wanted "to do something about welfare," who argued that we "couldn't keep supporting bad 'choices.'" And, of course, all year we were reading the contributions of our authors, as well as other writing about poverty, welfare, and what was happening politically in the county.

It was also the year the Republican Congress took control and welfare reform became a national issue as well as one where state after state, including our own, competed to create "the most restrictive welfare reform plan in the country." There was tremendous attention to welfare. Many liberal groups began to think that there was more to talk about than the old false promises to replace welfare with jobs—as long as some childcare and health benefits were included.

As other proposed cuts in immigrant rights, Medicare, Medicaid, and affirmative action were debated, there was real room for discussion. Liberals and progressives were honestly puzzled that it "could get so bad so quickly," and moderate audiences wondered if we were "going too far."

So the rooms in which we spoke were often full of energy, and sometimes we even had the special feeling that if we could just make the right arguments, and have long enough to talk, we could make a difference. People in the audiences asked questions that challenged us and helped us be more aware of how hard it is to make certain arguments, and why many people are afraid to think about certain things. We were heartened when participants would come up to us after discussions and say: "Yes, I see that I was blaming welfare recipients for seeming to have what I need too. That doesn't really make sense." We were pleased when we could help people see things differently, and when we felt the spirit move people to organize. Yet, at the same time, the tenor of the country, the level of talk-show venom, and the dangers posed by the real policies being proposed kept us terrified of the real implications for real women and their families, and the long-term effects on the security for everyone.

This chapter makes suggestions, drawn from our experiences, about how real coalitions to defend welfare recipients can be built. Our image, again, is one of talking across tables: kitchen tables, seminar tables, meeting tables, and negotiating tables. Here we put our suggestions "on the table" to continue the process of discussion, dialogue, strategizing, and negotiation that we hope will open options for the next round of talks across tables all over the country.

Words of Caution

But before we can make suggestions, we must bring to the table the most frustrating rejoinders that we still hear, even from friendly audiences. They are hard to respond to exactly because the answers take time, and yet, if they are not engaged, the discussion never proceeds and "new business" can never be attended to.

♦ *But what will work to get people off welfare?* This is the moderate response that often emerges, no matter how hard we try to explain that the problem is *not* to get people off welfare. The goal is to help people move out of poverty or, if we don't know how to do this, to provide income and other support that makes poverty less grueling, destabilizing, and demoralizing, by providing welfare or something like it, but better.

◆ *But don't we still have to do something to stop all the teen pregnancy, family dissolution, and child neglect?* Isn't getting women into the "normal" world of work better than the isolation and self-perpetuation of welfare? This is the "humanitarian" response that begs the question of whether society's very real problems are automatically perpetuated by providing income when women ask for it—rather than jobs that they can't keep.

◆ But all women have to work now. We just can't defend income programs any more, can we? This is the standard liberal response, based on an assumption that "public opinion" won't allow us to talk about welfare anymore. The logic follows that the only option is to keep pretending that somehow this economy can, with a little government help, actually create enough jobs to allow single women to join the working poor.

◆ *But, we all know that the real issue is unequal taxation, the maldistribution of wealth, economic injustice, the world economy, or how the rich get welfare, so don't we have to broaden the issue beyond poverty?* This leftist response is frustrating because, while true at one level, at another it can become a progressive way to triage welfare in favor of more "universal" issues, such as health care or taxes. And it denies the need to defend the crucial role that the defense and maintenance of a welfare state play in any strategy for building the foundation for a just society.

For us, and for all welfare rights activists, any answers to the above questions must be calibrated to the specialized concerns of the differing groups with whom we need to be in coalition. Yet each of these potential allies must be approached with care, while we listen to their issues, too.

Basic Elements for Coalition Building

Very briefly, we want to report on the lessons we have learned from talking across different tables, in very different settings:

With *labor groups*, we had good luck talking about how "you're next."

◆ As discussed elsewhere in this volume, union members see the threat of Workfare to wages and employment—this, after all, is the AFL-CIO's own position. They will usually support a discussion that sees welfare as another level of social security that backs up unemployment insurance. However, unionists, especially the men, are a real challenge when it comes to the deeper discussion of valuing women's work in the home, and the barriers that keep them from employment. Here women in labor have a crucial role to play, and are useful in providing forums for discussion. We have also had luck arguing that, just as grievance officers must defend every worker's rights—even those whose behavior is not ideal—so we must stand up for all parents' rights to receive welfare, even when a particular woman on welfare may "behave badly." There is often an opening for understanding when we talk of the far greater pain it causes women on welfare to be looked down upon by working-class cousins or uncles than by rich politicians.

♦ And we have learned that any fruitful discussion of women's poverty must include an analysis of the insecurities of the employment system, the inadequacies of benefits, hours, and wages for so many families. In dialogue with unions, the most interesting questions have been how to create a real floor of security for all workers. Would it be by a system of wage subsidy, such as an expanded earned income tax credit? Or a basic income scheme, where all people would receive a basic grant, which would be supplemented by wages without penalty? These are some of the intriguing questions that should bring folks together.

In talking with middle-class *women's groups,* we have found that both feminist and other organizations now understand that women are profoundly threatened by the loss of options when welfare is taken away, or made so problematic that women will stay in abusive situations rather than accept assistance.

♦ The problem with women's groups is usually one of style, of too easy identification. Not all women on welfare see childcare, education, or even health insurance as their only barrier to employment, yet so many middle-class women will assert this commonalty without learning how recipients prioritize their needs. Abortion, which is a vital option for women, can also be seen as a profound threat by poor women. When abortion is presented as a better choice than poverty or single motherhood, then many women on welfare can hear their very own lives being challenged. And if women are unaware of the class privilege that their personal style may project, then they are not going to win allies. Failure to provide women on welfare who are invited to meetings with real money, not vouchers, for childcare or transportation often makes women on welfare believe that "feminists just don't get it." Travel and housing accommodations for recipients need to be pre-paid and as comfortable as any arranged for more wealthy speakers, if meetings are to be attended and respectful coalitions are to be built. We say this to groups, and sometimes they listen, but often we get the feeling they think we are focusing on petty details, not signs of respect that allow people to talk to each other.

♦ On the other hand, talking with organized women's groups has taught us to try very hard to make the case for motherhood without essentialism, without seeming to argue that all real women are mothers. We have learned that it is still central to talk about women, despite the great temptation to talk about the needs of children or families as a way of making the issue safer. We now know that more work needs to be done in talking about the fathers: Somehow we haven't figured out how to talk clearly about how men both must be responsible to their children and yet respect women's options to live without them. And we surely have more work to do in addressing both women's legitimate rage at male behavior and the reality that many women on welfare are, or want to be, reconnected to "good men." These confusions can make discussions among women's groups especially fruitful and important to creating a clearer direction.

In talking with scores of *liberal, and mainstream religious groups*, we have learned that they serve a critical public role when they insist on society's moral obligation to protect children and mothers.

◆   Religious communities have vital roles to play, first, in linking welfare to basic notions of love and charity, and second, in leading the challenge to the religious Right. In Boston, for example, the work of a religious taskforce on welfare reform was critical in stopping some of the worst proposals. They created an insert for church bulletins on Mother's Day. And the untiring work of some ministers, rabbis, nuns, and priests has helped recipients to be heard by new audiences, and to feel less demonized. We have learned from Diane's experiences especially that it is best to send speakers who share some of the religious background of their audiences, because they can use familiar metaphors and call up similar notions of obligation. For the same reason it is critical, but far harder, for religious allies to stand up to the Christian Right. Here even our best friends sometimes want to avoid the fray—because they don't like to fight with other co-religionists, because they fear splitting members of their own communities, and perhaps exposing their own marginality. This is where religious allies must be pushed: A sympathetic minister, for example, can be far more effective on Christian talk shows by saying, "my Bible does not say that mothers have to be punished for bringing life into the world—it says they should be helped," than can those of us who make moral arguments about secular rights.

◆   Here the dialogue must go on. Women on welfare need the support of people of faith, but they must push to be portrayed not just as victims, nor just as innocents. Honest discussions must be held about how to work together around issues of morality when single moms do not choose to marry or are lesbians. Moving people to see welfare rights as a major domestic human rights issue can hold promise. Here, many of the women who are redefining spirituality from a woman's perspective can be especially helpful.

Professional advocates, especially lawyers, academics, doctors, and social workers, remain crucial to support and defense efforts.

◆   Talking with advocates is critical, especially as a means of helping them
    hear the strategies that feel most comfortable for recipients. As the
    Welfare Warriors suggest, sometimes advocates try to defend recipients
    in ways that are confusing: What does it mean to prove that most
    recipients are white, have only two kids, and were once married? Does
    that mean that it is O.K. to defend welfare recipients because they really
    are "good women" after all? Professionals sometimes need lessons in
    working with women on welfare as equals, and in respecting their
    leadership, even if they may seem "unrealistic." Advocates who play
    lobbying roles are especially vulnerable to trying to manage recipients
    so that "friendly" legislators aren't offended. Often academics can play
    a useful mediating role between recipients and professionals. If they
    have taught recipients and worked with them in more collaborative ways,
    they can sometimes help people to hear each other. And, of course,
    academics should organize themselves—as many have—to be available
    to engage in participatory and respectful research to defend poor
    women, and to seek media attention when they do so.

◆   On the other hand, even as they are themselves under attack, legal
    services attorneys and other professional advocates continue to be true,
    essential friends: by compiling and processing information on the latest
    round of state legislators and U.S. Congress proposals and actions; by
    discussing the uses and limits of legal strategies; by literally defending
    recipients from lawless welfare departments and workers. The goal of
    discussions has to be to keep open communication so that recipients
    can be heard when they express their strategic priorities, so that
    advocates can be respected when they give strategic advice, and so that
    some level of mutual give and take can occur. As national- and state-level
    experiences of discord have taught us, accomplishing this is surely an
    ongoing agenda item.

Talking with *African-American groups* has been especially rewarding, and indicates to us that critical connections are being made.

◆   Racism is so deep in all the talk about women and poverty. Most
    African-American groups understand that AFDC has been at its most
    destructive within their communities: Workers are most hostile and
    inflexible; fraud is always suspected; and no one has really tried to
    develop meaningful employment options. At the same time, welfare is
    so stigmatized because it is associated with black people. So often, male
    and female leaders of black groups haven't wanted to be highly visible
    as "welfare rights" advocates—they know that if white people thought
    all people on welfare were white, the whole debate would be different.

◆   But, as Diane has found at several national conferences focusing on poverty and people of color, as well as at community meetings here in Boston, African Americans usually understand what the assaults on recipients mean for their communities, and they are not fooled by promises to get people off welfare and into jobs. Indeed, we have both found that you have to be more radical to be heard by black audiences. It is before such audiences that we get to talk about guaranteed income proposals, and about the deep racism that taints even some of the less punitive "welfare reform" ideas. At the same time, we both know that black audiences will not let us romanticize recipients. Residents of low-income communities are angry at the crime and dysfunction within their neighborhoods, which they see as directly linked to destabilization by "the system." To talk about welfare there, we must face how angry people are that social workers do not really offer help to women who are in trouble, and have both neglected and abused low-income families. The discussions are intense, and we both experience them as the most open about the costs of poverty, the ways in which oppressive systems operate, and the absolute need to make change.

Sometimes we have spoken before *legislative or congressional hearings* or to "friendly" politicians and their staffs. These are hard but necessary encounters.

◆ The best hope we have here is to try to get them to stiffen their backbone and remember that there are still *voters* who expect government to play a role in helping people. We have given them advice and first-hand accounts of how voters in their districts are affected, and asked them to sign a "Pledge of Respect" that they will not engage in debates where all recipients are insulted. But it is always hard not to feel managed in such encounters. Even if politicians seem polite to individual women who tell their stories, we often feel they don't really listen, because they keep assuring us that "everybody wants to reform welfare." Church allies have been most helpful in cracking this, but we are sure that nothing will really change until a broader social movement emerges to demand as well as ask, to disrupt as well as plan lobbying days.

Finally, we always feel supported by self-consciously "progressive" groups but still want to push them further.

◆ Many progressives are working hard to revive a viable leftist populism, by exposing the increasing disparity of wealth in the country, and by reviving labor and grassroots demands for economic justice. We are gratified by this and support it, but we hope that this time people will find ways to build in demands for an expanded welfare state into the rhetoric. Populism can often fall into a kind of anti-government politics that acts as if we would all be fine if people just had jobs. Issues that are seen as primarily affecting people of color, or women, or the poorest can be viewed as divisive, so we are told once again to wait. At first, in the heat of the welfare reform debate, this old pattern seemed to have broken. We just cannot squelch all our doubts that, when some other more "unifying" issue (such as health care) becomes tactically critical again, women on welfare and their advocates will find themselves one more time relegated to the back table of seedy, somewhat embarrassing relatives, whose issues are "important but not central to core concerns." We don't have time to take this step backward again.

Talking the Real Talk, Walking the Real Walk

At another level, we know that what is going on politically has nothing to do with welfare and AFDC: It has to do with the victory and consolidation of the hard Right. It is clear to us that right-wing politicians, activists, and writers are simply using welfare as their first wedge in building their broader base for creating a society where no one, not just welfare recipients, has any security if they are outside the norms and behaviors of the national community. We hear this "anti-vision" as commands to everyone:

- Work at the wage you can get, with the benefits deemed affordable by the employer.

- Live in an appropriately behaving family, do not tell secrets about what happens there, and do not challenge the authority of Christian family values: regarding sex, male authority, or discipline.

- Do not claim any rights except those to live free or die, own guns, and do what you want with the money that alone can allow you freedom.

- Forget any social vision that expects support for living as securely as possible, that sees freedom from fear as basic, and that puts forward the goal of society as not profit but the most democratically determined security for all. Indeed this is an anti-American, socialistic vision that hurts people by promising a security that does not come from conformity to the norms set by employers, fathers, and church.

Our horror at this alternative agenda, and our sense that it is coming closer to achievement, drives us to end with a brief proposal of strategies for what needs to be done that go beyond defensive coalition building.

- In the short term, linking other issues to poverty and the diversification of alliances especially at the state level, that has been the dominant welfare rights strategy for several years should continue. It has been effective at building state and national alliances, and at regaining national attention to welfare rights issues, at least among feminist, church, and progressive organizations.

♦   In the long term, it is time to hunker down and prepare for the worst while building a new base for resistance strategies. We need to teach ourselves more. We suggest reading about the American Right and the history of fascism, so that we are able to face how bad it really can get in countries with "core values" like ours. We also suggest working harder to understand the "necessities" created by this phase of international capitalism: such as structural reductions in the workforce, the limits and social outcomes of a service economy, the isolation of computerized off-site workplaces, and a global decline in wages. If we don't understand how the whole world is shifting, we can come up with solutions and organizing strategies that make no sense. We need to know more about the changes in the European welfare state, which is adapting to changes in the economy in very different ways than is deemed inevitable in the United States. And, we need again to look at all the organizing history and strategies—from those of Abolitionists to labor to civil rights and feminists—in order to reinvent ourselves as movement builders for the 21st century.

New Abolitionist Movement

♦   Finally, as we have anticipated earlier, we seek our strength in a vision of a new Abolitionist movement, based on popular education, sanctuaries for the victims of poverty, and militant action. Just as it was hard for white Northerners to comprehend that there really could be people who would take babies from their mothers and sell them, or to hear how common rape was on the plantations, it is hard for many people today to believe how dangerous the radical Right, which has now gained and is consolidating power, truly is. They cannot believe that a woman is forced to give up her children because they live in a car; or to go back to an abuser if her two years on welfare are up (or never leave if she is an immigrant). And, just like the Abolitionists, we must keep educating ourselves about the fact that there really is another view of the world, and a different set of ideas about what we can tolerate in society, out there.

♦   There are lots of folks with another set of standards for acting than many of us want to accept—look hard at the photograph of the Citadel boys as Shannon Faulkner was hounded out. Their faces and their body movements were the same as the smirks and gestures of those who poured mustard on the sit-down strikers at southern lunch counters, or those who smiled and ate their picnics at lynchings, or those who made slave auction day a holiday in ante-bellum towns. Just as there were journalists and "scholars" who wrote extensively in defense of the superior southern culture and the institution of slavery, so today there are right-wing "scholars," funded by right-wing think tanks, who are attacking welfare recipients, government bureaucrats, teen mothers, and poor people as undermining the moral fabric of the society, personified in the unfettered capitalist economy, the patriarchal family, and the existing racial hierarchies.

♦ So to build our movement, we too must understand better the interweaving threads of the arguments that are so triumphant today, if we are going to abolish this scary and dangerous world order. (In fact, we would argue, today's right-wing anti-vision is not so new, and not so different from the old order that grew out of a Slave Power that only lost its particular *means* of oppression—slavery—when it lost the war. Its legitimation of class, race, and gender hierarchies never died—but that's another story.) We are going to have to put some new ideas into people's heads—ideas that make more sense in explaining the world than those that "naturally" come to mind. And we are going to have to give people new ways to act like responsible citizens.

♦ One of the ways to do this today is embedded in a new initiative begun by the National Welfare Rights Union: the establishment of Survival Sanctuaries around the nation. Building directly on the Abolitionist and human rights models, NWRU is seeking to create stations, with an activist leadership focus, where Runaways from Poverty can receive refuge, advocacy, shelter, clothing, food and other resources. Churches, women's groups, peace activists, universities, and unions are asked to give leadership in accumulating needed material. In addition to soliciting resources, members of NWRU will themselves collect hotel gratuities from their speaking engagements: so that women in the shelters can bathe themselves with Sheraton soap, wash their children's hair with Marriott Shampoo, and use lotion, coffee, tea and toilet supplies from Holiday Inn. Maybe someone will even donate Helmsley chocolates for the pillows. Students from area colleges and schools will be recruited to offer "community service" to families in the sanctuaries.

♦ Like the Underground Railroad, Survival Sanctuaries will make a symbolic point as they serve real needs. They will be a center for community outreach and organizing. There will be meetings to discuss the ideas, concerns, and visions of poor people and their friends. Sanctuaries will sponsor Freedom Schools offering community education to all, with a liberation curriculum and seminars on theory, strategies, and tactics. The ultimate goal will be to recreate a broad vision of a loving, humane, and nonjudgmental society where people meet each other to address common needs.

Visions and actions such as this are not "realistic." They won't stop the federal abandonment of AFDC and the continued state-by-state assaults. Yet it is something of a miracle that any woman on welfare gets out of bed every morning, feeds her kids, gets them to school, and gets herself to the welfare office to find out about yet another erosion of her plans. But hundreds of thousands of women do this, and still manage to kiss their kids, laugh with their friends, and plan for birthdays, holidays, and another day. If women with the most strikes against them can do this, then, in our view, anybody with any more resources has no excuse. We have to get up and move, because as that hero of the Civil Rights movement, Ella Baker, said:

> To me, I'm part of the human family. What the human family will accomplish, I can't control. But it isn't impossible that what those who came along with me went through might stimulate others to continue to fight for a society that does not have those kinds of problems. Somewhere down the line the numbers increase, the tribe increases. So how do you keep on? I can't help it. I don't claim to have any corner on an answer, but I believe that the struggle is eternal. Somebody else carries on.

ABOUT THE CONTRIBUTORS

MIMI ABRAMOVITZ is Professor of Social Policy at Hunter College in New York City and a long-time welfare rights and women's activists. She has written numerous articles and two noted books on the topic, *Under Attack, Fighting Back* (1996) and *Regulating the Lives of Women*, Revised Edition (1996).

RANDY ALBELDA is Associate Professor of Economics at the University of Massachusetts/Boston and the author, with Nancy Folbeare of *The War on the Poor a Defense Manual*.(1996) She is a speaker and activist in the Boston area where she is cofounder, with Ann Withorn, of the Academics Working Group on Poverty.

LISA CATANZARITE is assistant professor of Sociology and Urban Studies and Planning at the University of California, San Diego. Her work centers around social stratification and labor markets, with special attention to occupational segregation by gender and race/ethnicity. Her most recent research is on segregation of recent-immigrant Latinos.

MARGARET CERULLO teaches cultural studies at Hampshire College in Amherst, MA and is long-time activist and writer on feminist, lesbian, and left issues. She is an editor of *Radical America* magazine.

DEBORAH CLARKE is a board member of Solutions at Work, a homeless women's organization that coordinates the Cambridge Furniture Bank and Move, a moving company run by homeless individuals. She is formerly homeless, a bachelors degree student in Community Planning and a former intern at the Women's Institute for Housing and Economic Development.

CLAIRE CUMMINGS is finishing her doctoral dissertation, "Profiles in

Survival: Women and Class Identity at the End of the Welfare State" at Clark University Women's Studies Ph.D. Program. She has been an activist in the Women's movement since 1968, and has taught sociology and psychology at Newbury College for the past 21 years. She has been happily coediting *Survival News* for 10 years within a feminist, cross-class, cross-race intentional community.

MARTHA F. DAVIS is director of the NOW Legal Defense fund and a long-time welfare advocate.

DELORES DELL is formerly program manager of the Women's Drop in Center for Shelter Inc. in Cambridge, MA. and cofounder of *Spare Change* newspaper. Formerly homeless herself, she is working to establish a support group for homeless women and serves on the City of Boston's Homeless Advisory Group. She is earning her bachelors degree in Human Service Planning.

ELAINE DONOVAN teaches economics and women's studies at Merrimac College. She is the single mother of two children. She writes and researches questions about economics, employment, and women's poverty.

SUSAN EISENBERG is a Boston poet and electrician. Her poems have been published in many places including *Prairie Schooner, The Nation,* and *Utne Reader.* A recognized speaker and writer on issues facing women working in "non-traditional" jobs, she is currently working on a nonfiction book about women and construction.

MARLA ERLIEN is a Boston area activist who has worked in many areas of feminist, socialist, and anti-imperialist politics, and with women in Cambridge, MA public housing. She is an editor of *Radical America* magazine.

BRENDA FARRELL is cofounder of the Community Outreach Project in Framingham, MA., a coalition of current and formerly homeless women that advocates to improve policies affecting their lives, and conducts empowerment sessions for homeless women. She is earning her bachelors degree in Community Planning and Management.

SANDY FELDER is a former president of Local 509, the social workers local of Service Employees International Union in Massachusetts. Currently she is on the national staff in support of organizing and mobilization campaigns across the country.

LAURA FLANDERS is executive producer and host of "CounterSpin," the syndicated radio program from the media watch group FAIR (Fairness and Accuracy in Reporting). She is also coordinator of the Women's Desk at FAIR in New York and a widely published freelance writer.

NANCY FRASER is Professor of Political Science at the Graduate Faculty at The New School for Social Research. She is the author of *Unruly Practices: Power Discourse, and Gender in Contemporary Social Theory* (1989) and the co-author of *Feminist Contentions: A Philosophical Exchange* (1994). Her new book, *Justice Interruptus*, will be published in 1997.

LINDA GORDON is Professor of History at the University of Wisconsin and a long-time writer and activist for women's rights. Her most relevant recent works are *Pitied But Not Entitled* (1994), *Women, the State and Welfare* (1991) and *Heroes of Their Own Lives* (1989).

MARION GRAHAM has been a union steward and was a cofounder of ARMS, the student welfare rights chapter at U-Mass/Boston. She raised five children while enduring a battering husband and then using welfare and low-wage jobs to survive. She is currently an administrative assistant at the U-Mass/Boston.

DEBORAH GRAY is a family counselor at a comprehensive program for homeless families in Dorchester, MA. While homeless she joined a homeless empowerment group that gave her the inspiration to form a similar group through RWARM. She is earning a bachelors degree in Human Services and serves on the board of directors for Parents United for Child Care.

BETH HARRIS is an activist and political scientist in Seattle. Her interests include legal mobilization for economic rights and the contradictions in the states' welfare and social control functions. She has collaborated on a number of organizing projects for Central American solidarity, battered women, and economic justice.

SUSAN JAMES has worked in Seattle as an advocate and therapist for battered women and sexual assault survivors. She cofounded The Therapy Network for Sexual Abuse Survivors, which provides low-cost therapy to sexual abuse survivors. She is currently recreating and developing as a writer in San Francisco.

ERIKA KATES has been researching issues on low-income women many years and has a PhD from Brandeis University. She facilitated a family preservation and evaluation project at Tufts University and is now a research associate at the Project on Women and Social Change at Smith College.

MARIE KENNEDY is Associate Professor of Community Planning at the College of Public and Community Service at the University of Massachusetts in Boston. One of twelve researchers recognized in Profiles of Participatory Action Researchers, she has many years experience conducting participatory action research, has published extensively on community development issues and is on the board of Grassroots International, among a wide range of other activities.

MARIAN KRAMER is currently co-president of the National Welfare Rights Union. She is a long-time civil rights, labor and poverty activist based in Detroit. She has spoken at rallies, demonstrations and conferences around the country. She was a delegate to the NGO Forum on Women in Beijing and has been arrested for civil rights, welfare rights, housing takeovers and most recently, with Patricia Ireland of NOW for protest in Washington D.C. against the Contract with America.

FONG YEE LEE is a Chinese immigrant who has been active on refugee and immigrant issues for more than 20 years.

BETTY REID MANDELL is a retired professor of Social Work who is a long-time welfare rights activist. As founder and editor of *Survival News*, she has been locally and nationally recognized for her work in allowing women's voices to her heard. She has published many books and numerous articles on poverty, social welfare, and social issues.

VILMA ORTIZ is associate professor of sociology at UCLA. Her research focuses on the social condition of Latinos in the United States. With Edward Telles she is currently conducting a 30-year longitudinal and inter-generational study of Mexican Americans in Los Angeles and San Antonio.

FRANCES FOX PIVEN is a long-time welfare rights activist and writer, as well as a national cofounder of Human Serve, an organization founded to promote voter registration among low-income people. Among her most important books on welfare, with Richard Cloward, are *Poor Peoples' Movements* and *Regulating the Poor.*

ROBIN A. ROBINSON is director of the Adolescent Voices Project, a national evaluation of adolescent pregnancy and prevention programs, within the Department of Health and Human Resources in Washington D.C. She is formerly Assistant Professor of Social Work at Rutgers University. She is also a former teen mother and a public service librarian in inner-city libraries in Massachusetts. She is currently at work on a book on delinquent girls, *Violations of Girlhood: The Lives of Delinquent Girls* to be published in 1997.

NANCY ROSE is Professor of Economics and director of the Women's Studies Program at California State University in San Bernardino. She is a long-time activist for women's and welfare rights and the author of *Workfare or Fair Work,* as well as numerous articles and another book on the topics of women, work, and welfare.

BETSY SANTIAGO is a formerly homeless woman who is a member of Homes for Families, the Dudley Street Neighborhood Initiative and the board of Project Hope in Boston, MA. She is studying Human Services Planning and has worked on the Boston Foundation Aspen Project.

VICTORIA STEINITZ teaches at the College of Public and Community Service at the University of Massachusetts at Boston. She is the director of the Human Rights Project that is monitoring the implementation of welfare reform in Massachusetts as a case of human rights abuse. She is the author, with Ellen Solomon, of *Starting Out: Class and Community in the Lives of Working Class Youths* and other articles on women and education.

DOTTIE STEVENS is President of the Massachusetts Welfare Rights Union and National Vice President of the NWRU. She is a long-time activist for poor people's rights in Boston and has served on the boards of *Survival News*, the Coalition for Basic Human Needs, and Advocacy for Resources for Modern Survival. She ran for governor of Massachusetts in 1990.

MARY HUFF STEVENSON is Associate Professor of Economics at the University of Massachusetts at Boston, where she teaches courses in urban, labor, and gender economics. She was raised by her mother in as New York City public housing project and is herself a single mother with two children.

CHRIS TILLY is Associate Professor in the Department of Policy and Planning at the University of Massachusetts at Lowell. A long-time activist for economic rights, Chris has been a Fellow at the Sage Foundation in New York, and is the author with Randy Albelda of a book on women's poverty in Massachusetts to be published in 1997 by South End Press.

TESLEY UTLEY is a formerly homeless women who joined the *Spare Change* newspaper project six months after it started. She is currently planning arts and crafts workshops for the Women's Drop In Center of Shelter Inc., in Boston and is studying Human Services Planning.

NOEMY VIDES is an immigrant woman who has been reborn in Boston by being exposed to education, freedom, and awareness. She believes that continuing education will help her overcome oppression, poverty and outrage.

LAURA WALKER is a divorced mother of two teenaged boys and has been both a paid and non-paid welfare rights and community organizer in Massachusetts. She has served as a board member for the Coalition for Basic Human Needs, president of *Survival News*, president of the Saugus Commons Tenants Organization and treasurer of the Massachusetts NWRU.

DIANNE WILKERSON is the first African-American female to serve, since 1992, as a Massachusetts State Senator, representing Matttapan, Dorchester, Roxbury, Jamaica Plain and Back Bay neighborhoods. She is a lawyer who has represented the NAACP and obtained partnership status with a major Boston law firm. She is a former welfare recipient and pays special attention to welfare, labor, and childcare issues in the Senate.

PASS THE AMMUNITION
The Best Sources For Crying Out Loud

The literature on welfare and its meanings is very large. For our purposes here, the most useful sources are:

Abramovitz, Mimi. 1996. *Regulating the Lives of Women*. Boston: South End Press.

Abramovitz, Mimi. 1996. *Under Attack, Fighting Back*. New York: Monthly Review Press.

Albelda, Randy and Nancy Folbeare. 1996. *The War on the Poor: A Defense Manual*.

Gordon, Linda. 1994. *Pitied But Not Entitled*. New York: Free Press.

Gordon, Linda, ed. 1991. *Women, the State and Welfare*. Madison: Univ. of Wisconsin Press.

Gordon, Linda. 1989. *Heroes of Their Own Lives: The Politics and History of Family Violence*. Viking Press.

Handler, Joel F. 1995. *The Poverty of Welfare Reform* . Yale U.Press, 1995.

Jennings, James.1994. "Persistent Poverty in the United States: Review of Theories and Explanations", *Sage Race Relations Abstracts*, vol 19, no.1, February.

Katz, Michael. 1989. *The Undeserving Poor*. New York: Pantheon.

Katz, Michael. 1986. *In the Shadow of the Poorhouse*. New York: Basic Books.

Katz, Michael. 1983. *Poverty and Policy in American History*. New York: Academic Press.

Quadragno, Jill. 1995. *The Color of Welfare*. NY: Oxford U. Press.

Schram, Sanford F. 1995. *The Words of Welfare*. Madison: University of Wisconsin Press.

Schein, Virgina E. 1995. *Working from the Margins: Voices of Mothers in Poverty*. Ithaca: Cornell University Press.

Sidel, Ruth. 1996, 2nd edition. *Women and Children Last.*. New York: Viking.

Skocpol, Theda. 1995. *Protecting Soldiers and Mothers*. Belknap Press.

Skocpol, Theda. 1991. "Targeting Within Universalism" in Jencks and Peterson, *The Urban Underclass*, pp. 433-34.

Sullivan, K. 1995. *Days of Hope: Race and Democracy in the New Deal Era*. Cambridge: Harvard University Press.

Survival News, the National Welfare Rights Newspaper. Boston.

Tufts University Center on Humger, Poverty and Nutrition Policy. 1995. *Statement on Key Welfare Reform Issues: The Empirical Evidence.* Medford, MA.

For the best information about what is happening with congresional welfare reform see the constant stream of depressing updates provided by CLASP, the Center for Law and Social Policy in Washington DC.

KNOWING THE ENEMY
The Best Sources for Reading about the Right

The best overview of the history of conservatism in America is a set of three articles by Alan Brinkely, Susan Yohn and Leo Ribuffo, in the *American Historical Review* (April, 1994), in a forum on "the Problem of American Conservatism."

For a useful review of the social science literature, see William B. Hixson, Jr., *Search for the American Right Wing: An Analysis of the Social Science Record, 1955 - 1987* (Princeton , N.J: Princeton Univ.Press 1992).

For treatments of the media and conservatism see Howard J. Gold, *Hollow Mandates, American Public Opinion and the Conservative Shift* (Boulder: Westview, 1992) and Peter D. Hart and Linda DiVall, "Public Attitudes toward Welfare Reform," (1993), available through the Center on Budget and Policy Priorities, Washington D.C.

See also:

Bennett, David. 1995.*The Party of Fear: The American Far Right from Nativism to the Militia Movement*, 2nd. ed. NY: Vintage.

Berlet, Chip. *Eyes Right: Challenging the Right Backlash*. Boston: South End Press, 1995.

Cantor, David. 1994.*The Religious Right: The Assault on Tolerance and Pluralism*. NY: ADL.

Diamond, Sara. 1989. *Spiritual Warfare: The Politics of the Christian Right*. Boston: South End Press.

Hardisty, Jean. 1995. "The Resurgent Right: Why Now?"available through Political Research Associates, Somerville, MA.

Himmelstein,Jerome. 1990.*To the Right: The Transformation of American Conservatism* (Berkeley: U.of Ca.Press.

For the best examples of how the Right thinks about welfare see:

Arnn,Peter P.and Douglas Jeffrey. 1993. *Moral Ideas for America*. Claremont Ca: The Claremont Institute.

Auster,Lawrence. 1993.*The Path to National Suicide*.

For the view that immigration is not so bad, just the welfare states support of aliens after they arrive, see Ron K Unz, "Immigration or the Welfare State: Which is the Real Enemy?", *Policy Review*, (Fall 1994). For a lively and revealing debate on the issue, see comments on Unz' article in the

Winter 1995 *Policy Review.*

Gilder, George. 1981. *Wealth and Poverty.* ICS Press.

Mead, Lawrence. 1992. *The New Politics of Poverty.* NY: Free Press.

Mead, Lawrence. 1986. *Beyond Entitlement.* NY: Basic Books.

Murray, Charles. 1984. *Losing Ground; American Social Policy 1950-1980,.* New York: Basic Books.

Olasky, Marvin. 1993. *The Tragedy of American Compassion.* Regnery, Washington D.C.

Reed, Ralph.1994. *Politically Incorrect.* Dallas: Word.

Robertson, Pat. 1993. *The Turning Tide.* Dallas: Word.

INDEX

reform, 158-159, 292-293

Republicans: and media, 31-32, 36.
See also Conservatives; Social
policy; Traditional family; Welfare reform

Right wing. *See* Conservatives; Republicans

Roofless Women's Action Research
Mobilization (RWARM), 42, 54,
55. *See also* Homeless women

RWARM. *See* Roofless Women's Action Research Mobilization

S

St. Petersburg Times, 37

SEIU. *See* Service Employees International Union

Service Employees International Union (SEIU), 213, 216, 217, 218,
221, 283. *See also* Unions

Service workers. *See* Social workers,
female

Sexism. *See* Gender issues

Sexual abuse, 110, 111, 117. *See also*
Domestic violence

Shelters: for domestic violence victims, 41, 60-61, 62; for homeless
women, 41-42, 43, 45, 48-52, 53-54

Social class: middle class tax deductions, 35, 217; middle class welfare programs, 156, 289-290; and
social workers, 272-273, 276;
and welfare activism, 175-180.
See also Cultural attitudes; Immigrants; Minorities; Racism

Social policy: and cultural attitudes,

89-92, 335-336; and economics,
69, 71; leadership for, 370-377;
and minorities, 121-122, 123-124,
136; and state power, 189-191;
on teen mothers,108-109, 114-119, 290-291; and voting, 114,
377; and welfare dependency,
237-238, 239, 241-242, 244-246,
250-251, 255-259; and welfare
myths, 29-39, 163, 351-353, 364,
365, 368-369, 371-372, 374-376.
See also Conservatives; Democrats; Government work programs; Liberals; Media; Public
opinion; Republicans; *specific;
legislation*; Welfare reform; Welfare system

Social Security Act (1935), 156, 287

Social workers: class/race issues of,
272-273, 276; client disassociation with, 273-274, 276-277; client subservience to, 269,
272-273, 277-279; and client
unity, 281-285; and cultural values, 275-276; and human service
arena, 270-272, 385; negative attitudes of, 269-270, 271-272, 274-275; relationships among,
279-281; unionization of, 213,
216, 217, 218, 220-221, 283

Students: Advocacy for Resources for
Modern Survival (ARMS), 163,
164-165, 174, 316-317, 318, 320,
321-322, 325; as welfare recipients, 315-317, 319, 325, 327. *See
also* Education

Survival News: as collective, 172-173;